PSYCHOLOGY WORLDS ISSUE 32

CONNOR WHITELEY

AVAILABLE AT ALL MAJOR BOOKSELLERS!

INTRODUCTION

If I'm being completely honest, I have no idea how to describe August 2025. Normally, when I do these introductions, I talk about what I'm excited for, how brilliant the month has been and why I'm really looking forward to the month ahead.

And whilst this is still true for the most part because I flat out love the summer weather, having time to work on my projects and I did my first-ever podcast interview on male sexual violence this month, there have been a lot of things I haven't enjoyed.

For example, I've left university, I've left my job as a Student Ambassador for my former university's Outreach and Widening Participation Department because I've finished my degree, and I had a lot of lovely moments with all of them as we cried, said goodbye to each other and more.

Then there is the small matter of me leaving an emotionally abusive situation and I am having to deal with the fallout of me being emotionally abused for over a year without realising it.

Anyway, I am okay, I am happy and as much as I allow myself to process my emotions (the good and the bad and the extremely painful), I still have a lot of things to be grateful for in my life.

Including you, dear reader, and this magazine.

Therefore, to kick off the August 2025 edition of The Psychology Worlds magazine, you get to enjoy some brilliant psychology articles. Firstly, you get to learn about social graces, learning about our own biases in clinical work and why this area is so important for aspiring and qualified clinical psychologists to understand in *What Are Social Graces in Clinical Psychology.* Personally, I really enjoyed this article because I had seen social graces mentioned time and time again in job applications, but it wasn't until this article that I learnt what they were truly about.

If you want to become a psychologist then this is a critical article to read, understand and apply to your daily life.

Secondly, you get to learn about *How To Reduce Conflict Between Parents.* This is an important article to read because parental conflict can increase mental health difficulties in children, it can erode self-esteem and their relationship skills. Parental conflict can have lifelong implications for a child so knowing how to manage this conflict effectively and in a healthy way is beyond critical.

Thirdly, you get to read an insightful, fascinating and heart-wrenching article on *Lessons From Rape 1 Year On.* Like so much of my rape content, this article is deeply personal, I reveal my own struggles and everything I have lost and gained in the past year. There is a lot you can learn from that tragic article for sure.

Stepping away from rape and sexual violence, the penultimate article in this issue is *Why Psychologists Do Not Only Deal With Crazy People*. For our next article, I wanted to deal with a slightly lighter topic so this is a fun, insightful reflection on the different clients that clinical psychologists see, support and interact with.

Finally, in *How Does Childhood Trauma Impact Relationships*, you get to develop your understanding of the wide range of psychological impacts trauma can have on childhood. Specifically, this article looks at boundary difficulties in childhood between a child and abusive caregivers. If you're interested in developmental psychology, mental health and social relationships then you will love that article.

That's all before *Clinical Psychology Reflections Volume 5* makes another enthralling return to the magazine. Containing 20 exciting, engaging and thoughtful reflections on clinical psychology, this book gives you even more food for thought about my favourite profession.

You'll learn a lot for sure.

Finally in this issue, *I'm Not A Victim, I Am A Survivor* makes its debut in these pages. This is a brutally honest, personal and deeply tragic book about the first five months after my rape. You can see my mental health rise and fall, everything I was struggling with and some tips and tricks that I used just to survive.

It was really hard to reread and prepare for publication and putting in these pages but I am proud of this book, I love this book and I definitely think you will learn more than you ever thought possible.

Because this book is my truth, my defiance and me reclaiming the events of my rape.

Let's turn over the page and start exploring some fascinating Psychology Worlds.

WHAT ARE SOCIAL GRACES IN CLINICAL PSYCHOLOGY?

Whenever a client comes into our therapy room or whenever you meet a psychologist, they have certain privileges and disadvantages that you don't have. Also, you'll both have different life experiences, perspectives and focuses that you will share and you will differ in. This is because every one of us is wonderfully unique with our own thoughts, feelings and lived experiences. Yet as aspiring and qualified psychologists, we need to acknowledge that we have certain social graces or privileges that our clients don't have and vice versa. Therefore, in this clinical psychology podcast episode, you'll going to learn what are social graces, what are some types of social graces and how social graces can impact the therapy process. If you enjoy learning about psychotherapy, clinical psychology and privilege then this will be a great episode for you.

What Are Social Graces in Clinical Psychology?

Social graces is an acronym that helps us to understand the visible and invisible aspects of our identity, so this allows mental health professionals to examine the elements of our identity that impact our behaviour and lives. This is what each letter of the Graces in social graces mean:

- G- Gender, Generation, Geography and Gender Identity
- R- race and religion
- A- age, appearance and ability
- C- culture, caste and class
- E- education, economics and ethnicity
- S- sexuality, sexual orientation and spirituality

In addition, social graces is a framework designed by Burnham (1993) and updated in 2012 that asks mental health practitioners to be aware of how their identity influences their thinking and approach to work. Since social graces focus on how different aspects of our identity impact our practice.

Some academic definitions of social graces include:

- "A mnemonic that separates out different aspects of identity into separate categories." (Butler, 2017, p. 17)
- "Mnemonic for aspects of difference" (Jones & Reeve, 2014, p. 2)
- "A suitable framework […] through which therapists can reflect on their own beliefs and prejudices in order to understand how they might bring these into the therapy" (Totsuka, 2014, p. 106)

Therefore, some quick examples of how thinking about social graces can impact clinical practice is, if you're a young and beautiful young woman (age, appearance and gender) how might these social factors impact your clinical practice compared to a middle-aged woman with an average appearance? The middle-aged woman would likely have more clinical experience than the young woman, yet the young woman would probably be treated better and have advantages because of her youth and attractive appearance. Yet both women because of their gender would be unlikely to face one or two gender stereotypes compared to male therapists. Due to the myth in society that women are more sensitive, caring and better therapists than men.

On the other hand, men would have a lot of benefits compared to women because of the patriarchal society we live in.

Personally, if I look at myself briefly, I am a young 24-year-old white non-binary person who was assigned male at birth and I look male in appearance. I am from a middle-class background, I'm gay and in terms of sexuality, I am not very active and I have only ever had one relationship. All these different social factors would impact my clinical practice in different ways. For example, whilst I'm aware of a lot of social issues, especially those faced by people from lower socioeconomic backgrounds, I will never be able to fully understand the impact because I have not experienced them myself because of my class. Also, when I work with heterosexual clients, again I have a great awareness of heterosexual relationships but because I'm gay and I've only ever had one relationship, my understanding will be limited. However, because of biological sex and appearance, I get a lot of male privilege that other clients and practitioners don't get and I'll be able to help and support autistic, LGBT+ and trauma survivors a lot in my clinical practice because I've lived those experiences too.

What Is The Purpose of Social Graces?

The social graces framework is useful because it allows psychologists, counsellors, educators and therapists to talk about aspects of our identity and how they might impact how we relate to other people. Therefore, it's designed to make identity factors a part of our clinical discussions about our personal privileges and disadvantages that we face in society. This includes our own implicit biases because once our biases are identified, we can help neutralise them so we can become more thoughtful, fair and effective practitioners.

Nolte (2017) page 4 mentioned:

"provides a helpful way for us to become intentional in our developing awareness of, reflexivity about and skillfulness in responding to sameness and difference."

Because I want to lead by example here, I know I can sometimes be biased against different classes, which is weird because I come from a very, very deprived area. Therefore, because I make myself aware of my classist attitudes, I'm able to catch myself and stop the thought and biased attitude in its tracks.

Moreover, Partridge and McCarry (2017) argued that the framework can help psychologists to use our reflections to inform our future actions so it gets us to think about how we can ensure that we are fairer in the future. Social graces can help us to reflect on our actions in the first place so we can think about how our identity influenced a situation, and social graces allow us to subvert the dominant discourse. This involves psychologists considering how to rethink ongoing behaviours that give privilege to dominant social identities, like white, male, middle-class, able individuals. Lastly, social graces allow us to consider new alternatives for future actions so we can come up with new ways to behave that are fairer.

Going back to my classism example, when I find that I've been classist against someone or a group of people then this is me reflecting on my action and realising is my own class that is making me behave this way. Therefore, in future, I need to make sure I am fairer and I need to subvert the dominant course. This is one of the many reasons why I love my Outreach work because every week I get to work with students and young people from deprived areas and help them realise that university is a great and achievable option for them if they want to go. This helps rebalance the social scales so university isn't reserved for dominant social identities, and anyone can go and apply regardless of their age, race, gender, socioeconomic status and more.

What Are The Key Features of Social Graces?

Firstly, all aspects of identity are equally important to the social graces framework. Burnham (2003) proposed that all the aspects of our identity should be considered equally important because whilst Gender, Geography and Generation come before Race and Religion in the framework, this does not mean they are more important.

Each of the Graces are meant to be examined individually without being drowned out by any of the others.

Secondly, the social graces framework is always evolving because people will naturally add and subtract from it. Since psychologists can use the framework practically by starting a therapy session by asking people what other aspects of identity they could add to the framework. For instance, if you're working with a refugee then they might add their refugee experience and status to the framework, and if you're working with an indigenous person then they will add their indigenous experience to the framework because they are core, fundamental parts of their identity.

These new aspects are still just as important as any of the pre-existing aspects in the framework.

Finally, the social graces framework makes the aspects of our identity explicit and visible. As a result of our identity and the different aspects of it isn't often spoken about or given room to be discussed inside or outside the therapy room. This means the framework gives us a chance to discuss our thoughts on the unsaid aspects of our identity in addition to the aspects that we wear on our sleeves. For example, some unsaid aspects of my identity generally my thoughts on religion, my sexuality, my sexual orientation, my gender identity amongst others. Whereas I happily wear the age, generation, biological sex, education amongst others on my sleeve.

On the whole, when in therapy sessions, social graces can be discussed with clients to get both the client and therapist thinking about how each aspect of identity impacts their thoughts and behaviour. For example, when clients and therapists talk about education, they can talk about how their education background influences their views, and when people talk about generation, they could talk about their lives growing up and how the attitudes and behaviours of different generations impact their views nowadays. Such as, if my Grandad who was born in the Silent Generation was to discuss his generation then he would talk about how you didn't show emotion, you didn't show that you were upset and you certainly did not talk about your feelings or complain as part of that generation. Then a therapist would explore how those attitudes impact his daily life and behaviour now, and whether these are still adaptive or maladaptive attitudes to have these days.

What are The Advantages of the Social Graces Framework?

Firstly, a great benefit of the social graces framework is that it helps us to see our own implicit biases because when we examine the aspects of our identities, this allows us to think about how they shape our actions and views about our self, others and the world. Then by talking about these aspects we can eliminate or, at least, minimise implicit biases in our clinical practice.

Secondly, the framework is great because it helps people to understand identity. I would add that this is very useful as a potential psychoeducation tool for our clients because identity is a very abstract concept, so by providing a framework to our clients that helps to facilitate a discussion. This is a really useful way to make an abstract concept slightly more tangible for our clients. As well as the framework is a useful way to examine with our clients how aspects of our identity impact our beliefs and perspectives.

Lastly, another advantage of the social graces framework is it makes us talk about the invisible and unsaid aspects of our identity. I mean without this framework, we wouldn't talk about a lot of aspects of identity, because most aspects are often overlooked or ignored because they're invisible. It's really common to talk about gender, sexual orientation, race, age and education because we largely see these social factors. Yet it is rare to talk about generation, sexuality amongst others. This means it's useful that clients and psychologists can talk through each aspect one by one to make sure nothing is overlooked.

What Are The Disadvantages of The Social Graces Framework?

The first major disadvantage of this framework is the very fact that it is a framework and not theory. This means that whilst it is a useful tool for thinking about identity, this isn't a theory that offers us an explanation of how the world works. In other words, social graces should not be considered the same as Critical Whiteness Theory, Critical Race Theory or Intersectional Theory because each of these valuable and insightful theories offers us an explanation for how the world works. Instead the social graces framework only offers us a chance for important discussions to be had about social identity biases, so some people argue the lack of explanation about the world is a disadvantage.

In addition, a final disadvantage of the framework is that it completely fails to understand just how complex our identities are. At some point in the next year, I have a book coming out called *Your Unshakable Self* and I'm really looking forward to that book being released because it explores a lot about our sense of Self, our identity and all the different ways how it impacts our behaviour. This social graces framework doesn't cover the majority of what I talk about in this book, and another sub-issue of the framework is that it is the complete opposite of Intersectional Theory according to Bulter (2017). Intersectional Theory sees the intersectional identities as unique, impossible to talk about separately and you cannot neatly separable out our identities.

I completely agree with Butler (2017) because if we talk some aspects of my identity. You cannot talk about the sexuality part of my identity without talking about my sexual orientation, my gender identity, my biological sex, race and my class. Since the very fact that I am a gay non-binary person assigned male at birth who's white and young who has very little romantic or sexual experience. Fundamentally means all these factors insect and interact to inform my views and perspectives about myself, others and the world. Equally, you cannot talk about me being a clinical psychology Masters student (education) without considering how I'm white, from the south of England and from a nationally deprived area. All those social identities impact on my educational journey and impact my views.

Those are only some examples about how you can't treat aspects of identity separately.

On the whole, Butler (2017) argued that breaking down our identity into separate categories fails to understand just how complex our identities are. As well as the framework seeks to look at identity as a "sum of its parts" instead of an indivisible and holistic concept.

Conclusion

After struggling for a few months to understand social graces and what they actually were because in my lectures, the social graces framework was always just skipped over. I am really happy that I took the time to think about social graces because they are flat out critical to understand, we should be having these conversations and we should be reflecting and always wanting to be fair. And having social graces doesn't make us a problem in society, people will always have social graces that others do not have and vice versa, but if we do not reflect on our biases and think about how our social identities impact us and if we are not proactive in becoming fairer. Then this is where our social graces become a problem because we should always be striving to make society better, fairer and more equal for everyone regardless of their social graces.

Ultimately, Burnham et al. gave us a very useful way of looking at how our social identities impact our implicit biases. As well as this is a valuable discussion tool to help mental health professionals think about how best we can counter our own biases so we can better achieve social justice.

Everyone deserves to be treated fairer, compassionately and equally in society, let alone our therapy rooms. So if having discussions about social graces is the way to achieve these outcomes then it is something we absolutely have to do.

And you'll likely learn a lot of fun, interesting and surprising things along the way.

Clinical Psychology References and Further Reading

Birdsey, N., & Kustner, C. (2021). Reviewing the social GRACES: what do they add and limit in systemic thinking and practice?. *The American journal of family therapy*, *49*(5), 429-442.

Burnham, J. & Roper-Hall, A. (2017) Commentaries on this issue. *Context*, 151, 47-50.

Burnham, J. (1992) Approach-method-technique: Making distinctions and creating connections. *Human Systems*, *3*(1), 3-26.

Burnham, J. (1993) Systemic supervision: The evolution of refl exivity in the context of the supervisory relationship. *Human Systems*, *4*, 349- 381.

Burnham, J. (2005) Relational reflexivity: A tool for socially constructing therapeutic relationships. In: C. Flaskas, B. Mason & A. Perlesz (eds.), *The space between: Experience, context and process in the therapeutic relationship*. London: Karnac.

Burnham, J. (2012) Developments in social GRRRAAACCEEESSS: Visible-invisible and voicedunvoiced. In I-B. Krause (Ed.) *Culture and Reflexivity in Systemic Psychotherapy*. Mutual Perspectives. London: Karnac.

Burnham, J. (2018). Developments in Social GRRRAAACCEEESSS: visible–invisible and voiced–unvoiced 1. In *Culture and reflexivity in systemic psychotherapy* (pp. 139-160). Routledge.

Butler, C. (2017). Intersectionality and systemic therapy, *Context*, *151*, pp. 16-18.

Cockell, S. (2017) Exploration of attire as an unvoiced 'GRACE'. *Context*, 151, 19-22.

Jones, V. & Reeve, D. (2014). *DISsing the Social GGGRRAAACCEEESSS*. Paper presented at the AFT Conference. University of South Wales.

Jones, V. (2019). Diversity IS GRACE–Using the'Social Graces' to Promote Reflection on Diversity. *Working with People with Learning Disabilities: Systemic Approaches*, 243.

Nolte, L. (2017). (Dis)gracefully engaging with diversity learning – reflections on the SGs as a training tool. *Context*, 151. pp. 4-6. ISSN 09691936

Partridge, K. & McCarry, N. (2017).

Graces that bite: Unleashing the GRR in the graces. *Context*, 151. pp. 7-10. ISSN 09691936

Totsuka, Y. (2014). 'Which aspects of social GGRRAAACCEEESSS grab you most?' The social GGRRAAACCEEESSS exercise for a supervision group to promote therapists' self-reflexivity. *Journal of* family Therapy, 36, 86-106. DOI: https://doi.org/10.1111/1467-6427.12026

HOW TO REDUCE CONFLICT BETWEEN PARENTS?

If you're a UK listener living in Kent then you might have heard on the radio recently an advert by Kent County Council about the awful and damaging impact consistent arguing and parental conflict can have on child development. After hearing this advert a few times, I wanted to learn more and it's really interesting how parental conflict negatively impacts a child's development at no fault of their own. Therefore, in this social psychology podcast episode, you'll learn how parental conflict damages a child's development, how to reduce conflict between parents and more. If you're interested in child psychology, conflict reduction and social psychology then this will be a great episode for you.

Why Do We Need To Talk About Conflict Between Parents?

I'll explain in the next section the damaging impact that parental conflict has on a child, but I want to start off this psychology podcast episode by mentioning that it is normal to argue and for there to be conflict in a relationship. There will be things in your life that just annoy you. Be it work, home life or just being a parent, these things can cause you to become stressed and agitated. It's okay, and this can cause a lot of friction in a household so arguing and shouting happens.

Unfortunately, there are times when this happens in front of children.

I want to stress that some conflict is normal because it truly is and not all conflict is damaging to children. If parents didn't argue at all then I would be more suspicious of that because I don't know a single couple, a single group of parents and a single friendship that has not argued at least once.

However, there will be times when this parental conflict can increase to unhealthy levels. This could be screaming at each other and shouting without a resolution, communicating to each other in disrespectful ways or periods of silence. This is not healthy communication at all and it is this is persistent and/ or extreme source of conflict that damages child development. Not only in terms of their mental health, but it can damage the relationship between the child and parent too.

No parent wants interparental conflict to harm their relationship with their own child so that's why we need to learn about how to reduce it.

How Does Constant Parental Conflict Harm Child Development?

There are a lot of significant ways how constant or consistent parental conflict can harm child development. For example, it can harm a child's emotional and psychological well-being since persistent exposure to parental conflict can lead to a child becoming emotionally insecure. This can manifest as depression, anxiety or behavioural difficulties (Cummings & Schatz, 2012; Hess, 2021; Sarrazin & Cyr, 2007). These harmful effects can become worse because typically children feel caught in the middle of their parents' conflict so this increases feelings of stress and helplessness.

In addition, the sheer levels of stress and other difficult emotions caused by persistent parental conflict can harm academic performance in children. The associated stress can impair a child's cognitive functioning and concentration so they can't focus on lessons so this academic performance worsens.

Another negative outcome of persistent parental conflict is it harms a child's social development. Since research shows increased parental conflict correlates with reduced prosocial behaviour and an increase in problems with same-age peers in children (Sarrazin & Cyr, 2007). As well as these social difficulties can become worse because of parental behaviour. For instance, if a parent doesn't show a child emotional warmth or positive communication then the child won't know how to show emotional warmth and positive communication either. This continues to only harm their relationships with other children and people.

Finally, for this section, it's important that we realise these harmful effects of parental conflict aren't short-term that only lasts a few years. These damaging, awful effects can last well into adulthood and it can and will continue to harm a child's self-esteem, social relationships and their overall mental health (Hess, 2021).

Personally, I know at the end of the day all

of us are only human, we all make mistakes and there are times when we just want the other person to listen to us just for once in their life. We want them to pay attention and hear our side of the story. Sometimes, it feels like shouting, screaming and having a real argument is the only way to possibly get through to them. And sometimes when the other parent is talking to us about silly things after a hard day's work, we snap.

We are only human.

However, I have just listed four ways how persistent parental conflict impacts our child's development. I am not a parent and I can only imagine how hard it is to raise a child, but we need to try to reduce parental conflict as much as possible. There are other ways to sort out conflicts because conflicts will always happen in relationships, but there are healthy ways to sort out conflicts that do not end up damaging your child's development.

How To Reduce Parental Conflict?

Now we know the damaging impact parental conflict can have on children, let's look at some ways we can reduce parental conflict. Although, it's important to remember that whenever it comes to conflict within relationships, you need to keep yourself safe. This means if you ever feel threatened or unsafe by your partner, then this is not okay. No one should ever feel unsafe or threatened by their partner and if your relationship has become abusive, then please seek support for domestic abuse.

You deserve and need to feel safe in your own home.

One way to reduce interparental conflict is to avoid using the "you" word. As I've been researching and learning a lot more about attachment and how to deal with conflict in relationships, this is a consistent piece of advice that I've seen repeatedly. The issue of using "you" statements in arguments is that these statements make the other person feel targeted and like you're accusing them of something. This leads the other person to become more defensive, so try to use "I" statements instead.

For instance, let's say your co-parent is meant to pick up the kids every Tuesday and Friday because those are the days you have to work longer for your job. Yet every Tuesday and Friday your co-parent never picks up the kids like they're meant to so you need to rely on a friend at the same school to take your kids to your co-parents. Instead of saying "you never pick up the kids when you're meant to and you annoy me," try saying something along the lines of "I feel annoyed when you don't pick up the kids on Tuesdays and Fridays like we agreed."

You see how that's less accusatory than the "you" statement version.

Thirdly, in relationships, it's important to recognise how you argue. At first this idea might make no sense because surely everyone just argues and there are no different types. In reality, all couples and parents need to understand how they communicate to each other and how you communicate arguments and disagreements to each other is an important part of this process. Especially, if you and your partner both approach arguments with very different styles. For instance, you might be a very calm, collected person who deals with conflict and arguments in a calm, logical manner where you focus on solutions instead of negative emotions. If your partner is the exact opposite and they prefer to shout and scream and they get even more angry when you don't show negative emotions as well. Then this can only make the arguments worse so it's important to recognise how you both argue and how best to deal with your different approaches.

Two final aspects of this recognition part of parental conflict is to make sure you think about what triggers you and your partner. It will definitely take some time to think about and identify some of the issues that might trigger a strong reaction in you or your partner. Most people just go through their entire lives without giving this much thought and this leads to a lot of negative relationship patterns because the couple aren't able to identify triggers and adapt their behaviour to deal with these triggering topics in a healthier way.

Finally, my main audience on The Psychology World Podcast are aspiring or qualified psychologists or people interested in psychology. Active listening skills are a massive part of our profession and whilst I strongly discourage you from bringing your therapy skills into the home because no partner wants to feel like a client. Yet listening to your partner or co-parent without interruption is flat out critical for reducing parental conflict because everyone wants to feel heard. Therefore, even if you have an important point to make or counter what they've said, just allow your partner to finish what they're saying and try to see the conflict from their point of view before responding.

<u>How To Reduce Parental Conflict By Taking A Break, Being Open To Compromise and Choosing the Right Time?</u>

Three more ways to reduce parental conflict includes if you can't stay calm during an argument or conflict, then please take a break. I don't think it's possible to avoid conflict with heated emotions forever. Even for myself who never really tends to get angry or show heated emotions, there are times when I do get angry and I can show a lot of heated emotions. When these situations arise, it is normally a good idea to take a break so both people in the conflict can take some time to cool down so when you next come back to the conversation it will hopefully go better.

Penultimately, in any sort of conflict, it's important to choose the right time to address issues and this is something I've learnt over the past few weeks. It turns out that a major difference between people with anxious attachment and avoidant attachment is that a person with anxious attachment tends to want to resolve conflict immediately even if this is a bad time when the other person doesn't want to engage in conflict. Whereas an avoidant person will avoid discussing and resolving conflict at all.

I mention these attachment facts because I recently learnt with some conflict in my house that I wanted to resolve conflict immediately but the moment I picked was not a good time for the other person and this made the conflict even worse.

Therefore, if you want to talk to your partner or co-parent about an important issue then it's best if you make sure you give yourselves enough time to talk about the issue. Ideally, this discussion will happen somewhere where you won't be interrupted or overheard, so it's a good idea to set aside some time to have a proper conversation when it suits you both.

Finally, you can reduce parental conflict by being open to compromise. I know from experience that when we're in an argument with heated emotions, we can just focus on "winning" an argument and making sure that we are the ones who walk away with the best result. The problem with this approach to arguments is that it means we don't tend to reach a solution with our partner, so this isn't a helpful way of resolving issues. Therefore, it's more helpful to be clear with your co-parent about what you're willing to compromise on and what you won't. Boundaries are critical in all relationships and this is another boundary exercise, what are you flexible on and what aren't you.

Interestingly, once you start thinking about compromise you'll probably realise some of these areas that you could never originally compromise on are actually less important than you thought.

Conclusion

Life is stressful and I cannot imagine how hard it is raising a child with the stressors of work, home life, friendships, relationships and so many other factors on top of that. Parenting and life as an adult is not easy. Therefore, it is normal for parents to argue because sometimes we all just need a release when our stressors get to unbearable levels.

That isn't the problem.

The problem is when parental conflict and arguments become often and extreme. This only damages your child's development by harming their physical, emotional and social development. As well as it harms their academic performance and parental conflict has long-term effects that can ensure the harmful damage effects conflict inflicts on children lasts long into adulthood.

This is why it's critical that parents learn how to reduce conflict by focusing on keeping themselves safe, understand how both parents argument, avoid using "you" statements and use "I" statements instead, if parents cannot stay calm then take a break, and choose the right time to address issues and listen without interrupting your partner. As well as it's helpful to know what triggers you and your partner and most importantly, be open to compromise in conflict.

Parental conflict doesn't have to escalate to damaging levels, it is avoidable if parents take a step back, learn how to deal with their emotions and conflict better and focus on doing this for the betterment of their child. Reducing conflict does take work and a lot of effort but if it means ensuring your child has the best and healthiest start in life, doesn't that make it all worth it?

Here are some questions to get you thinking at the end of this social psychology podcast episode:

- How often did your parents argue when you were a kid?
- How do you argue now?
- What triggers you and your partner in a relationship?
- What unhealthy ways of communicating might you and your partner have?
- How could you and your partner reduce conflict in your relationship?

Social Psychology References and Further Reading

Amjad, M. J., Nawaz, A. H., & Zubair, M.

(2024). Parental Conflicts and Child Socialization: An Impact Analysis of Parent Stress in Southern Punjab, Pakistan. *Review of Law and Social Sciences*, *2*(4), 09-19.

Bate, J., Pham, P. T., & Borelli, J. L. (2021). Be my safe haven: Parent–child relationships and emotional health during COVID-19. *Journal of pediatric psychology*, *46*(6), 624-634.

Cummings, E. M., & Schatz, J. N. (2012). Family conflict, emotional security, and child development: translating research findings into a prevention program for community families. Clinical Child and Family Psychology Review, 15, 14-27.

He, D., Niu, G., Hu, Y., Song, K., Zhou, Z., & Fan, C. (2024). The relationship between parental conflict and adolescent cyberbullying: the roles of parent-child attachment and core self-evaluation. *Current Psychology*, *43*(9), 8230-8240.

Hess, S. (2022). Effects of inter-parental conflict on children's social well-being and the mediation role of parenting behavior. Applied Research in Quality of Life, 17(4), 2059-2085.

https://www.kent.gov.uk/education-and-children/kent-family-hub/mental-health-and-family-relationships/reducing-arguments-and-conflict-between-parents

Jones, J. H., Call, T. A., Wolford, S. N., & McWey, L. M. (2021). Parental stress and child outcomes: The mediating role of family conflict. *Journal of Child and Family Studies*, *30*, 746-756.

Özaslan, A., Yıldırım, M., Güney, E., Güzel, H. Ş., & İşeri, E. (2022). Association between problematic internet use, quality of parent-adolescents relationship, conflicts, and mental health problems. *International Journal of Mental Health and Addiction*, *20*(4), 2503-2519.

Sarrazin, J., & Cyr, F. (2007). Parental Conflicts and Their Damaging Effects on Children. Journal of Divorce & Remarriage, 47(1-2), 77–93. https://doi.org/10.1300/J087v47n01_05

I SURVIVED. HIGHS, LOWS, LESSONS LEARNT FROM RAPE ONE YEAR ON.

Rape and other forms of sexual violence is beyond awful. It is one of the worse, most traumatic and devastating things that can happen to a person. During sexual violence, someone takes everything away from you, your control, your consent, your ability to do anything at all. You just go into survival mode and the consequences of sexual violence are immense. There isn't a single area of your life that sexual violence isn't impacted by. Therefore, in this clinical psychology podcast episode, to mark the one-year anniversary of my rape, I want to explain the highs, lows and lessons from the past year as I survived my rape and everything I had to deal with afterwards. There were a lot of awful, horrific things that I had to deal with as a rape survivor in the past year, but there have been some highs too. By the end of this clinical psychology podcast episode, you'll know some of the negative mental health consequences of sexual violence, how sexual violence can destroy lives and how people can deal with sexual trauma. This is a great, deeply personal episode that you're going to learn a lot from.

Note: whilst this psychology podcast episode will talk about rape and other forms of sexual violence, I will not include any graphic details about what happened to me during my attack.

One-Year Anniversary Of My Rape

On the 13th April 2024, I was raped and as much as I know some people will call me a liar because of the societal myth that people Assigned Male at Birth never get raped and they are always the rapists. That is a lie and I have done a lot of research over the past year about the truth behind sexual violence, and how and why men and women can be both the sexual predator and the survivor. Hence, I am just going to be honest and tell you about my experience and if people call me a liar or a fake just seeking attention then so be it. I've been called it all over the past year so it won't be anything new to me.

Therefore, on the 13th April 2024, I was raped in a hookup that went very wrong. After a lifetime of being abused, hated and never being accepted for being gay, and with my friends all in happy relationships where they could do whatever they wanted without the fear of death and being beaten. I just wanted a single night of being gay, a single night where I could experience something that was perfectly natural and normal for other people, and a single night where I could be free.

It really didn't work out like that at all so I was raped. Contrast to all the myths and lies about sexual violence, I didn't scream, fight back or try to stop him. I simply went into survival mode and I fawned because I didn't want to make him angry, I didn't want him to hurt me anymore than he was already and I wanted to escape as soon as possible.

I survived.

I was in denial for two days about what had happened to me because I thought that was simply how sex worked. Then as more and more trauma responses manifested themselves, I realised I was raped and then everything happened. I developed Post-Traumatic Stress Disorder along with intense social anxiety so I couldn't really go out by myself because I was so anxious and terrified of being raped again.

And I have discussed a lot of what happened to me over the next seven-months in different episodes of The Psychology World Podcast.

Now I want to focus on the lows and the lessons learnt before wrapping up with the highs of the past year along with a few final lessons.

The Lows of The Past Year After Being Raped

The Post-Traumatic Stress Disorder

There have been a lot of different factors and mental health consequences that have not been fun in the past year. I think the worse because it encompasses so many different facets of my mental health was the Post-Traumatic Stress Disorder. That was seriously horrible to experience because the majority of people think it is just soldiers who can experience PTSD. Yet I did because whenever a rape memory was triggered or I was reminded of my rape whether this was through something I saw, something I hear or an intrusive thought or flashback. I had severe trauma reactions.

I would literally run away at times. I would get so fearful and scared that I was going to die, be raped or get beaten. Or I would go into survival mode and once I was safe, I would have a full-on breakdown because it was simply too much for me.

One of my triggers was seeing fat men, and I don't say that to be fatphobic but because my rapist was a fat man. I couldn't actually stand to be in the same room as a fat man because it would cause me to have a breakdown and enter fight-or-flight mode. The same went for hearing or thinking about the name of my rapist or experiencing any sort of sexual or romantic attraction.

Which was really tragic because when I thought a guy was cute or attractive after my rape, I would have an extreme trauma reaction. That was really horrible, because I was raped in April and then it was summer, and I won't deny that I like summer because men can look very hot in shorts and t-shirts.

Sleep was another major issue because of rape dreams. There wasn't a single night for the first six months or more when I didn't have a rape-related dream. It wasn't even related to what actually happened, it was just how my mind twisted everything. I had dreams about my rapist killing me, my friends raping me, people I had only seen briefly at social events raping and beating and killing me.

The First Lessons: Rape Has No End of Impacts, Need for Processing Trauma and Self-Compassion

On the whole, there were other aspects of the PTSD that I flat out hated, like the intense social anxiety and the depression that I've spoken about before on the podcast. Yet the stark impact that sexual violence has on a person was unreal and I couldn't believe how many different ways it impacts you. From my work to my friendships to my ability to go outside and everything else, my rape and my mental health impacted so much of it.

As a result, this massive negative aspect of 2024 where the entire year was basically taken up me healing from my rape and recovering from sexual trauma. This aspect taught me the importance of having good friends and a good social support network, as well as never underestimating the power of trauma. In one of my books coming out in the next few years, I include the line "if you don't deal with your trauma, your trauma will deal with you," and that is so true.

You need to keep healing and processing what happened to you otherwise your trauma will make you process what happened to you in the worse ways possible. As well as this low taught me the important of self-compassion too, which has become an important part of my life now. I used to beat myself up so often for my mental health, for feeling so depressed and anxious and having such severe trauma responses that I couldn't do anything for days or months at a time. I essentially didn't have a life in 2024.

And that made me feel even worse about myself, my life and my mental health. Thankfully learning self-compassion helped me deal with those negative self-critical thoughts.

I still use all of these important lessons in my life nowadays to help my mental health whenever it dips.

Self- Blame and People Who Know Less Judging Me

A second major low of the past year was that at first I didn't blame myself for my rape because it wasn't my fault. Rape and other forms of sexual violence is never the survivor's fault because there was nothing they could have done to prevent it. That is the simple truth of it.

However, when I started reading things online, seeing how certain people who were very dear to me started blaming me, judging me and making me feel awful for what some rapist had done to me. That only made my mental health worse. For example, two people very close to me who were meant to love me no matter what couldn't handle the fact that I was raped. So they blamed me, they wouldn't allow me to call it rape, they wouldn't allow me to talk about it and they were very firm that it was my fault. I shouldn't have done it and I shouldn't have been gay.

And as whilst researching rape and sexual trauma more and more was very healing for me because it allowed me to see everything I was going through was normal. It reminded me of the world I actually lived in and how society saw people like me. It reminded me that sexual violence is extremely common, society always blames the survivor and the world is always against the survivor because of lies, myths and misconceptions. And the extreme rare cases of false allegations of rape don't help matters.

Therefore, as I was exposed to those societal judgements and certain people in my life judging me and blaming me for being raped, my mental health only declined. And what really annoyed me about these people was that I am unfortunately an expert by experience when it comes to rape. I was raped. These people were not, and yet because of their egos, and what they've seen on the news. They believe it is their God-given right to tell me, the rape survivor, how I am meant to be feeling, how I am meant to be behaving and how I am not meant to be getting raped.

It is outrageous and disgusting that people think they know better than rape survivors.

Second Lesson: You Learn Who Your Friends Are After Rape

The second major lesson I've learnt in the past year is that after being raped, you really learn who your friends are. You learn who you can rely on, who you can't and how people can deal with certain news. My best friend could certainly handle the news about my rape and they were great to me for the longest of times and I will always be extremely grateful for everything they did for me. Yet honestly, because of my disorganised attachment and their avoidant attachment styles and other traits about my best friend, we both turned the friendship very toxic and our friendship has never really recovered from my rape trauma and everything we accidentally did to each other during that time.

There have been friends who I've told and they act like it never happened and they let me talk about it whereas others let me talk about it but they don't know what to say at all.

I don't blame them at all because rape is awful and it is hard to know what to say.

As a result, in the past year, I really have learnt the different levels of friendship that you can have with people, what you can and what you cannot say to others and I have just learnt a lot about attachment and friendships in the last year.

At the time of writing actually, I'm doing a lot of work on my own disorganised attachment style because even though I am making great progress, I want to deal with it as much as I can so it doesn't harm any more of my friendships and relationships.

Self-Harm and Suicidality

This is probably the lowest part of the past 365 days because I self-harmed a lot in the past year. I haven't self-harmed since the 30th December because I can deal with a lot more things than I could previously and I really have worked hard to deal with whatever happens. Including learning that certain people who I'm close to where having sex. Again, even thinking or learning about sex was a major trigger for me up until recently.

Even though a year later, sexual contact is still to much of a trigger at the moment for me.

I think I self-harmed because I wanted to punish myself for being raped. A lot of important people in my life were telling me that it was my fault, that I should have done things differently and I interpreted certain things that being my fault. For example, I remember last June I was driving to the university in the evening for a social event and I parked my car, it was a beautiful evening and I was listening to the radio. And I listened to a news report about a cop congratulating a rape survivor for coming forward because they were able to arrest the rapist because of it.

I cried so hard, and self-harmed in the end of it.

For me, because other people had already told me that I was a failure for not reporting it, for not going to the police and a whole bunch of other factors. I felt that I needed to be punished and control was another factor too. I self-harmed because I wanted to be in control and feel something instead of depression, anxiety and other trauma responses.

And as my mental health continued to decline, I went to kill myself three times. I won't explain how but I tried to kill myself three times and this was how I learnt how strained my relationship with my best friend became. They were so badly hurt, in so much pain and I later learnt that this is the point where they started having panic attacks over me because they really didn't want me to die.

I really did destroy our friendship with these suicidal attempts.

However, contrast to popular myths and lies, I didn't want to do suicide because I wanted to. I tried to kill myself because I didn't think there was another way out. My quality of life was so low and I couldn't go outside, I couldn't do anything with my life and my mental health was so bad that I couldn't do anything I enjoyed. I doubted I could ever form a good relationship, I doubted I could ever have sex and so many other factors.

I just couldn't see another way out and I suppose I knew that it would hurt my friends and my housemates. Yet I just didn't want to be in pain anymore.

I wanted it all to end.

Third Lesson: Life Actually Does Get Better

There have been other lows in the past year, like my anorexia, but I'll talk about them in one of the books that are coming out in the next few years. As a result, in the past year, I have learnt that life really does get better in the end. It will take a while, believe me, it seriously will take so much longer than you want.

Nonetheless, your life will get better overtime. It will be small changes at first and you will be able to do more and more over time, and it will never seem enough. You will be angry, upset and depressed that you cannot just magically bounce back from your sexual trauma, but you will get there.

If you keep putting in the therapy work, if you keep healing and if you intend to survive this, then you will in the end.

And now as I transition onto the highs, I am really looking forward to sharing with you the positives of the past year since I was raped.

The Highs Of One-Year On From Being Raped

Becoming An Expert By Experience

I fully understand that this is a very, very weird benefit of the past year but as an aspiring clinical psychologist, honestly I am glad to have the mental health and counselling experiences that I have. Now I understand what it's like to have PTSD, to have intense social anxiety and to have major depression. Of course, everyone's experience is slightly different but I can now understand and empathise with future clients because I vaguely know what hell they are going through because I have lived through it too.

I am grateful to know how to survive these awful mental health experiences and I am really happy that I went through specialist rape counselling, and my anorexia counselling. I have learnt so much about myself, self-soothing and trauma recovery because of my two excellent counsellors. I have had such lovely and powerful conversations with both of them and I have learnt tips and tricks and techniques that I can now use with future clients once I'm qualified.

Without my rape, I never would have learnt those things.

Of course, I am not saying I am grateful to be raped. I will never be grateful to having gone through that but I could look back on the past 365 days with hatred, bitterness and I could not focus on any positives. Yet that isn't actually healthy. Still, grieve for everything that you have lost, been through and allow yourself to feel all the painful emotions that you're experiencing. Yet as part of positive psychology and compassion for ourselves and others, we should try to focus on the positives.

It is actually a great way in my personal experiences to push away suicidal thoughts. Even on the really, really bad days if you can name three or five positive things that happened then you really do start to feel better.

It's a simple but very powerful technique.

So the past year has taught me a lot of valuable techniques, life experiences and mental health experiences that will serve me in the future. It means I can relate to clients more, come to clinical work with a unique insight and it gives me more experiences to draw on when I'm writing these podcast episodes.

I am a survivor, not a victim.

Healing, Healing and More Healing

The penultimate high is a great benefit of the past year because I am finally healed from all sorts of different traumas that have happened to me in my life. I explain more about this in my upcoming book *Healing As A Survivor* but the vast majority of my rape trauma responses were actually just heightened trauma responses that I got from my childhood because of my child abuse. I was able to deal with all of that and I was able to learn healthy boundaries and how to be empowered for the first time in my life.

I flat out loved resetting my boundaries and resetting my relationships so many people, because I am not perfect at it. Yet I want to stop the harmful, toxic relationships that have ruled my life for so many years and I am already reaping the benefits.

Furthermore, I'm healing in terms of my anorexia too. My rape really did refuel my anorexia to new levels and I was losing a kilogram a week for months, I was making myself really ill and fatigued all the time. My health wasn't the best because of the condition, but in the past year, I've healed more because I've targeted my anorexia. Sure I still have anorexia because you can't eliminate mental health conditions, but I know how to cope with my sense of control, strong emotions and my anorexic thoughts.

I'll continue to have flare-ups in the future, but I seriously doubt my anorexia will ever get bad again. I know how to manage it and because I know who I am, what my values are and everything that anorexia threatens. I really don't want my anorexia to return.

At the end of this psychology podcast episode, I'll share one of my favourite quotes of all time with you because it hits this topic right on the head.

New Friendships and I Had A Partner

In the past year, some of the highs have definitely included the new friendships I've made along the way. A good few of them haven't lasted because of my mental health, my disorganised attachment and a few factors related to the people themselves. Yet I've still really enjoyed making those friendships because they were all great people and I honestly wish them all the best with the future.

Equally, now I have my friends who I spent almost every Saturday with playing board games and/ or Dungeons and Dragons or another RPG system with. It was only yesterday I met up with three of them and we played board games outside in the sun for a few hours before moving inside to play for another four-ish hours before we went to dinner at Wetherspoons in Canterbury.

I really enjoy hanging out with my friends on Saturdays because I never would have met or become friends with them otherwise. I have a lot of fun with them, we always have great conversations and it's how I met my partner.

Which is certainly something I never expected.

After I was raped, given all my mental health struggles, how bad I was at social relationships and my low self-esteem, I never expected to have a relationship for 6-weeks. 6-weeks full of laughter, fun and just enjoying being someone's partner. I had my first kisses, I held someone's hand in public for the first time and I was just able to do things that I had never done before, and things that I never would have dreamed of a few years ago because I would have been too terrified because of trauma.

We even both stayed up until 4:15 in the morning one day just talking and hanging out and cuddling.

I really enjoyed that relationship more than I wanted to admit, even though it was casual and I was able to do casual.

We didn't even break-up after 6-weeks because we weren't into each other. We broke up because making out with my partner brought up a lot of trauma for me, and my partner had been repeatedly assaulted in their last relationship so they were struggling too at times and they weren't in a good place themselves.

My partner agreed if they were in a better place they would want something deeper, committed and longer-term with me. And ever since we got together, they kept saying how they didn't want to hurt me.

It was sweet.

There's a lot more to it than that but considering this a public podcast that is all I'm going to say.

However, I still really enjoyed it and after I was raped, I never ever imagined forming new friendships, certainly not playing dungeons and dragons for hours upon hours with them, and I truly never imagined someone as beautiful as my partner would say yes to me.

There really is always hope.

It doesn't matter if you were raped, it doesn't matter how much trauma you've been through, it doesn't matter how dark you think the world is. There is hope that great, wonderful things can happen to you in the end.

It may take far longer than you imagine, or it might take no time at all, but it can happen in the end.

Brief Guide To Actions We Can Take To End Sexual Violence

In the future, I have another episode on the actions we can take to end sexual violence once and for all because it is possible. Yet I want to briefly mention three things we can do at the end of this podcast episode to work towards ending sexual violence.

You Need To Learn About Sexual Violence And Share It With Others

I know I'm preaching to the converted here but if we're going to end sexual violence then you need to learn about it, what it is and the truth behind sexual violence. In other words, you need to overcome all the myths and misconceptions that we've created for ourselves in society, because these myths are harmful and extremely common. Therefore, it's good to know that online resources, like this podcast, have made it easier than ever before to get accurate information about sexual violence as well as how common it is within our communities and how it devastates lives.

Knowledge is power against sexual violence, so please, make sure you read about it and learn about sexual violence.

The next step is sharing what you've learnt with other people.

You Can Advocate For Youth Prevention Programs

As I've spoken about before on the podcast, the majority of perpetrators of sexual violence are teenagers and young adults. Therefore, if we're going to stop sexual violence then we need to give young people the knowledge and tools for healthy relationships. This includes tools to help them understand consent and to help them have a healthy sexuality.

Thankfully, over the years, there has been a lot of work done on the development of youth prevention programs to help give young people the tools to have healthy relationships without them believing they have to commit sexual violence.

You Can Identify Organisations And People Working With Sexual Assault Survivors In Your Community And Connect With Them

To help take action against sexual violence within your community, you can see who's doing prevention and response work in the local area. For example, this can include a family justice centre, a rape crisis centre and local political groups in charge of legislating against sexual violence. This can be a powerful way to take action to end sexual assault because by reaching out to these organisations and people you can get involved in their networks and be an active member of them so you can use your interests, skills and abilities to support them. For instance, if you identify a gap in their resources, like there being no way for people to donate to the local cause, then you could help them fill that gap in the community's network.

Conclusion

In all honesty, I probably haven't scratched the surface of all the highs and lows from the past 365 days. For instance, I haven't mentioned all the good things about university, my transgender mental health studies, my Outreach work, my family, my new Irish citizenship and more. Yet that's a good thing. The past year has been hellish. I don't wish my past year on anyone because of everything in my life that has fallen apart, been smashed and annihilated and everything I have had to go through and do just to survive. No one should ever have to go through it. No one should ever have to go through the Post-Traumatic Stress Disorder, the rough and eye-opening experience of learning who your friends actually are in your darkest moments, and the self-harm and suicide.

No one should have to go through that.

However, me and so many other amazing, bright people survived our trauma. There were great benefits of the past year too and 2024 will be extremely transformative for me in some bad ways but a lot of good ways too. The past 365 days have allowed me to reset my relationships and actually learn who I am through doing a lot of healing, it has given me some great real world experience about mental health difficulties and how to cope with their maladaptive effects, and I've forged some great friendships.

I had a beautiful partner for 6-weeks, and we might not be together anymore. Yet my partner's still happy to kiss, hold hands and hang out, so I'm happy. I can still experience stuff for the first time in my life.

Ultimately, I want to end this podcast episode by saying, if you're an aspiring or qualified psychologist or a psychology student. There will be times when you meet a client who has experienced a type of trauma, be it sexual trauma or not. The past year has also taught me how outrageously high the number of sexual trauma incidents are, and when this happens in your clinical work. It is important that you remember it is possible to survive and you believe it yourself.

My anorexia counsellor and my old private counsellor who I forgot to mention earlier, they have no training and no real awareness about sexual violence. Yet there were still great things they did to help me and just help me through my time. The best result is always to refer rape survivors to rape crisis centres because East Kent Rape Crisis Centre is flat out amazing and they helped me to save myself.

However, aspiring and qualified psychologists should get some awareness in psychological trauma and stabilisation. You will come across a client with trauma one day and trauma is specialist work but you can help the client more than you possibly know.

And finally, if you're a survivor, then please keep going, keep fighting, keep working towards healing. It will be painful, it will be slow and there will be days when you want to die because it seems so much easier.

Please don't though.

If I had managed to kill myself any one of those three times, I wouldn't be here right now talking to you wonderful people. I wouldn't be able to share my experience, I wouldn't be able to learn all the great things that I flat out love, and I wouldn't be able to write, read fiction and do all the other thousands of things that make me happy.

And I wouldn't have been able to meet my partner, have my first kiss and just be with someone. We're still friends now and I've cried a lot over that relationship because I hate that someone raped and assaulted my partner who is such a lovely and caring person.

Sexual violence has to end and it will one day.

"As long as I have my unshakable self, I can dig in with both feet with all my might. As long as I know who I am, all my doubts, hesitations and frustrations will disappear. And no demon on earth can escape my descending blade,"

-Tokito, Demon Slayer anime Season 4

If you think about that quote from a mental health perspective then you'll realise why that is my favourite quote of all time.

Just keep going yourself and remember it gets better in the end.

Forensic Psychology References and Further Reading

What To Do When Depression Makes it Impossible to get out of bed?

What is window of tolerance?

What's it like to experience a major depressive episode?

What is Post-Traumatic Stress Disorder?

Why An Erection Isn't Consent?

Armatta, J. (2018). Ending sexual violence through transformative justice. *Interdisciplinary Journal of Partnership Studies*, *5*(1), 4-4.

https://www.psychologytoday.com/gb/blog/awareness-action/202203/3-ways-take-action-end-sexual-assault

Kirby, P. (2015). Ending sexual violence in conflict: the Preventing Sexual Violence Initiative and its critics. *International Affairs*, *91*(3), 457-472.

Tutchell, E., & Edmonds, J. (2020). *Unsafe spaces: Ending sexual abuse in universities*. Emerald Publishing Limited.

Wessells, M. G., & Kostelny, K. (2021). Understanding and ending violence against children: A holistic approach. *Peace and Conflict: Journal of Peace Psychology*, *27*(1), 3.

Wright, H. (2015). Ending Sexual Violence and the War System–Or Militarizing Feminism?. *International Feminist Journal of Politics*, *17*(3), 503-507.

WHY PSYCHOLOGISTS DO NOT ONLY DEAL WITH CRAZY PEOPLE

I don't think anyone can go through their psychology journey without encountering any myths about psychology. A few years ago at a gender reveal party, I was talking to my brother's dad (we have different ones) and he explained how he needed to see a psychologist because of an injury before he could go to work. Yet when he was younger and even now, he wouldn't do it because everyone back then knew psychologists only saw "crazy" people. After I explained the types of people who psychologists actually helped, he was more relaxed about going. This is just one out of the millions of myths that psychology and psychologists face every day. Therefore, in this clinical psychology podcast episode, you'll learn about the "crazy people" myth about psychology, who psychologists help and more about clinical psychology in the real world. If you enjoy learning about psychology myths, careers in psychology and mental health then this is a great episode for you.

WHY PSYCHOLOGISTS DO NOT ONLY DEAL WITH CRAZY PEOPLE? (Extract from Myths About Clinical Psychology by Connor Whiteley COPYRIGHT 2025)

If there is any psychology myth that is going to get me on my soapbox then it is definitely going to be this myth because there was so much to unpack and I'm actually really excited about this chapter. Therefore, in this myth chapter we're going to be focusing on the stupid idea that psychologists only deal with so-called crazy people.

This is going to be a lot of fun.

Little Recap

So the main reason why this myth is automatically wrong is because it builds on the idea that only mental health professionals and clinical psychologists are psychologists. Also, this myth completely forgets there are other types of psychologists. For example, business psychologists, social psychologists, experimental psychologists, academic psychologists, and on and on and on.

Therefore, even if this myth was true and psychologists only saw crazy people (I absolutely hate saying that) then it would just be impractical for psychology to only see crazy people. For example, you might be able to argue that a social psychologist and an academic psychologist might meet with a crazy person for academic research. But I would have no idea and no explanation as to why the hell a business psychologist would want to work with a crazy person because business psychologists only really working HR departments.

Therefore, this myth is just unpractical from a practicality standpoint and how the psychology job market actually works.

What Even Are Crazy People?

Now then if we jump on my soapbox for a moment what the hell are crazy people. I have no idea what crazy people actually are because it just comes back to this myth in general society that only crazy people like Psychopaths, murderers, evil abuses and paedophiles have mental health difficulties. It is one of the most disgusting myths ever that if you have a mental health difficulty then you're a crazy person, you're dangerous, you're insecure, you are unstable, you're going to hurt someone or kill someone.

Like forgive my language but is absolute bullshit. I absolutely fucking hate this myth because it is so dangerous, disgusting and these people just need to learn what psychology actually involves.

And even if someone was apparently crazy in terms of being psychotic for example. It doesn't mean that they are a bad person, it doesn't mean they don't deserve support, it doesn't mean they deserve to be helped any less than anyone else. Because people with psychosis can live good lives, they can receive mental health support and they can do really good things about their lives if given the right mental health support and treatment.

The very idea that just because someone's crazy according to this horrible societal myth or idea about what a bad person looks like. It's just horrific because even a psychotic person still deserves good treatment, good support and to live a good life. I just absolutely hate this myth that says certain people just because they have sudden conditions are lesser or dangerous or they're evil.

Of course, I am not saying that psychopaths, sociopaths and some people with psychotic disorders are perfect or nice and they don't commit crimes. Yet the idea that you would want to tarnish an entire clinical population with the same brush and say all of them are bad people that are going to commit crimes and hurt people is disgusting.

Anyway, that is my rant over and that is me jumping off my soapbox because I hate this idea that there are crazy people in the world and it is absolute fucking bullshit.

What's the Truth?

Let's now look into what clinical psychologists actually deal with and the amazing people that they help. So in reality clinical psychologists help and they deal with anyone has a mental health difficulty or mental health condition. Some examples of these mental health conditions or difficulties can include suicidal idealization, depression, anxiety, self-harm, eating disorders, or disordered eating to be honest. Trauma survivors with Post-Traumatic Stress Disorder is another possible group too.

As we can already see clinical psychologists deal with a lot of different conditions and people and some of them are really normal. For example, neurodivergence, like ADHD and autism, and clinical psychologists can also deal with learning disabilities. And it is this really wide range of people that you get to deal with and you get to help that makes me love psychology and really makes me love clinical psychology even more because you can do so much with it.

Since at the time of writing in February 2024 so far, I've done two major bits of psychology work experience and I've done tons of different bits and pieces on the side. I've worked with people with learning disabilities and this was quite wide-ranging and if you go check out the backlist of The Psychology World Podcast, you can actually find the episode that I wrote about my experience. And then I've also worked with transgender individuals at a Gender Identity Clinic, which I really loved. So as you can see just from those two really simple examples I worked with such different people with different needs, different mental health difficulties and they were in very different situations.

And then a final example before I start making my point about the truth behind this myth is that I've also spoken about this on the podcast before and I do have A Memoir and it might be out by the time this book's released, but I've also been through some trauma and abuse and I went for mental health support I went for person-centred counselling. And the very idea that I'm crazy, I'm messed up and I have a problem just because I needed some counselling, I think it's very disgusting to be honest. Not so much hurtful because I've heard it all before but I think the fact that people want to judge me for what I went through and how I dealt with it is beyond disgusting and I just don't understand it. Like the very idea that someone says I'm a bad person for what other people did to me and how other people traumatised me and how others abused me, I think is laughable. Due to you can tell that these people who are saying these things just don't understand what it's like to go through certain stuff.

And if you've read any of my books, if you listen to my podcast and I hope that you've understood this through my tone and how passionate I am in these chapters, I hope you know that I'm a lovely person, I love helping people and all I want to do is support our amazing clients in the future when I do become a clinical psychologist.

Overall, this serves as a great segway into my point about what the truth behind this myth is, in reality, clinical psychologists deal with normal people with normal mental health difficulties in normal situations, and sometimes extremely abnormal situations, like abuse and trauma. Clinical psychologists deal with people that laugh, that love their families, have children, are sons, mothers, daughters, and children, and maybe trans. They are just normal people. These clients that clinical psychologists have to deal with like going out with their friends at the weekend and they might drink. They like having fun with their friends, they like watching TV, they might like reading, they might like watching movies just like you.

All these people that clinical psychologists have to deal with that makes them different from other people is just that they're brave enough, they're courageous enough and they are amazing enough to admit they need mental health support to improve their lives, decrease their psychological distress, and give themselves power. To me that makes them flat out amazing and I will not have anyone saying they're crazy or bad or evil people just because of some stupid myth.

And if my passion in this chapter has offended some belief of yours. Then I'm not sorry because this is such a dangerous annoying myth that I do want to stamp out because it's not fair on our client so it isn't fair on people like me who've had mental health experiences and it's just a disgusting myth that Society does need to remove.

Clinical Psychology Reference and Further Reading

Whiteley, C. (2025) *Myths About Clinical Psychology: A Psychology Student's and Professional's Guide To Myths About Clinical Psychology.* CGD Publishing. England.

HOW DOES CHILDHOOD TRAUMA IMPACT BOUNDARIES?

After something personal happened last night, all I can think about today is trauma and considering this psychology podcast episode is already likely to be late going out, I didn't want to argue with myself. I just wanted to do an episode on something I was already thinking about because what we experience in our childhood can have a massive impact on our relationships. For example, what *we* think a healthy relationship and boundaries look like and how we believe the social world works. Therefore, in this clinical psychology podcast episode, you'll learn about how childhood trauma impacts relationships, how trauma survivors can improve their relationship boundaries and a lot more useful and insightful information. If you enjoy learning about mental health, trauma outcomes and a bit of social psychology then this is a great episode for you.

How Does Trauma Impact Relationships?

Not a single one of us is born with an innate understanding of healthy boundaries. We learn what boundaries are healthy and what isn't healthy in a relationship by trying out different things, learning about social relationships and unfortunately, getting hurt along the way. All of us go through life thinking we know what healthy boundaries are until one day or one moment, we realise what we thought was a healthy boundary actually isn't. For example, you might have a fight with your best friend and it doesn't go the way you expected and you or your friend is hurt. Equally, you might find relationships really overwhelming and other people might believe that you're simply too "sensitive". Finally, and this happens to me somewhat often, you find out that you aren't actually as close to someone as you thought and you start to feel like an outsider.

Personally, I'll be the first to say that I find interpersonal relationships quite overwhelming at times because of my disorganised attachment style that I'm working on. As well as having childhood trauma and autism makes it difficult to do the entire social relationship part anyway, especially with neurotypical people who don't exactly have the same communication style as me. I have no problem talking with anyone and I love forming those relationships, but honestly, it is hard for me to form deep and meaningful friendships and relationships.

Boundaries are sometimes a major problem for me because I don't understand them. Also, I didn't really have great role models in my life to model these behaviours from.

On the whole, we all learn in the end that boundaries are a fine balance between feeling safe and vulnerable in a relationship where we can share our authentic emotions whilst asserting our personal limits and needs with other people when we feel we need their support.

However, when childhood trauma is added into the mix, this adds additional layers of complexity into trying to understand what healthy boundaries in relationships are, because of their traumatic experiences.

How Does Childhood Trauma Affect Relationship Boundaries?

Unlike when adults experience trauma and their perception of healthy boundaries aren't always affected, children who experience trauma are different. Since children living in dangerous, neglectful or abusive situations nearly always have their sense of boundaries negatively impacted because they have to depend on untrustworthy adults just to survive. These children don't have any choice and as part of this survival process, a child's brain has to do some very intense work. Especially as, Jannia Fisher (a trauma specialist) explains in her book Healing The Fragmented Selves of Trauma Survivors:

"When attachment figures are abusive, the child's only source of safety and protection becomes simultaneously the source of immediate danger, leaving the child caught between two conflicting sets of instincts. On the one hand, they are driven by the attachment instinct to seek proximity, comfort, and protection from attachment figures. On the other hand, they are driven by equally strong animal defense instincts to freeze, fight, flee or submit…before they get too close to the frightening parent." (Fisher, 2017 p. 24)

In other words, as much as a child knows their caregiver is abusive or being neglectful, the child still wants to form an attachment and bond with them because the child innately knows they need the adult in order to survive.

Yet as the child tries to do this more and more, they experience a powerful and (I would say) almost horrific stress reaction that signals to their nervous system that a threat to their very survival is incoming so their body gets into fight-or-flight mode constantly.

To the child this means they learn very quickly that relationships are helpful because they are key to survival, but relationships are dangerous too. Therefore, the child adapts their perception of boundaries to fit this really weird paradox.

At the moment, I'm doing a lot of research and writing regarding attachment styles so this is really clear and tragic to read about in a trauma context.

Personally, I would love to say that this is wrong but it isn't. Based on my own experiences of having a very homophobic social environment and a lot of other things going on in other social situations. It's hard. You don't know what's safe, who to trust and you are always on edge just waiting for something bad to happen. It's horrible and over time, you can convince yourself that it is simply safer to be alone because if you don't let anyone in then no one can hurt you anymore.

Of course, your life gets really alone, isolated and awful if you continue that pattern of behaviour for too long.

In addition, I know we've never looked at Schema Therapy on the podcast before but within this form of psychotherapy, there are "mistrust/ abuse schemas" which can leave a person with more tolerance for being mistreated and have weaker boundaries. All because the person doesn't know any different. Making it quite the powerful revelation when the person realises that healthier boundaries are actually possible.

As a result, when a child makes a connection between their abuse or neglect that causes a traumatic stress response from their brain, so they either fight, flight, freeze or attach or feign with their attachment style or sense of boundaries. This leads to five different effects on the child's boundary style and as an aspiring or qualified psychologist it's important to understand these boundary styles so our approach to mental health work can be more trauma informed. Ultimately, helping us to support our clients feel safer and more in control in their relationships.

<u>What Are The Five Boundary Styles?</u>

As I mentioned in the last section, our mind and body have five reactions to trauma that impact how we perceive healthy relationship patterns. For example, firstly, there is the "fight" reaction where we believe we need to push our needs onto others, impose our own version of events or even attack other people if we think that it's necessary to preserve our urgent needs. This can lead to someone becoming self-absorbed in a relationship.

Secondly, you could react with a "flight" response where your childhood trauma has caused you to have anxiety around closeness and intimacy where you always find reasons to avoid getting too close or directly expressing an emotional need. This can lead to social and emotional isolation.

In my opinion, this second point definitely fits me because it's clear I have an anxious attachment style because I get stressed in close relationships. I find them scary and I get concerned about getting close to someone because I'm always scared they're going to abandon me like everyone else in my life. Thankfully, this is something I'm actively working on and I recently learnt I have disorganised attachment as my main form of attachment too.

Thirdly, there is the "freeze" reaction where a client might passively detach themselves or zone out from a situation and find ways to avoid conflict. This leads the client to being impulsive, procrastinate and experience self-alienation.

Penultimately, a client might have an "attach" reaction where they are overwhelmed with a strong, painful need to be close to others but they're always stuck feeling lonely, sad and other people might call them emotionally needy and desperate.

This is something I can partly relate too as part of my attachment style because when I do find someone I want to be close to, and this is even more true when I'm struggling myself. Yet I used to get as close as possible to someone and I didn't want to be lonely and I did come across as emotionally needy.

Finally, a client might have a "feign or submit" reaction to other people where they only think about the other person's needs so they degrade or they become blind to their own needs. Or they feel guilty or criticise themselves for having needs of their own.

I won't say too much because as someone who regularly interacts with someone who fits this description. I understand that it's a trauma response and it is just something that they have learnt, but it is hurtful and almost "annoying" to see someone not recognise this when they're calling you out for your own attachment and boundary issues. Since when someone with a "feign or submit" reaction does recognise their own needs and they stop supporting the other person without warning because they didn't realise how much they were degrading their needs. It's hurtful and it really sucks.

How To Cope With Boundary Styles Using Positive Self-Talk?

As a result if we're ever working with a client who might fall into one of these five reactions, even though they are likely to have a single main or dominant reaction but still dip into the other types of boundary styles depending on the situation. It's important that we help clients to learn how best to cope with their boundary styles, in addition to any trauma work that needs to be done.

Therefore, there are three things that clients can do to help themselves with their boundary style. Firstly, they can use journaling with a sense of curiosity and control as a way to track their relationship patterns. I'll be the first to admit that you will be blind to your relationship patterns because they are so normal for you and you don't know anything else. As well as you often only realise that you have unhealthy relationship patterns because someone has pointed it out to you. Yet if a client doesn't have access to someone who will point it out to them, they can use journaling to identify their feelings around staying present with emotions in relationships. And clients could explore what not submitting or feigning would be like for them. Also, they could explore the thoughts and feelings that going against their boundary style brings up. So the client can ultimately find out what they are most afraid of when it comes to changing up their boundary style.

Secondly, it's critical that clients learn to trust their body. This was a major part of my sexual trauma counselling because your body, your senses and your nervous system are a brilliant tool to help you survive and it picks up on so much more information than you even realise. Yet your body is the first thing that will tell you when your boundary style is being triggered so you can trust your body and learn from it. For example, if you enter a certain situation and you start feeling dread, anxious and like you're going to get shouted at or punished. Then notice these signs and figure out where you learnt them based on your trauma. Then you can identify areas to work on.

For me, at times my boundary styles can be triggered when I get close to people because I'm scared they're going to hurt me, betray me and I'm going to lose everything again like I have in the past. I never want to go through all that pain, suffering and conflict ever again.

Finally, clients can use self-talk to cope with their boundary style because after a client has noticed and identified their triggers. They can start talking to themselves and instead of being your scared traumatised child self, they can show themselves compassion, love and attention as an adult that the client might never have received as a child.

Internal Family System Therapy is essentially built around this idea and I have some experience with a few techniques from this therapy because of my private counselling in 2023. I found it really helpful.

Conclusion

On the whole, when it comes to childhood trauma, or as I found out last night all forms of trauma, it will affect you in a million different ways. It will affect you from your relationships, your attachment styles, how you relate to others, your mental health, perhaps your ability to work and so many more areas.

However, just because childhood trauma causes you or your client to have a certain boundary style, doesn't mean you're messed up, you're doomed or you can't change. The traumatised part of yourself is still inside you, it will be scared of being close to others because you don't want to risk going through your childhood again. I understand that, and that's okay. It really is.

Nonetheless, you're an adult now. You don't need to depend on neglectful or abusive adults anymore, and what you really need, what that child part of you really needs, is for you to compassionately care for that child part. Provide it with the love, comfort and reassurance that you probably never received as a child.

Once you realise this you can and probably should work on it in therapy with a trained trauma informed mental health professional. They can help you work through your trauma and most importantly, how to safely manage your relationship boundaries so you can grow and thrive instead of just survive.

Here are some questions at the end of this psychology podcast episode:

- Have you ever experienced childhood trauma?
- Do you or anyone you know fit into one of these boundary styles?
- How could you identify any triggers or situations that activate your boundary styles?
- Could you find a mental health professional to help you work through this?

Child Psychology References and Further Reading

Erozkan, A. (2016). The Link between Types of Attachment and Childhood Trauma. *Universal journal of educational research*, *4*(5), 1071-1079.

Fisher, Janina (2017) Healing the Fragmented Selves of Trauma Survivors: Overcoming Internal Self-Alienation. Routledge.

Fuchshuber, J., Hiebler-Ragger, M., Kresse, A., Kapfhammer, H. P., & Unterrainer, H. F. (2019). The influence of attachment styles and personality organization on emotional functioning after childhood trauma. *Frontiers in psychiatry*, *10*, 643.

MacDonald, K., Sciolla, A. F., Folsom, D., Bazzo, D., Searles, C., Moutier, C., ... & Norcross, B. (2015). Individual risk factors for physician boundary violations: The role of attachment style, childhood trauma and maladaptive beliefs. *General Hospital Psychiatry*, *37*(5), 489-496.

Skinner-Osei, P., & Levenson, J. S. (2018). Trauma-informed services for children with incarcerated parents. *Journal of Family Social Work*, *21*(4-5), 421-437.

Valeras, A. B., Cobb, E., Prodger, M., Hochberg, E., Allosso, L., & VandenHazel, H. (2019). Addressing adults with adverse childhood experiences requires a team approach. *The International Journal of Psychiatry in Medicine*, *54*(4-5), 352-360.

Walker, Pete (2013) Complex PTSD: From Surviving to Thriving: A Guide and Map for Recovering from Childhood Trauma. CreateSpace Independent Publishing Platform.

Yilmaz, H., Arslan, C., & Arslan, E. (2022). The effect of traumatic experiences on attachment styles. *Anales de Psicología/Annals of Psychology*, *38*(3), 489-498.

BESTSELLING AUTHOR OF FORENSIC PSYCHOLOGY
CONNOR WHITELEY
CLINICAL PSYCHOLOGY REFLECTIONS VOLUME 5
THOUGHTS ON CLINICAL PSYCHOLOGY, MENTAL HEALTH AND PSYCHOTHERAPY

CLINICAL PSYCHOLOGY REFLECTIONS VOLUME 5

Thoughts On Clinical Psychology, Mental Health and Psychotherapy

INTRODUCTION

Clinical psychology is an amazing area of psychology. It can improve lives, transform them and save people for the better, and it can decrease psychological distress too. That's why I love this great area of psychology.

However, the problem with how clinical psychology is taught in lecture theatres and formal education is that there are only so many topics you can teach, only so many debates you can talk about and there is only so much research in the world so you cannot have lively, heated debates at university.

I wanted somewhere to address this issue.

Therefore, I decided to write these clinical psychology reflection books where I can use evidence and research and my own fact-based opinions to explore some of the hottest debates in clinical psychology. As well as explore other topics from a clinical psychology perspective.

All these books are extremely fun to write and are fascinating so I know you're going to enjoy them as well. Also, this has to be the best book in the series so far, because it explores topics in a lot more depth and we tackle some truly thought-provoking topics that impact the highest levels of clinical psychology practice and research.

If you're looking for an engaging, fascinating and easy-to-understand book exploring the edges of clinical psychology as well as other topics that you would never be taught at university, then this is the book for you.

You won't regret buying this book.

Who Am I?

Personally, I always love to know who the author is of the nonfiction I read so I know the information is coming from a good source. In case you're like me, I'm Connor Whiteley, the internationally bestselling author of over 40 psychology books.

In addition, I am the host of *The Psychology World Podcast,* a weekly show exploring a new psychology topic each week and delivering the latest psychology news. Available on all major podcast apps and YouTube.

Finally, I am a psychology graduate studying a Clinical Psychology Masters at the University of Kent, England.

So now we know more about each other, let's dive into some great clinical psychology reflections.

RETURNING TO CLINICAL PSYCHOLOGY AS A NEW PERSON

To kick off this 5th clinical psychology reflection book, I really want to explore a very personal topic in relation to clinical psychology. If you've read one of these books before or you're familiar with me, then you know I champion and encourage people with lived experiences of mental health conditions to go into clinical psychology. Due to we need people with lived experiences of therapy, mental health difficulties and more in the profession to help comfort and support our clients.

However, when I started my clinical psychology Masters with a lecture on the theory and introductory information to my Masters, I realised that I am coming back to clinical psychology as a completely different person to who I was during my undergraduate degree.

For context, I am now very much of the people with lived experiences and I always have been but I have been firmly denying my abuse and trauma up until the August of 2023.

What happened was that for about a decade I've been going through prolonged and intense emotional and verbal abuse in the form of homophobia from family and my general social environment. Then add in a number of traumatic events in-between that led to extremely bad mental health that I was never able to deal with, I really shouldn't have been surprised that I was going to have a mental health breakdown at some point.

That happened in August 2023 where I resumed a number of extremely negative coping mechanisms and I basically burnt my life to the ground because all my pain and suffering from a decade of abuse and trauma then exploded.

I simply couldn't continue living as I was so I changed my life forever, I went to therapy and I basically gave my family and friends an ultimatum in a fashion. Love me and support me or get out of my life.

Thankfully, they chose the love and support route which I am extremely grateful for because I do love them and I didn't want to lose them.

Anyway, I talk more about this in my memoir *Healing: A Gay Man's Journey to Happiness, Joy and Recovery From Abuse and Trauma.* In the book I go into the details of my struggles, what happened to me, my therapy sessions and how I recovered.

Therefore, I was sitting in my lectures surrounded by 30 other Masters students and some of them were talking about their experiences of mental health difficulties. For instance, I know one person in the cohort has experience with domestic violence and another person has experience with extreme anxiety.

Then it just hit me that I was one of these students too now. I have lived experience of abuse, trauma and what it's like to go through therapy.

And I don't know but there was just something rather unsettling about that realisation. I think it comes from me having to admit that everything happened and me having to acknowledge all the pain, suffering and all the ways that my life is better after the summer.

However, as we went through the lecture, there was something about the language that other psychology students were using that started to annoy me a lot. Long time readers of the series know I always like talking about the importance of language within clinical psychology, but this was starting to annoy me.

I have never been a fan of the term mental health "problems" because that is very blaming. You are basically saying to a client that their depression, anxiety, suicidal ideation is their problem and they shouldn't burden anyone else with it.

That is what the term "problem" means because in life, if you have a problem then *you* need to fix it.

Instead myself and a lot of other clinical psychologists prefer the term "mental health difficulty" because it is a lot less blaming. We all have difficulties and we can all support each other with whatever we find difficult.

Anyway, we were talking in the lecture and the more the term "problem" was thrown about, the more annoyed I got. Since yes, I have been suicidal (and before you ask I would never ever ever do it), I have self-harmed and I have suffered extreme trauma at the hands of other people.

But does that make *me* a problem?

Of course not.

I am not a "problem" that needs to be solved and fixed and cured. Sure, you might argue that the ways that I dealt with my abuse and trauma was problematic and they could be considered "problems" in their own right. Yet even then if we say those coping mechanisms were problems then there is a very real risk a client would see themselves as a problem.

That isn't good in terms of psychotherapy.

As a result, I just hate the term "problem" because it isn't helpful, it makes a client feel bad about themselves and it doesn't help us, as current or future therapists, to create a space, welcoming space were clients can come and reveal their deepest, darkest secrets to us.

I am so grateful that my therapist didn't call my or my coping strategies a "problem" because I know I would have been more likely to shut down. Instead she was welcoming, friendly and she didn't judge me for one moment.

And as much as we bang on about being non-judgemental in clinical psychology, when we use words like "problems" and "disorder" that is exactly what we are doing. We are judging our clients, calling them problems and making them feel like crap when they have gathered up the courage to come and see us. Something that would have terrified them.

Overall, I am rather excited for the rest of the lectures, modules and discussions that will happen over the course of my Masters. Not only because I love clinical psychology and I am always excited to learn more, but because now I have lived experiences so I can understand and comment on different topics I learn about from both a psychology student's and a person with lived experience's perspective.

Something I fully believe will be invaluable and interesting and maybe even a little annoying in the future.

And even if you don't have lived experience of mental health difficulties, still love, learn and study clinical psychology because we still need amazing people like you. Just make sure that you listen to other people whenever they talk about lived experience because you never know how valuable that information will be in the future.

It's always better to know information and not need it than need information and not have it.

HELPING YOURSELF BY HELPING OTHERS

Every so often I like to write a reflection that isn't aimed at mental health or clinical psychology in particular, and this is one of those reflections because the "problem" with clinical psychology is that there is a good chance you will experience burnout at some point. Having to deal with tons of people with various mental health conditions, hearing the horrible and tragic things that happen to them and having to deal with the impossible working conditions all leads to a high chance of burnout at some point.

That's why it is even more important in clinical psychology that everyone looks after themselves and that is the angle that I'm working from in this reflection since volunteering can have a lot of great mental health benefits.

For example, research shows that volunteering decreases depression and increases self-esteem, happiness, life satisfaction and physical health (Thoits & Hewitt, 2001). As well as a massive European study shows that volunteering can help people have the health benefits of a person five years younger than themselves (Detollenaere et al., 2017).

Also, research shows that people who volunteer have better mental and physical health, have more sense of purpose and increased general wellbeing (McDonald et al., 2013). As well as they have lower mortality risks, better cognitive health and better social and emotional functioning (Shmotkin et al.,

2003).

Therefore, as you can see there are a lot of great reasons why we should all volunteer more.

In the rest of the chapter, I'm going to expand on this a little more, link it to clinical psychologists and comment on some of the challenges to volunteering because that is something important to acknowledge.

Personally, even though I haven't done any form of volunteering in about five, six years. I did enjoy it a lot. I was involved in Scouts for over a decade and I did a lot of volunteering through them and I did work with organisations like Youth United Foundation, went to King Charles's 70th Birthday Party (he was Prince back then) and I went to Malta with the Scouts too to work on an EU project.

Volunteering does present a lot of fun opportunities that I never would have gotten to do normally. As well as I know I only got these opportunities because of the amazing Scout leader who knew I was very capable and responsible. Hence there is a privilege element here which I will talk about later on.

Overall, the entire point is that volunteering is valuable, great and it honestly does make you feel like you are making a positive difference in the world.

Consequently, if we link this to clinical psychology then it is important that maybe those working in the profession do actually start volunteering more. They get involved in local projects, local groups and local campaigns to help them get these mental health benefits.

Then maybe this will start to decrease the high rate of burnout and psychological distress in the profession. Volunteering could help psychologists to relax after a hard day or week at the office and they might feel like they are more than their work, because of how overwhelming being a psychologist can be at times.

I know that working in clinical psychology settings can be exhausting, overwhelming and extremely tiring. Volunteering could help psychologists get back that positive attitude, feeling of control over their life and improved mental health that has probably been negatively impacted by their work in the past week.

Also, it is very much worth noting that being affected by what clients have to say is completely normal, it is to be expected and it really doesn't make a psychologist a bad one. It doesn't make them bad psychologist material, a weak person or any of that rubbish.

To have a reaction to the heart-breaking stories a psychologist has to hear at times is normal, and it makes them human.

Therefore, we do have to acknowledge that volunteering isn't perfect for everyone and there are systemic reasons for this, because people do need to be supported to volunteer. Especially in a high-demand, high-stress and full-time profession like clinical psychology.

Since most clinical psychologists I've spoken to work a full day, have a long or longish commute then they have to make dinner, do their housework, spend time with their kids if they have any and do X, Y and Z before bedtime.

Where's the time to volunteer during the week? There isn't any.

When it comes to the weekend, you probably want to relax, catch up with your family, your kids, spend time with your partner and just not do volunteering. I completely understand that and hell, I would be no different at all.

Even more important is that Poulin (2014) did some interesting research on how sometimes people volunteer to hide and manage the stressful life events that plague them in their personal life or work life. This very much sounds applicable to clinical psychology because of our high-stress and high-demand job.

This isn't a healthy way really to go about work-related stress. Instead we, as a group or profession, should be trying to help and manage work-related stress and decrease it so no one is experiencing a lot of stress at work, because that only makes burnout more likely.

Therefore, we have to be wary of that and we need to acknowledge that as a profession, we have a good way to go in helping to make the clinical psychology workplace less stressful for workers.

Although, I have to admit I sort of think this is outside of our control. Since until governments, NHS bosses and more make a concrete effort to decrease workload and improve working conditions, we are very stuck in our workplace at the moment.

I could be wrong, but I doubt it.

A final point to note is privilege because not everyone has the same opportunities to volunteer as everyone else. Two simple reasons are that a single mother couldn't volunteer like a rich, wealthy couple raising kids. Equally, people from lower socioeconomic backgrounds are less likely to have the resources to volunteer their time for free.

For example, middle class people compared to lower class people have more time and resources to dedicate to volunteering (Sundeen et al., 2007). As well as there could be a perception amongst richer people that they need to help the lower, poorer people as a way of a "needy others" handout. This reinforces power inequalities and perceptions about lower-class people, and it could make lower-class people resent the volunteers (Ganesh & McAllum, 2009).

Overall, there are a lot of great and powerful benefits for people who volunteer and I do think that clinical psychologists, if they can, should take up volunteering because it could really help them maintain their mental health and decrease burnout. Yet volunteering isn't as easy as you think and there are barriers to volunteering that we have to overcome.

In time I really hope we will work out a way to overcome these barriers, but until then we need to be aware of them and try to think of ways to combat them, so everyone can enjoy the great benefits that volunteering brings to our lives, our communities and most importantly, our mental health.

References

Sundeen, R. A., Raskoff, S. A., & Garcia, M. C. (2007). Differences in perceived barriers to volunteering to formal organizations: Lack of time versus lack of interest. *Nonprofit Management and Leadership*, *17*(3), 279-300.

Ganesh, S., & McAllum, K. (2009). Discourses of volunteerism. *Annals of the International Communication Association*, *33*(1), 343-383.

Poulin, M. J. (2014). Volunteering predicts health among those who value others: Two national studies. *Health Psychology*, *33*(2), 120.

Thoits, P. A., & Hewitt, L. N. (2001). Volunteer work and well-being. *Journal of health and social behavior*, 115-131.

Detollenaere, J., Willems, S., & Baert, S. (2017). Volunteering, income and health. *PloS one*, *12*(3), e0173139.

McDonald, T. W., Chown, E. L., Tabb, J. E., Schaeffer, A. K., & Howard, E. K. (2013). The impact of volunteering on seniors' health and quality of life: An assessment of the retired and senior volunteer program. *Psychology*.

Shmotkin, D., Blumstein, T., & Modan, B. (2003). Beyond keeping active: Concomitants of being a volunteer in old-old age. *Psychology and aging*, *18*(3), 602.

AN UPDATE ON HOW ANGER DRIVES ACTION

I have to admit that this is a very interesting reflection for a few reasons even before we start talking about the topic itself. Since out of the five reflection books so far, I have never ever really "revisited" a reflection before, but this is a critical topic that I want to reflect on again. It is very important for reasons I will talk about in a moment.

Another reason why this is an interesting reflection is twofold. Firstly, this is one of the reflections that I wrote long before I wrote the rest of this book, which is weird in itself. Secondly, I had massive procrastination problems with this reflection as it is so personal and important to me that I really didn't want to write it for the longest of time.

Now let's talk about what this reflection actually means.

What Is How Anger Drives Action?

Back in Volume 4 of the series, I wrote about how anger drives us, as humans, towards doing some kind of action. And how anger isn't actually a bad thing if we use it in a positive way since anger can be a very, very powerful force for good.

Below is a 463-word extract from the longer reflection in the last volume, and I've included it because it gives a real flavour for why anger is a force for good. In the reflection itself, I did include a clinical psychology focus, but I will explore that angle anew in this reflection.

Enjoy.

"For example, if we start off generally before narrowing in on clinical psychology, the world is filled with anger and injustice at times, and at least that is what the news definitely makes us feel at times. And whilst the news is designed to get a rise out of us and make us angry, it isn't always a bad thing that anger turns into action.

It is bad if we watch something on the news for example and that drives us to violently protest, smash up shops and burn down buildings. That is wrong, but equally I do understand that certain things do provoke enough strong emotion to drive people to do that sort of thing. As well as like always the debate about right and wrong is subjective and very much beyond the scope of this book.

Yet if we look towards anger bringing about positive change and action then this has always been the case throughout history, or at least modern history. For instance, if black people and LGBT+ people didn't get annoyed, feed-up and outraged by their constant mistreatment, murder and being treated differently from other law-abiding citizens. Then this never would have led to the stonewall riots, what Rosa Parks did and the events that followed and everything that allows civil rights and equality to function today. That was in the 60s and onwards.

Then if we go back even further towards the start of the 20th century with the suffragettes and the suffragists (the difference is very interesting so I do recommend researching it for yourself), then if women didn't get angry about their mistreatment and how they were barred from doing almost everything in society. Then women would never be allowed to vote, be more than mothers and be more than a mere sex object for men.

Of course I am flat out not saying that modern society is perfect because it's seriously not, but these are just some historical examples about how anger leads to positive action and change. Granted some of the suffragettes did have questionable methods at times.

Then this is still something we can see in society today from the peaceful climate change protests, to the protests surrounding Scottish Independence and the protests surrounding Black Lives Matter and more. All of these are peaceful for the vast, vast majority of the time and this all came from anger about a situation and people wanting to change it to improve their lives.

Overall, anger is a powerful force for good if used correctly and anger can definitely bring around a lot of good action that improves society. Of course at the time, these protests and these people are seen as crazy, weird and far-left nutters, but history thankfully remembers the suffragettes and others as heroes."

Why Did I Want To Revisit This Topic?

I've decided to revisit this reflection because of a lot of things that have been happening in my personal life lately, and I think there are a lot of lessons that I can apply to clinical psychology here. Even more so because a lot of the lessons themselves are based in clinical psychology.

Therefore, to start at the beginning, a few weeks ago as I write this, I went out with a friend of mine. He's a trans man and he's great. Really good friend, really nice guy and it is impossible not to like him.

Me and my friend had been talking for a while over Instagram ever since we met at a university Outreach event, and he wanted to have an in-person catch-up. So that happened, I had a great time and it was so nice to be another friend that I could just talk about things with that I simply couldn't talk about with my own family or other straight friends.

Later on, what happened was we continued to talk throughout the week afterwards, and I realised that because I have been looking at getting some work experience anyway. I already have my learning disability work experience in September 2023 but I wanted some more.

So I was thinking about working with trans people, because since meeting him I sort of fell down the rabbit hole of learning about it. Since honestly, it is really interesting to learn about and you quickly realise how all the anti-trans myths are complete and utter lies.

Anyway, I made myself leave the work experience alone in case I was just wanting to do it because I had had a nice time with my friend. I normally have a four-day rule, meaning if I'm still excited after four days I give myself permission to actually do it.

Now that weekend there was a lot of homophobia and transphobia at home and in my family more generally. As well as it was the same weekend that my friend, who was Latvian, was upset because Russia signed their stupid law banning legal and medical changes for transgender people. Meaning it negatively impacted how his extended family saw him.

And I am no stranger to homophobia, hate and bad mental health because of it. I seriously am not a stranger to it all.

However, this weekend caused me to be extremely, extremely angry, almost rageful I would say on the Monday and Tuesday. Now the nice thing about me being angry is I am passive aggressive to the extreme. It is honestly impossible for you to tell that I am angry because I do hide it.

It's a survival strategy that I learnt years ago.

Yet I was so angry and rageful, and it actually took me ages to realise why that was. Since as I mentioned earlier, intense hatred towards me isn't new at all, and I do realise that social psychology teaches us that our own self-knowledge is very, very poor. Still, go with me here because there is a clinical psychology point shortly.

On the whole, I think I was so angry because I had just had a great week of going out with my friend, talking to him through the week and just enjoying having an accepting friend that didn't judge me, hate me and most importantly, he understood me.

So when at the weekend I had to put up with even more homophobia than usual and I had a good friend that was upset too. I was just so angry that my family couldn't be supportive, happy and accepting towards me like my friend had (and to be honest everyone else at university).

Also, I think I was so angry because, whilst I am used to homophobia myself. I've come to realise in recent weeks that my life is all about helping people. Whether it is through providing knowledge and entertainment through my books and podcast, to me giving blood and being an organ donor to save lives. As well as me wanting to be a clinical psychologist in the future, I am happy to say that my life is all about helping people.

Meaning I don't like seeing or hearing other people suffer.

Now I do realise that this makes me sound like a very emotional person, but I am seriously not. It is definitely one of the more interesting parts of being autistic, it doesn't exactly make you the most expressive of people. Except when I'm writing, like I would never say even a tenth of this reflection in public.

So I suppose that's a clinical psychology point straight away. This reflection helps you to understand the struggles and life of an autistic person.

In addition, another part of my autism is that I don't "care" about a lot of people. I like tons of people and I love my readers truly, but it is hard to explain. But there aren't a lot of people I would bend over backwards for or destroy my routine for.

That's a better way to explain it as routines are the lifeblood of autistic people.

Therefore, when I heard that my friend, which I do care about, was upset and everything else was going on was happening at the same time. This made me furious with my world, myself and my friend's parents as well as a ton of other people.

I was furious.

How I Used Anger To Drive Action?

Now, of course like any normal person, I

could have simply allowed my anger that surprisingly enough lasted for two whole days to simply go away. And I did do that for the most part but I allowed my anger to cement my positions too on certain topics.

It made me believe even more how much I respect and are not bothered by trans people, because I can promise regardless of whatever the myths say. Trans people aren't nutters, they seriously are not doing this for attention and the trans community is a tiny, tiny portion of the population.

However, it also made me a lot more determined to do work experience and work with trans people, and I developed a real, real passion for this clinical population.

So much so that I actually surprised myself.

Since if you've been a long time reader of mine or a listener of The Psychology World Podcast then you know I flat out love clinical psychology and everything within the discipline. I do want to do clinical psychology, I want to help people and improve lives. Yet I have never ever felt as passionate and fired up about wanting to work with any clinical population than I did about trans people.

Meaning I set out to apply to a lot of public and private sector services that worked with clients with gender dysphoria. By the time, this reflection book comes out in 2025 I definitely should have done a lot of stuff on work experience and whatnot on The Psychology World Podcast. So if you're interested in work experience definitely check out the backlist of the podcast.

In total, I used a letter template that I adapted for each of the 13 places that I applied for, and I will admit I learnt a hell of a lot about trans people during my research for this work experience.

Nonetheless, my point about this section is that my anger drove me to spend a good few hours of the week of my anger to researching, writing out letters and submitting them to different organisations. Therefore, not only could I work with a clinical population I am extremely passionate about, but so I could continue to develop clinical skills (ideally in an NHS setting) that will benefit me in my future clinical psychology career.

<u>Over To You</u>

Overall, the entire point of this updated reflection was to show you a practical example of how being angry isn't a bad thing at all, if you use it in a positive manner. Therefore, if there is something that angers you about a clinical population, if there is an injustice in clinical psychology you want to sort out, or something else entirely. Then do something positive to help that clinical population.

Of course, you could argue that work experience with a clinical population doesn't help them. Maybe you're right, but it will still help you gain clinical experience, an understanding of how to work in clinical psychology and you never know the impact you will have on a client.

I always come to the realisation that therapy, a psychological assessment and formulations are always a scary, scary time for our clients. We are asking them to open up to us, complete strangers, and reveal things that society has told them are wrong, messed up and flat out weird.

You never know, your friendly face, your positive actions and your younger presence in the therapy room might be exactly what the client needs to feel more relaxed.

I don't know, but my point is never underestimate the positive contributions you can make to a clinical population if you want to.

I know not a lot of people will want to help trans people due to the awful social and political climate we find ourselves in, but even if I get a single week of work experience and I can make a positive impact on a single person's life. Then those hours of researching, writing up letters and submitting them will be more than worth it.

People in clinical psychology help people, improve lives and give people a future. And if you do it right, anger can certainly help with that ambition in very surprising and wonderful ways.

MENTAL HEALTH CONDITIONS AS REACTIONS

Whilst in the next chapter we're going to be focusing on this idea using trauma, I wanted to explore this fun idea I first heard in one of my undergraduate clinical psychology lectures. The idea comes from the psychological and socioconstructivist viewpoint that mental health conditions aren't strange, abnormal signs of madness like the biomedical model proposes but instead they are reasonable if not maladaptive reactions to different situations.

Now I will admit I love this idea because I think there is a large amount of truth to this idea. As well as this is why I like these reflective books because they allow me to reflect and use fact-based opinions to talk about some of these things.

Social Anxiety

Therefore, let's take anxiety as a first example and a young kid has a terribly embarrassing experience at a party that led to a lot of humiliation. This would cause any young person a lot of psychological distress and I wouldn't be surprised if this was a major cause if they went on to develop social anxiety disorder.

Okay, then we would have to ask ourselves if social anxiety could be a reaction to this feeling of psychological distress and the associated experience.

I think there is an argument to be made for it. I don't think anyone would like to be humiliated yet again in another social situation and experience high levels of psychological distress. Then if this person had other risk factors for social anxiety then I don't think it is a silly idea to propose that being socially anxious, rapid heartbreak, intense nervousness and panic attacks when going into a social situation, could be a reaction to this unpleasant event.

In addition, social anxiety could be a reaction even more if the negative experiences in social groups were repeated with different people and across time. Then if a person keeps having bad experiences (according to their perception of the event if we tap into the cognitive approach here) then I think being socially anxious and avoiding social groups is a reasonable reaction.

There isn't a particular point I'm trying to make here except that maybe mental health conditions aren't signs of madness, craziness and inadequate social functioning after all. Maybe they're just maladaptive reactions to bad situations.

Depression

For our second example, let's look at depression that is traditionally characterised as low mood, low energy and not getting as much pleasure from activities as you used to. Yes, I appreciate there are other symptoms of depression but still, this is an exploratory reflection to be honest so let's keep things relatively simple here.

A depressed person has negative automatic thoughts about themselves, others and the world after a particular event triggers their vulnerabilities, at least according to the Diathesis Stress model.

Therefore, for the sake of this reactions argument, the depression that is caused by the triggering event could be a maladaptive reaction to whatever happened. For example, I know one the major changes between the DSM-4 and 5 was now you can be diagnosed with depression if a loved one has died recently.

If the death of a loved one caused the person's depression vulnerabilities to express themselves. Then the low mood, low energy and loss of enjoyment could be a normal reaction to the loss of a loved one. I don't think any of us feel that great after a loved one dies, I know I don't.

Another factor to consider is one of the cognitive biases that reveal themselves in depressed people. For instance, depressed people generalise their failures so they might fail one subject at school and the depression makes them believe they'll fail everything at school. In terms of thinking about this as a reaction, I don't think it's futile to argue that if a depressed person fails at something and they already feel bad about themselves, isn't generalising a normal reaction to failing?

Is it actually any different to non-depressed people lecturing others about how they'll never find love after they experience a breakup?

Not really.

On the whole, of course this reaction argument isn't foolproof but I think it is a useful tool in helping us to realise that the maladaptive coping mechanisms and consequences of mental health difficulties are actually logical reactions to have in bad situations.

Mental health difficulties don't make a person bad, messed up or needing to be "cured". They are just trying to function in response to a bad situation and our clients need more adaptive and helpful ways to react in different situations.

This is another analogy we can use to explain this idea.

Post-Traumatic Stress Disorder

The final example I want to look at is PTSD because I think this is the clearest example of mental health conditions as a response to bad situations. Since PTSD develops when a person has been through trauma and they experience intense psychological distress, intrusive flashbacks and memories and they experience impaired functioning in different areas of their life.

Let's say a soldier went overseas and saw their friends ripped to shreds by a bomb and then they had to fight for survival, pinned down by the enemy for an hour until help arrived.

If seeing your friends ripped to shreds isn't trauma then I really don't want to know what is.

Leading to the soldier later developing PTSD with the symptoms I mentioned earlier. I forget the theory off the top of my head but I know there is literature on it, yet there is an argument that the intrusive memories and flashbacks are the mind trying to get the soldier to confront their past and deal with the trauma.

Therefore, in that sense the intrusive memories are a reaction to the trauma by the body because the mind wants to help the person deal with the past so they can move on with their life.

The psychological distress would be a reaction to the horror of the war, seeing their friends die in front of them and the stress of staying alive whilst waiting for help to arrive. The soldier would have spent that hour thinking that they were going to die, just imagine the horror and sheer stress that would have caused.

Finally, the impaired social functioning would be a consequence of the intrusive thoughts and memories and the distress caused by the trauma. Yet I still think (and know because of my own trauma experiences) that we all have to deal with trauma in our own ways and if we come across as socially awkward, rude or distant. Then they might be a reaction the soldier has to not wanting to get close to anyone again in case they get ripped to shreds like their last friends did.

In conclusion, I appreciate a lot of this chapter has been hypothetical discussions and theorising about different mental health conditions. There is no literature on this argument to the best of my knowledge, except the PTSD stuff, and I don't care enough to have a look.

However, my point is that in case you are of the persuasion and therapeutic orientation that believes people with mental health conditions are strange, abnormal and a little messed up. Then just start questioning this damaging and harmful belief because as someone with lived experience, I can promise you, we are just trying to survive in the world after experiencing bad stuff.

Sure the things people do with mental health conditions might be strange and confusing to other people but to a large extent, all the symptoms and consequences that we see in people with mental health conditions are just reactions and maladaptive coping mechanisms they use to get through the day and live.

One day at a time.

TRAUMA AS NORMAL REACTIONS TO ABNORMAL SITUATIONS

As we continue our look at a new way to look at maladaptive coping mechanisms and the different ways that our clients might show behaviours that are harmful to themselves and others, I want to use this reflection to focus in on trauma a little more using a more general approach to clinical psychology and then drawing on my own experience in the second half.

Therefore, there is a wide range of trauma and behaviours that a client can show. Some trauma might be caused from child abuse, violence, a car crash, being a soldier in a war zone, being victimised in a crime or going through secondary victimisation and so on.

There is a wide range of what can traumatise someone.

In addition, I think whilst there are a lot of

similarities between trauma victims and survivors, there is room for variation too about their behaviour and the different ways that they cope. A lot of trauma survivors do have intrusive memories and thoughts, they have increased levels of anxiety and panic attacks when they encounter a situation similar to the traumatising one. As well as they show avoidance behaviours towards something that might remind that of their trauma.

However, there are differences in how they cope with the trauma. Some people might disassociate from the trauma completely, others might block out the memory, others might choose to partake in substance abuse, alcoholism and self-harm or suicidal ideation.

Furthermore, others might withdraw from the world as well.

All of these different maladaptive coping mechanisms are harmful, damaging and should be addressed in therapy whenever the client admits they need to change, and they have the capacity to change. Since we cannot help someone that doesn't want to change their ways.

Nonetheless, if we really think about it, none of these maladaptive coping mechanisms make a person crazy, insane or whacky. They are all reasonable reactions to abnormal situations.

I've already used the soldier example so let's use the example of a rape victim. Something that is extremely distressing, flat out outrageous and beyond disgusting. I have never really looked into rape trauma in any great depth so I might get small details wrong and I apologise for that, my expertise and experience lay with child abuse and trauma more, but my point will still be clear.

Therefore, if a person was raped at a university party by three men and the person was about to leave when it happened and they were raped in a dark alley. This might lead to the person becoming depressed, having social anxiety about parties and a fear of going out after dark, even more so if they live on the university campus. As well as to cope with the feelings of shame, guilt and helplessness that rape makes a person feel, they might start drinking excessively to black out the memories of the rape. As well as they might experience emotional numbness that makes them want to self-harm so they can feel something and punish themselves for the rape.

I know I've drawn on a lot of different concepts that I'm familiar with but I want to make a point now.

Normally we would see these behaviours as messed up, unhelpful and the drinking would bring a lot of stigma to the victim that a lot of people wouldn't be interested in helping them. Due to the strong stigma that alcoholism is associated with.

However, when we consider these behaviours through the lens of the person being a victim and the person going through the trauma of being raped. Then things start to make a lot more sense because if a person has gotten through something extremely traumatic causing them to have intrusive memories and they are constantly forced to think about the rape. Of course they are going to want to forget about it and block it out of their mind.

Hence, the alcoholism and it makes sense because alcohol can be used to help someone blackout and forget. It isn't healthy but still.

Furthermore, after going through the traumatic experience of rape attack at a party in the dark on a university campus (something for the sake of honesty is very uncommon) then it is reasonable to be socially anxious about parties, going out after dark and being on a university campus. You would want to engage in avoidance behaviours so the traumatic experience doesn't happen again and you don't have to go through it again.

In addition, if we think about trauma I know from experience that it is emotionally exhausting and I imagine (because mine was prolonged) that a single "short", sharp traumatic experience would be emotionally crippling and because the emotions would be too intense, too negative and too awful that a person would be emotionally numb after the experience.

And people want to feel good, they want to feel alive and they just want to feel something, anything. I know I felt like that after a month of my negative mental health.

Therefore, it is possible that self-harm might be an "attractive" option for the person so they can feel something. It would be painful and extremely unhealthy but it would allow them to feel a reaction and an emotion.

Drawing On My Experience

Before I conclude the reflection and explain why this is a powerful exercise to think about, I want to "briefly" draw on my own trauma experiences and why what I did were reasonable reactions to my situation.

I've mentioned before that my trauma experiences led me to self-harm, become emotionally closed off and experience suicidal ideation at times. As well as I've explained the context before so I'm not going to do that again.

Therefore, I used to self-harm because I could never get angry, shout and scream at my home environment whenever they would say "you need to beat the gay out of them", gay people should die and that all gay people are rapists and paedophiles. I couldn't fight them with words on these disgusting beliefs because I needed them more than they needed me, I needed their support for other aspects of my life, I needed shelter and food.

I was angry that my home environment (who didn't know I was gay) considered me a rapist and that I needed to die. I would be rageful at times, but I would internalise my rage because I couldn't disrupt the boat because I needed them.

So I would scratch myself until I bleed to get the anger out of me. I served its purpose, I felt like I was doing something useful with the anger and it made me feel okay.

The abnormal situation in this case was being told repeatedly, almost weekly for a decade that I needed to get beaten so my reaction was self-harm. And I have no doubt there was a punishment aspect to this self-harm too. Yet it was reasonable in my eyes to self-harm given the hate, shame and guilt that was constantly being thrown my way.

This connects to the suicide aspect too as a reaction, because my family and wider social network never would have supported me being gay and being me. They all believed that gay people were abominations, they were against God and they should have been beaten.

Just imagine hearing this about you time and time again, week after week for a decade.

Then throw in some other trauma from friendships and family problems as well as complications caused by undiagnosed autism then things get tense real quick. And I was completely alone to deal with all of it so I just wanted things to end so I could get a long moment of peace and quiet.

Therefore, the abnormal situation was the intense stress, fear and shame caused by the beliefs of my wider social network and family. So it would be reasonable to want to escape it all and want to die so I didn't have to deal with all this anymore.

I would never ever kill myself, but I used to want to.

Then the emotionally closed part was just a way to cope with other violate and unstable friendships and close-to-legal things that happened during my life based on the lies and misunderstandings of others. Therefore, it is simpler not to be close to people so they couldn't hurt me anymore.

On the whole, I won't lie and say that self-harm and suicide aren't some of the most serious coping mechanisms you will see, but there are always reasons for them. No one wants to die but sometimes people feel like it is the only way out.

Thankfully, in reality, it never is.

The Entire Point Of This Reflection

Overall, the entire point of this exercise is to get us to realise that maladaptive coping mechanisms don't make our clients whackos, messed up or deranged. It is them trying to function after a traumatic experience that they don't know how to cope with.

Humans are designed to cope and survive and thrive no matter what. Sometimes we have to turn to "darker" means to do just that but everyone wants to survive and just live one day at a time. And if alcohol, self-harm and other extreme traumatic responses help them to do that then it is reasonable but something that has to be addressed in therapy at some point when the person realises they don't want to continue like this.

It's an empowering realisation for sure, I know that, but it takes a lot longer than it should but that's a reflection for another day perhaps.

A STATISTICS AND ARTIFICIAL INTELLIGENCE RANT AND HOW IT RELATES TO CLINICAL PSYCHOLOGY?

Considering by the end of this book, I would have done exactly 100 of these clinical psychology reflections, I am very impressed with myself that this is the only one that will ever be a rant. I know some of the other reflections might have seemed like I was having a go at something in the world or clinical psychology or something else related to mental health, but they weren't rants.

They were honestly me being passionate about something wrong with the world and how we needed to fix it to improve mental health.

Anyway, this is a full-on rant but it is very relevant and very important to the future of psychology education and clinical psychology in turn.

For the purposes of this chapter, I'll explain what happened and why this is important to talk about and then I want to dissect some of the examples my lecturer gave because they really annoyed me and I might even argue they are dangerous with possibly deadly consequences.

Let me explain.

So I had my first statistics lecture this week

because I've started my clinical psychology Masters, and like always, the lecturer in the first week goes through all the introductory stuff. Yet this lecturer might have had a background in clinical psychology, but his "real" main background was in artificial intelligence.

Therefore, within the first hour of the lecture, he basically turned round and said to us something along the lines of "in a few years all this statistics stuff won't be needed because AI will do it and more,"

Okay then, I was not impressed as soon as he said that but let me explain what else he said so you can understand my frustration even more.

I am paraphrasing in this entire chapter but the point is scarily clear.

"AI will allow us to do more with data analysis and it will allow us to explore data in more depth than statistics allows us to,"

Why do I need to learn statistics then and why am I "paying" (with taxpayer money) to listen to you talk for four hours a week if I don't need this stuff?

Also and this is what really annoyed me and this is why even after two days I am writing this with a bit of anger.

"universities and employers want people who can code and can work with AI on their CVs. The university said to me, I got this lecturer job because I have experience with AI,"

What the fuck!

So the university in its infinite wisdom is not only making me and my cohort learn statistical knowledge that will be useless in a few years because AI will be so good (it is actually good enough now to be fair) and it will be so mainstream that AI will do the data analysis for me.

Also, the university isn't going to teach me about AI, it will not teach me coding and it will not teach me a whole host of other computing skills that the university itself has said employers want.

What is the fucking point of my statistics lectures?

Personally, I just do not believe there is a point even more so because I have no intention of working in the poorly paid, high stressed and abusive working environment of academia. I have no interest in working in computing or data science. I have no interest in any of that.

And yes, I know full well clinical psychologists need to know about statistics and research methods. Research is the lifeblood of clinical psychology after all.

But when a former clinical psychology turned academic preaches to an entire cohort saying that statistics won't be needed because of AI in the future, I just don't know. I don't see the point in learning any of this except it allows me to pass my Masters.

That is it.

Nonetheless, in all fairness, the lecturer did mention that he asked the university about officially teaching psychology students about AI. The university said no for this year but they might next year onwards.

Again, not exactly useful considering I will not be at the university next year and I hope to be out in the psychology job market, but with several computer skills less than other graduates it seems.

And before anyone asks, I am too annoyed because of what I'll mention below to self-teach. As well as I am a psychology person, if I wanted to do computer programming I would have done a computer science degree, also I have trouble learning advance computer topics without someone teaching it to me. That's why I like having lectures about R because I tried self-teaching (granted I was having a mental breakdown at the time but still) and that just failed miserably.

However, my real problem with the AI revelations was the fact that his clinical psychology examples fucked me off.

The Problems With AI In Clinical Psychology

For the sake of ease and to give you a layman's explanation of how Artificial Intelligence works and how Machine Learning works, it takes millions of datapoints, creates a model to predict behaviour and then it gives you an outcome.

Firstly, there is one problem I have straight away. Behaviour is not something you can simply predict with 100% certainty. If that was the case then everyone that had ever been abused as a child should go into therapy because we know abused children are at an increased risk of developing mental health difficulties.

That is an increased risk, not an absolute.

We also know that when people are depressed, there is an increased risk of suicide. Again that is not an absolute.

Equally, I know from personal experience that someone who looks to have the perfect life, perfectly happy and has high school grades should seem like a clinically normal person. But fuck is that not the case at times.

Therefore, the very assumption that you can create an AI model that is more accurate than the current research and that model can predict behaviour more than a clinical psychologist, I just have trouble believing.

Especially because there is no causal research in mental health to be honest. We can say abuse may lead to an increase risk of self-harm and suicide but it cannot say with empirical certainty sexual abuse causes self-harm. Since it doesn't, people self-harm for tons of different reasons.

However, the main example my lecturer used and this is the only one that stuck in my mind because I was so annoyed by it, was he said that Machine Learning will allow us to predict exactly when clients are likely to commit suicide.

Again, there is that magic word "exactly" but I have already spoken about that.

I have no doubt that Artificial Intelligence based on the current research could create a model that is just as good as a clinical psychologist or maybe, maybe slightly better at predicting suicide risk with a client.

However, when it comes to a client and being assessed with suicide risk, the data put into the machine and into the model is not subjective. A client cannot know with 100% if they will commit suicide at a given time in a given week in a given situation. They might have intense feelings of suicidal ideation but they might not go through with it.

Also, the client is most certainly (notice I didn't use a more definitive statement) depressed so they have cognitive biases impacting their self-perception, knowledge and this is going to have an impact on the model. As well as this model will likely miss the human factor, the body language, the tone of voice and all those other small indicators that help form a part of the risk assessment that a human psychologist would do.

I know AI isn't about replacing human

therapists, but still.

In addition, what about the clients like me when I had my mental health breakdown back in August 2023. I knew for a fact even when I was at my worse and I truly wanted to die, I knew I would never do it. I still know I wouldn't do it in the future and that's before I remember how great my life is now.

However, I can promise you according to all the research I've read over the years on suicide, I would be shocked if an AI model said I wasn't a suicide risk. Yet what would have happened if an AI model did say I was a suicide risk, would I be ripped away from my family? Would I be institutionalised? And if we're going to be extreme here, would I be drugged up so I was too docile to do anything?

Of course, I will admit I am taking the mick here, but these are all good questions. If an AI model believes someone is a suicide risk based on research and it lacks the human connection and human factor that a conversation with a therapist can bring. Then what will the consequence be?

I can promise all of you that if I was ripped away from my family, my life, my routines and I was placed in some strange environment that I didn't want to be in. That would only decrease my mental health even further and who knows, maybe I would have actually considered doing it for real.

There are consequences for giving people labels based on cold, hard science.

My last comment or example is about the sheer imperfection of the data we give mental health professionals. Since I went for a counselling assessment last week and I didn't like the woman doing it, she was too smiley and giggly and interrupting me. She asked if I had ever actually attempted suicide, and if I had liked her, I would have told her the truth saying "No but there have been three times in my life when I have actively wanted to and come very close to actually making an attempt". Yet I didn't like her and I didn't trust her so I simply said no.

If that simple "No" had been plugged into an AI model then its risk assessment of me would be completely different.

When it comes to gathering data and information in clinical psychology so much of it depends on the client, the therapist and their therapeutic interaction. And clients might feel uncomfortable talking about certain things for a while so they might bend the truth, the therapist might realise this, but would an AI model?

I simply have no idea because the university refuses to teach us about AI at this moment in time.

And I certainly think that this is when clinical psychology becomes as much an artform than a science. We absolutely have to listen to the science about how to improve mental health and create an intervention that will almost certainly work. Yet our clients are individuals, random variables of data and they are amazing in their own right.

I think if we boil them down to pieces of data to feed into a model then we are betraying everything clinical psychology has been trying to build since its creation. We are moving towards a place in our profession that focuses on individualised formulation that puts the client as an individual at the heart of everything we do.

And if we see them as data then, as someone who has been through hell and back, then that is a fucking disgrace and that is unforgivable in my opinion.

TRANSFORMATION THROUGH TRAUMA

In the April 2023 issue of The Psychologist magazine, there was a brilliant article or book recommendation or something that spoke about how trauma can be a positive transformation experience after recovery, and I love the framing of this recovery.

Since as long-term readers and listeners of my books and podcast probably know by now, I am a positive person that focuses on helping people, I like modern thinking and I like being positive about mental health conditions and extremely negative experiences, including trauma because of my own experiences.

Therefore, I do want to take the time here to help show you that trauma might be extremely negative and it can result in a ton of negative mental health outcomes for an individual. Yet there is a great sense of hope and exploration and transformation that comes from trauma too.

Of course, the ideal situation is for a person never ever to go through any trauma in the first place, but sadly that just isn't possible. Especially, for certain sexual, racial and gender minorities as well as certain jobs like being a soldier.

I strongly believe this is an important reflection for us, as future or current clinical psychologists, because we understand the importance of trauma-informed practice and we are starting to understand that through formulation and the biopsychosocial model as well as the cognitive approach to mental health, that it is our perceptions and societal beliefs that impact our mental health too.

This is certainly true when it comes to trauma, because if society somewhat rightly tells someone trauma is *only* negative and there is no hope for them then the client will believe it. And even if they do thankfully seek professional help and the therapy works, they might miss the transformational aspects of trauma.

Furthermore, I tend to find there are two board types of trauma recovery and regaining a sense of identity after trauma recovery. There is returning to the identity you had before the traumatic event if you had a stable identity beforehand.

Or if you had childhood trauma and abuse like me then the question of identity becomes a lot harder to understand. Since identities are changing and developing in childhood and adolescence so the trauma just becomes part of that identity. So when it goes, you don't understand who you are and there is nothing to return to because you didn't have a fully developed identity in the first place.

Anyway, most trauma recovery that I've seen and read about focuses on the first aspect and returning to some identity that the survivor had before.

And yet, this doesn't mean that the client cannot experience transformation because recovery from something as negative and awful as trauma, does have the power to be transformational and that's what I want to focus on now.

As a result of as I've mentioned before my trauma recovery meant for the first time in a decade I was pain-free and my trauma and abuse was no longer holding me back. That was a massively scary, hopeful and exciting thing about my life because I could actually start to live my life how I saw fit and I could live my life without the constant fear of beatings and more.

That is very powerful.

Also, trauma recovery allowed me to start building a new identity that is very similar to who I was before. Since I am still someone that loves learning, writing, helping others and trying to save lives in small tiny ways. Like giving blood, being an organ donor and being on the Bone Marrow Register.

Yet in other ways, I am a completely different person. For instance, I now feel like I can date, I am no longer scared of the world and my own family, I know I won't kill myself, I'm pain-free and there is nothing holding me back anymore amongst a whole host of other things.

Therefore, trauma can be very transformational for a client. It converted me from someone who was scared, scarred and traumatised and who was terrified to be who they wanted to be, and made me into someone who loves life, has a social life and is playing around with their new identity.

It's fun and it's exciting.

Of course, I would have liked never had had to go through the trauma in the first place but it all worked out. I'm alive and safe and I am really hopeful and excited about the future because anything could happen now.

I am not trapped in the past, I am not in agony and I want to do things that I never would have done before.

It's exciting.

And that's the point.

As future or current psychologists, we do have the power to help give someone back their life, we have the knowledge and tools to give to someone so they can use it to help them take control of their life back so they can live the life they always wanted to.

It will not be easy for the client at all but it is possible. I am proof of that and so many other amazing clients all over the world have found transformation in their traumatic experiences.

They can rebuild their lives in whatever way they see fit and I think almost every single client will admit to knowing that their life is so much better now after trauma recovery, because they're back in control, and they've shredded the bad aspects of their life away.

It's an interesting thought exercise to think of trauma as a force for good in someone's life, and whilst trauma is bad, the recovery aspect after working through the traumatic event can focus on the positivity, excitement and all the brand-new possibilities that therapy has allowed them to explore.

And that should be very exciting for a client and a therapist, because we are the people that helped our clients realise it for themselves. And that is a wonderful feeling indeed.

IMPORTANCE OF EXPLORING OTHER THERAPIES, EXPLAINING YOURSELF TO A CLIENT AND MORE

After having a bad mental breakdown in August 2023 and then a few smaller ones when the new academic year started I applied for free counselling at the university and when I started it, I was inspired enough to draw a few parrels with other forms of psychotherapy. As well as I want to reflect on the experience so much in a general sense because we can all learn from this.

Especially because this is lived experience that goes beyond our textbooks, lecture theatres and maybe what our lecturers can tell us.

The Importance Of Exploring Therapies

I'll link this to my new therapist in a moment, but something I am starting to discover more and more as I continue to explore psychology is that you need a very playful attitude towards therapy at times. Since I have said time and time again in different psychology places that no one therapeutic model has all the answers for every single client, and all the therapies even the most woo-woo ones can have good elements you can take in case they work with a specific client.

And this playful attitude is flat out not taught at universities and I would almost say that it's discouraged. Since again, I will never ever argue against the Scientist-Practitioner model. Clinical psychologists MUST use science and empirically supported methods of working.

This is why I like Cognitive Behavioural Therapy so much because it is highly effective, there is great research to support it and it is a very accessible therapy.

However, there are other therapies available in the world and for different therapists to use. Also, you might have a client with depression and the vast majority of CBT works great for your client, but there is just something missing or something holding them back from "completing" the therapy and the CBT tricks aren't working for this particular client. That's why having a good knowledge of other therapies is useful because you can borrow tricks and tips from them.

In addition, all the therapeutic models are basically saying the exact same thing in different versions of the same flowery language. You only need to listen or read The Psychology World Podcast "What is Person-Centred Therapy?" episode and the other therapy-based podcast episodes around that time to see the similarities between the cognitive-behavioural approach and the humanistic approaches.

Anyway, my point is that you might learn a lot about CBT in your Masters, but don't limit yourself or your knowledge to that single therapy. Don't limit your knowledge to a single therapy period, whatever it is.

I know you need to keep learning, you'll learn more in the future as you gain experience and if you're in the UK, then you are required to train in at least two therapeutic models to the best of my knowledge.

And instead of seeing this as an exercise in learning about a main therapy and then a minor one that you might use a little but not a lot. Take this learning as an exciting exercise that will allow you to explore mental health more and help improve lives.

The reason why I talk about this is because my therapist uses tons of imagery and metaphors in his therapy work. He mainly focuses on integrative work, and my mind immediately pushed against that (without him knowing) because I wasn't convinced that imagery and metaphor had a place in psychotherapy.

It turns out it does.

And I've learnt a lot about how he works,

how he uses metaphor and imagery to help clients and it can be used a lot to help explain concepts or emotional states that are hard to describe with "simple" words. I wrote about it earlier in the day for another book but that will form a chapter after the next reflection because I do believe it is really useful in helping us, current or future, clinical psychologists to understand how this other form of psychotherapy works.

Since imagery and metaphor, in my experience, isn't something you learn about because it can be woo-woo, unempirical and everything else.

This is why at times therapy is as much an art as a science.

The Power Of Explaining Yourself To A Client

Something I always remember from my undergraduate clinical psychology lectures is the importance of explaining yourself to a client before you start therapeutic work. For example, you would explain the limits of confidentiality, the importance of saying "no" if the therapist is wrong, explaining how the therapy will work and just general stuff like that.

That was really interesting to see as a future clinical psychologist, because it was useful to see how to easily and almost carefully he did it. He was careful in the sense that he knew he had to be confident but delicate at the same time because therapy can be overwhelming for a lot of people.

Moreover, as a client myself in that situation, it was a relief to know he wasn't arrogant, he was supportive and he was a great person that I could work with because it was clear he was there to support and work *with* me. Instead of just thinking that he knew stuff and whatnot.

I know from my own learning that therapists are not *meant* to presume they know everything and they are meant to work with the client and everything. But I think everyone still has the fear or what if they don't act like that.

As a result, I just wanted to mention that I know this will seem unimportant, annoying and just a silly little necessity you need to do at the start of working with each client. Yet I can promise you, your future clients will find really useful, really hopeful and it is more powerful than we could ever know from our lectures and textbooks.

This is why listening to real-world lived experience is important and why it is a lot of fun to read or listen to people who have been through things, you hopefully will never have to go through.

MEANING OF THE WORD TRAUMA, DOING IDENTITY WORK WITH CLIENTS AND MORE

As you'll be able to tell from the tone of this reflection, this wasn't necessarily written at first as a clinical psychology reflection as this is a reflection on my first counselling session at my university.

However, I wanted to include it in these pages because it is a massive reflection on my experience of a counselling session, so you will be able to learn from that alone. Yet there are plenty of concepts, explanations of other therapy-based reflections that you'll be able to learn from too. You'll be able to understand and see some of the techniques the counsellor used on me, and what I as a client thought about them.

Of course, nothing in this book is any sort of official advice but you might like an idea and it might be useful for you in your future or current practice. I don't know, but I found this interesting and I think this has the potential to be useful for you whatever stage you are at in your psychology journey.

***

I have to admit that currently as I write this reflection, I'm not entirely sure what book this will be seen in, because my memoir is already written and it's set to be published. Yet if you're reading this then I must have found somewhere to slide this reflection in.

However, I am probably only saying that because I'm procrastinating about doing this reflection. Due to it reflects a larger truth that I lie to myself about constantly, it is the fact that I still need to be careful with my mental health and I still need counselling. Which isn't a bad thing at all and I only feel like this for the various reasons that we'll reflect on throughout this first counselling session.

In addition, just for a bit of context, the counselling was provided for free by my university's mental health support service and the counsellor I was assigned I really like. He gave me a few things to reflect on as an aspiring clinical psychologist, but he was great as a counsellor and I'm looking forward to my sessions with him.

He uses a lot of imagery, metaphor and he does interrupt at times but he only does that for two reasons. One, I expect he's autistic like me so he can't really help it. Two, whenever he does interrupt he only does this to be helpful and useful to me so I really don't mind it.

In terms of context for myself, if you're read my memoir then you've familiar with my pain, trauma and child abuse that I experienced for about a decade. That made me feeling suicidal at times and I self-harmed a fair bit over the years.

Although, after the events and mental breakdown discussed in my memoir and my journey towards healing and trauma recovery, I would never do those things anymore and I'm no longer in pain.

This is important for the context because no longer being in pain, no longer being held back by my trauma and abuse and past made me feel really lost, fragile and my entire world had changed. Since it led to a lot of honest conversations with my family so they now support me.

That's the context for the rest of the reflection and why I wanted counselling, so I knew how to deal with this new reality.

Meaning Of The Word Trauma

One of the first things we looked at in this first counselling session was an interesting take on trauma as a concept, and he wanted me to know the meaning of the word trauma. Then he mentioned how he was giving me this information and I could do with it what I willed. I don't think he really had a specific idea or desire for me to use the knowledge in a certain way.

Then again the entire point of counselling or at least person-centred work is that the client has all the answers, and they just need guidance and encouragement to find the answers for themselves.

Anyway, the word "trauma" comes from the German word "to dream" and we spoke for about a minute about what that could mean. And this was fascinating to me because in clinical psychology, there is an approach called the cognitive approach to mental health. The founding idea of this approach is that it isn't the event themselves that are traumatic or cause us to have negative mental health. It is our interpretation and perception of these events.

For example, if we take social anxiety for a moment that was caused by you getting humiliated at a party leading you to develop an intense fear of parties. It isn't the humiliating part that gave you social anxiety, it is your fear surrounding wanting to make sure that never ever happens again, that's the cause of the social anxiety.

At least in a layman's explanation.

Therefore, when it comes to trauma, it isn't the traumatic event that makes you have all the negative mental health consequences and the maladaptive coping mechanisms. It is how you interpret the events that makes it traumatic.

This helps to explain how two people can go through the exact same event and one can have good mental health and the other doesn't.

Personally, this is useful in a therapy context because it means when it comes to me relating and remembering my trauma of my home environment telling me "you have to beat the gay out of them" and everyone in my wider social support actively hating and wanting to hurt gay people. It means yes, this is extremely traumatic because I heard this constantly for ten years and I was in fear for my life most of the time.

Yet, it wasn't the words and things that were said to me that was traumatic. It was what I reasonably believed the words to mean and the possible consequences.

Of course, this might sound like I'm blaming myself and other trauma survivors but I flat out am not. Instead, I am saying that whenever it comes to a traumatic event humans have a good, survival-based habit of imagining what could happen and what might able if these situations are allowed to repeat.

And that is where a good amount of the negative mental health comes from.

This is why therapy is flat out critical in helping a trauma survivor to move on and help them to move on so they aren't constantly engaging in this extreme imagining.

<u>Identity Changes On Context</u>

One of the reasons why I went to counselling and one of the main aims I have for this round of counselling is that because I am no longer held back by my pain, trauma and abuse I no longer really know who I am.

Since my counsellor likes to use imagery and whatnot I described it to him as a container which is my identity, being filled with water that represents my trauma and then the water being emptied out. Leaving only a few peddles that represents different aspects of my identity, but now there is a lot of empty space and air in the container where I feel I am missing parts of myself with my trauma being dealt with in therapy.

Therefore, I felt really lost before this counselling session because I simply didn't know who I was anymore.

And he didn't say this but this would be too judgemental for a counsellor, but he challenged me on the concept of identity because I now know I was looking at identity wrong.

Which is rather interesting considering I

know all this from social psychology research anyway. But identity changes depending on the social group we're in. For example, I engage in a different social identity when I'm at university compared to at home, and when I'm with friends compared to with family, as well as when I'm doing a podcast episode compared to talking with a lecturer.

And so on.

Our social identities are constantly changing and being switched about depending on the context. There is a lot of social psychology research on the topic so if this interests you then definitely check it out.

However, for me in a therapy context, I think what I was looking for was for me to realise that I have a core identity that is *me* and then I have all these different social identities around my Core Self that reflect different aspects of who I am. Yet before, all these different aspects were bound by my pain and trauma and now it isn't there, everything felt disjointed.

I thought I was looking for something to help me out there.

Nonetheless, that wasn't the case because being reminded of such a basic principle in social psychology was really useful for me in figuring out who I am, or at least starting to.

Since at my very core, I am still the same person with or without my trauma. I am a gay person who writes, podcasts, loves their family and I love psychology, writing and transgender stuff (that's a new interest). As well as I am kind, helpful and I always want to keep learning in the areas I am interested in.

That hasn't changed.

And as for the idea that I feel lost because the pain and weight of my past isn't holding me back anymore. That connects with a lot of different things that I will talk about below, but fundamentally, this takes time to learn who I am these days and it is okay to switch social identities.

It is normal and it is critical to functioning in a social world.

Switching social identities doesn't mean I don't know who I am anymore, it is simply me focusing and trying to fit in in a social world.

That's the basic idea and now I'll explain some other ways how this counselling session helped me with my identity.

Being Reborn and Traveling

Continuing with the idea of metaphor and imagery, at one point in the therapy session, my counsellor started using this weird metaphor for travelling through life events by focusing on nomadic people. Me being me was very unsure on the idea but I turned out loving the idea and it was really interesting.

So we all know that nomadic people move around a lot and they travel from one location that has depleted resources to another area with a plentiful supply of resources.

In addition, nomadic people travel in four stages. Firstly, the nomadic people arrive in a location and they set themselves up comfortably and they basically find themselves and where they fit in that new environment.

Secondly, they get use to that new area, they farm, they work and they live their life in that area.

Thirdly, as resources start to dry up and the environment starts to become less plentiful and useful for the nomadic people, they pack up and they leave the environment that they have called home for so long.

Fourthly, they are travelling and they

eventually end up back in a new plentiful environment with new resources. Basically arriving back at stage one again for the cycle to continue.

Now this is useful for exploring and explaining life rolls to people because this is how life works. For example, let's take a fairly basic example of a young person going off to university.

Stage one and two would involve the young person being at home, living their life, going to school and going out with their friends. Then they would start to feel like they need to go to university for self-growth, to improve their career prospects and they might want to take advantage of the university clubbing scene, for instance. This would make them need to pack up their life and travel towards their new destination of university for three years where they need to settle down again, create a new life and live their life at university during their degree.

That sort of idea.

Personally, it is useful to hear him talk about life in this way because he explained how I was in the Fourth Stage and I was traveling. I was traveling from my old life which was defined by pain, trauma and abuse towards my new life where I could be anything I want without pain, trauma and abuse holding me back.

I have no idea where I will end up, who I will become and what social network I will end up with, but I am traveling.

And considering how lost, hopeless and uncertain I felt about everything to do with my identity after my last round of private therapy. It was really useful to have someone tell me that I was traveling and I need to try and enjoy the journey and focus on the fact that this will take time.

Something I struggled with horrifically.

Furthermore, another useful concept he mentioned that helped with my identity crisis was the idea of "being reborn" and this is how I feel to some extent.

At the end of the day, I am not the same person that I was. The old me was filled with self-hate, pain, trauma and they were extremely scared of things not in a pathetic way but they were scared of being discovered and living life how they wanted to.

In addition, the old me had no problem self-harming, wanting to die and they were a "tortured soul" some might say. And they would be right to.

Nonetheless, I am none of those things now and I would never ever commit suicide or self-harm again because I understand it serves no purpose now and it is stupid for me to self-harm because of the faults of others.

As a result, I am a new person that has been reborn to a large extent. As well as there were some interesting connotations that my therapist mentioned during the session, because if you've been reborn then this means that there's a certain level of infancy about you.

For example, you're vulnerable, uncertain and you have a lot of learning to do to understand how the world works similar to how a child has to learn how the physical and social world works.

That is similar to how I feel and I think I agree with the metaphor for the most part. I am an infant in the sense that the new-me has only recently been born and I am very much trying to figure out my place in the world and how this new world works around me considering every single little thing changed for me during my mental breakdown.

It had to and I am glad it did, but I am very unsettled at the moment.

As a result, I am really grateful that he gave me these concepts to focus on and he helped me to understand what everyone else was saying to me about the importance of giving yourself time. Since I now understand using this metaphor that children and infants don't grow over night or over a few weeks, they need to explore the world, test what they like and dislike and slowly build up an identity as they start to understand everything around them.

I do feel a lot, lot better and secure in myself and my identity a few days after the therapy session and I'm looking forward to exploring myself and my new identity as time goes on. I'm even going to start playing Dungeons and Dragons with my friends in the coming weeks, something I never ever thought I would do and I have been known to vow never to play a game like that.

But I am different and it will be fun and interesting for sure.

Transitional Friendships

A final major lesson from this counselling session was the idea of "transitional friendships" because if you're read my memoir *Healing: A Gay Man's Journey to Happiness, Joy and Recovery From Trauma and Abuse.* Then you'll be familiar with how I lost a dear friend during my mental breakdown because I developed emotional dependency and I basically made that friendship toxic because of my trauma and abuse.

And I do miss them and I have always felt a lot of guilt and uncertainty and pain and… a lot of different emotions for how badly I hurt them and his boyfriend because of everything I went through. But definitely check out my memoir for more information on that and everything else.

Therefore, I spoke to my counsellor about this and he mentioned the normal stuff about it's clear I want to make things right and everything, and they weren't saying I should or shouldn't try to recover this friendship. But they did mention something about transitional friendships.

In other words, this friendship's purpose was to take me from one place and hold my hand until I reached another place and that was the job of the friendship.

This does make perfect sense about the friendship because this friendship did exactly that. It gave me so much support and it forced me to go from my old life of trauma and abuse into my new life. Without this friendship I never would have gone to therapy, have the honest conversations I did with my family and so on.

And I wouldn't have the friends I have now that I met during a social group I joined after starting my trauma recovery.

Therefore, that friendship did take me from one place to another, and I wasn't sure what to make of this idea for ages. But it is helpful to think about this friendship that I murdered because of my pain and abuse and think about it through the lens of there was purpose in it and it did achieve everything it needed to.

It's hard to explain but I did like the idea that transitional friendships exist. As well as whilst I don't know what book this will end up in, I want to mention this concept just in case you find it useful for the future.

Overall, I do enjoy therapy sessions and I love reflecting on them even more because they help me process everything, they help me learn and they help me love my new life and psychology even more.

THE KEY METAPHOR FOR FRIENDSHIPS, IDENTITIES AND WHO WE ARE

Two reflections ago, I mentioned how my current therapist uses a lot of metaphors and imagery in his work and there was a particular metaphor that I really liked and I think this is a really useful metaphor for our future work. I think this is a great metaphor in case you work with autistic people in the future because it can take the abstract concept of friendship and make it more tangible.

And in the words of my therapist, the idea that autistic people cannot engage in imagery and metaphor in the vast, vast majority of cases is "bullshit", so please don't dismiss this automatically.

In addition, I think this metaphor has a lot of potential applications in identity work, definitely with trauma and abuse survivors and I think this could be applied in a thousand more situations if you'll willing to stretch and bend the metaphor enough.

Please enjoy.

***

Following my second therapy session I quickly realised that in the first reflection on my counselling sessions at the university, I didn't mention one of the most useful things I had ever heard. It was a brilliant metaphor that I wanted to focus on more in this reflection because it is really useful and you can expand it and use it in your own friendships.

However, first of all I just wanted to mention that overall I am doing surprisingly well after the last session. I no longer feel lost in who I am, I don't feel like the my identity is empty and shattered because I no longer have the abuse and pain and trauma holding me back. As well as what I am most interested in is some of my resilience is coming back.

All trauma and abuse survivors are naturally highly resilient because you just have to be to survive, but when my pain and everything was dealt with. I didn't need to be resilient anymore or I didn't know how to be resilient anymore. Thankfully, my natural resilience is starting to return which is a wonderful feeling.

Also, I am just starting to learn a lot more about friendships, who I am and my identity in general. Mainly, because I'm playing around with small changes to my look, some really, really subtle feminine changes. Like I brought myself a small rose gold bracelet that I wore to Trans group and then to a university social this week.

No one noticed and no one cared.

So I am slowly growing and learning who I am nowadays. As well as it is great to have finally realised that this identity work is just a learning process and it will take time, and that isn't a bad thing.

That's the overview of how I'm doing, the realisations since the last counselling session and everything else in general.

Now let's move onto the metaphor.

<u>The Key Metaphor</u>

I mentioned before that my therapist really likes to draw on metaphors and imagery in their therapeutic work with clients. And towards the end of last session, he was talking about imagine you're in a house and someone who you haven't met before comes up to your house (which represents you and your life) and you both start talking.

If you feel a connection and want to become friends with them then you might give them a key to your porch area, so you invite them into your life a little more.

If you don't like them or if a friendship doesn't develop then you don't give them a key at all. Since they're staying outside your life and they don't deserve to come in.

Then overtime as the friendship develops, you might start giving them more and more keys so they can come deeper into your life and they can be taken to different rooms that represent or are metaphors for different things. For example, if you'll willing to give your friend a key to the living room then this might represent for you (these are always what these rooms mean for you) that you're comfortable around them to socialise and entertain them. But you might not give them a key to the kitchen (the heart of the home where some of the most important functions happen perhaps) or your bedroom or another private, personal space.

Overall, so far, the metaphor is really useful in understanding how friendships work in the sense that there are different levels to friendships, and friends take time to evolve and grow so you gain enough trust and consent in the relationship to move through each other's lives or houses.

In addition, this doesn't have to be a real house or based on one, because you can add as many rooms as you like that represent different aspects of yourself. This is important for something I'll mention later on.

For example, in the session, because I used to be really into Warhammer 40,000 and now I'm going to be starting Dungeons and Dragons in a few weeks, because my friends are playing. We added a gaming room to my house and this was important, because let's face it, there is a good level of vulnerability to your gaming room (if you have one). You tend to act silly, authentically and without a care for what other people think of you as long as you're all having fun when playing a game. Especially a wargame like Warhammer or a roleplaying game like D&D.

Therefore, if I'm willing to give someone a key to the gaming room then this helps me to understand that I am close with this friend. And that's a good thing.

Over To You

Before I explicitly focus on why I find this metaphor so useful and how I use this in my everyday life (I've used it a lot over the past week), I want to say that in your own metaphorical houses you can add any rooms that you want, as well as you can decorate them however you want.

For example, one thing we did in the session was we focused on my bedroom, because I was stressing that was a very, very personal space where I slept, it was where I had had breakdowns and a lot of my mental health was tied up in that room.

As a result, he got me to describe this room in detail and thankfully, my real bedroom reflects who I am and how I feel currently very well, so I just described my real bedroom. Therefore, because I'm feeling good it's very well-lit with beautiful photo artwork on the walls that adds beauty and nature to the bedroom, as well as my bedroom is practical but it is spacious and airy and it doesn't feel negative or depressive.

That imagery reflects who I am with my subtle interest in beautiful real artwork that are photos, I focus on being practical or I want my spaces to feel positive because I am a positive person.

On the flip side, when I'm down or when the Gay part of me was being abused, traumatised and wanted to die. I invoke the imagery of a scared 16-year-old boy in a very dark bedroom terrified of what was going to happen next and if it was going to get beaten or killed.

That simple piece of imagery explains a lot about my feelings and thoughts when it comes to trauma and abuse.

To bring this back to you, if you want to make this imagery or metaphor in therapy then do it but make sure you customise the imagery to how you feel. It might take some practice but if you're finding it hard to describe what you're going through, imagery is great to fall back on.

Furthermore, when it comes to your own rooms, you can create whatever rooms you want. For example, if you seriously love gardening then have a massive garden. Yet if there is a section of your garden that contains your most prized plants or a bunch of garden toys for the kids or something then maybe have a metaphorical fence around that stuff. Since you might sit outside for a coffee with a friend you like but don't love. Yet you might only show your best friend, your most prized plants.

I don't know but you need to use the metaphor as you see fit representing the important aspects of yourself that are personal and who represent you.

This includes rooms that you might not show anyone besides from yourself or even a romantic partner that you're committed to for the long term. For instance, I'm not really sure how many secrets I have these days but there are things, certain opinions and other interests that I wouldn't just share with anyone. Some of these opinions I might keep to myself period and these might be represented by small rooms with doors covered in shadows on a floor with a staircase that only I have the key to.

It's just an idea.

Then finally for the theory or setting up the metaphor, this is a great metaphor for understanding that certain friendships belong in certain places, and certain friendships function in some domains but not others.

The example we used in the therapy session was how the garage of a house is where you tend to be practical, make things and be resourceful. So you would only want practical friends in there that are good with their hands, so you might not want some other people in the garage. For instance, I would want some of my old scouting friends in the garage because they're good with their hands and they are good at creating things and that's a fun activity. But I wouldn't always allow the same people into my living room because I don't want to socialise and entertain them outside the garage.

Some more general examples include, I'm a Student Ambassador at my university and I have a few friends from that domain of my life. Meaning it is normal to see them in my Outreach room, but it would be wrong to see them in my living room or bedroom. Those friends don't belong there. It doesn't mean they aren't my friends, it just means they don't belong there.

Equally, if my university friends come into my writing room or something that would be wrong too, because my university friends aren't my work or writing friends. They flat out don't belong in this area of my life.

Therefore, in a way, I guess this helps me to understand that friendships can be limited to a certain area of your life and that's okay. There's nothing wrong with that and I think that is healthy too. You need your own space and you don't want your friends to dominate every aspect of your life.

That's enough of the theory side for now so let me explain how I use this metaphor in practice.

How I Use The Metaphor In Practice?

Overall, I really like this metaphor because it allows you to check in with friendships, see how they're developing and generally, they allow me to understand that I'm making more progress than I thought.

For example, over the past week I've spent a lot of time thinking about friendships, talking to friends and going out with them and I've realised that the definition of friend is a lot looser than I imagined.

This is a good thing.

Since I used to believe that a friend was only a person who I had a really close bond with. That is still true but there are other shades or flavours or types of friendships that are different but still no less valuable.

For example, I was at Trans group Wednesday night and I spent a good two(ish) hours talking to a trans man friend that I hadn't really spoken too much, because they had bad mental health before and listening to their experiences caused me to have a breakdown later that night.

Yet it was great to talk to him and it was fun and it was just nice.

Later on I had a conversation with another friend for about 30 minutes, and it was the first time we had probably spoken just the two of us but it was fun. I learnt exactly how much I don't understand or know about D&D but she's going to help me create a character idea.

And yes, I still have no idea what that means.

So anyway, I was back at my great aunt's that night because I was staying with her after taking my Grandad there after his eye operation. And I was laying in bed and I just realised that I am starting to build a good little group of friends because the trans man and trans woman I was talking to I would happily give them the keys to my living room.

Then there's another person I talk to weekly who these two people are great friends with, and I would give them keys to my Gaming Room and a whole bunch of other spaces too that these two people don't have access to.

For now.

Therefore, I like how this metaphor can be stretched and adapted for whatever you need. The house can be added to more and more to reflect the rooms and spaces and aspects of yourself that you need.

Overall, this is a metaphor that I use to evaluate and monitor friendships and it helps me as a survivor and an autistic person to understand how complex friendships are in a way that is easy to understand. Because I can see it and this metaphor helps make the complex nature of friendships more tangible and real.

My unofficial advice for you if you're trying to work out who you are and anything to do with friendships would be to give about your own house and then see where you would allow your different friends to go within that house.

And a final tip I learnt from this session, it is perfectly okay and normal for friends not to have access to all the rooms. We always have aspects of ourselves that hide and change depending on the person. We probably need to hide certain aspects of ourselves otherwise we would be extremely vulnerable if we were completely, completely open without a single secret to other people.

So it's okay if you don't let anyone besides yourself into certain rooms.

Because that's healthy.

THE STUPIDITY OF OUT OF AREA PLACEMENTS

Something I am seriously known for amongst the long term readers of these clinical psychology reflections is that I am a famously bad reader of The Psychologist by the British Psychological Society. I have issues of the magazine that I got over 14 months ago and still haven't read, so that's why I enjoy these reflections because it makes me actually read the magazine. Since every so often I get a very interesting idea for a reflection.

This is one of those times.

Interestingly enough, a few days before I read this article, my mother actually mentioned to me that one of her friend's wife's (who's a clinical psychologist) mentioned how in England the county of your birth has to pay for your mental health care. Whilst I have no idea if this is true, I have a good sense that it is.

As a result, when a person needs psychological support, one of three things happen. A person who is struggling with mental health support is treated in their local area where they live, they are returned to their birth county for treatment or they are sent somewhere out of their local area because there's room there.

Of course, the UK Government pledged to ban Out of Area placements for people receiving mental health treatments in March 2021. Yet as everyone in the UK knows, this current UK Government lies about everything so since March 2021 (the proposed month this was to be scrapped), another 209,000 people have received Out of Area placements.

That figure came from an article in the July/ August 2022 issue of the Psychologist. That means in basically a year and a quarter 209,000 people have been ripped away from their social support networks and everything they knew just because of the stupidity of this idea and scheme.

That number has most probably doubled at the time of writing this reflection.

Therefore, for the rest of this reflection, I want to reflect on why *I* think this is stupid but to be a little balanced, I'll reflect on the possible reasons behind this scheme. Then I'll propose ways to fix these reasons.

Why I Think Out Of Area Placements Are Stupid?

We know from a lot of different research studies that social support, friends and family are critical for our mental health. For example, a person who has a lot of friends and family members with good, high-quality relationships with them is less likely to have mental health difficulties than people with fewer connections and experience loneliness.

We can all agree on that.

Also, for certain mental health conditions and for certain people, routine, structure and being in a familiar environment is important. As well as I would ever say that whenever everyone is going through hell and experiencing clinically significant levels of distress, we want to be somewhere we know and are familiar with.

Therefore, this is where the stupidity of Out of Area placements lie because we are taking people with mental health difficulties, hundreds of miles away to a brand-new city, town or hospital, whatever to receive treatment. They won't be able to see their friends, their family, their entire lives will be disrupted.

That will only add to their distress and the distress of their families and friends.

Since no one gets an NHS appointment these days unless the situation is dire. I know to get access to psychological treatment in Child and Adolescent Mental Health Services (CAMHS) a child needs to do two *believable* suicide attempts. And even adult services because they are so underfunded and stretched, if a person gets an appointment, it is only because they're been on a waiting list for years or they are so "bad" or so distressed that they need to jump the queue for lack of a better term.

As a result, the people who get NHS appointments are extremely, extremely distressed to the point of self-harm, suicide or a number of other "risky" mental health difficulties. So the very notion of that we want to add to their psychological distress by taking them away from their friends, family and routine is beyond stupid.

Let me add a personal example that really explains why this would be beyond stupid for someone like me.

<u>Why This Would Be Dire For Me?</u>

I mentioned before that in August 2023 I had a major mental breakdown because of years of trauma and abuse that led me to self-harm and there were even some thoughts of suicide but no real plan and definitely no attempt. Let's say by some fantasy miracle that I got an NHS appointment when I needed it. That's funny to think that might happen.

Then that's say the NHS wanted to send me to Cornwall or Cumbria (two counties on opposite ends of the country and at least 4 hours away from my home) because those Trusts have some space in their mental health services for me.

Well, I can promise you, the very idea of my routines, being away from my family and friends and being away from what little normality I had left. That would not have helped whatsoever and that would have made me worse.

It was actually the tiny things that really helped me during my breakdown. I could still write, I could still do online classes and the associated assignments, I could read and I could do some small things when I was feeling like I was dying inside.

If I couldn't write, watch my online courses or read or just do anything that I loved to do because I was in a strange, new environment. That would have been even worse for me.

Therefore, as annoyed as I am at the NHS, no actually the government for crippling the

NHS so much that mental health services in the UK are next to useless unless you have tried to kill yourself. I am glad I barely managed to deal with everything alone, I burnt my life down in the process, but I managed to stay alive.

I managed that but if I had been sent to an Out of Area placement then I doubt the results would have been the same. And I fairly sure I would have been retraumatised because I just wouldn't have that sense of routine, structure and safety that I depended on during my breakdown.

I would have been surrounded by strangers, new medical things in a hospital or wherever people end up and I would have hated it.

I would hardly be the only one.

Possible Reasons For Out Of Area Placements And Their Possible Solutions

To be honest I think Out of Area placements really come down to funding and capacity issues and the solution is the same.

The lack of funding in the NHS and its mental health services means that different NHS Trusts have to decide how serious someone has to be before they are seen too because it is flat out impossible to see and treat everyone with mental health difficulties.

Also, there is limited funding available so if a Trust can transfer over to another NHS Trust so this other Trust has to spend money then I think all NHS Trusts would prefer that option. Especially as the NHS Trusts are run like businesses like public sector healthcare settings.

On the whole, the solution is simple (they say smiling) there has to be more funding for mental health services so the NHS Trusts can expand their services and keep people inside their local areas where they still have contact with their friends and family members and hopefully their normal lives.

But I know the UK Government always bangs on about funding and yet we need "real funding". We need the funding and extra money from central government to go to the services themselves instead of being used on Managers and all the other stupid ways that money in the NHS is wasted by the people at the top.

That is definitely an interesting area you might want to look at in your own time. It's called Managerialism in the NHS in case you're interested.

And I was listening to a podcast yesterday at the time of writing and this woman (who was yet another victim of US gun violence) and she was explaining how her medical bills might come to $200,000 at the end of her treatment and she was curious about how her money would be used.

Would the great nurses and specialists that treated her use it? Or would it be used to line the pockets of other higher up people that didn't help her much?

It is a good question for healthcare systems around the world but that is beyond the scope of this reflection.

Overall, Out of Area Placements are stupid in my personal opinion because they mean taking people with severe mental health difficulties away from their normal lives, their friends and their family members that offer them love and support, and stick them in a strange new environment that only adds to their distress.

This shouldn't happen and things can be

changed to make sure this doesn't happen, but it requires solving a lot of problems that I doubt the government and the highest tiers of the NHS are interested in solving.

ARE ALL BARRIERS IN CLINICAL PSYCHOLOGY THE SAME HEIGHT?

When I was flicking through the December 2022 edition of The Psychologist Magazine, there was this article from a man talking about him feeling out of place and almost like an imposter on the UK's NHS "Aspiring Clinical Psychologist" scheme.

It's a scheme designed to help people who cannot undertake a Masters nor undertake unpaid work experience to get work experience and a partial education towards becoming a fully qualified psychologist.

In the article, the man was talking about how much of a fraud he felt because he was white, wasn't from an ethnic minority and he didn't have any other characteristics that would disadvantage him. The only reason he was on the scheme was because he was from a poor background so he couldn't undertake unpaid work experience or do a Masters degree.

And then the article went on to talk about how he realise he did belong on the scheme but it still made him think about his own privileges and that not all the barriers in clinical psychology are the same height. The barriers to the profession were a lot lower for him compared to a black person from a poor background.

Personally, this got me thinking about my own privileges and disadvantages, but firstly I want to mention that this man might have been white and he didn't have any other disadvantages besides the fact that he was from a poor background. He still 100% deserved to be on this scheme because he met the criteria, he needed the help and it benefited all the future clients he was going to see.

He was suffering from self-doubt and imposter syndrome, which is understandable, but he shouldn't have felt that way about himself.

Furthermore, I think the reason why this really got me thinking is because of my own appearance, status and disadvantages. Since I am a white male from a middle class family in a poor area. Those are my advantages and those have been very useful to me in my life.

Also, I am gay but you would never know from looking at me so I can hide that part of myself very well if needed. As well as I am part of the trans community as a non-binary person but again, you would never be able to tell.

Then finally, I have suffered really bad mental health and I had tons of lived experience of mental health difficulties behind me. You would think that would certainly be an advantage in clinical psychology and it very much can be, but people are still weary. And there are still unconscious biases at play during the recruitment process, even within clinical psychology.

Yet again, you would never know I have had horrific mental health in the past, because I hide it very well.

Therefore, what got me thinking about this article was that I definitely know how this man feels. Since there have been times I have wanted to apply for minority-focused bursaries, opportunities and more but I have stopped myself because I don't *feel* disadvantaged at times.

Of course, I am perfectly aware that I am disadvantaged and there have been times when people in positions of power have made that perfectly clear to me in very non-subtle ways.

However, I keep telling myself the same lie over and over again about how I don't need these things. Even though it would have helped me, my future and my career if I had applied for these things a few years ago.

It's interesting that I try to convince myself that I am perfectly okay even now, but I am not because I am disadvantaged and I shouldn't be scared to recognise it.

On the whole, when it comes to myself, in the future if there is an opportunity that comes up for minorities. Then I need to be more open and honest with myself about looking into it and allowing myself to apply if I think I meet the criteria.

For everyone else reading this, if there is an opportunity that you meet the criteria for, whether it's aimed at minorities or not, you should go for it. Getting a job in psychology is hard enough for all of us, but it is even harder for other people that face more barriers than most.

Look for opportunities, exploit them and help yourself to build a Resume or the career that you want.

Don't let self-doubt, imposter syndrome or anything else hold you back.

IN VULNERABLE TIMES WE REMEMBER WHAT OTHERS SAY

Sometimes when it comes to the Psychologist magazine, it's the content that gets me interested, sometimes it is very much the writer (like the amazing Lucy Johnstone) but other times it is simply the title that gives me something to reflect on.

Therefore, in one of the late 2022 issues, there was an article titled the same as the name of this reflection, and whilst I didn't really read the article itself because I didn't find it too interesting. I still really liked the title.

Since it is very true and I think we can reflect on this both personally as well as professionally.

<u>The Personal Perspective</u>

When it comes to being vulnerable, I think there are two main types that we can focus on here, psychological distress during a mental health crisis, or the being vulnerable outside of a crisis.

What I mean by being vulnerable outside of a crisis, this might be what happens during a breakup, the loss of a loved one and generally when you feel really vulnerable and you want other people to support you.

This is a time when we remember who was there for us, who made us feel good and who made us feel safe in amongst the chaos of everything that happened. I remember when my Nan died a few months and my mother received a lot of great support from her friends even though their relationship was both dead and extremely complex.

In that time of emotional uncertainty where my mother was processing her feelings for that awful woman, she remembered and loved her friends and family for supporting her despite the logical reaction to be nothing. But she did have an emotional reaction because she still lost her mother physically.

Anyway, whenever we have a friend or family member going through stuff, it is important to remember to support them, be there for them and just check in. I don't believe for a moment it has to be very grand or important, it can simply be a check-in.

They will remember that simple gesture of kindness when everything has passed, and it will pass in the end. That applies just as much as to you as it does to your friends and family members.

On the flip side, if you, your friends or family members are having a mental health crisis then they will certainly remember who was there for them and who wasn't.

I remember a lot of what my friend said to before just before the worse my breakdown. I remember what my therapist said when I was trying to rebuild my life and I remember a fair amount of the kind, supportive words that my parents said when they finally decided to take my mental health seriously and actually support me.

I'll always remember and appreciate them all for that, and it helps to remind me that I am loved, supported and appreciated. And me and my parents are now a lot closer after those honest conversations and I really do remember what we said and how I felt during that time.

Overall, when it comes to vulnerable times, it is perfectly okay to experience these feelings because they are natural and a result of something bad that happened. It is okay to lean on people to support you and it is okay to be annoyed at people that don't say things to you, and it is even better if you remember the people that were great and kind to you.

You might be surprised where the sources of support come from.

I know I was.

The Professional Perspective

When it comes to clinical psychology and being a future or current therapist, we see amazing people that are having very vulnerable times and moments, they're experiencing clinically significant levels of distress and they're dealing with a lot of mental health difficulties.

Therefore, like I have mentioned millions of times before on the podcast and in these reflections, what a therapist says matters. Yet it isn't only *what* they say, it is how they say it, how they interrupt or don't and how they make a client feel.

As a result, we really can expand the title of this reflection at its heart because what a psychologist does *with* a client during difficult times matters a lot. Psychologists have the power to help them, to support them and help to feel better for the first time in ages.

However, in the very rare event that a psychologist isn't great, if we say something dismissive, cold or we misunderstand something to an extreme degree then a client will remember this. They will probably remember the negative of what was said, of how bad they felt afterwards and they will probably find it helpful.

Of course, most of the time this won't happen because being compassionate, knowing how to talk to clients and how to think about responding to clients will be covered in your training and you will improve with experience.

That's why something I learnt from my counselling sessions from a clinical psychology perspective is it's okay to take an extra few moments to think about responding to a client. It's better to spend an extra five seconds thinking about a good way to phrase it than to say something completely unhelpful.

And I also learnt from my counselling session that if you say something that might be pushed back against by the client because they might see it as unhelpful. Then you might want to say something along the lines of "I want to gently challenge that idea and you can push back if you want" in a careful tone.

When he said that to me, it was useful in understanding that I was an equal in the therapy session and what he was doing was out of respect and he wanted to help me.

See, it's been a few days since that session but I still remember it.

Overall, when it comes to clinical psychology being able to be respectful, sensitive and aware of our client's thoughts, feelings and behaviours are really important when it comes to helping them through vulnerable times because they will remember what was said.

Words have the power to change lives for the good and for the bad. Training helps us know a lot about how to talk to clients but it is us that speaks the words at the end of the day.

So we have to be aware, not scared, not nervous or overly concerned, but just aware that our words have power and our clients will remember what we say, we do and how we make them feel.

WHAT'S MISSING FROM MENTAL HEALTH CAMPIGIANS?

Something I think is great about the past few years, and especially the COVID-19 pandemic, is that mental health campaigns have become really important, easy-to-see and they have received a lot of support.

As an aspiring clinical psychologist myself, I am really happy to see that mental health (at least in the public eye) is finally getting the recognition and attention it deserves. Granted, in the mental health settings and different levels of government it is still not being treated as seriously as physical health but that's a topic for another time.

However, in the September 2022 edition of The Psychologist, there was an interesting focus and spread on the idea that mental health campaigns in their current state aren't actually that great. Due to they're effective at reducing the stigma and helping to raise awareness for how common various mental health difficulties are, but they are still missing a critical piece of the puzzle.

They don't motivate people to get professional help.

I'm very much in two different minds about this article, because I think it is largely true. I will never argue that mental health campaigns are not effective at making mental health conditions known, and laypeople are starting to understand how common they are and their negative side effects.

There are so many I cannot really focus on just one but I think Pringles did a good advert a while back about just asking and focusing on how someone *actually* is. It's a great advert considering in the UK the question of "how are you?" is the biggest waste of time ever. The response is always the same and it is always a lie, everyone says "they're good thanks," without thinking about it even if their life is terrible.

It is just a cultural factor.

Nonetheless, that sort of preventative mental health advert definitely has its place in the world, because it is useful to give people tips and tricks to help the people around them with their mental health before it develops into a "full-blown" mental health difficulty that causes clinically significant levels of distress.

Then another type of mental health advert I see a lot is the focus on statistics and facts that highlight how common different conditions are. Again, these are badly needed to help normalise and reinforce the idea that it is okay to talk about mental health and get help.

And there lies the factor that is missing from mental health campaigns and it is only now after reflecting on the different campaigns that I've seen, I realised how true this factor is.

There is no real focus on getting professional help and dealing with the mental health difficulties surrounding that aspect.

I've spoken in my memoir, on the podcast and probably in these clinical psychology reflections that going to see a therapist and getting professional help is scary as hell. It takes so much courage, so much determination and so much fear that it stops a lot of people.

And that's before we consider the stupid myths surrounding mental health that society has created.

Therefore, I really do agree that I think we have reached a point where the "commonality" and "preventative" types of adverts should take a backseat for a while. We still need them to be about and people still need them, but I think we now need to move towards campaigns and adverts that deal with getting professional help.

It is all well and good us telling people that 50% of people get depression in their life time (I just made up that number by the way) if we don't tell them what to do next and we help them gather up the courage to seek professional help.

I firmly, firmly believe that people will only get professional help when they are ready but I know from personal experience, it only takes one push in the right direction from people to help a client get on the therapeutic journey towards changing their life for the better.

And if we could develop an advert or campaign that helps inspire that change or the start of the client's journey then that is going to be immensely, immensely powerful and we could help a lot of people.

Advertising definitely works for products and services, so let's turn our attention towards helping people help themselves to improve their lives.

So they can experience less psychological distress, less emotional pain and less maladaptive coping mechanisms. Let's help give them their lives back.

BE SURE NOT TO INTELLECTUALLY GASLIGHT SOMEONE?

One other article I want to reflect on from the September 2023 issue of The Psychologist is a great article focusing on intellectually gaslighting the public and someone by saying that the only threats to humans were from the natural world. Granted, the article was slotted into another series of articles focused on COVID-19 but the article was still wrong.

Therefore, because this article has a lot to do with mental health, the NHS and clinical psychology as a whole, I will certainly be reflecting on it in these pages.

However, just for the sake of clarifying, below is a definition of Gaslighting taken from an episode of The Psychology World Podcast.

"Gaslighting is a form of emotional abuse where someone uses psychological manipulations to cause another person to question their reality. It can happen between two people in any relationship. Like friendships, working relationships and romantic relationships. The gaslighter preserves their own sense of self and power over the other person who ends up adopting the gaslighter's version of reality over their own.

The reason why we need to look at this is because it's important to distinguish gaslighting from normal and healthy behaviours. Like disagreeing and we need to understand when a conflict turns into gaslighting."

In the article, the author proposed that the only serious threats to humanity would come from the natural world in the form of diseases that was the general jist of the article. Then something I rather like about The Psychologist in more recent issues is they publish criticisms and responses to previous articles and the response to this really got me thinking.

Since I completely disagree that the natural world will produce the most serious threats to humans in terms of health, mental health and basically everything else.

I will not lie. COVID-19 and other pandemics are beyond horrific and they sadly kill millions of people, but these are thankfully rare and considering what humans do to themselves in terms of mental health, the natural world cannot hold a candle to us.

For example, as all of you know, I live in the UK and this is not a good country to live in. It is better than other countries for sure, but in recent times, we are experiencing cost of living crisis that is worse compared to the USA and most EU countries, many people are struggling to pay their bills, many people are having to go to food banks just to survive, there is a mental health crisis in the country and we have a free (at the time of writing) health service that has been degraded so badly by the UK Government that my healthcare system is always strained and close to breaking point.

And that's all before we talk about the climate crisis and how human activity is making that worse than it ever would have been without human involvement.

Also, war's a massive human factor that is upending lives, causing mass migration of refugees and war causes a lot of negative mental health outcomes for those affected and Post-Traumatic-stress disorder.

Furthermore, we have a government that is trying to restrict legal protections for minority groups, waging a culture war on trans people, reducing our Right To Protest and actively arresting people who *might* protest and *might* make a disruptive protest.

That isn't how democracy works but that is certainly beyond the scope of this book, as well as I have reflected on these disgusting laws in previous volumes.

In addition, there are plenty of other facets of everyday life that are not ideal and have gotten worse over recent years according to research and so far, I have just rehashed what the response to the article said in The Psychologist.

However, notice how all of those problems come from human activity and human political decisions.

As a result, I firmly believe that to say that the natural world is the only source of threats and dangers to humanity, is stupid at its best and downright gaslighting at its worst. Since if you ask any British person then they will say that the UK Government is useless and it is destroying the healthcare system that so many of us rely amongst their many other faults.

So for a leading psychologist to say in this article that human factors, political factors and the decisions taken by governments aren't important and doesn't cause 99% of these real-world problems that are impacting the mental health and lives of innocent people, is gaslighting I think.

We all know that if governments made different decisions that supported the most vulnerable, supported us and were based on research then the problems might not go away entirely. Yet the psychological distress they caused would be lessened.

One such example would be if the UK Government listened to psychologists and other healthcare professionals about what needs to happen to fix the NHS. They need to restructure it were there is less managerialism, mental health is taken more seriously and the NHS has real funding so we can actually reduce some of these waiting times.

It will never happen and I do suspect the UK Government wants the NHS to collapse so the US health insurance companies (that donate massive sums of money to their party each year) can come in and expand into the UK market. You really should read into that if you're interested.

Anyway, the media has covered these stories, politicians have called each other out for causing these problems and at the heart of it regardless of your political orientation, we know that political decisions have the power to negatively impact the mental health and lives of innocent people.

So to say that this doesn't happen is gaslighting and very cruel.

Thankfully, all of these can be reversed in time, but not by politicians to be honest because they don't tend to change their minds once they're made a decision that harms people. The past three UK Prime Ministers have proven that beyond reasonable doubt (and for our international audience I'm talking about the 3 Prime Ministers we had in a single year in 2022).

Instead I think the change and hopeful improvement for the lives of innocent people, that will have a knock-on effect for their mental health and us as future or current clinical psychologists, will perhaps come from a new UK Government but I sort of doubt it.

Instead I think as psychologists and psychology organisations continue to battle for recognition and different policy changes, I think over time (and I'm being negative here and I am going to say years and years) psychology, research and an understanding of the importance of mental health will become more important.

Therefore, the impact on mental health of political decisions and human activity might be given a little more weight in the future.

On the whole, the entire point of this reflection was to show you that intellectual gaslighting is a thing and you shouldn't do it. Whenever you make a psychological claim, make sure it is real and you aren't gaslighting people that know the truth, because human activity and the decisions made by others that impact other people's lives are massive threats to our mental health and they happen a lot more frequently than pandemics and other threats from the natural world do.

Finally, this is why I am a massive believer in the therapeutic principles of our client is the expert in themselves, they know themselves best and we can challenge them and their beliefs of course but we should never dismiss them. What they believe is valid, and it might be biased, reflective of a faulty thinking pattern or something else entirely but it should always be believed.

Don't gaslight your clients just because you think you know what's best and you think you know what happened to them in their life even though you have never met them before.

HOW DO WE MAKE PSYCHOLOGY RESEARCH MATTER?

The vast, vast majority of people reading this book have done at least a psychology undergraduate degree, if not a Masters in clinical psychology, so we are all well aware of the importance and how to do psychology research.

However, psychology research is all well and good but there is still the critical problem all research faces, we need to understand how to make the psychology research matter to the general public, policy makers and other stakeholders so the research can have a real-world impact.

This was the focus of an article in The Psychologist in March 2023 and I want to reflect on it, because it is flat out critical. Since one of the many reasons why I love psychology is because it is useful, it can save lives and it can give people such hope in their darkest moments, at least clinical psychology can do that. Yet all the other subdisciplines of psychology have their own "superpowers" too.

However, it is great psychology can do all those things but that only happens if the people in charge of these services, in government and the general public can understand, appreciate and apply these psychology findings.

And academic psychology does not help itself at all.

As a result of psychology research is done by academics, which are people that focus on academic writing because this is required to get it academically published in a good journal, so they can advance their careers. Academics have never ever been trained in how to make their research accessible for the masses and most of them have no idea at all how they would go about explaining their research to the general public.

This is certainly a massive problem within academia, because it is a massive bubble that is almost an echo chamber. They create and do their research for each other and their precious journals. Even though if you talk to them, they will almost always say they do research so they can have a real-world impact.

And there lies the disconnect between academia and the real-world. The real-world is run by non-psychology people that don't really understand research, academic writing and they have their own agendas. This means you cannot approach them or talk to them like fellow academics, if you want them to listen to you and take you seriously and even take your ideas onboard, then you have to talk to them like a real person.

As well as play up to their egos, their ambitions and what makes them look good. It is simply how those in power work.

In addition, this has been spoken about a lot in clinical psychology over the years. The academic researchers work away on clinical psychology topics finding out useful things for clinical psychologists to use with clients, and then they write up their pretty little reports without any regard for any useful or practical advice or steps for how this can be used in the real world to improve lives.

As you can probably tell I am really annoyed by this disconnect, but it is how academia works.

Academia and academics aren't always based in reality and the real-world. I am not trying to disrespect academics because they are lovely people if not a little too passionate at times about their research. Almost to the point where everything else in life becomes lesser than their passion for their research.

Anway, I am highlighting this problem because if psychology academics ever want to have a real impact in the world then they need to help make this more accessible to non-psychology people.

I know a lot of people are trying to do this in different ways. For example, it is why I write my books and I host The Psychology World Podcast, it is me breaking down psychology topics into easy-to-understand episodes. It is still aimed at psychology students and professionals but it is written in a way that makes it easy to understand in case anyone else finds it too.

Furthermore, this is why with my current mental health research on the gender-affirming clothing on transgender youth, I'm trying to make it useful in both the academic and practical sense. I'll be including recommendations and practical findings for mental health practitioners and those working with transgender youth when I write up the academic paper in the vain hope of publishing it in a journal.

If not, I'll transfer the knowledge and the findings into a book so it is still available for people to learn from. As well as I will convert some of it to a podcast episode so the practical stuff is available for free to people who might benefit from it.

Of course, I know I am only able to do these things because of my amazing readers and podcast listeners (thank you by the way), but I guess this is me trying to fight the good fight and help make psychology research matter. So I can share this knowledge and show and prove to non-psychology people that psychology research can improve lives, be useful and help decrease psychological distress.

Yet if no one writes about this in an accessible, engaging and interesting way then people will never know the power of psychology research and nothing will change in the world.

That is sad, tragic and something that has to change in academia, so if you want to go into academia then please, bear this reflection in mind. It might help you make more of an impact than you ever thought possible.

WHAT DO YOU WANT TO BE KNOWN FOR ON SOCIAL MEDIA?

Of all the different inspirations and articles and real world things that get me thinking and reflecting, I have to admit that this idea from the October 2023 issue of The Psychologist Magazine might be an outlier of sorts. Since there was an article that was talking about digital legacies and wanting to be known for something on social media long after we're gone.

I think this is a logical next extension of legacies because currently and in the past, everyone has been so focused on *doing* or creating or building something to form their legacies. For example, we know Van Gogh, Picasso and Da Vinci because they created stunning art amongst other things as part of their legacy. As well as I am sure in your own country there are famous examples of people that have done great things and built impressive features of a country. One example that comes to mind is Effiel who created the Effiel Tower in Paris.

Anyway, I believe that as we continue to move into the digital world, there will be a growing emphasis on digital legacies.

All of these ideas and drives behind creating a legacy will have clinical psychology and mental health implications. You only need to read my book *Social Media Psychology* to understand the positive and negatives of social media on mental health.

Therefore, I want to reflect on this idea for future and current clinical psychologists, because one of the aims of the profession is to help us impart our knowledge to the next generation of psychologists. This is why in an ideal world clinical psychologists split their time between working in clinical practice and teaching at universities, but the time constraints and work pressures make that balance impossible.

As a result, social media is another good avenue for clinical psychologists, and us students once we have qualified, to share information. And to be honest, of course non-qualified people cannot call themselves clinical psychologists, they can still help share knowledge, insights and inspirations to people across the world.

That is the beauty of social media.

If we take myself as an example, I host The Psychology World Podcast every Monday without fail and in each episode, I talk about psychology news, a personal update that touches on university or my own psychology experience briefly and then a main psychology topic.

Then on a Monday this goes out to YouTube and all major podcast apps allowing people around the world to listen and learn about psychology. As well as I share the podcast episode on Twitter, Facebook and LinkedIn and Pinterest.

Therefore, I tend to use social media as a way of sharing knowledge, getting engagement and helping people learn more about psychology. Of course, I sometimes do this a little half-ass considering I used to be a lot more active on Twitter before He took it over and ruined the platform. But I do try to be a person people interested in psychology can come to so they can learn interesting things.

There is a larger point I want to make in a moment.

In addition, in terms of me as a fiction author, on Facebook and Instagram, I always try to share a book recommendation, something interesting about me, a Weird Word Wednesday thing and a film or TV recommendations. I do this because I want my fiction author accounts to be entertaining, interesting and a place where people can come to to get good recommendations.

I want to be remembered as an entertainer, a storyteller and a person that makes people smile and find interesting.

Therefore, I cater and craft my social media accounts accordingly, or I try to at least.

Finally, if I really encourage you to find out about the social media accounts that you come coming back to. What do you like about them? Will you remember them? What makes them interesting enough that you keep returning?

I know I don't follow too many social media accounts, but for the ones I do, I have good reasons. For example, USA Today Bestselling author Kristine Kathryn Rusch shares a lot of funny stories, interesting life events and book news that I enjoy looking at. Her cats make us laugh and that's great.

When it comes to Mae Martin's Instagram account, it is always great, funny and fun to see what they're up to as a comedian.

Then in terms of psychology, there are some LinkedIn accounts that I look at on occasion because I know there are a great place to look at if I want certain information on clinical psychology careers and so on.

As a result, I hope this has shown you that social media isn't all bad and it can have benefits for us. It can provide us with a fun, interesting place to learn about the things we're passionate about.

In addition, the entire point of this reflection was to help show you that you might want to cater your professional social media accounts (if you have any) to help form a part of your legacies.

You seriously don't need to be a podcaster, blogger or writer like me. You could be known as someone who posts little inspirational psychology quotes that makes people feel good, you could be known for posting a paragraph a day about your favourite psychology topics, or something else entirely.

If you want to have a digital legacy or even if you just want to use social media more purposefully then maybe be a little more conscious how you post and the type of things you post. We all have ten or more accounts we can randomly think of that we avoid like the plague because they're toxic, awful and their legacies are beyond horrific.

But as future or current clinical psychologists, our social media accounts don't have to be bad or overzealously filled with psychology-related stuff. There is the 80/20 rule so 80% psychology content and 20% personal stuff.

As we move into the new digital age, there will be one question that impacts us more and more, what will your digital legacy be?

COULD INCLUSIVE-LANGUAGE BE IMPORTANT IN THE ADOS AND OTHER MENTAL HEALTH SETTINGS?

Every so often in The Psychologist Magazine by the British Psychological Society, I come across an article that I seriously, seriously like because it's interesting, thought-provoking and it sticks with me for a while after reading it.

I had one of these times when I was reading the November 2022 issue and there was this tiny little article about the Autism

Diagnostic Observation Scale because the woman was saying she had watched a training video with her cohort and a five year-old child was asked this question "do you have a girlfriend?" and she acknowledged that the question itself doesn't matter for the clinical task because it is the child's response that is more important than the question. It is to see how the child thinks and responds about human relationships.

Yet I do agree with her point and I will go one step closer.

For starters, in my personal opinion, why the hell would a 5 year old boy be dating? I don't care if they're dating a boy or girl, why would a 5 year old be dating?

Of course that probably makes me sound hardline or something about children dating, but I think it is weird that we have that sort of expectation. That a kid would be dating and even if they were "dating" they wouldn't know what that really means or the experience that we later experience as teenagers or young adults or adults.

Again I know the question itself isn't important and it is effective for knowing how the child thinks about relationships, a major factor in autism that I am still learning about even now.

The Real Point Of The Article

Getting back onto the real point of the article, the woman is openly gay and she pointed out how the question was strange when we consider the world we live in and the research itself. The original question is "do you have a girlfriend?" and I imagine if the video was about a five year old girl being tested using ADOS, the question would be "do you have a boyfriend?"

Why shouldn't the question be more open and more telling to be honest? The question should be "do you have a girlfriend or boyfriend?"

I think this for three main reasons.

Firstly, I think this is a lot more telling and useful for the ADOS test itself, because in the event that 5 year old boy (I would still be surprised if a 5 year old was dating) was asked about dating a girl and they weren't, they would just say no and respond a little.

Then depending on the severity of the autism, and judging on my own experiences of even mild autism at that age, chances are if the five year old boy was "dating" another boy then they wouldn't know that they should understand the question is about social relationships and they should reveal and respond on having a boyfriend.

Now at the age of 22, I can understand most of the time the real point behind a question even when it's worded wrong, like this one would be. Yet a five year old wouldn't be able to if they had autism.

Therefore, I strongly believe that the ADOS question was more inclusive by containing those two extra words that might take someone an extra second to say. Then the Scale might get more information to use in the assessment.

And surely, that's the entire point of ADOS?

Important Side Note: No This Will Not Turn Kids Gay

In the very, very rare event that a homophobic person has made it to this section of the book, I can promise you that simply asking a five year old boy "do you have a girlfriend or boyfriend?" will not make them gay. That isn't how it works.

It seriously doesn't.

Also, I think what people need to understand is kids don't care about gay, straight and everything in-between. They only care about what parents, adults and society tells them later on that this is something to be upset by, disinterested in because you're okay with it and want to support people regardless of their sexuality, or it's perfectly okay and actively encouraged if the person has that interest.

And if they do have an interest in same-sex relationships in the future then you're benefiting them and their mental health by telling them from an early age that it doesn't matter if they like boys or girls.

Because it just doesn't.

Considering The World We Live In

Secondly, we live in a world that is generally more accepting and this is something we need to continue to work on and work towards. And because of the general acceptance, the safety young people feel now and how positive compared to previous decades people are towards LGBT+ people. There are more people in general identifying as LGBT+ and it is still a tiny, tiny minority of the general population, but it is still present.

Therefore, considering psychology is part of the world and society that we want to make more equal, fairer and accepting. It is a little odd that we are implying that opposite-sex relationships are the only options for people at such a young age.

Wouldn't it be a brilliant and such a subtle way to teach children that it's okay to like girls and boys regardless of whatever their preference ends up being?

Just like how we tell girls from a young age that they can do anything they want, they can become engineers, IT people and all the other job roles that are typically male-only. Wouldn't it be good to teach kids the same thing about relationships?

I think it would.

And this would serve two purposes too. It would teach kids if they later discover they're LGBT+ that it's nothing to worry about because you've taught them from that young age that no one cares by asking a simple question in a normal way.

However, for kids that don't discover their LGBT+ then it helps to promote tolerance. Since from that young age you've taught them that it doesn't matter if someone likes boys or girls or both by asking a question in a normal way.

Language has immense power in clinical psychology and so do our questions.

It's A Weird Question Considering The Research

To wrap up this reflection, the original article in The Psychologist mentioned how this was a weird question considering there is an overwhelming amount of research that shows that LGBT+ people are more likely to experience mental health difficulties.

Done that and brought the t-shirt.

Therefore, if we apply this idea of using more inclusive language in other mental health settings and the ADOS itself, then this is only going to benefit people. I know from my own experiences of therapy, it is awful, awkward and just flat out weird to have to "come out" to a therapist because they don't ask things.

It isn't a "normal" or "typical" question in clinical psychology settings.

And considering that a lot of therapists

will see LGBT+ people in their practice at some point in their lives because of the mental health difficulties that society and family factors creates for this population. It seems strange that we want to bake into mental health services another factor of distress.

If a therapist had asked me, was I gay and what are my pronouns? I would have bit a little awkward still because of my trauma, abuse and everything that happened to me. Yet it would have been nice to be asked and not have to awkwardly "come out" when explaining why I was there and I was seriously stressed out about it in the time leading up to my first appointment.

Update

In addition, I'm adding this little section in a few hours after writing this reflection because I had my first counselling session at the university, and there is something I want to comment on about this topic.

We were talking about identity and because he didn't ask me anymore about my sexuality and gender identity (because it isn't standard practice), I couldn't really tell him about my trans identity as a non-binary person.

Granted I am not blaming him at all because he is brilliant as well as he knew I was gay anyway because my referral form, and I mentioned it during me talking about why I wanted counselling. Yet since my "new" gender identity (it isn't new at all but I only realised it 6 weeks ago), it was really hard to talk about it and "come out" as a non-binary person.

So I didn't.

And I think I should and it will be helpful but I just felt awkward disclosing it because it is something I am still learning about and that part of myself is still very much developing.

Therefore, my point is that this extremely harmless question of asking "what is your sexuality?" (if it is relevant of course) and "what are your pronouns or what's your gender?" in a therapy setting would be very, very helpful to me in this personal example.

It would have given me an "in" to this disclosing and this is something that all of our clients want at different times. It is no different than clients or therapists building on the comment or conversation the other person has just mentioned.

At the end of the day, psychological therapy is about the exploration of mental health, the client's psychological process and any psychological distress they're experiencing. And all exploration requires us, as future or current psychologists, to have an "in" with a client to start talking about a topic, any topic.

So just in case someone wants to talk or express or declare their sexuality or gender identity, let's give them the chance. It might be important, it might not be but this would only take an extra 10 seconds.

And that simple question could have immense power, something I talk about more below.

Conclusion

Overall, I strongly believe that inclusive language should be used more in mental health settings, because it isn't hard but the impact could be immense for our clients. It could decrease their psychological distress in the future, it could help promote tolerance in society and it could seriously help put our clients at ease when they first come into our services.

And considering the entire point of

clinical psychology is to help our clients improve their lives and decrease their stress. It seems weird that we aren't doing such a simple trick that would only take an extra ten seconds to do but it could have an immensely positive impact for us, the therapeutic alliance and most importantly, our clients.

DO CLINICAL PSYCHOLOGY COMPLAINT PROCEDURES NEED TO BECOME EASIER?

As future or current clinical psychologists, there will be times when we have a client that we aren't a good fit for, we no longer want to see because we don't believe we can help them or we just don't want to see them because we can't work well together.

That is okay because at the end of the day, a therapeutic relationship is a relationship between two different people and sometimes relationships work out. Yet sometimes they do not.

However, I was reading a really good article in the September 2023 edition of The Psychologist about an awful experience that an autistic client had been through were the therapist had said by email that they no longer wanted to see the client. There was no reason given, no explanation and no offer of another service instead.

This was, of course, a private therapist and the entire article was focused on how damaging this was to the client because there was no more support for them, they couldn't understand why this was done and then when the client tried to find out why. She threatened harassment against the autistic client.

And before I continue I want to jump in here and mention that ending a therapy correctly is flat out critical in clinical psychology. I've reflected on this before in one of the earlier volumes, but if we don't end a therapy correctly then this has immensely damaging effects on a client.

It can even undo all the good work you've done with them over the sessions so the client ends up being back at square one.

Whereas a good ending can leave a client feeling happy, relaxed, engaged and ready to take on the world with their newfound sense of freedom, happiness and their new coping mechanisms. At least that's how I basically felt.

Although, as you can expect this autistic client was really shocked, confused and deeply hurt by the actions of the therapist and this is where we come to the problem within clinical psychology.

Who do you complain to?

Since The British Psychological Society cannot act until they receive an "Unfit To Practice" judgement from the other professional bodies depending on who the person is registered with. As well as the only judgement that can be passed by the other professional organisations is "Unfit To Practice".

Of course, if you go to the NHS and have a course of therapy through them then I sort of imagine the complaint procedure is easier. Due to you could write to the NHS Trust, NHS England or go to the Department's head.

But when it comes to private therapists in the UK and to be honest aboard. I have no idea.

I know when I had private therapy, I wouldn't have a clue about who to complain to. I didn't even really take note of the three or four professional bodies the therapist was registered too.

Then another problem is that writing to a professional organisation, launching an official complaint and taking part in an investigation takes a hell of a lot of courage. No one likes complaining, no one wants to do this so they only really complain to a professional body if they have the courage to do this.

Not a lot of people do.

In addition, another problem is that "Unfit To Practice". That is an extremely high bar to set when dealing with a complaint and if someone is Unfit To Practice then that leaves a lot potentially questionable behaviour that can go under the radar. All because it doesn't meet the threshold for "Unfit To Practice".

I'm not saying that the therapist was wrong in the article to drop the client, the autistic client wasn't saying that either because they highlighted how there were two sides to every story. Yet the problem remains, in clinical psychology there are no easy ways to complain about a private therapist if they do something "bad" or damaging to a client.

In addition, "Unfit To Practice" is sort of the ultimate punishment too. Most clients don't want a therapist to get struck off just because of one really damaging mistake due to most of these are just one-off mistakes. Yet they want some sort of apology or acknowledgement that what happened was flat out wrong and it should never happen again.

However, because certain actions that have damaging impacts on clients fall below the threshold of "Unfit To Practice" it means that acknowledgement or judgement by a professional governing body never comes.

Personally, I would need to look into this a lot more and the different rules and regulations to make an even more informed judgement on the topic. Yet as someone who has been through therapy twice for different reasons and different things, I think there should be something that isn't quite "Unfit To Practice" but a judgement that means a therapist has to admit what they did in this incident was wrong. It doesn't mean that they were Unfit To Practice, it doesn't mean they're a crap therapist all-around. It just means what they did with a particular person was flat out wrong and it shouldn't have happened in the first place.

Especially as the article in The Psychologist sort of read like everyone was trying to gaslight them into believing being dropped by email by a therapist was perfectly okay, normal and expected.

Is it?

Maybe that is the case, but it doesn't make it morally right considering how we can make clients feel supported in their time of psychological distress. Or at least given them a reason for ending the therapeutic relationship and maybe sign post them to other services that might be able to help them better.

That would at least help stop some of the feelings of abandonment, but this is a very tricky topic that depends on so many different factors between the client and therapist. Yet I do believe complaints within clinical psychology should be easier and more accessible because I think a lot of clients can agree, in the rare incident they need to complain, they have absolutely no idea who to complain to.

And that is dangerous if something does go wrong.

AN UPDATED LOOK AT ENDINGS IN THERAPY

In the last reflection, I spoke about an ending of a therapy that went badly and left the client feeling hurt, damaged and confused about what the hell had gone wrong in the therapy for the therapist to just drop them like that.

In this reflection, I want to reflect on my own personal experience of ending a therapy and how it made me feel as a client. This is useful for all future and current clinical psychologists because it will help you to understand how a client feels coming to the end of a course of therapy that has helped them, transformed their lives and given them hope.

Nonetheless, first of all, I want to include this small extract from CBT For Depression that covers some of the psychological theory behind ending therapy as a whole.

Enjoy.

"How Ending The Therapy Works?

Now this is a critical part of the overall course of treatment because if there is a jerking ending or an unsatisfying end then this can be just as damaging as no therapy at all. For example, one of my lecturers told us how her client had had so many therapists and they just ended up leaving him that it confirmed his cognitive processes about how everyone leaves him in the end.

That isn't what an ending is meant to look like in CBT, so that's why we need to focus on it now. There's no point doing therapy if the ending is only going to undo all the hard work of the client and therapist.

Therefore, the ending of therapy should be like the beginning in terms of it being structured and collaborative. As well as when a therapist does end of a piece with a client they would revisit the goals they set with the client set at the beginning.

To make sure that they've gotten everything they've set out to achieve, and it's nice that you can go to the client, something along the lines of "Look, a few months ago you told me these were all impossible to achieve and now look at you,"

And this links into making the client realise how much *they're* done and why *they're* amazing.

And that's the magic thing about CBT, it is a therapy where the client is always centre-stage because the therapist might give them great tools, but at the end of the day, it is the client that put in the work and made the change all possible.

Sometimes it only takes the skilled hand of a therapist to make them realise just how incredible they actually are."

My Personal Experience of Ending A Therapy

The first major feeling you experience when it comes to ending a therapy is a sort of weird combination of happiness, nervousness and even a little anxiety. Since you're a happy because I was better now and I felt able to go on and live a brilliant life filled with love, healthy relationships and I was pain free for the first time in my life. As well as I was happy I was no longer going to be spending £50 a week on therapy.

I was a little nervous and anxious because ending this therapy meant a major source of psychological support was going to be gone from my life. And that was a very scary thing because I didn't know, or I wasn't sure I was going to be okay with it.

Therefore, your client will most probably have these sort of feelings about ending the therapy regardless of how amazing the work has been. For example, my therapist was flat out amazing and she helped me transform my own life for the better, but I was still experiencing all these different emotions.

Furthermore, when it came to the therapy session, it was really good in the sense that it was very relaxed and we went through a list of about six things that she wanted to wrap up and suggest I continue working on in the future. Since we did some short-term work together and there was more to cover.

I really liked how my therapist just took her time and we spoke about all the different expects of the list she had put together, she warned me against boxing stuff up and it was a good, positive and hopeful therapy session that set me up for the future.

And it's that sense of hope that I really, really liked. She was helping me to realise that I am only 22 and I have my entire life ahead of me. I am going on this massive journey, this massive experience of finding out who I am and everything surrounding me no longer being held back by my pain, trauma and abuse.

She helped me to realise on my own how much hope and great things there are in the future.

Then when it came to ending the final session, she mentioned stuff like how nice it was working together, how interesting it was and there were some empowering reminders about how *I* am the one that did the therapy work and everything like that. I had started therapy as a scared, traumatised, wreck of a person who was spiralling badly.

And I left a new person who was excited about seeing the world for the first-time not through the lens of abuse and trauma.

That's good therapy.

<u>What Does This Mean For Us?</u>

I think for us, as future or current clinical psychologists, it means we need to acknowledge that our clients will be scared, nervous and anxious about the end of psychotherapy. This is normal and it seriously doesn't mean we've done a bad job. This is an extremely normal human experience I think when it comes to ending something that has been so positive and life-changing for them.

Of course, not every client, not every therapist and not every course of therapy will feel this way. If you have not really enjoyed working with a specific client, you might be almost grateful to see them go or your client might never have truly engaged with the therapy.

But as long as we all try our best in psychotherapy then that's okay.

Anyway, I think my experience teaches us that the final session should give the client hope for the future and it should hammer home that we've given the tools to be their own therapists at home and in their life. This means they can go on and live their own lives without having to fall back on their maladaptive coping mechanisms that brought them to our service in the first place.

And to wrap this up, I don't actually think "ending" is the right term to use for this, because yes this is the end of therapy. But it isn't a real end.

In fact, the end of psychotherapy is

actually the beginning of something. For me, it was the beginning of being pain-free, being happy and being able to live a life without trauma and abuse controlling every single aspect of myself.

Every client will be different but the end of therapy isn't the end for a client. It is the beginning of a journey towards a new and exciting and hopeful life filled with joys, wonders and a lot of happiness.

But sometimes it takes us giving the client a few reminders to make them realise it.

WRITTEN BY RAPE SURVIVOR
CONNOR WHITELEY
I AM NOT A VICITM, I AM A SURVIVOR
A PERSONAL, CLINICAL PSYCHOLOGY AND SOCIAL PSYCHOLOGY GUIDE TO SEXUAL VIOLENCE AND RAPE

I AM NOT A VICTIM, I AM A SURVIVOR

A Personal, Clinical Psychology and Social Psychology Guide To Sexual Violence and Rape

INTRODUCTION

On the 13th April 2024, my life changed forever because I was raped. This is what happened over the next 5 months before my specialist counselling started.

This is my truth.

Whenever a person experiences sexual violence (the ultimate violation), we need to start our healing journey and healing from sexual violence is a journey that takes time, as annoying as that is to realise. Since as this book shows there'll be a lot of twists and turns, highs and lows, heart-warming and heart-breaking moments as you start to heal.

During healing you can have a breakthrough, a time of happiness where most of the trauma responses go away, then you remember a new detail or realised you have a new trigger, and this can feel devastating. Almost like you will never heal fully, never get better and you are doomed to be ruled by your trauma forever.

Healing is very possible, even if it feels like it's taking forever.

Nonetheless, as this book shows as I talk you through my life and mental health week-by-week for the first 5 months after my rape. You can see that the healing journey isn't linear, and there is no such thing as a finish line. You will heal in time, as you learn, go to therapy and try to recover, but it is a journey.

In this book, you'll be able to see my highlights, my low points and how I helped myself survive with the help of my friends. As well as on your own healing journey, you will encounter something that you think is a setback, this will be another piece of trauma that your body and mind are revealing to you so you can heal. It is annoying when this happens but it is a good thing because it means you can heal it and recover over time.

It is these small healing pieces that allow you to be successful over time and allows you to face more and more challenges. Trauma is essentially the gift that keeps on giving and it is exactly like an onion or artichoke, you peel back layers then you find the centre. The centre of you that wants to live, wants to be healed and the centre that can never be defeated.

A lot of people might believe that me writing about my rape as soon as it happened is strange, but I am a writer, I am a researcher, I am a psychology Masters student. For me, writing and researching rape was how I dealt with it because I knew I couldn't heal from this alone.

At the time of writing this introduction, it's 7-months since my rape and now I am at the point where I can confidently say that I am healing because I still go through hell-and-back some days, but my triggers are decreasing and everything is getting better very slowly.

However, this book shows that wasn't always the case, so I want you to know that are never alone in your feelings, your experiences and whatever you're going through.

What Is The Purpose Of This Book?

Personally, I call this book a mixture of memoir and psychoeducation information. A lot of the book focuses on my experiences, my PTSD, my mental health after my rape. I wrote about these topics with you in mind and whenever I can, I focus a lot on tips and tricks that helped me survive these periods.

In addition, there are chapters in this book that are solely dedicated to providing you with psychology facts and information about the sexual violence and therapy options, so you can understand the topic for yourself if you're comfortable. Even though I talk more about sexual violence in my book *Breaking The Silence.*

This book is designed to help you in small ways so you don't feel alone, but professional help is always best.

Furthermore, if anything in the book starts to overwhelm you then please, give yourself permission to stop, use the self-soothing exercises I introduce in a moment and come back to the book later.

Never forget you, and only you are in charge. You have choice in what you read, what you do and how you relate to this book.

Lastly, whenever you're healing from sexual trauma, it is perfectly okay if you don't, but it might be useful to include a dear friend or family member or therapist in the process. You may feel vulnerable at times, but their support will help you heal.

Who Am I?

In my other psychology books, I include this section because I like to know who the author is so I know the information is coming from a reliable and good source, but I'm including this section for a different reason.

I'm Connor Whiteley, the internationally bestselling author of over 40 psychology books, I am the host of *The Psychology World Podcast,* a weekly show exploring a new psychology topic each week and delivering the latest psychology news. Available on all major podcast apps and YouTube. As well as I am a psychology graduate who studied a Clinical Psychology undergraduate and Masters at the University of Kent, England.

I am a survivor, not a victim.

I love psychology, spending time with my friends, going out and living. Also, I like fiction books of all types especially books by Dean Wesley Smith, and I like watching films with my friends.

I am a normal person with a normal, fun, exciting life but when I was raped, he took everything from me.

I thought I was a weak, victim but I am not. I am slowly rebuilding my life, I am slowly living again and I am recovering from what he did to me.

I am a survivor, not a victim, but it wasn't always that way.

This is my story and this is my truth.

WHAT ARE SOME SELF-SOOTHING STRATEGIES?

I'm almost embarrassed that I didn't think to include this chapter when my sexual assault counselling started (that's the focus of another book), but I wanted to include this first chapter so in case you get overwhelmed, triggered or distressed by anything in this book then you have some strategies to help your body relax.

The very last thing I want is for you to get triggered or distressed by anything in this book and for you not to have tools or strategies to help you.

As a result, the ability to self-soothe is beyond critical to mental health because it allows us to calm ourselves down, we can relax and return to our window of tolerance. Yet some people aren't able to self-soothe so to relax, calm down and maintain their mental health they need others to soothe them. This is a strategy that works for a time but it is far from perfect and it doesn't solve anything.

I struggle a lot with my inability to self-soothe because this was the focus of the topic this week in my specialist counselling session. Therefore, in this chapter, you'll learn what is self-soothing, how can you self-soothe and why it's so important to your mental health.

What Is Self-Soothing?

A person's ability to self-soothe is their efforts to calm themselves down when they're in an emotional state as proposed by Wright (2009). As well as this is beyond critical for our psychological well-being because it helps people to stay calm and emotionally regulated.

I know this is a massive issue for me because my ability to self-soothe has always been bad, but after my rape, over time it got worse and worse. Currently, at the time of writing, I essentially cannot self-soothe at all, which is a massive problem. This is why I'm focusing on this in therapy.

Moreover, a lot of people learn how to self-soothe when we're babies because when our caregivers soothe us, we internalise this soothing and learn how to do it ourselves (Wright, 2009). Yet there are a wide range of reasons why people (like me) are unable to learn these self-soothing skills and use them as adults.

Thankfully, it is perfectly possible to learn how to self-soothe as an adult and that's the focus of this chapter. Granted, self-soothing requires self-insight, we need to develop our skills and we need to be able to effectively use these skills in an effort to calm ourselves down.

This is an important bit I believe because we can read and learn everything we want to about self-soothing. Yet unless we practice and get better *over time* then we will never actually improve our self-soothing skills.

What Are Some Self-Soothing Strategies?

Take Some Deep Breaths

I wanted to start us off with an extremely simple one because I know from personal experience, it is this extremely simple and extremely useful technique that we tend to forget the most. As well as I want to take advantage of the primacy and recency effect. Therefore, whenever we want to self-soothe we need to deactivate our sympathetic nervous system. This means we need to activate our parasympathetic nervous system because this nervous system helps to stop the fight-or-flight response and helps us to calm down.

Thankfully, the parasympathetic nervous system can be very easily activated by taking a few long, deep breaths, including box breathing. Box breathing involves you breathing in for a count of 4 then you hold for a count of 4 and breathe out for a count of 4. Finally, you hold for a count of 4.

You do this a few times until you start to feel calmer.

Again, you need to practice this, so let's try it right now together.

- Breathe in for a count of 4.
- Hold your breath for a count of 4
- Breathe out
- Hold

You would do this a few times but I hope you already start to feel calmer. I know I do.

You Need To Listen To Relaxing Music

Something I've only just realised is that when my mental health is bad and I cannot focus on doing something on my laptop, I play relaxing music as a matter of habit. I never do it when my mental health is good, but I still do it to self-soothe. I never realised that until now. In fact, on YouTube, I'm currently listening to *"Cozy Autumn Vibes, Beautiful Relaxing Music, Peaceful Soothing Instrumental Music, By Tim Janis"*.

It's very good by the way.

Anyway, listening to relaxing music is a good idea for self-soothing because this type of music helps to reduce the stress hormone called Cortisol (Khalfa et al., 2003). As a result, if you're feeling distressed and you're spiralling, try listening to relaxing music because this calming music might help you change your mood, help you to breathe deeper and decrease the negative emotions that you're experiencing.

If you have a Go-To music service that you love (my friends still don't understand why I prefer YouTube for my music over Spotify), then maybe create a playlist of relaxing music so you can listen to it when you're distressed.

Then remember to actually play it and listen to it.

You Should Do Pleasant Activities To Self-Soothe

Personally, I know how difficult, impossible and awful it can be when you're depressed, spiralling or in a mental health crisis, because we all know we need to do pleasant activities to maintain our mental health. Yet when we're spiralling and urgently need to self-soothe, it can be so impossible to do these things that we enjoy.

However, Dialectical Behavioural Therapy suggests that we can self-soothe by doing activities that bring us joy and make us happy (Linehan, 1993). Especially as us doing a pleasurable activity when we're distressed can make us feel better.

As a result, when you're distressed, try to do activities you enjoy. Be it reading, gardening, exercise, whatever. Just try to do something that makes you happy.

When I'm distressed, I try to watch something I'll enjoy, listen to podcasts, cook, read or hang out with friends. Since these are the activities that make me happy and they help to make me feel better. Of course that doesn't mean they're easy to do in the slightest when I'm distressed but over time as you practise to self-soothe more and more then these strategies become a lot easier.

Conclusion

In my opinion, none of these strategies are useful alone and in isolation. In reality, whilst all these are highly effective self-soothing strategies, they feed into each other. For example, when you're distressed you cannot simply start doing pleasurable activities because in my experience, you cannot focus and you cannot enjoy them. Therefore, you can start to self-soothe by doing box-breathing to activate our parasympathetic nervous system so you can calm down or listen to relaxing music. Then you can start to do pleasurable activities to help you self-soothe for longer.

So much of psychology and mental health advice can never be done effectively in isolation.

Therefore, to end this chapter, I want to finish by saying that having an inability to self-soothe can be very damaging to your mental health, and it is so annoying. Yet it is more than possible over time to practise and improve your self-soothing skills. I never thought I would be able to self-soothe but last night I got triggered by a stupid sex ad on YouTube and I got distressed yet I practised box-breathing and managed to self-soothe for the first time in my life.

And I am very proud of myself for managing that.

Now I just need to keep practising, keep trying and keep strengthening my ability to self-soothe. It is possible regardless of how impossible and scary it seems. Just keep trying and using the strategies included in this chapter and one day you will get there.

And it will be a wonderful feeling when you do.

PART ONE: MY PERSONAL EXPERIENCE OF RAPE

THE EFFECTS OF SEXUAL ASSAULT

Trigger warning: this following reflection contains references to sex, sexual assault and the aftermath of the assault and mental health. If the following will trigger you then please skip this reflection for the sake of your own mental health.

Straight after my assault and before I knew I needed to write a book on my experience as a survivor and the first 6-months of my recovery, I wrote what I call "clinical psychology reflections". This is one of the psychology series I have and they're easy-to-understand experience- and fact-based reflections written to inform and educate aspiring or qualified clinical psychologists.

This is one of those chapters.

However, please rest assured that nothing in this book is going to be dull, academic and unreadable. This is a very personal and insightful chapter that you're going to learn a lot from, so please sit back, relax and read how I was sexually assaulted.

***

Sometimes things happen in my personal life that make me want to write these clinical psychology reflections a lot earlier than I normally would. For example, I know I won't write the rest of these reflections for another few months but I need to write these two now.

I was sexually assaulted two nights ago and I had an appointment today to discuss it at my university, the very nice woman helped to me to understand that it was sexual assault. I wasn't making it up or overreacting and she was really helpful.

I easily cried 2 or 3 times during that 30-minute appointment.

There is a clinical psychology point in the next chapter that I might be able to generalise to our profession. Yet I want to explain the effects of sexual assault on a victim in this chapter because I was surprised to learn what was normal behaviour in these cases when I spoke to the specialist at the university today.

Disclaimer

I've been watching the news, looking at social media and I've heard a lot of conversations with different people over my lifetime. I know I will get slated for writing these next two reflections, I know people will say I was asking for it and I know people will say I am disgusting and all that shit.

But honestly, unless you have experienced sexual assault then you don't have a leg to stand on.

I promise I am not having a go at 99% of readers because I know my audience are genuinely lovely and I love you all, you allow me to write and do what I love.

I am instead talking to the 1% of people that will read this and want to bully me because of it. To you I say kindly fuck off.

What Happened?

Before I explain what the effects of this event on me were specifically, I want to explain what happened in a way similar to how I described it to the woman at the university. I will brushstroke some stuff because what actually happened was too detailed for a book.

Therefore, if you're familiar with me and if you've been listening to The Psychology World Podcast then you might be aware that I was abused and traumatised as a kid for being gay. My social environment was extremely homophobic, I was in fear for my life for a decade that led to a lot of bad mental health outcomes. So I was never ever allowed to be gay at all. Much less hookup, have sex or kiss someone.

Thankfully, in that department my life is a million times better than it was and I'm generally happy with my life. It was so much better than before.

So I was free at the weekend, my friends have a lot of relationships and my best friend is currently abroad visiting the woman that They really want to start a relationship with. So I thought yeah it would be great if I could experience something.

I went on Grindr (for people who don't know that is a gay dating app but it is a more sex-focused one) so I had some nice conversations with two people that wanted to have sex with me. They couldn't do that particular night so I started talking with a third guy.

He seemed nice enough, he knew I was a virgin and had never ever done anything before with anyone. His photo seemed nice enough (something that was a minor con in the end) so we arranged to meet and I went to his house.

For starters, I realised he had lied on his profile because the photo he sent me he had hidden his body in such a way that he was very overweight.

For clarification I am not fatshaming, I am simply raising a point that he made sure to hide that fact and he used his weight to his advantage later on.

I went inside the house and he grabbed me and started kissing and grinding himself against me. I said "No, I haven't done this before". Expecting him to stop and we could talk about this hookup, what I wanted and we could go slow.

That didn't happen.

He stopped for a moment and then he grabbed me again and started *really* grinding himself against me, kissing me and forcing his tongue down my throat. And let me tell you, considering I have never kissed anyone in my entire life before, that wasn't nice and it is awful having someone force their tongue down your throat.

I hated it.

Now typical stereotypes would make you question why I didn't punch, kick, scream in this situation if I hated it so much. I have been a survivor my entire life and I was always focused on doing what I needed to do to survive, so I simply let it happen because once it happened this would be over and I could get the hell out of there without anything violent happening to me.

When I was talking to the woman at the university, this is a very normal response. The vast majority of sexual assault and rape victims do this strategy because this is what happens.

So the guy kept touching me, taking off my clothes, he kept kissing me and getting really really excited.

Only an idiot couldn't tell I wasn't enjoying it because I wasn't touching him back, I wasn't smiling and I wasn't doing anything to him in return. Mainly because he was massive. I might have touched him on the head to be nice and polite but that was it.

Then he took my boxers off and this is where I skip over some details. Let's just say he really, really liked my manhood so let's skip over that section.

Afterwards he ordered me to lie down and I am very thankful for the next bit. Because he was so fat, his dick didn't work in the sense that it didn't get long so this couldn't graduate from sexual assault to rape (the legal difference being rape requires penetration).

He grabbed me and covered me in his hulk in a tight hug as he tried to penetrate me and once he realised he wasn't able to. (He wasn't even using a condom or lube which is extremely bad sexual practice but I was too numb and feeling bad to mention it) He stopped and called it over.

I got out of there.

The Effects

During this entire process, I felt very numb, uncomfortable and I expect this is the autism here. I didn't feel in danger or too distressed at the time.

Interestingly when I spoke to the woman at the university, she said that this is also very normal because victims go into survival mode. Similar to fight or flight response, there is "fawn" or "freeze" response and I think I did both of these in the moment. Since fawn is about being a people pleaser in the end where you just allow shit to happen because it would make the other person happy and that reduces any unseen things happening to you. Like him getting angry and lashing out.

Equally, "freeze" is definitely what I did once he grabbed me for the second time.

In addition, something I notice with myself and I expect this is an autistic trait, so autistic people don't always know what they're feeling in the moment and there can be a delay between what happened and an emotion. Turns out, according to the woman at the university, this is common for victims too.

Since when I got home the night it happened, I felt numb and uncomfortable but I didn't feel distressed. Yet my problem was I couldn't sleep, I couldn't stay still in my bed and it wasn't awful. I woke up with a massive headache the next morning.

Also, the next morning I was really distressed, scared and I started to spiral. In other words, my brain and emotions caught up with the reality of the situation.

I cleaned my teeth a lot yesterday because I wanted to make sure my mouth was clean after he tongued me. Also, I had my normal trauma reaction of whenever I ate or drank it felt like swallowing glass. I've experienced that before whenever I'm distressed.

And the most major one and you might want to skip the next few paragraphs if you're sensitive. Because the guy liked my dick so much, I really hated having a dick. Yesterday morning I wanted to cut it off and just get rid of it forever.

Thankfully, that only lasted yesterday morning and then it shifted into a case of "I don't like seeing my dick but I don't want it gone anymore". Even now, I'm *better* with my dick but I still haven't looked at it and I haven't really touched it.

So going to the toilet is a bit annoying.

Moreover, something that is distressing as hell is yesterday when I was trying to keep myself busy and focus on everything but what happened (it didn't work). I could be doing something, like lying on my bed playing Duolingo or reading something, and I could *feel* him touching me.

Then I would get scared and almost cry because my body literally felt like he was touching me exactly how he did the night before. I know there's a name for this in psychology but I don't want to look it up.

It was weird and scary and awful.

Finally, the last major effect of the assault was I had a very weird panic attack last night in my own bed. Now this guy didn't try to have sex with me in a bed, it was in his living room.

Therefore, I was very surprised that when I went into my bed last night in my normal way of only wearing boxers. I had a panic attack because I wasn't wearing many clothes and I had to use grounding techniques about what I could feel, hear, smell and taste (I couldn't use see because I had my bedroom lights off) to make me focus back on the present moment.

And where I actually was.

So I'll admit I am very nervous about going to bed tonight but if I have another panic attack then I'll do what the woman from the university said and wear more clothes going to bed. That's a good idea to be honest and it's easy.

The Response From Others

Yesterday I was spiralling, trying to focus on what had happened and I was just scared because of a bunch of other trauma and what had happened before in my life (it wasn't sexual assault related but my brain didn't care), so I contacted one friend. The problem was they're in another country and they were away so they didn't have access to Wi-Fi (we communicate via WhatsApp a lot), so they didn't get back to me.

Also, my other close friend is very innocent and they wouldn't have any clue about this. As well as my other close friend is a sexual abuse victim from childhood so I couldn't talk to him about it.

Therefore, this morning actually did contact my friend that had been sexually abused as a child with the massive caveat that he needs to say no if he isn't comfortable with this. He messaged me back hours later saying we could take this conversation slowly and thankfully he didn't get triggered but he confirmed this was rape.

Before that though, I contacted my university because they have a Specialist Support Service as part of their mental health team. I had a 30-minute appointment with her and she's great and I told her what happened, she told me about my options and some support I could get.

The only real support I am concerned I might need is academic because I have two stats exams coming up and I'm concerned that I can't seem to focus. I know I'm getting ahead of myself because it was only two days ago but I am scared that I won't be able to focus on revision for the exams next month.

Thankfully, she said mitigation is an option and she can help with that.

Then she mentioned the name of a service with an extremely problematic name and we spoke about groups and some interesting stuff including some denial about terms on my part. Like I didn't want to admit I was a sexual assault victim until three people confirmed what happened was sexual assault.

I really didn't want to admit it but that is what happened.

Finally, I had a lovely, deep conversation with my best friend who finally read my messages and I'm looking forward to seeing them in a few weeks when they're back.

Ending Note

I'll admit that it took a lot for me to write this reflection because I didn't want any of this to happen, I am better than I was in the morning but that's only because I spoke to people about it. I feel better that I'm supported and the people important to me socially are aware of this.

Like, I'm seeing a friend on Thursday (it's Monday today), I'm spending a few days with my best friend anyway, I'm hoping to see my innocent friend next week so I thankfully have the social support.

Will I be 100% okay?

Of course not. No one ever is but I am better than I was and I'm happy about that.

Now, because this reflection is a little longer than I intended I will leave the rest for another reflection. Which will be a lot more general towards clinical psychology and mental health as a whole.

Let's check it out.

GROUP IDENTITIES AND PROBLEMATIC NAMES OF RAPE AND SEXUAL ASSAULT SERVICES

Trigger warning: *the following clinical psychology reflection contains details and references of rape, sexual assault and the stories of victims. Please do not read this reflection if you would find it distressing.*

Originally, I debated whether to include this chapter in or not but I want to. Since our next chapter touches on how us survivors can be in denial about what happened to us, as well as how the names of services can stop us from accessing them.

In other words, this chapter, like a few other chapters in this book, is about letting you know that you aren't alone and if you're experiencing things that you might call "weird" then chances are, you are far from the only one.

You are never alone.

The Group Identities and Labels

As a clinical psychology student, author and podcaster, I've thought a lot about the stigma and social perceptions surrounding labels and names. It's one of the reasons why I hate the diagnostic system with a passion and it's why I've spoken a lot about the damaging impact of labels in these reflections before.

However, I was a little surprised by my own denial and resistance to terming myself as a victim or a sexual assault victim. I think mainly because I thought maybe only someone who's been kicked, punched, beaten with an inch of their life could say they're a victim of rape or sexual assault.

Again, just me going off the societal myths about this sort of crime.

Maybe I thought only certain people get raped and assaulted. Maybe I didn't want to admit what had happened and how serious and bad that was.

Then as the woman at the university said along with my good close friends, this was rape and this was bad and this never ever should have happened.

I slowly had to acknowledge that this was sexual assault and I was a victim.

Therefore, as a clinical psychology person, I find it interesting that people don't want to attach certain labels to themselves. In all honesty, I know this from my previous lectures and comments on labels because they are stigmatised. I bet you're thinking I am a very specific type of person because I've been sexually assaulted.

Some of you are probably thinking I'm weak, not manly (I'm non-binary anyway) and I'm a failure because real people fight back.

You would only be going off cultural

stereotypes so I hardly blame you. I might even do the same if I was in your shoes.

And I think the reason why I was so resistant to terming myself as a sexual assault victim was because I didn't want to see myself as a victim anymore. I've been a victim my entire life from child abuse and trauma, living constantly in fear for my life and so on.

I just wanted to live a little and then this happened.

And I know from my family and my social environment that being a victim of sexual assault isn't always something you get supported in. Like I know I will tell my family but I won't at the moment because that will make me a victim in their eyes and they will look at me every day like I'm a victim.

Also, there is a lot of stigma and social pressure on victims. People will say I was asking for it, I should have fought back, I should have done X, Y and Z. or even well, I'm gay so this was bound to happen (an utter bullshit comment if there ever was one but I have heard a variation of it in real life).

So I was very resistant to it.

Overall, when it comes to clinical psychology work in the future and you have a client that refuses to be termed or included in a group of people. I would unofficially recommend respecting them and maybe even gently question why.

Since when the woman at the university said in a paraphrased way "Something-Something Rape Services for victims of sexual violence, I don't know if you would include yourself in those groups,"

I said: "I don't want to but I know the definition is anything that isn't consensual sex is rape. But I *know* I'm a rape victim but I don't want to admit it,"

That is perfectly okay and she respected me and I later admitted it in my own time. That is something you can and should do with clients too.

Naming Services

Continuing with the same vein of thinking and reasoning, I wanted to comment on the name of a charity or mental health service that offers counselling and other support for sexual assault and rape victims. I can't say its actual name for privacy reasons but it was "Something-Something Rape Crisis Centre"

I didn't like the name and the name immediately put me off the service.

As well as the woman at the university admitted the name was problematic because for starters, it implies only rape victims can go there, not sexual assault victims.

Also, the name is very loaded because it suggests that if you go to this place then you are a victim of rape and sexual assault and it carries all that social stigma with it. I did not want to contact or deal with this charity whatsoever because I didn't want to admit to myself that I was a victim and I did not want to go there and be seen to everyone at this charity as a weak victim.

Again, this isn't me being difficult. This is me just using what limited knowledge I have about victims from what I've seen on TV, the news and social conversations over the years. I only researched it more this afternoon after others confirmed and helped me to realise what had happened.

On the whole, I think if this service and charity didn't have such a loaded name then I would have considered it. I might have contacted them, and the woman at the university wouldn't have had to explain that other people have had similar reactions to me. And then she gently made sure I explained what support network I have in place at the moment as she knew I wasn't going to contact the service.

In future, I think, as future or current clinical psychologists, if we ever rise to a position of power where we are in a position to name mental health and support services. Then we need to be mindful about the words we use in the name so they aren't loaded, they aren't going to turn people away and they aren't going to stop the people we aim to help.

Just an interesting thought-provoking idea that I would have liked never to learn or have to think about.

WHY ISN'T AN ERECTION CONSENT?

This is the psychology article that started everything, because without this podcast episode, this book would not be possible. Also, this article allowed to subtly talk about what had happened to me, it made me want to speak up about rape and male rape more generally so I could educate people against the many myths and misconceptions about rape.

Even though any podcast episode on sexual violence is going to do badly because 99% of people just want to avoid the topic of sexual violence and pretend it doesn't exist, I am proud that I did this podcast episode.

It gave me a chance to find my voice, get comfortable talking about my experience and it gave me a drive to fight. It gave me hope that I could fight against the veil of silence that society created for itself around this topic and it gave me hope that I might be able to help at least one single person in case they're experienced something similar.

Please enjoy the psychology article that started everything.

***

Research suggest that men get raped and sexually assaulted as often as women by both men and women. Yet male rape is a lot less reported because of societal factors, gender roles and a whole bunch of horrible myths that stop men from reporting rape and sexual assault. Also, it's important to note that talking about male rape isn't about stopping or taking the focus away from female rape, instead it's actually about highlighting something that isn't spoken about in society. All rape and sexual assault whether it's against a man or woman is flat out wrong and it should never happen. Therefore, in this forensic psychology podcast episode, we'll explore male rape and why an erection isn't consent. If you like learning about forensic psychology, sexual crimes and why people do this crime then you'll enjoy today's episode.

Why Am I Talking About Male Sexual Assault and Rape?

Just as a little introduction to this episode and why I'm personally doing this, I wanted to be upfront and honest with you about my own personal position. So I'm a victim of sexual assault, it happened about three weeks ago and I cannot emphasise how distressing, awful and foul it was. I don't wish it on anyone and whilst you won't hear any major details about my assault in this episode, this did happen to me. As well as I will add in my personal thoughts like always in this episode to help it come alive.

Since one of the awful things that

happened after my assault was that I worked an Open Day at my university and I was talking to a lecturer that I always talk to. I really like her, she's great and she studies forensic psychology. Even though I completely forgot her topic was sexual violence so she started talking about it and I just couldn't listen not one week after what had happened.

And the entire reason for this podcast episode was researching sexual assault and rape really did help me during that first intense, horrific week. It helped me to understand what had happened, this was common and it really wasn't my fault.

Therefore, even if I can help one person or inform a few people about male sexual assault then I would have done my job with today's episode.

Some Data On Male Sexual Assault

Before we start talking about the content in any more depth, let's look at some data, the Rape, Abuse and Incest National Network found that 1 in 33 men have experienced a completed or attempted rape in their lifetime and 1 out of every 10 rape victims are male. And remember, these figures are out of the reported figures, so the real numbers could be a lot, lot higher.

Furthermore, the US's Centre for Disease Control and Prevention have shown in research that men and women are equally likely to be sexually assaulted and victims of sexual violence. Yet sexual assault against men has been severely, severely underrecognized, undertreated and underreported.

Finally, the National Crime Victimisation Survey shows that a lot of men report being sexually assaulted by women through forced penetration and coerced erections.

Overall, I hope this goes to show that male sexual assault isn't rare and it is a lot more common than any of us realise.

Male Sexual Assault And Rape

Whilst it is very rare that male sexual assault is reported in a given year, it is true that men are victims of sexual harassment, rape and molestation on a daily basis. Also, whilst it's tempting to think that male sexual assault is *only* committed by other men, in reality, it is actually an even spilt with female and male rapists.

As a result of male rape by women is a lot more common than we will ever see in the Criminal Justice System and the news as well as social media. Part of this underreport is shame and the stigma of a man "not being manly enough" because of the stupid idea that "only weak men get raped". Yet another reason is that when women rape men, they generally get the man to have an erection and even ejaculation so this confuses and paralyses the man.

Mainly because society teaches us that if a man gets an erection then they enjoy it and that isn't rape.

I actually remember one of my schoolfriends saying this back in my secondary school years and back then I sort of knew that wasn't 100% right, but I had no idea how flat out wrong it was until three weeks ago.

Also, on the underreporting, why I didn't report it was because I was embarrassed, I felt dirty, I felt so violated that I didn't want many people to know. And I was scared to be honest. I was scared of getting hurt yet again, I was scared of the stigma and I was scared about what my friends and family would think. Of course, they loved me, supported me and they have been great since they found out. Then there is the legal issue too because I had cleaned my teeth when I got home and I had showered the next morning because I was in extreme denial. And it took me two days to admit I had been sexually assaulted and by that point there was no one DNA left on me.

There were other reasons why a prosecution would have been difficult but that isn't the focus of this episode.

And I didn't want to go through the whole legal process, but if someone listening does want to do this that is very important, critical and you should. If you want to press charges then you absolutely should.

In addition, having an erection isn't consent or a sign that the person is willing or ready to have sex because an erection and ejaculation are physiological responses that we cannot control. Also, these physiological responses can occur due to pain, anxiety, fear and sexual desire or excitement.

Lastly, a final note on the underreporting, a lot of men don't label themselves as sexual assault victims and they don't call it what it is. Since typically when men learn that other men have been sexually assaulted they meet the disclosure with insensitivity and mockery.

Personally, it took me two full days, my two good friends and a specialist at the university to help me realise and call my assault what it was. I was in such extreme denial that I refused to label myself as a victim of sexual assault because I knew how those people were viewed in society. Yet I am a victim and once I "accepted" or realised that, it got a little bit easier because I could talk to people, contact my therapist and start recovering.

This podcast episode is part of that recovery because I want to help someone possibly.

What About Male On Male Sexual Assault? A Brief Look

So far in the episode, we've looked at what happens when women assault men, but let's focus on male-on-male sexual assault. When a man is sexually assaulted by another man this carries another strand of stigma as the victim fears that other people might question their sexual preferences and their sexual orientation and there is a concern about they might be seen as "less manly" because of the assault.

This is why I don't understand gender roles and the whole idea that men have to behave a certain way. Male mental health would be so much better if these gender-based rules of behaviour weren't around.

Anyway, a lot of men don't report male-on-male sexual assault because of the shame and humiliation or the perception of being weak for not fighting their attacker.

That's actually an interesting myth about sexual assault and rape that I learnt from the specialist at the university. Everyone thinks that when someone is raped or sexually assaulted, the victims screams, fights and tries to break free. But that is very, very rare. In reality, and this happened to me, you basically get so numb and cold and an emotion that I lately realised was fear, that you don't want it to happen, you say stop but when the attacker keeps grabbing you and carrying on. You get it over with so you can escape and run like hell after towards. Since my fear was my attacker was a lot larger than me unfortunately, so I was scared if I tried to fight back he would grab me, hurt me and the situation would be even worse.

That is why people rarely fight back.

It doesn't make them weak or stupid and

it doesn't make what happened to them any less traumatic.

It just makes them a survivor.

Myths That Contribute To The Challenge Of Recognizing Male Sexual Assault

Below are some myths in society that contribute to people not talking, recognising and treating male sexual assault as seriously as female sexual assault (And yes, I realise there is still a long, long way to go before female sexual assault treatment is perfect).

- Men are only raped by other men.
- Erections only happen when the man is excited.
- Erections are a sign of consent.
- Men always want sex no matter what.
- Men can never have enough sex.
- Men secretly like being sexually assaulted.
- There is something wrong with a man if he doesn't want sex.
- Ejaculation is a sign of sexual enjoyment.
- "Real men" don't get sexually assaulted.
- Men like to be in charge in the bedroom.

All these myths are extremely harmful when it comes to recognising male sexual assault, but they don't help the aftermath of the assault too. Since our culture views sexual violence against men as disenfranchised abuse and this means men don't get the same emotional, legal or medical support as women do.

Therefore, these myths about men only being sexual predators that have an extreme need for sex that is engrained in the mental health, public health, medical as well as Criminal Justice Systems, they only hurt men. Since having an erection and ejaculation makes people debate if it was actually assault or not, because people believe they had to be aroused and enjoying it for that to happen.

I can personally protest that this isn't the case. Sure, I was rock hard during my assault but I was never ever going to ejaculate and I was not enjoying it. I did not enjoy being grabbed and having a lot of different things done to me.

Interestingly, as I'm an aspiring clinical psychologist, in psychotherapy, a therapist might question the validity of the rape claim by the male victim and they might not be very convinced of the traumatic effects of the incident. So the therapist's behaviour and attitudes tend to leave male victims feeling undermined and delegitimatized.

Another factor I want to add here is that after a sexual assault, it takes even more courage to reach out to a therapist than normal. Since I have a great relationship with my therapist and she is brilliant because I work well with her and she helped me with my child abuse trauma. Something that was slightly connected to my assault. Yet I didn't want to contact her because I didn't want to admit that my assault had happened. I only contacted her and had a brilliant session with her because a good friend basically ordered me to see her.

Thankfully, it worked out well.

Conclusion

Before I wrap up the podcast episode with a little more information, I want to mention that I have really enjoyed this episode. It has been tough and at the moment, I've only written the episode out. I am a little nervous about saying this stuff because I think having to say the R-word and the A-word so many times will be hard. But I'm still proud of myself for doing this really hard episode, because I'm revealing to the general public what happened to me and some people won't like what I'm saying because of the myths. Other people will thankfully support me and it's those people that I will listen to and treasure.

But ultimately, I'm doing this episode to help people. There might be another listener who has experienced an assault, rape or they might know someone who has been. I hope this episode shows these people that it's okay, things do get better and it wasn't their fault. This is a common experience and it flat out doesn't make you a failure.

Society and the myth spreaders, they are the failures.

And for people who have never been a victim, I seriously hope that never changes, but I hope you now know the truth and you'll actively challenge these myths when they pop up. Then if you work with clients and if this happens to a friend or loved one then you know more facts to help them.

Just love them, support them and listen to them. Those are my biggest takes from my experience.

Anyway, on the whole, we need to realise that when our systems don't make victims feel like they're taken seriously and they minimise the assault and don't tend to take action. Then this continues the harm and suffering that male victims experience from the trauma of sexual violence.

As a result, as a society, we need to stop this minimisation and break this stigma of male sexual assault because it isn't helpful and it certainly isn't right. A lot of this can be done by deconstructing traditional gender stereotypes because the main problem is that currently men aren't allowed to demonstrate their feelings besides anger, and this isn't good. Especially when people see pain and trauma responses as a degradation of manhood and this isn't helpful to us achieving true feminism.

In other words, true gender equality where men and women are true equals.

Additionally, we need to continue to work on deconstructing traditional ideas about what it means to be a victim. Since it's important to note that "force" isn't always about physical strength and being overpowered. Rapists and predators typically groom, coerce and emotionally manipulate or threaten their targets into nonconsensual sex.

Most importantly, this podcast episode and the entire point of advocating for male sexual assault victims isn't about delegitimising or undermining violence against women. Instead I am highlighting that men can be victims too and the gender stereotype that women are helpless victims is another unhelpful and undeserved gender stereotype. In turn, this only reinforces silly ideas what about it means to be a man or woman and even more outrageous ideas that male victims are "failed" men.

No victim of sexual violence is a failure. They are a victim that needs to be supported, helped and listened to.

Overall, when it comes to male sexual violence (or women for that matter) using gender-sensitive approaches in our work is critical. We need to understand that societal norms and expectations will always impact men and women disproportionately, and this should never come at the cost of undermining boys and men that have been sexually abused. Instead we need to use inclusive approaches to our work that allow us to advocate and support victims regardless of their gender, so we can enable a culture shift to happen.

Ultimately allowing us to have more conversations about healing, prevention and providing good care for victims whatever their gender is.

TRIGGERS CAN COME FROM ANYWHERE

Within clinical psychology, we are all well-aware that clients with different mental health conditions can be triggered in a few different ways. For example, if we take the most obvious example of anxiety, then we know that clients can be triggered in limited ways.

For instance, clients with social anxiety will likely be triggered in social situations whereas clients with a spider phobia will likely only be triggered in a situation involving a spider. Also, clients with generalised anxiety disorder can get anxious about everything and anything.

This content we all learn through our clinical psychology lectures, textbooks and we can hear about it from service users. Yet this comes back to the previous point I made in another reflection, I did not truly understand this idea of triggers and how extremely distressing and random they can be until my assault.

I'll briefly and lightly tell you some things that happened to me this week and then I'll reflect on them in terms of clinical psychology. Although, this is more of a lived experience post compared to a "hardcore" clinical psychology reflection.

What Happened?

It was my birthday over the bank holiday weekend and my best friend stayed with me at my parents' house, and because of my Great-Aunt was staying, They couldn't sleep in the room they normally did whenever they stay over.

They had to sleep on a camp bed in my room, and I had been concerned about that for a different reason for weeks after my assault. I was concerned how I would react to have someone I really like sleeping in the same room as me.

I just never expected it to trigger me as much as it did.

Since my friend was wearing jeans with a belt and when we turned the lights off my friend started to get undressed for bed. Like any normal person would and I was trying to get to sleep because I had undressed and got into bed when they were cleaning their teeth.

Yet the sound of them undoing their belt and taking their clothes off was beyond awful. I wrapped myself up so tightly in my bedsheets just so nothing could happen.

And in hindsight I should have gone downstairs and slept on the sofa. Yet I stayed in my room with my friend and it was a rough night. My friend slept fine but whenever they moved in the night, whenever they made a sound and whenever they did anything. I would get so anxious, so scared and so hypervigilant that I couldn't sleep.

On the second night, I slept downstairs

but I still couldn't really sleep because our sofa is a lot less comfortable than it was 2 years ago at Christmas. And the camp bed was on a dodgy floorboard so again whenever my friend moved in the night I would hear it.

Thankfully, the third night, I got a better night's sleep because I was sleeping again in my room but closer to my friend. And I trained my brain to tell me that if there's a noise in the night, my friend would never ever let anything bad happen to me. They would protect me.

That worked for the most part and the only bad part was the floor next to the camp bed was, well, a floor so I wasn't perfectly comfortable.

Anyway, so you can see how just something as normal as two friends sleeping in the same room can be triggering. As well as simple sounds or movements can be triggering to assault survivors.

Personally, I found this a logical thing to be triggered by because in my sexual assault, there were no clothes on, the assaulter was wearing jeans and he had to take them off and the rest. So I can understand why this was triggering.

Yet I was surprised how this trigger had spread to other domains in my life. Since my assault did not happen with a friend, it did not happen in a bedroom and it did not happen with someone that I trust with my life. Much less someone I'm romantically into.

However, I think this trigger is a good example of how traumatic events and what reminds victims of them can spread into other areas of their lives to the point where they are extremely distressed.

It was horrible not sleeping for those three nights then it took me another two nights to start sleeping normally again.

The Tube Incident

On my actual birthday when my friend stayed with me, we both went up to London to do this Virtual Reality escape room that was brilliant fun and I seriously recommend it. The day was lovely, I really enjoyed the VR thing and I had a great time with my friend.

Yet I was already tired from not sleeping for two nights and then we were on the Tube in London to get some dinner. And there was a sign, a very noble and innocent sign on the Tube opposite me.

Pressing Up Against Someone On Purpose is Sexual Harassment. Then it was something like *Don't Do It* or *Stop!*

And my body and mind just got scared and triggered to my utter annoyance. I tried to make myself as small as possible, I could only look at the floor and my friend had to call my name to make me look at them. They told me things were okay, we didn't have long left and they were asking if I wanted to get off the Tube for a breather.

They are a brilliant friend.

But I really didn't want to be on that Tube, because in my mind, pressing up against someone is the same as grinding against something. Which is something my assaulter did to me constantly so I was tired, stressed and seeing that sign really didn't help.

I hated it and when me and my friend were back in my room, I asked them point blank *what was it like seeing me like that*? They could only say it was concerning and they worry about me enough anyway so to have their worries confirmed probably really wasn't nice for them.

Overall, I'm really annoyed that I was triggered by such a stupid sign. I hated how I was triggered that easily and I think there is an embarrassment aspect because I was crying my eyes out on the Tube and all this happened in front of other people who didn't know me, didn't know what had happened and they were judging me. Especially this elderly man with grey hair and big bushy eyebrows. He was seriously judging me.

So I hated that I could be triggered that easily since there is a disempowering element too.

Part of me no longer knows if I can go up to London by myself, because what if I get triggered and there's no one around to help me? What if all the assault memories flood me and I'm trapped? What if someone hurts me again on the Tube?

Of course the last one isn't a logical or realistic thought, but it happens. As well as I know giving myself time to heal needs to be my main focus but it is still annoying.

<u>Reading Survivor Stories</u>

Finally, on the Wednesday, I was still tired and I was at university away for a revision lecture and I had a social group thing that evening. I was still a bit distressed because after I dropped my friend off back home, they experienced something really bad because of their housemates. And I know it's bad because they refuse to tell me over text and we can have massive text conversations lasting hours at times.

Anyway, the distress from my birthday weekend was still lingering so I thought in my eternal wisdom to look up male sexual assault survivor stories. So I wouldn't feel so alone, so I would know other people were coping and surviving and they were thriving.

Note to self, do not read stuff like that less than a month after the assault.

I found a story exactly like mine down to every detail accept the ages were slightly different. And that was distressing as hell to realise that had happened to someone else and it was even worse that 5 years later they couldn't really date, they couldn't have sex and they couldn't live a normal life.

My mind didn't want to accept that, because when I was really distressed I was in the mind of "I want everything to go back to how it was before the assault". Of course that can never happen.

Reading that story was so triggering and distressing that I was crying and I had to do something very stupid to stop the pain.

Then I tried to read another story (clearly not learning my lesson) about a guy who had a completely different assault to me. The last line of the opening paragraph was "now I've lost everything I love" and that really sent me over the edge because I don't want to lose everything.

I know I won't but reading that survivor story wasn't helpful to me personally at this moment in time. Because this has always been my fatal fault, I try to do healing things before I am ready for them because I want to be further along than I am.

I never give myself time to heal and that's a massive mistake on my part.

Overall, when it comes to this triggering experience, I think we can all understand why this was triggering. It was reliving in words what had happened at a point where I was already distressed, tired and I hadn't slept in days.

Although, the interesting thing about this is that it shows that feeling that you aren't alone and that there are others like you, that come with time. Since some survivors and clients aren't ready for that straight away (I don't think anyone is straight away) and I think sometimes in clinical psychology when the conversation does turn to a sense of community, the nuance about whether this is right for a client or if they're ready for this, is missing at times.

I know I miss it in my personal life and my clinical psychology interests, but every client is different. That is what I've learnt from this week even more than normal, so some clients will enjoy and benefit from hearing stories and feeling apart of a larger community of victims. But some clients aren't ready at the moment and maybe they never will be.

That's okay because there are still so many ways to help them improve their lives, take back control and decrease their distress.

WHAT IS INTENT TO SURVIVE?

"You need to have the Intent To Survive this,"

Those were the words of my therapist towards the end of our session shortly after my sexual assault. They were powerful words to hear both as a clinical psychology student and a sexual assault survivor. I think a lot of their power came from me not understanding what it meant and me still reeling from what happened, but I also think they're powerful words because they are so true.

To be able to survive any traumatic event, you need to make sure you want to survive it.

As a result, I want to take the opportunity of this reflection to explain what Intent To Survive means to me personally as a survivor, but first I want to talk about this as an aspiring clinical psychologist.

What Is Intent To Survive In Clinical Psychology Terms?

As we know from our clinical psychology experiences, lectures and various conversations with professionals, we all know that we can give a client a lot of psychological help and support yet until a client is willing to change and use the tools and techniques we give them. Then our help only has a limited value.

For example, we can teach our clients ways to change their biased cognitive processes in depression and other mood disorders. Yet unless a client puts what they learn in therapy into practice in the real-world then the client cannot improve their lives.

To some extent, I think "Intent To Survive" is the trauma term of capacity to change, because a trauma causes a lot of psychological and physiological changes within a client. For instance, my sexual assault caused me to have a lot of panic attacks, rapid heartbeats, shaking and more.

Those were the physiological changes.

When it comes to psychological changes, I have a fair amount of social anxiety, my mood changes from normal and positive to depressed so I can't move some days, and as bad as this sounds I do have a minor fear of overweight people. Since my attacker was severely overweight so I might overweight people triggering.

Therefore, the term *intent to survive* means that a client has to do double duty when recovering from trauma. Since not only have they got to want to change and improve their life so they don't "suffer" from the physical and psychological manifestations of their trauma, but they have to want to survive it and move past it.

I know that won't make sense for people, because surely it is perfectly obvious that our clients will want to survive their trauma.

No.

Trauma really doesn't work like that in my personal experience and conversations I've had with some survivors.

Due to in trauma, death really can seem so much easier, and surviving trauma seems so pointless. It really does.

One example I had in May 2024 about 3.5 weeks after my assault was I had had a few panic attacks at a social group I go to normally and my friends and some of the other people at the social group went to a local pub in Canterbury. They asked if I wanted to go but I just broke down a little and ran out of there.

I texted my best friend and another friend about five minutes later saying how I just wanted to kill myself, I didn't want to do this anymore and death just seemed so much easier. I wasn't really suicidal that night but the thoughts were starting to come up.

This is rather normal in trauma survivors because surviving something traumatic just seems impossible and such a far away future that it doesn't seem real at all.

Therefore, as aspiring or qualified clinical psychologists or other mental health professionals, you might benefit from thinking about trauma in terms of *intent to survive.* Since helping a client focus specifically on surviving instead of healing straight away might be really, really useful.

Of course, the process will and should always be on the healing as well as recovery process. Yet healing takes a long, long time and it is that time in-between that is stupidly difficult.

Also, even though me and my therapist aren't really focus on the concept of *intent to survive* too much in my session. I still found those three words useful over the past few weeks because whenever I was struggling or in a "dark place", I could say to myself "I need to have *intent to survive* this,".

It was useful.

Overall, the concept of *intent to survive* within clinical work might have two places. Firstly, it is an effective way to reframe initial trauma sessions even more so when a client has just recently suffered the trauma. This is where (to my knowledge) survival is the main priority as healing seems so far away and impossible and trauma survivors aren't really in a position to heal at this point in time.

Secondly, *intent to survive* might be a useful phase to say to clients so they can remember they need to have an *intent to survive* their trauma whenever they're struggling or in a really dark place.

What Does *Intent To Survive* Mean To Me?

This is something I have seriously struggled with over the past few weeks because as an aspiring clinical psychologist, I know what this means. I think it is a great term and way to frame our own thinking about trauma like I mentioned above.

However, as a two-time trauma survivor, I have struggled to work out what this means to me as a human being. When my therapist first mentioned this, I didn't really register it because of course I wanted to survive this, I wanted to move past this and I thought I was going to be fine.

Because come on, it was only sexual assault.

Then May happened with my panic attacks, meltdowns and everything else that went negatively with my mental health. So it was nasty and I didn't know if I had the *intent to survive* because I wasn't sure what it meant.

Nonetheless, it's been 7 weeks exactly since The Event and I have a *better* idea about what it means to me. I've had my counselling assessment, I'm on the waiting list and I've learnt how great my friends are, so I have built a social support network around myself.

I think in the beginning *intent to survive* literally meant I wanted to see my best friend again because they were in Switzerland. I know this sounds odd because I wanted to see my best friend and I wanted to spend my birthday with them. I wanted my family to meet them, I wanted to go up to London to do the virtual reality escape room and I wanted to catch up with them.

They are my best friend for a reason.

Also, to me *intent to survive* initially meant just processing and dealing with it, because I was having a lot of physical reactions and problems. For example, the shaking, the fear of going to sleep and the problems of having a toilet.

After this happened the definition of *intent to survive* changed as I started to experience more and more psychological symptoms and trauma reactions. Like the depression, the meltdowns in public because of triggers, the intense social anxiety and so on.

When this happened *intent to survive* meant rather sadly just putting one foot in front of the other, taking each day as it came and trying to live as normal as a life as I possibly could.

This was really hard because there was another minor change in the definition as I couldn't see a future. The future and the idea of healing seemed so extreme and so impossible that I did not believe I could have a future.

This wasn't helped by my exams, my best friend experiencing awful harassment and accusations by their psychotic exboyfriend, and then a whole bunch of other things were going on in my own life.

Therefore, *intent to survive* took on a very meaningless or opaque definition. Since I sort of wanted to live and survive my assault but I also couldn't see a future. I couldn't see how I could ever have a relationship, I couldn't see how I could ever have sex, love someone or how I could ever not feel like a weak, pathetic, violated victim.

Thankfully, I did meet with the specialist at the university again and it was nice to have that referral.

This is where the definition of *intent to survive* changed again to what it currently means, and it's actually rather lovely to think about it for a change.

I know me and my best friend we are still operating on the assumption that I am a moderate suicide risk until we move into together at the end of June 2024 (exactly four weeks away). Personally, I think if I can make it after Pride weekend (that triggers a lot of past child abuse and trauma for me) then I should be okay.

Also, there will be a lot of people at Pride and a lot of couples and my concern is my mind will twist seeing couples and lots of happy people enjoying their day as "you can never have this because of your child abuse and your sexual assault so what's the point of living,"

Thankfully, me and my best friend have a plan in place anyway for Pride weekend and we're going with a lot of other friends too.

Anyway, going back to *intent to survive,* because I've had my counselling assessment and I'm on the waiting list with East Kent Rape Crisis Centre, I have a sense of hope. I am not 100%, I am still not completely sure that I can date, I can have sex and I can have relationships in the future.

But I will get the support I need, even if it takes two or three months.

There is hope.

So for me that is what *intent to survive* means at the moment. It means I have the hope to live and survive my sexual assault long enough to see what happens to me in the future.

Additionally, it means I have the curiosity as well as capacity to change because I want to survive this, so I can explore relationships, dating and what consensual sex actually looks like. That would be lovely. Also, I am curious about the therapy process as an aspiring clinical psychologist because I know sexual violence work is very specialised so I want to see how this differs from "normal" clinical work.

And it is perfectly okay if that is a reason that increases my *intent to survive*. As long as I can intend to survive my trauma then that is okay.

Lastly, *intent to survive* means to me that I want a future. I have no idea what this future will look like, I don't know if it's filled with relationships, love and respect. I don't know if it's filled with trauma, pain and suffering. I don't even know if it's filled with job possibilities and me having a successful career in clinical psychology.

Yet I want to try and I want to explore my future what it might be.

That is what *intent to survive* means to me because if I don't survive this trauma then I will never ever know what my future will be and hell, right now this is a half-joke to myself but I hope in a few months this will be something I truly believe in.

If I don't survive this then I might deny a hot, sexy guy or masculine person a chance to meet me, and come on now, that really would be cruel.

HOW CAN SEXUAL VIOLENCE IMPACT YOUR SEXUALITY AND ATTRACTION AND A POSSIBLE WAY FORWARD

First of all, when I included sexuality in the title of this chapter, I flat out do not mean that going through sexual violence will make a straight person gay and vice versa. Everyone has a sexuality whether you're straight, gay, bisexual-plus, etc. You have a sexuality no matter what so in this context I am talking about how sexual violence impacts your relationship with your sexuality.

Secondly, if you ever wonder what chapter or idea made me want to do this book, it is this chapter. Since originally, I was never really going to talk about this with anyone until my specialist counselling started but then I brought it up with my best friend and we spoke about it.

Now I want to talk about it in an effort to normalise what happens to sexual assault survivors, because I've read a lot about this topic and every sexual assault survivor goes through this in one form or another.

Therefore, in this chapter, I'm going to talk about the information more generally then I'll talk about my relationship with my sexuality and my attraction since my sexual assault. Then I'll finish off discussing something my best friend said about as a potential way forward, because right now, that is helping me.

It might help you, and just for the sake of context, I am writing this chapter as a sexual assault survivor at the 9-and-a-half-week mark since The Event happened.

General Information

I would include a lot of different references and links to different websites and articles, but if you type in something along the lines of "dating after rape" you'll find out a lot of this information. Since I made the massive mistake of reading up all about this one night when I was on holiday in Wales and my parents were asleep.

My mind wandered and I looked up assault stuff instead of happy stuff. I have to admit this is probably the topic I've handled best but it's taken me this long to be relatively okay with it.

Anyway, generally speaking, after experiencing sexual violence, a survivor's sexual behaviour and attraction can either go to the extremes. For example, all they want is sex, porn and masturbation. They're basically obsessed with it. Or a survivor can go to the extreme of swearing off all sexual contact, all members of their attacker's gender and they don't want to be attracted to anyone ever again.

Those are the two extremes and whilst some survivors do fall on the extreme ends of the spectrum, most people fall in between these extremes.

That's a good thing.

Another issue about sexuality, attraction and sexual violence (and this is something that upset my best friend because they weren't impressed by it) is even when you are ready to start dating, you face the massive challenge of finding someone who can support you when you need it and you have to tell them about your sexual assault at some point in the relationship.

There is no right or wrong way to do this.

Also, you are NOT damaged goods whatsoever, because you are a wonderfully bright, caring person who deserves love, romance and everything you could ever want in a relationship.

And if someone can't see how brilliant you are, then they don't deserve you.

Furthermore, from what I've read, there are different ways of telling people about sexual assault, but it's important to remember you don't have to tell them everything. You could simply tell them you are a sexual assault survivor and leave it at that, and tell them more over time as your level of emotional intimacy increases.

Equally, you could tell them before the first date, during the first date or you could not tell them at all until you're ready or before something physical happens.

The whole idea about telling someone is that you want them to be understanding if you freeze during a physical act, you get nervous or you have a meltdown.

Also, you want your partner to be understanding that you might (more like) will have certain needs that they HAVE to meet, because you are a brilliant person and you need to be respected.

Personally, thinking about it now, some of

my needs at this week-9 point, would be I would want sex in a bright room that isn't the living room and I couldn't do kissing, I couldn't have my frontal private area dealt with and I don't want my partner kissing my body like it's the most amazing thing on earth.

Even now it's making me upset and anxious and awful just thinking about it.

It is okay to feel like that and your partner needs to respect these boundaries and your needs.

In addition, I am really scared and nervous about telling a future partner about my sexual assault, because they will have to know on my timetable. They might be really into me and try kissing me and I might freak out and feel sick. So that would be a good time to tell my partner why I reacted like that.

But how the hell do you tell someone that that happened to you?

That is hard and it is why you have to be kind to yourself and you need to respect yourself and your boundaries no matter what the partner wants.

Also, the thing that upset my best friend was when I told them, there are three typical reactions that a partner has when you reveal your history of sexual assault to them:

- They're shocked and speechless and they ask if you're okay.
- They're stupid and fall into the myths and they ask moron questions that subtly blame you.
- They're pathetic and leave you.

My best friend used the c-word to describe people who fall into the latter two reactions and I agree. Therefore, it is hard to deal with this aspect of sexuality and attraction after experiencing sexual violence, but you will have to deal with it.

A part of the healing process is knowing you are valuable, you are amazing and you deserve to find a partner that loves you.

You deserve to be loved.

That's the general information.

My Experience With My Sexuality and Attraction After my Assault

Please know I am going to share extremely non-graphic but personal details about my own journey in this regard. I am feeling very vulnerable and honest but I am doing this just in case you find this useful and relatable.

I know a lot of people will find this relatable but still, I am nervous to share my story.

Immediate Aftermath And The First Week

For the first few days after my assault, I flat out couldn't look at male private areas at all and I couldn't look at dicks. I seriously couldn't because looking at a dick was way too triggering for me and I hated my own dick to be fair.

As I've mentioned before for those first few days, I wanted to cut my own dick off.

Personally, this was really annoying and concerning, because I am gay. I normally find dicks and men and male private areas very attractive and I am a massive fan of them. Yet given how I couldn't get hard, looking at male private areas made me feel sick and experience a lot of physical sensations.

This was a major problem for me and it was distressing.

It made me feel hopeless for the future because it made me think I could never date, never love and never ever be in a relationship. A fear that was only compounded by my child abuse and homophobic family.

As you can guess, this took a massive, dangerous toll on my mental health.

That's the sexuality angle.

In terms of attraction, I seriously couldn't be attracted to anyone for a few weeks after my assault. I go to a trans group (because I'm non-binary) and I have friends there and there are some trans-girls I find attractive (okay, okay I'm technically androsexual- attracted to masculinity and there are a few transwomen that are a little masculine at my group) and I'm normally attracted to them, but I wasn't attracted to them.

I'm still not particularly, so at this point in my journey, attraction was basically dead.

I was still attracted to what I call my "Core Four" and this is such an autistic thing (at least I hope so otherwise, I'm really weird) and these are the four people I love, trust and want relationships with. In other words, I know without a shadow of a doubt that these four people in my life (two of them aren't in my life anymore) would never ever hurt me.

I was glad about this attraction because I found reassurance in the fact that I could still feel attraction to some extent.

<u>Between The Second Week Of My Assault And Now</u>

Then as I've mentioned before, for the next few weeks, my attraction to my best friend was causing me a lot of distress, panic attacks and utter fear because they were going to be staying with me over my birthday weekend. This was going to be hard for me and it was as I mentioned before.

Therefore, in this sense, being attracted to someone was extremely distressing and it was triggering all my assault stuff really badly. Thankfully, this has abated completely when it comes to my best friend but it has morphed into something else now.

Additionally, I went through my massive disempowerment part of my journey where I felt so disempowered to do anything in my life. I felt like I couldn't do anything, I couldn't make any decisions and my life was in complete and utter freefall. This was awful as I've spoken about in previous chapters and this did connect to sexuality and attraction.

Even now one of the massive areas I feel disempowered in is anything to do with dating, being attracted to someone and wanting some kind of relationship in the future. I seriously do not feel like I can do this.

Therefore, me and my best friend (because my best friend knows I'm attracted to them and want to be with them) we're always said I should try to be proactive and date. Granted that was a tiny reason why I got raped in the first place, but that's life.

Anyway, my best friend has a friend that I think is really attractive and I find them rather hot. So I've been trying to get an introduction with this person for ages and my best friend has been trying (but failing a lot).

So a few weeks after my assault, my best friend was hanging out with this person and my best friend tried to put a plan in motion by getting this person to come to our trans group (we're all non-binary). This person said no.

Now I was angry and annoyed even though I didn't really have a right to be.

I was really angry during this period of time because whilst this person did not know about my assault, they didn't even know my best friend was inviting them so we could meet. I was really angry because I was trying to make a choice to make me feel empowered after what my bastard attacker did to me, and this person was denying me that choice.

I always knew I had no right to be annoyed but I was just angry and upset that I was trying here to be empowered and make my own decisions, something I can barely do at times, and this person said no.

That's another way experiencing sexual violence can impact attraction.

Current Relationship With Sexuality And Attraction

As a result, if we fast forward to this current point in time, my relationship with my sexuality and attraction is very difficult in some areas and easier in other areas.

Personally, I'm okay again about being gay (that was mixed in with my child abuse) and I have no problem being attracted to, loving and wanting to be with men. That is no longer a problem thankfully and I do want a boyfriend and partner.

This want and acceptance of my sexuality again was encouraged by me not committing suicide a few weeks ago. That is a good thing and I know I have a future, I am just not 100% sure what that future is yet, but I want to find out.

In terms of attraction, the reason why I wanted to talk about this topic in the first place was because I realised recently my attraction has gone to the other end of the extreme. I am trying to find a lot of people attracted to try and feel more empowered.

For example, I am not trying to be offensive here, it is just personally I do not find feminine women (or 99% of women) attractive whatsoever. This is simply down to my personal taste and preference. I am flat out NOT hating on women.

Last Wednesday, I had to quickly pop up into my best friend's DnD session to give them a birthday card and present for a friend of ours before I left Canterbury for the evening. I was going on holiday to Wales the next day so I couldn't see our friend.

Yet I went in there, saw the DnD game because my friend was talking to me in the corner and there was a woman and she smiled at me. She was only one that acknowledged me entering the room (turns out everyone was way too into DnD to even notice me) and I only saw her for a second or two but I thought she was really attractive and pretty.

Granted, looking back I realise Wednesday I had been crying, had a lot of social anxiety and I was a delicate wreck (more on that next chapter).

I was talking about her the next day with my best friend, I learnt her name and later on I checked her out on Facebook to see what she looked like. And I wasn't attracted to her, but she was lovely so I do wish her the best of luck in that department.

It still made me realise that I was being attracted to people a lot more than I actually should have been, and it made me realise something was a little wrong with my attraction in general.

So I thought about it more and more over my holiday and realised, my attraction was moving towards the extreme because I feel like I want to be attracted to someone, anyone so I can pretend to have a choice about my attraction, relationships and everything.

This isn't healthy.

And it is all fake.

As I said to my best friend when we went out for dinner and had this conversation, I'm not really attracted to anyone at the moment in any real sense. And even if this was "real" attraction, I am seriously not in a mental position where I could even consider dating and getting into a relationship.

Ultimately, this is me unhealthily wanting to feel in control because I still feel so disempowered in this area of my life. And I have no idea whatsoever about how to date as a sexual assault survivor, and that is annoying but I need to stop trying to be attracted to someone just so I can feel empowered for a second or two.

That seriously isn't healthy.

And as my best friend said, it can lead to some pretty risky situations if it goes to the extreme and if I don't have self-control. This connects to the sex obsession I mentioned earlier.

A Potential Solution

As an aspiring clinical psychologist, you know I'm going to say the only real solution for this sexuality and attraction issue caused by sexual violence is professional help. There is no way around that and you will need professional help no matter what, so do it as soon as possible.

In the meantime, I am going to tell you what me and my best friend are currently doing and this helped me in the sense that, it gives me a little bit of practical hope to focus on. So I don't get hopeless about relationships, my mental health doesn't die and I won't get suicidal again.

My best friend is demisexual and pansexual. In other words, they can only be attracted to you if they're friends with you first of all (not that it helped me get with them anyway. Ha) and they're attracted to all genders, and they're on the asexual spectrum too.

I'm mentioning these facts because it helps put this into perspective and why I understand this solution but I am not entirely sold on it, because I am not demisexual at all.

Again, I am still writing about this in case it helps others.

Therefore, me and my best friend are going to go to the LGBT+ coffee morning and other events during Freshers Week next academic year, we're going to go to new societies (adult social clubs formed around a particular interest) at our university and we're going to keep meeting people.

Then the plan is overtime, hopefully I will become friends with someone I am attracted to, and because friends hug, I can get used to hugging someone new as a friend first, and then if they're attracted to me I can enter a relationship that way.

This would solve a few issues for me in terms of sexual violence stuff, because I cannot abide the thought of being touched or hugged by anyone else at the moment. I only let my best friend touch me regularly when we hug goodbye, and I let my Mum hug me from time to time after she shouted at me a week-and-a-half after my assault for not letting her hug me.

Supportive and understanding as always. Not.

Also, it would allow me to form a relationship with someone I trust and I think it would help a lot of stuff generally.

Of course, the only problem with this is going from friend to relationship, I think is somewhat uncommon and unlike my best friend, I am not demisexual. Meaning I would like to go out, maybe use dating apps and whatever to meet people in the future.

However, for now, I think this is a solution that will help me focus on the future and realise that a future is possible.

Mini-Conclusion

Overall, I wrote this chapter to show you that after experiencing sexual violence, it is perfectly normal for your relationship with your sexuality and attraction to change and keep changing for a while. As you heal, it will change and it will almost certainly go back to whatever it was before your trauma as you near the end of your healing journey.

Just be kind to yourself, be careful and if you realise you are heading towards or you are at one of the extreme ends of the spectrum. You need to talk about it, get professional help and keep yourself safe.

And most importantly, you deserve to be loved, in a relationship and have everything you ever wanted.

It will take time, but it is very, very possible.

ACCEPTING THE WEIRDNESS OF TRIGGERS

In previous chapters, I've spoken about various triggers I've had and how distressing, upsetting and awful they are. One such example was a few chapters ago when I discussed what happened on my birthday on the London Tube, that was a surprising trigger that distressed me a lot.

Another surprising trigger soon after my assault was how whenever I thought of my best friend, it would trigger all the rape stuff and how horrific it was.

Therefore, in this next chapter, I want to focus on triggers itself in terms of how surprising, annoying and disempowering they can be at this point in my healing journey. Again, please, it has "only" been 9.5 weeks since my sexual assault so everything said in this chapter is a reflection of this point in my healing process.

In addition, as my best friend said the other night, from what they know from other sexual violence survivors, the triggers do get less common and distressing over time. Yet for now, triggers are a major part of the aftermath of sexual assault.

This brings me to what happened last week.

What Happened In Week 8?

In week 8 after my sexual assault, I only had three days to do things before I was going on holiday to Wales for 4 days, and I couldn't do anything the weekend before because I was at Canterbury Pride then I stayed at my best friend's house.

I only had three days to do a lot of business and writing things. To say I was busy was an understatement but I was really happy because I was busy and I was so focused on getting things done that I didn't have time to think about The Event or something assault related.

Anyway, so the night before I went to Wales I needed to go down to Canterbury anyway to pick up a psychology book from the library that my supervisor wanted me to read. Afterwards, I was going to go to the trans group I always go to because it was at the university.

This is where the triggers started.

I was so happy that it was Wednesday evening and I hadn't been triggered whatsoever this week, and I was so excited about maybe this was the week where I would be okay. A stupid idea if there ever was one.

This is my first tip for you.

Tip

You need to accept or find a way to accept that maybe the first three months or longer, there will probably be distressing stuff that pops up every single week without fail. This is scary, distressing and it might seem hopeless, but I promise you I am living proof that you can survive this and life is seriously worth living.

It gets better over time.

Back To Week 8

I was driving down to Canterbury and in case my best friend was done with their DnD game at 6 pm (they weren't really sure when they were going to be free and I needed to see them anyway to give them our friend's birthday card and present), I didn't have time to connect my phone to my speaker so I could listen to podcasts. So I was stuck listening to the radio.

I listen to Heart by the way.

There was good music, good adverts and good other stuff. Then Heart does the 6 pm news and it's always local rubbish that I don't really care about until the news told a local story about how a rapist had been convicted after abusing a young boy for years, and the police were praising that young boy for having the courage to report it. I won't say anymore because it made me feel awful so it might trigger other people too.

Thankfully I was just finishing up parking my car when I had to turn off the radio so I had a panic attack, I cried and I just shattered in my car. It brought up all my feelings about feeling worthless, a failure to other survivors and my mind went mad at the idea that I was a bad person for not reporting my assault and prosecuting him.

I managed to calm myself down enough so I could get out of my car, then I started walking out the university car park and towards the library.

Now the problem is that there were a good amount of people so I was really anxious anyway. I wanted to cry again so badly and my mind turned against me again saying that because I wasn't like that young boy, I was setting up other people to be attacked and assaulted because I was a failure.

I went to the toilets in my main university building and I just cried my eyes out, and I used Bing Co-pilot (just think ChatGPT) to answer some questions about reporting rape.

I Need To Stress

Now, I need to stress here that it is totally up to you if you report your sexual assault or rape to the police. It does not matter what other people do, it does not matter what other people say to you and it certainly does not matter what other survivors have done.

It is your choice.

And if someone tells you, you HAVE to do something then tell them to fuck off.

It is your choice. No one else's.

Furthermore, all my thinking was wrong after I heard that radio report. It is perfectly okay that I did not report my assault and my attacker because to legally prove it was sexual assault would have been extremely difficult, I did not want the public shame and embarrassment of a trial and I did not want to be ripped apart on the stand by a solicitor.

Also, I have no proof that what happened that night actually happened at all, much less that it was non-consensual and there was no informed consent. Not that there was consent at all in the first place.

If you want to report it then please go ahead, but if you did not report then that is fine too. You did nothing wrong and if you want, you can always report it in the future.

Back To Week 8

After I finished crying and I spent easily 25 minutes in the toilet, I went to the library. That was a nightmare in itself because I could not find this book for love or money so that took another 30 minutes to find a single bloody book.

Anyway, I was about to call it quits when I found it because I realise I hate narrow and enclosed spaces these days. I hate narrow library rows of books because they make me anxious and my mind goes "hey you know if anyone wanted too, they could grab you, pin you up against the bookshelves and do whatever they want to you,"

This fear was also reinforced on my trip to Wales when I was walking under a short tunnel with a narrow walkway with a canal next to it. That was an enclosed space and my traumatised mind loved it.

Not.

That was difficult then I realised how anxious, scared and panicked I was about going to my trans social group. This is a great group of people, I have a lot of friends there and I like talking to people there.

However, as I was talking to where the social group was, I was getting more and more socially anxious so back to the toilets I went. I spent another 20 minutes in there and I was scared, panicked and all my triggers were popping up again. Because there are a lot of people there, there are some fat people there and in my mind, any one of them could hurt me.

That wasn't nice for me.

If we fast-forward to three days later, me and my parents had had a lovely day in Wales doing some hiking, exploring and we went to the local town. We came back early, my parents had a crime drama on and they feel asleep.

I kept on watching the crime drama and it turned out that the killer was getting revenge on her rapists. I got distressed, I couldn't change over the channel so I shouted and got even more distressed. My parents woke up, helped me change over the channel and then they shouted at me, because I was overreacting, I woke them up and I was being an idiot.

Yeah, my parents are amazing supporters of me after my sexual assault. (They are great in a lot of other areas though)

That was annoying that I got triggered by something as simple as a crime drama, and I didn't have the social support from my parents.

I know there were other triggers on my trip to Wales, I think there were daily triggers because all the distress, fear and depression mixed into one. I know I was distressed on the Sunday because in Wales they do horse-drawn canal boat trips and the guy leading the horse was a spitting image of my attacker.

I made sure just not to look at him and I was with my parents so I forced myself not to react. I was dying inside but I dared not show it.

I didn't want to get shouted at again.

One Trigger For This Week (So Far)

Lastly, a final trigger I want to mention from this week is, and this goes back to social anxiety, is me and my best friend are working what's known as Summer Core at our university. We're both student ambassadors for the Outreach and Widening Participation department. This means we help out and support events that ultimately help to promote the idea of coming to university to students from schools that have a below-average number of pupils that go on to university.

For example, yesterday I helped out with a finance talk at a local secondary school, on Tuesday I helped out at a Future Human day that gets students to do a small research project at a university for the day and gets them to experience a lecture and what a seminar is (helps develop a sense of belonging amongst other pedological outcomes), and next Thursday, I'm helping at a World Languages Day.

Anyway, there is Outreach every working day for the next four weeks.

Therefore, on Saturday, me and my best friend are working a KS3 (just think 13 and 14 year old students) Family day so students and parents come to the university to do fun activities. Thankfully, when Outreach emails us from time to time I can see who else at the university is included in the email and I recognised one of the names.

Let's call him Rory (not his real name) and I know Rory because we used to do scouts together, he's about 5 years younger than me and our parents get on great. We haven't really spoken for years but we did talk when I was Session Lead at another Future Human event back in May.

So I was going to offer him a lift down to Canterbury, because we live in the same town in Medway, and this would mean I could get an extra 5 pence petrol allowance, so it's a win-win for everyone.

Then I thought about it. That would mean I would be alone in a car for over 40 minutes with a man that is slightly overweight and I haven't seen and spoken properly with him for ages.

Just thinking that again made my anxiety shoot up.

Equally, I know if I made this offer, I would not sleep for the next three nights, in turn this would make my mental health worse and I would be even more triggered again and again.

So even offering an old friend a lift and car pooling like so many people do every day (hell I know a few people carpooling at the moment and I'm picking up my best friend anyway on Saturday), is something that triggers me.

Especially as my mind when I'm getting triggered imagines Rory doing stuff to me. Stuff that would never ever happen in real life, Rory is straight for starters.

That's annoying. It makes me angry and it is so fucking disempowering that I cannot even do those simple, nice things for people like I used to be able to.

<u>What Was The Point Of This Chapter?</u>

On the whole, the point of this chapter was to help normalise how random, annoying and common triggers are. I found the triggers were more intense for the first few weeks after my assault but now they are a lot more common and random.

This is disempowering because I just want to live my life and do whatever I want. Yet I know and mostly accept that this cannot happen until I get professional help in the future so I hope that comes sooner rather than later.

Furthermore, I want to help normalise how common and random these triggers can be. I want you to know you are normal, there is nothing wrong with you and triggers are an unfortunate part of Post-Traumatic Stress Disorder. This is just something that will happen to us for a while until we get professional help and we can work through it.

And you can work through this.

Life can get better. Life is worth living and you are an amazing, brave survivor who will recover and heal.

REMEMBER AND FOCUS ON THE GOOD TIMES

Before I talk about the brilliant topic of this chapter (I'm really excited to be back writing after having to deal with a lot of Real Life stuff for the past week), I want to take a moment to be honest about why I want to be truthful that I have no idea where this chapter is going in the book.

I don't want everything in this book to be perfectly organised, structured and flow without a single problem.

That isn't how sexual violence recovery works in the slightest.

Therefore, I strongly believe it would be a massive disservice to myself and you wonderful readers if I pretended that this subject material wasn't chaotic at times. It is and that's okay.

Your life might be chaotic on certain days, certain hours or certain minutes. But you will be fine, you can recover and you will survive this.

And most importantly, please remember that you are never going insane when experiencing the effects of trauma.

You are simply experiencing normal effects to an extremely abnormal situation.

Why Do You Need To Remember and Focus On The Good Times?

If you're a survivor or if you know a survivor then you are probably way more aware than you want to be that there will be tough times ahead. I'm currently writing this chapter at week 11 after my assault, and it is tough.

There hasn't been a single week since my sexual assault that there hasn't been something major pop up. And hell, for the past four days, it has been major.

However, I'm doing okay at the moment because I'm focusing on the good times because they make me smile, they make me feel like a teenager again (which is a weird saying for me because my teens weren't that great) and they remind me that life is brilliant.

I'm not going to pretend that you're going to be able to focus on the good times when/ if you experience panic attacks, nightmares and flashbacks.

Even though, please make sure you ground yourself by saying out loud what you can see, hear, touch, taste and smell. As well as make sure you do any other grounding techniques you want.

Nonetheless, in those moments where you feel safe, secure and you aren't experiencing a flashback or panic attack. Or do this straight after one, please remember and focus on the good times.

Personally, I would be extremely careful about focusing on memories and good times from the distant past and I would attempt to keep them as current or close to the present as possible. This is just my opinion and what works for me.

However, the reason why you might want to stay out of the distant past is because flashbacks, panic attacks and all the other trauma responses of sexual violence take you back to the past in a bad way. And sometimes focusing on the past can be triggering and it can take away from the external sense of safety of the present.

In addition, these moments don't actually have to be massive things. Like the examples I'm going to list below. They can be tiny positive things that make you feel good, grounded and positive about your life. For example, right now, I am finally back writing after dealing with moving house, dealing with the crisis of the Psychology Society at my university and working so much Outreach work as a student ambassador at my university. As well as trying to get two podcast episodes out.

I flat out love writing, I love my business and I love being back at my keyboard doing what I love. That is an amazing feeling and I am happy.

Moreover, I haven't had a Tassimo coffee for at least five days and I haven't had a Coke of some sort for a while. These were just part of my normal routines when I lived with my parents. So I'm introducing them tonight and I like them. I do recommend the Costa Cappuccino in case you're interested.

These might be tiny positive things but you know what, they make be smile, feel good and feel positive in between all the trauma responses.

That is worth remembering.

Penultimately, for this section, two things you might want to do is write down 5 positive things that happened to you today before you go to bed. I'm pretty sure I've already mentioned it in this book, but a woman I talked to a lot does this and I've started doing it (I need to remember it better) and it works. It makes you realise there are a lot more positive things that happen to you than you remember.

These can be really small things too.

For example, if I was thinking about today my five (you can try to do more too) would be:

1. I've started writing again.
2. I helped my best friend by driving them to and from work.
3. I had a Tassimo
4. I had some Pepsi Max
5. I listened to the Handsome Podcast with the wonderful Mae Martin.

On the whole, making yourself focus and remembering the good times, helps you to realise that life does have some great, fun, positive moments. Sure, sometimes they are tiny moments, but they can remind you that you are so much more than your trauma and there are moments in life that can make you smile.

It is those moments that are amazing.

What Was The Inspiration For This Chapter?

I want to write this chapter for a very specific reason but I want to use another example first. As I mentioned earlier I'm working a lot of student ambassador events at the moment at my university because it's the Summer Core period and the university is really busy.

Last week, I worked a lot of great events. Including a forensic science event where I got to support kids doing fingerprinting, indentation taking, a forensic search of a crime scene and more. Those were really interesting events because I never normally get to do them.

In addition, I got to work as a Lead Ambassador at a Care Leavers event at Mote Park. I was essentially getting paid stupid money to sit around for 8.5 hours. I didn't do much because the event was so quiet in the end (250 people were meant to turn up, only 50 people did) but it was fun. I got to have a lot of lovely conversations with my fellow students, care leavers and university staff.

It was a fun day.

There were other highlights of Week 10, but even now as I'm writing this section, I'm smiling because they were really positive times. And after the past few days and how bad my mental health has been, it is honestly lovely to think about good times.

Please make sure you focus and remember these good times too.

<u>What's The Second Reason?</u>

This is the real reason that I wanted to write this chapter because it reminded me that there will be positive moments in amongst all the chaos of recovering from sexual violence.

I sort of, kind of met someone yesterday.

There are a few points here I want to make in a moment after I tell you what happened.

I can't mention their real name (obviously) but let's call him Henry. Me and Henry were working as student ambassadors yesterday at a Business Challenge event (basically it was a day of just babysitting 17-year-old students because the school wanted to bring them to university for a day.

I arrived there early because I had dropped my best friend off too as their event started earlier than mine. I got to the meeting place and there was a cute guy sitting there, I didn't have a trauma reaction which was nice but I didn't give it anymore thought.

Until it turned out he was another ambassador.

Henry was cute so I was glad he was working the event but I did not think at all about him anymore in between sessions. I don't know why I just didn't, I was dealing with enough stuff that it seemed impossible to talk to them.

Anyway at lunch time, we were eating with the students outside, it was sunny and I put my hat on. It was a branded hat for Kent International Jamboree which is a major global scouting event. If you don't know what "scouting" is it's similar to Boy Scouts of America.

Henry started talking to me about it, we talked all throughout lunch and it was lovely. I felt good, positive and I actually felt like a teen again. And I admit I wasn't flirty but you could tell I was gay by how I was acting and yeah, I just wasn't acting straight at all.

We could to the end of the day, we spoke some more and Henry seemed really, really interested in what Outreach events I was working so he could see me again. We found out we were both working together for 3 days next week and he seemed really pleased.

I'm not doing the experience any justice but Henry is cute, he's really nice and I do want to explore something with him.

Now I do not know if Henry is gay, bisexual or even into males whatsoever. I also don't know if he actually likes me or anything like that, and on a serious note, I have no idea how dating works as a rape survivor.

Come on, who does?

However, it is still lovely to experience being seriously into someone and just feeling like anything actually is possible for a few hours. And I honestly thought this wouldn't be "real" attraction because as I've mentioned at other points in the book, I have been attracted to people before since my assault but it wasn't real. It was simply me wanting to be empowered in an unhealthy way.

This is different though.

My main piece of evidence for this "difference" is something that has happened over the past 24 hours. Whenever I talk about Henry, I feel really positive and I *might* act like a teenager with a first crush. Since I am not embarrassed (that much. Grin) to admit that below is a real extract from an email I sent earlier to the sexual violence specialist at my university. She emails every few weeks and I say I hate these emails, but they are lovely and they are really good. I just like talking to someone other than my best friend about life.

Honestly, I only say I hate them because it means I have to repeat everything that has gone on lately and it makes everything real. I know this is part of recovery and it is important and I want to do it, but it's annoying.

Here is the extract:

"Finally, I sort out of met someone yesterday. He's called Henry, and I know this is the rape survivor and trauma talking but I doubt he's gay or even into me at all. But he's cute, really nice and he really likes talking to me. He was really pleased to know we're working the same Outreach event for three days straight next week. It was lovely feeling normal for a few hours yesterday considering the hell of moving. But as I said, I doubt he's gay or even into me, and it isn't like I can date at the moment. My mind tried to imagine me and him doing stuff together and it turned into a full-on rape scene. Not very nice at all.

Overall, I am doing okay today and honestly, sure a lot of triggers are popping up. Yet I am focusing on the positives like my Outreach work, living and spending time with my best friend, meeting Henry even if it leads to nothing, and I'm slowly getting back into my routines."

So the fact that I mentioned Henry in an email to a mental health professional stresses how positive I feel, and I promise I am not the type of person to do this normally. I don't go round mentioning my crushes or people I find attractive. I seriously don't, but this time was different.

I just felt really good.

Chapter Conclusion

Therefore, whilst I have no idea if Henry is gay or into me or if a relationship is even possible. But I actually will ask for his phone number or social media just so maybe I can explore a friendship or possible relationship.

And honestly, I know in the dark times, I will just say what I said last night to my best friend (something I am not repeating in this chapter because this is a positive chapter), and most of the time I might believe I cannot date.

Yet yesterday proved me wrong.

I am capable of real attraction and want, and that is all you actually need for the seed of a relationship to form. Anything physical or psychologically intimate can change or develop and grow safety and securely over time in response to the boundaries YOU need.

That is the truth and as a survivor, I always need to focus and remember that because life isn't all doom and gloom.

It is amazing and there are certainly tiny, positive moments in amongst the darkness.

YOU HAVE THE RIGHT TO MAKE A CHOICE

One of the biggest themes of this stage of my sexual violence recovery is disempowerment, and one of the hallmarks of being disempowered is that you cannot make decisions. I originally wanted to write this chapter at the Week 9 mark but it's now Week 11. However, as I've switched the order of these chapters, you've already seen why it is important you remember "you have the right to make a choice".

Previously, you've seen how I wasn't going to make any sort of decision about where to put my kitchen items, and even deciding where to put my things in my bedroom at the new house was a major challenge. I needed to get my best friend to talk to me whilst I put stuff away so I could distract myself and continue to make progress and those sort of micro-decisions that this activity requires.

In addition, even though, technically, I could "only" manage 40 minutes of these micro-decisions before I needed a major break. That is actually brilliant progress compared to the day before, and sure it took longer than I would have liked, but I still did it.

And on a self-compassion note, I am proud of myself for doing it. I could have just thrown in the towel but I didn't. I made sure that I continued and *I* managed to put everything away for myself.

Therefore, this is a lesson for all of us, survivors. We need to be kind to ourselves when things go wrong, we need to reward ourselves when we accomplish things and most importantly, we just need to keep going.

That is the key to the aftermath of sexual violence.

Why Am I Talking About *You Have The Right To Make A Choice*?

As you might know already, after sexual assault or another type of sexual violence, you feel guilty, you don't trust your own judgement, have low self-worth and so on as I spoke about in the past chapter. However, you might find yourself having a moment when you can make a decision and you want to make it.

You can do that.

You can absolutely tell someone your decision and stick with it.

That is your right given as a human being and you have every single permission you need to make a decision.

If you want to decide something, just do it.

I'm talking about this because at the Week 9 mark after my assault, me and my friend had spoken earlier in the week about attraction and my best friend's relationship. My best friend was saying about they could keep it discreet, they could do it in secret so I didn't have to see it because it could be triggering. I'm missing out a lot of the conversation but you get the gist.

In other words, my best friend was willing to keep their relationship very secret so I wouldn't be triggered and rape stuff popping up.

I really wasn't sure and my best friend was brilliant because they let me make the decision entirely.

Of course, that is exactly what you should do when it comes to survivors. It is critical that survivors are allowed to make their own decisions.

Therefore, a few days later, originally me and my best friend had wanted to hang out on the Friday but they were tired so we didn't. Instead because I had made a decision, I sent the following text to them that night telling them about my decision:

"I want to tell you that rape-related thing now. I don't want to sit on it for another night and we might not have time tomorrow. That's just life though. I'm almost cried twice thinking of this message.

I don't want you being discreet with your partner because I want to make a choice for myself and there's 2 more reasons. So I am disempowered because of what he did to me. I can't start new social activities and I can't go to London because of my meltdowns and anxiety. I struggle going to something like Group because of the amount of people. I can't even drive a guy I've known for a decade down to campus tomorrow because I keep imagining me getting raped in my own car over and over.

There are a thousand more examples of me being disempowered and things I can't just do because they make me feel sick, have a meltdown or make me feel like I'm getting raped again.

But you are off-limits to him.

I am not letting him affect you and me. You're too kind, lovely and a great friend to let him do anything to us. I'm glad you'll never know how hard that first week was for me with whenever I thought of you it triggered all my rape stuff. My birthday was bad enough. I was terrified (Someone we both know) was right about us not being able to be friends anymore.

You are off-limits to my rapist affecting me. You can do whatever you want, live your life normally and let us just be us. Let us just be the great close friends we are without him making us change anything.

So I don't know want you being discreet because I will NOT let him affect us, your partners might not be that triggering for me anyway. And just let me make a choice for once. In a world where I can't do and make any choices please let me make one. I choose to make this one also because after all the shit you've been through, I want you to live normally with the freedom to do and have over whoever you want.

I'll be fine. If I haven't killed myself yet, there's a 99.9% chance I won't."

That was a very intense, raw message that fits who I am at times with people I am extremely close with, but it proves a point.

You can make a decision if you want.

If there is something you want to do, if there is something that you want to go a certain way then that is okay. You are allowed to say it, communicate it with others and you have the right for other people to listen and respect it.

Another great example was I'm writing this chapter in Week 11, and last night, me and my best friend spoke about anything and everything for about 6 hours straight. Something that popped up was my guilt about them being the only person I have, and me wanting to meet new friends.

I said to them (because they're half-French and I'm learning French on Duolingo) that I want to go to French Society at our university. This would mean I could meet French people and other people with an interest in French. It is something I've spoken about before but I want to do this, I have made the decision that

I want to go to French Society.

I'm partly joking when I say this but I want to go to French Society because I might meet an attractive French guy, fall in love and marry him. So I can have an EU passport again. (Hell, French guys can be attractive).

Joking aside, it is okay for you to say what you want and other people have to respect your wishes even if they don't agree with it. If they love you, care about you and support you fully then they will respect your decision even if they don't agree with it.

You have the right to make a choice.

Sometimes you might not be able to make decisions like me when it came to moving things into my new place. Yet sometimes you will be able to make a decision like me going to French Society and me wanting my best friend not to be discreet about their relationship.

You can make any choice you want. It might seem impossible at times but you seriously can.

I believe in you.

GUILT AS A SEXUAL VIOLENCE SURVIVOR

It might be Week 11 for me at the time of writing but I wanted to put this chapter earlier in the book, because guilt is a major part of the healing process and the aftermath of sexual violence. I've experienced guilt in a massive number of ways, and I've experienced a wide range of ways how I've dealt and overcome with this difficulty.

Therefore, in this next chapter, we're going to be exploring guilt after sexual assault, how it's impacted me and how I've dealt with it. Then I'll talk more generally about some other ways how you can deal with guilt as a survivor.

In addition, I'll talk about my experiences in a moment, but research shows (references included in the back of the book) that survivors feel guilt because of three main factors. Firstly, they feel guilt because of self-blame. For example, if they hadn't done something then it wouldn't have happened so they feel guilt about that.

I used to struggle a lot with the idea that "if only I hadn't been in a hurry and wanted to be gay" then I wouldn't have made the mistake.

Even though in reality, not a single survivor reading this book has made any sort of mistake whatsoever.

None of us are to blame, It is the bastard that attacked us that is the only person we can blame.

Moreover, another reason why survivors experience guilt is because of the cognitive impacts of sexual assault. For instance, the disturbed sleep and the intrusive thoughts. These trauma responses can make us feel guilty and this feeds into the self-blame too.

Finally, survivors can feel guilt because of their interactions with medical, legal and other professionals or people. This links to retraumaisation and if other people give us negative reactions then this certainly does not decrease the guilt.

Personally, the stuff that has been said to my face by people who should have loved and respected me has only increased my guilt, my self-hate and at times my suicidal idealisation. Thankfully, that doesn't pop up now.

How Has Guilt Impacted Me?

I've already hinted at a few ways how guilt has impacted me, but there are two ways that have had a major negative impact on me. I want to share them because I doubt I am unique enough to be the only person experiencing them.

The first one is dark, and the second one is very true that I know a lot of survivors experience.

Firstly, I used to get angry my attacker didn't physically beat me or just kill me when he did what he did to me. If he had done that then I would have had physical evidence and it would have made a prosecution easier, and if he had killed me then I wouldn't have had to deal with everything for the past 11 Weeks and onwards.

I wouldn't have to be in so much pain when everything pops up and I wouldn't have to deal and struggle and cry so much.

This is extreme guilt and I call it guilt because I feel guilt at times that this didn't happen.

Life gets better though.

If someone had told me that at the beginning of this book and shortly after my assault, I really wouldn't have believed them because life seemed impossible back then. And honestly, yes, life can seem a little impossible now at times.

But there are a lot of fun, joyous and exciting moments after sexual assault that is so worth living for.

In future chapters, I talk about how much fun I'm having with my Outreach work as a student ambassador, I'm having a lot of fun doing what I love with my writing, business and podcasting. And it was so, so lovely to possibly meet someone romantically on Monday at an Outreach event.

Even if meeting this guy doesn't turn into a relationship, it was still such a lovely moment because it proved that my sexual assault hasn't killed that part of me. I can still be genuinely attracted to people and that is a lovely thing to realise.

So please if you're suicidal, get professional help, contact a helpline and most importantly, remember that life is so worth living for.

Secondly, I experienced a lot of guilt as a survivor towards my best friend, because they are the only social support system I have in place. I don't have that many close friends I can lean on for support, my family doesn't know how to handle (or have a willingness to search online) me being assaulted. And they've said more than enough damaging stuff that it isn't worth it.

So I lie and say I'm perfectly okay whenever I talk to them, even if I've had the most hellish few days of my life.

Therefore, my best friend is literally all I have as a support system until my therapy starts and that is going to take another few months before that begins. To say I've felt extremely guilty about that is an understatement.

Because I felt like that was a hell of a burden on my best friend, knowing that they are all I have and if they leave or go back home for a few weeks then I have no other close friends. Thankfully, they are still living their life independently of me, which is what I want, but I still feel so guilty because they have to listen to me when I want to talk about my experiences and how I'm feeling.

There is no one else I can talk to.

And the following WhatsApp message highlighted how much guilt I had a few days ago towards my best friend:

"I'm really sorry about the hot water. If I wasn't so scared and traumatised, I could have listened and I might have heard something. I don't think he mentioned much. I know you know I'm trying and dealing with a lot but I want to be useful and I just still useless and draining at the moment. I promise I'll have more fun conversations soon."

I wanted to share this message because it highlights how as a survivor, there are times when you might feel extremely guilty for no reason, or you might feel really guilty about the smallest things. It's normal to feel that way and I hope this message shows you that if you feel guilt over the smallest "mistakes" then it doesn't matter, it's normal so you aren't going insane and most importantly just be kind to yourself.

In a future chapter, I'm going to talk about the importance of positive self-talk because you can see how negative I'm being towards myself here, and that isn't good for your mental health at all.

A final message is one that I typed out but I never sent it because me and my best friend spoke about this stuff later on in the night. The context for this text is on Monday, I had had a really rough day for reasons you'll read in a moment, I couldn't do any projects or anything because my desk hadn't arrived so I was left to ruminate about my assault and its consequences. I asked my best friend after an hour of giving them alone time if I could come up and talk, they said they wanted some more alone time (which is fair, they need their own space) so after three hours of really bad mental health I wrote out this message to send later on.

I'm sharing this message because it shows how survivors can feel guilt over the smallest of things and how I show immense guilt over this friendship. As well as I'm sharing this because it highlights how triggers can surprise you and it's normal (even if its really distressing) for triggers to surprise you.

Yet I am also sharing it because it highlights hope for future relationships (something I talk about in more depth in the future and before you ask Henry isn't his real name) and it shows how survivors can have very negative self-talk towards themselves. Again, this isn't good for mental health so I'm sharing this here for you to set up a future chapter.

"I'm sorry I bothered you earlier. I know it was okay but I'm not. I promise when I get my desk sorted, I'll be better. I'll be playing in stories and doing business stuff. You don't know the guilt I feel about you being my only support thing. It is not fair on either of us. Come September I promise I'll work hard to make more friends, be out more away from you and more.

I almost ruined a lot today. Um, I was in Wolfe Lecture theatre. Easily fits 400, we had 150 students. That was enough anxiety. But we were doing outreach registers and Wolfe has like 20-seat long rows so a group of girls had packed the back row. The second to last one was empty except for a stupid boy who stayed on the edge. I asked to pass him but he wouldn't get out of the row and stand to one side. He just stood up so there was a small gap between his front and his desk. I went past the first time okay. He just sat down. I got the registers from the girls in the middle. Maybe 10 just fine.

Then I went back.

I asked him to stand up again but he didn't give me much room. I slid past him, my ass facing his front and I think I had to bend over slightly to move past. Then it triggered anything because I was in a vulnerable position, I shot out of the row, I was tensed, I might have started to shake. Henry quietly asked if I was okay as he passed me his registers. He said it so quietly I just thanked him for the registers. Handed them to Judith, went to the toilet to calm down.

I just never want to have a public meltdown at Outreach. If they bench me because I'm a risk to the image of the uni or I "need time away from work to recover". Then I'm screwed. I need Outreach to keep me okay sometimes.

P.S- when I was downstairs, I couldn't find Henry on Facebook, Insta, LinkedIn, followers of ChemSoc or LGBTSoc on insta or the ambassador FB group. My mind tried to imagine some stuff happening between us but my mind turned it into a full-on rape scene. So I'm interpreting this, yes, I can find Henry as interesting as I want and in a fantasy world, he can like me too. But I can't do anything unless he's extremely patient and prepared to deal with so much shit. It's too much for 18/19 year to deal with."

The Solution For This Friendship Guilt

Thankfully, last night me and a friend spoke for hours upon hours and this was something we spoke about. We spoke about my guilt towards them and they reassured me that is was okay, they were happy to do it and we do have a healthy relationship. I am not so dependent on them and I am in no way so suffocating that they cannot live in their own life.

Also, they mentioned how this is what friendship is. Friendship is about supporting and enjoying the time with your friend even when they're going through hell and back. Friendship is just as much about the bad times as they are about the good times.

As a result, my unofficial tip for this experience of guilt, is please make sure you communicate with your friend about why you feel guilty. Your friend can support you, tell you why that isn't true and why you have nothing to worry about.

That conversation made me feel a thousand times lighter.

General Ways To Decrease Guilt In Survivors

After talking about my personal experiences, I want to mention some more general ways about how to decrease guilt within survivors. These are very useful ideas that you might want to try out.

Firstly, be fair to yourself and use self-compassion. Since we all need to understand that guilt is a very normal response to trauma but it is often biased because the guilt we feel doesn't reflect our responsibility.

I've mentioned that what happened to all of us wasn't our fault, we shouldn't feel guilty for something we didn't choose or do willingly or want.

There is nothing for us to feel guilty about because it wasn't our fault. This feeling of guilt is a trauma response, nothing more.

Also, in my experience, a very effective

and easy way to be self-compassionate is to be kind to yourself and imagine what you say to a friend in a similar situation. In other words, never talk to yourself in a way that you wouldn't talk to a friend.

Secondly, therapy is a great way to decrease feelings of guilt. I wanted to grab my old therapist for an appointment so she can help me with my feelings of guilt but she was on holiday, and my availability is too bad when she's back.

Still therapy is a brilliant way to get professional help with these negative feelings, and honestly, therapy is a great way to help you process what happened to you. As well as trauma-focused therapies like Eye Movement Desensitisation and Reprocessing (EMDR) and Cognitive Behavioural Therapy (CBT) can help us to process our feelings of guilt.

We all need therapy because of what people have done to us.

Thirdly, education is an effective way to deal with guilt and trauma as a whole, because we need to understand that guilt is a natural part of the healing process. As well as a lot of people find (myself included) that the more you learn about sexual violence and trauma, the more empowered you become and you can reduce self-blame.

Another added benefit is you find out what you're going through is normal and you aren't going insane.

Even as a psychology student who lives and breathes clinical psychology, this is still a very scary and annoying part of sexual violence. Since when everything pops up and everything gets intense and dark and you feel like your life will never be good again, you do feel like you're going insane.

Education helps to prevent the worst of that feeling.

Furthermore, support networks are a great way to reduce feelings of guilt. These include support groups, trusted friends and family members as well, because sharing with a support network can validate your experiences and decrease the feelings of guilt.

Mainly because you'll learn that there is nothing to feel guilty about because you did nothing wrong and people will support you.

Penultimately, using grounding as well as mindfulness techniques can be effective ways to reduce guilt. Since by practising mindfulness, you're helping yourself stay in the present and manage any overwhelming emotions you're experiencing. As well as I find grounding techniques some of the best ways to keep yourself in the present and remind yourself that you're safe whenever you go through a distressing moment.

Finally, journalling is a good way to write down your thoughts and feelings so you can process your guilt, trauma responses and it helps you to gain perspective. Honestly, that is one of the reasons why I'm writing this book because I want to help you and I want to record how I'm feeling and what I'm learning about clinical psychology, sexual violence and myself as I go along.

This is essentially a massive journalling exercise and I've found it helpful for me to process my trauma and what He did to me.

On the whole, as a sexual assault survivor, guilt is a normal and natural part of the healing process. All of us feel guilt for a wide range of different reasons, there are some general trends, but there are individual reasons too.

However, there are ways to overcome and

deal with the guilt so you can heal, thrive and take back control of your life.

Healing is possible if we deal with one thing at a time.

Useful reference:

Ullman, S. E., & Peter-Hagene, L. C. (2014). Social reactions to sexual assault disclosure, coping, perceived control, and PTSD symptoms in sexual assault victims. Journal of Community Psychology, 42(4), 495–512. doi:10.1002/jcop.21618

TRYING TO LIVE YOUR LIFE AS MUCH AS POSSIBLE AFTER SEXUAL VIOLENCE

It might seem impossible, but there comes a point when you need to try to live your life as much as possible after what happened.

As sexual violence survivors, especially if you go on to develop Post-Traumatic Stress Disorder like I have, living a life seems flat out impossible or it is extremely stressful. For example, going out, seeing friends, going to crowded places can all be extremely triggering and distressing.

But it can be fun too.

Since something I've noticed at Week 14 is that you do need to live your life as much as possible after sexual violence to some extent. The reason why it's taken me so long to realise this is because of a few different reasons. For example, I find new things distressing, I find small spaces very scary and triggering and I find one-on-one situations almost impossible and they make me want to cry.

Yesterday I returned with my best friend and another friend of ours (who's a housemate too and let's call them Ruby, again not their real name) from Brighton, because Ruby lives down there and we went to see them. Also, we went to Brighton Trans Pride, we stayed at Ruby's mum's flat and we had a lot of fun.

However, it was extremely distressing for me, because we went Friday to Sunday. It's bad enough that Pride was extremely busy and packed and there were some very large people there who triggered me badly. Yet it was in a new environment, the flat was very small and choking so I couldn't really sleep, but on Thursday me and my best friend went to a BBQ with some work friends and rape stuff was mentioned.

Including a very innocent joke that played on my mind for ages. And I want to mention here that if you ever hear someone make a joke, feel free to correct them or tell them that isn't okay. I didn't do that because I didn't want these work friends to know I was raped and I know it was from ignorance, it wasn't them trying to be nasty.

That BBQ content meant I didn't sleep Thursday night, so I didn't really sleep for three nights straight. This only added to my distress.

However, there are great moments too, and this is what I want to focus on in this chapter.

Yes, triggers, distress and PTSD can be a major part of life before you go on to get specialist rape counselling or another form of psychological support. The sooner you start that process and get onto a waiting list, the better in my opinion because you will need the support.

However, if you allow yourself to be controlled by the fear, the anxiety and the panic attacks then in my opinion, it only increases your suffering, your hopelessness and decreases your mental health even more. For example, whilst I will always describe going to Brighton to see Ruby as hellish and the same goes for the first week when I moved into my student accommodation. I always focus on the positives too, because there are always lovely moments.

When we saw Ruby in Brighton, I took some lovely photos of the three of us on the beach, we saw some great, affirming content and there were tons of other great or funny moments too. Including getting gelato, racing to get the train before it left without us and my best friend being nauseous and vomiting because of a bad chilli.

Therefore, whilst I don't know what stage of the healing journey you are at, I don't know how you're feeling and I don't know how your mental health is (it might be better or worse than mine). I do know that it is so tempting to simply stay inside and stay in your safe space forever, and there are times when being in your safe space is your best option. For instance, it is best for me to limit my "new things" this week to basically nothing, because I need to recover after the past few days.

And if Ruby wasn't staying with us for the week because they wanted to see the house before they moved in in September, then I seriously would spend days in my safe space without going anywhere. That would be okay because I'm not isolating myself away from the world, I am just taking a few days to recover.

Therefore, my point is, over time as you start to heal a little bit more, it is okay to try new things and do more social stuff. You can do baby steps and you can adapt it to whatever you need. You can ask a friend to come with you, you can tell a friend point-blank what you need and don't need (I've mentioned that earlier in the book) and you can simply take it one step at a time.

But please don't trap yourself away from the world.

For me, going to Brighton was one of the biggest things I've done since I was raped and it was mostly hellish, but there were great moments too. And I know if I didn't go or if I stopped myself from going out of fear then my mental health would have been even worse, because it would make me feel trapped, isolated and hopeless about the future.

In addition, Brighton is even more proof for the future, because by going out, you're proving to yourself that you can go out, you can live and you can have fun after sexual violence. You can be a person again who enjoys their life.

That is something that seems impossible at times.

Finally, at this moment in time, there are reasons why I talk about living your life as much as possible. Since for all of us survivors, there are different limits to what we can do at our current stage of healing. For instance, I cannot go out and do major things by myself. Like, I flat out cannot do one-on-one or group social situations with new people, I cannot go to London by myself and I cannot go on any trips by myself.

I just can't because it's too much, too scary and it kills my mental health too much. Also, in these situations, it's okay not to do these things because doing these things by myself will do so much more damage to me, my mental health and my recovery than me not doing it or doing it with friends.

That's why at the moment, my best friend

is the person I basically do everything with. Although, my best friend is going home to the Midlands for a month in a few weeks so I will be alone for a month. Granted, we need to have a conversation about a "safety plan" for when they go away, but we've agreed I need to see people, be social and have things to look forward to during that month so I don't become suicidal. Therefore, we have talked about me and Henry doing things as friends (it turns out he wasn't into me after all and he's straight), and that is something I am scared about, but in the interest of protecting my mental health and proving to myself I can do it, I want to try it.

And I do know Henry would never ever hurt me so going out with them and doing something will be fine and fun. Even though I will be taking me and Henry doing things together very slowly and one step at a time.

Overall, at the end of this chapter, I want to stress to you that it is okay to struggle, it is okay to take baby steps and adapt "going out" to whatever you need, and it's okay to go slow with reclaiming the going out part of your life.

In my experience, the going out part after sexual violence is scary, anxiety-provoking and it can be hellish. But I am reclaiming that small part of my life, so I can feel safe, secure and happy to be out in the world again living my life and showing my rapist hasn't taken that part of me.

I am my own person and I can do whatever I want given enough time. I am nowhere near "healed enough" (whatever that means) to do grand things on my own and that's okay. Yet slowly but surely, I am finding ways to go out, have fun and make great memories with great friends.

And that is a wonderfully powerful thing that brings me a lot of joy in dark times.

It could do the same for you.

IF YOU CAN'T MAKE DECISIONS, THAT'S A NORMAL TRAUMA RESPOSNE

For the majority of these experience-based chapters, I try to write them in chronological order because I want you to see the ups and downs of sexual violence recovery as the weeks and months go on.

However, this chapter I want to bring forward because it complements and improves a chapter and something that happened from Week 9.

What Happened?

On the 29th June 2024, I moved to Canterbury with my best friend and I was already struggling a little because it was a lot, my bedroom is basically an enclosed space and my self-talk was very negative. And I realise I should have stopped, focused on the self-talk going on in my head and changed it from "I don't want to get raped again now I'm living in Canterbury" to "You'll be fine by living in Canterbury. No one will hurt you".

Anyway, my best friend had their partner over so they were upstairs unpacking my best friend's room. I was downstairs I flat out could not handle going upstairs because it was too triggering for me.

I needed to unpack but I was struggling with triggers, flashbacks and I was really depressed. I cried a few times and I finally wanted to put my kitchen stuff away in a cupboard but I couldn't decide.

I seriously could not decide what I wanted

to do with my stuff. Should I put my stuff in the left-hand or right-hand cupboard? What should I put wear? What should I do at all?

I had also struggled to make any sort of decisions for that entire late afternoon and evening of moving in.

Afterwards I simply broke down and cried my eyes out and I Whatsapped my best friend immediately asking them to come downstairs alone, we hugged and I explained everything to them. All I really remember about that conversation was how I talked about how much I hated my rapist, He stole my ability to make decisions and he was stealing everything from me.

And so on.

Thankfully, my best friend just talked to me as we both put away our kitchen stuff together, and it was a lovely hour before they went back upstairs to unpack their room.

After a while, I forced myself to go upstairs into my enclosed space of a bedroom because I was going to make decisions and unpack. That did not happen for a single second because I listened to music through my earphones to distract me from my fear. Then my bedroom popped open by itself, hit me and I realised how seriously jumpy I am so I got depressed and I laid on the floor of my room with all my boxes around me for a few hours.

I will admit Duolingo is a brilliant break from rumination, so maybe try that.

The next day my friend talked to me as I unpacked a little and we both kept our bedroom doors open so and that helped a lot. Granted I could only manage about 40 minutes of decision-making at a time and it took me a lot longer than I wanted to finish unpacking but I managed.

Granted that is the tip of the iceberg of my mental health over the past four days, but I wanted to focus on the decision-making aspect of disempowerment.

In addition, whilst the above paragraphs capture what happened, the Whatsapp message below helps to highlight the sheer distress and emotion I was feeling at the time. And again, I'm sharing this message with you so you understand that it's normal to be distressed, you shouldn't feel guilty for being distressed or triggered and I'm trying to normalise what we all go through.

Also, please note, this message connects to chapters on negative self-talk and guilt. This is something we shouldn't say to ourselves because we should be kind to ourselves, so please note that the negative self-talk and guilt I feel in this message is something I have thankfully worked on.

Yet it goes to show how distressing new situations can be and negative self-talk and guilt is something we all need to work on.

'Before I try to get some sleep, thank you for comforting me earlier and helping me. I hate the disempowerment part of rape and making choices. I can decide on anything business or writing related, but not normal stuff. It's shit.

I never did anymore unpacking. I tried to listen to music to get upstairs then my door opened by itself, it hit me, I jumped and I got depressed. I hate how jumpy I am so I got tired and depressed and couldn't really move. I just laid on my floor for a few hours thinking and being depressed. Duolingo was a short relief.

I try to live my life. This week proved that with

Outreach, moving and the chaos of Psychology Society. But at this point in time, I can't make decisions, I doubt I'll ever have a relationship or anything like you and Nathan have. I'm going to die alone, unloved and useless. I just want to live but I've never been able. From my child abuse from intensely homophobic family leading to mental breakdown last August to my friendship abandonment to my rape. I only survive. I don't want this anymore. Honestly part of me would love to die, but I care about you too much and I'll never hurt you. There are lovely, positive moments too that I love. So I won't do it but it's annoying a small part of me wants to.

Tonight I wanted to do a fun thing with you. We write down 3 things we want in our lives by the end of the tenancy. I've seen different people do this for other things. The only thing I genuinely wanted on my list was still be alive.
It took me at least 10 mins just to undress tonight. Only managed because I listened to music.

I'm sorry you had to move in with a raped person. I'm sorry for everything that will come up. I'm sorry this always gets dumped on. I hate it. I hate I have no one else. I just want this to be better for you than your last house for you and I'm scared it won't be.

Now I try to sleep and hopefully I'll have energy in the morning. Sleep well.

Over To You

Whilst nothing in this book is any sort of official advice, I want to mention a few things I have read or found useful myself in case you are struggling to make "basic" decisions because these decisions do not feel basic or easy at all.

In addition, it is worth mentioning that the reason why sexual assault survivors have difficulty with decisions is because of a range of reasons. For instance, guilt and shame about their attack and the notion that it was somehow their fault when it wasn't, they have low self-worth, they become perfectionists, they no longer trust their sense of judgement and so on.

That is why us survivors feel disempowered.

It is also our job, our professional help, determination and our social support network to move beyond all this in time.

Even though it takes a hell of a lot longer than we would like.

Therefore, I believe there are two main important things to remember when it comes to making decisions. Firstly, be kind to yourself and I know how impossible this is in the moment but please try. Remember that isn't your fault, it is the fault of your rapist/ attacker and you ARE capable of making decisions. As well as you will only get better at making decisions in the future, and these powerless moments are simply that, mere moments in the grand scheme of things.

You will be empowered again because you are brilliant.

Secondly, get some support. This can either be professional help and/ or support from friends or family. Get a friend that makes you feel good to talk to you either in-person, over the phone or over a video call as you make decisions. Get them to support YOU making the decisions so you can make your own decisions with a little bit of support.

The worse and most disempowering thing for survivors of sexual violence is for other people to make decisions for you.

For example, it was lovely my best friend

just talked to me and helped me make decisions about where to put my kitchen stuff. It helped *me* to make the decisions and it was lovely to feel empowered for a while.

And the more you make decisions, the more natural it will feel and the more empowered you will feel over time. This will make you feel good, improve your mental health and it will help your recovery.

On the whole, if you're struggling to make decisions, even the so-called "most basic" decisions ever. Then this is a normal reaction to an extremely abnormal situation and you are seriously not alone. A difficulty making decisions is something the vast majority of sexual assault survivors experience and it never makes you flawed, a problem or anything else negative.

It makes you human.

And the fact that you're reading a book and looking for ways to help yourself and improve your life, that truly makes you a strong, amazing person that will recover in time because it is possible.

I remember that no matter how dark, lonely or isolating a moment is where I cannot make decisions, there is always a way to make a decision and steal back a little grain of power from my rapist. Sometimes I need a friend or something else.

But I can reclaim my power.

And so can you.

THOUGHTS ON VIRGINITY LOSS AFTER SEXUAL VIOLENCE

As a writer, I process and think about topics by writing about them, considering the perspectives and writing about them in a way that is useful to other people. Originally, I was going to put this chapter earlier in the book, but I wanted to keep this chapter around the Week 14 mark because I believe some people might not be ready or even consider this option until a lot of the "initial" trauma responses have decreased.

I wrote that line smiling because I still have way more trauma responses than I would like, but that is the mind trying to help me process what happened.

Anyway, when I was in Brighton and dealing with everything I was going through, I don't know why this popped up but I got very scared that I wasn't a virgin anymore and I had effectively lost my virginity to my rapist. This was something I did not want, I was scared and a little distressed. I think I would be more distressed if I wasn't so exhausted, so this was a topic I wanted to explore in this chapter from different angles to help me understand if I am a virgin or not, and I want to help other people decide this for themselves too.

Also, I will end this chapter with a specific "Over To You" section so you can get something aimed at you, the reader, from this chapter.

Note: in the second section of this chapter on Definitions, *there are references to sexual acts. I have tried to keep it as light and non-graphic as possible, but please be careful if sexual references are triggering to you.*

Why Am I Writing About This Topic?

I've done a lot of online reading about virginity loss through sexual violence over the past few days, and this is something a lot of survivors struggle with to process and it is something that a lot of people have differing opinions on. All these differing opinions are important and good, because they work for different people. Therefore, I'm going to be writing about all the major different opinions I've read about because it is hard after experiencing sexual violence to process the concept of virginity, due to the way how society puts such importance on losing your virginity.

A lot of people see losing your virginity as a rite of passage into adulthood. I talk more about the social aspects of losing your virginity in the next section.

Furthermore, for a lot of sexual violence survivors, their rape or assault or whatever term you want to use for it, the Event was their first sexual encounter. This is what happened to me and after spending years of my life hearing from classmates, friends and family members about how great your first time can be and how it is such a big, wonderful thing, having *that* as your first sexual encounter, it is fucked up and wrong on so many levels.

It is that tragic realisation where you can realise or consider your attacker has stolen something from you. That is what's distressing and it makes survivors struggle with the idea of virginity loss, and this is why we need to talk about it in this chapter.

Personally, I struggle with the concept of losing my virginity because after suffering a lot of homophobic child trauma for a decade, I built up the idea of my virginity as something exciting, precious and it kept me alive. When I was really struggling, suicidal and I lost all hope that I could ever be gay, the idea of having a boyfriend that might love me and want to be with me (including having sex) kept me going.

Moreover, the idea of losing my virginity was the ultimate act of defiance against my family. The idea of gay sex where two men love each other, have passionate sex and want to be together is every single thing that my family hates and despises and finds an abomination. So the idea of utterly defining them and doing something they found so disgusting was exciting and it kept me going.

On the whole, the idea of losing my virginity to someone who was attracted to me and I was attracted to back gave me such hope in a childhood that was often hopeless.

As a result, the very notion or idea that I lost my virginity to an idiot rapist is disgusting, outrageous and I fucking hate my rapist. How dare he take that from me, how dare he lives and how dare he touch me.

I still want to be a virgin but after reading some opinions, I think there is a chance I might not be a virgin.

And if that is true, if I am no longer a virgin then that will only add to my pain, my suffering and my profound sense of loss because of what that bastard did to me.

<u>Why Virginity Is A Social Construct And Its Social Purpose?</u>

I know as a university psychology Masters student, I shouldn't read Wikipedia but I read up on virginity, and it meant the social purpose and constructive nature of virginity.

In essence, we all know that virginity doesn't actually exist, and it isn't real. There is nothing biological, there is nothing you can touch and there is nothing you can actually measure about virginity.

In truth, virginity is just a concept that people have made up to give importance to an event that happens in someone's life. Sometimes this "Importance" is given for religious reasons and other times virginity is "important" for social reasons. For example, the silly idea that virgins are more pure, better and more moral than non-virgins. Also, the silly idea that virgins are worth more, having sex with a virgin can cure aids and other Sexually Transmitted Diseases (a horrible myth that leads to a lot of women getting raped in Africa), and there are a lot of bunch of other reasons.

Furthermore, especially when it comes to young women, virginity is a concept used to control them and other people. Since there are certain people that want women to remain virgins because they believe virgin women are more valuable, more worthy and purer than non-virgin women. Therefore, by stressing the importance of being a virgin, it allows men and other people to socially control women and their behaviour so *they* can reap the rewards instead of the woman herself.

The final reason I'll look at in a little more depth is that in western societies, losing your virginity is seen as a massive deal amongst young people because it makes you an adult. It is a way for young men to brag and bond with their friends, they can talk about their sexual conquests and there is a lot of pressure on young men to lose their virginity sooner rather than later.

This is even more true for boys belonging to the popular social groups or more "laddie" groups in my experience.

On the whole, the concept of losing your virginity is important in society for no "real" reason. Instead people believe losing their virginity is important because of a wide range of social and religious reasons. This doesn't mean wanting to lose your virginity isn't important and it doesn't invalidate you wanting to lose it to someone you love or have a fun time with. Yet I want you to know that it is only important for these social reasons.

And for some people, it might be immensely useful to know that virginity lost is a social construct as it might allow them to move past these non-existent social expectations and decrease its importance as a result.

This might work for some people, it might not for others.

The Different Ways To Lose Your Virginity According To Different People

Before the first 14 weeks of after my rape, I was very content with the definition that you needed something to be inside you for you to lose your virginity. Yet I must have read something that caused me to start questioning that definition, then I started reading things online and I realised that a lot of people have differing definitions of virginity lost.

Now I'm going to explain the top three definitions.

Firstly, you have the "traditional" definition as I'm calling it. This is where you can only lose your virginity if a penis (a real or fake one) has entered your body. The most extreme traditional version is when a penis enters a vagina, but that definition isn't useful for LGBT+ people. Therefore, you can lose your virginity if someone puts something in you.

Secondly, you can lose your virginity if you have any sort of sexual contact. For example, if someone performs oral sex on you, you're naked and you touch each other, you give someone anal or penetrative sex without them doing the same to you and so on.

Personally, this is the definition that caused me a lot of distress because this definition means I am not a virgin, and my rapist has already taken so much from me, I don't want him to take away my virginity too.

Finally, you can define it as you see fit and some people believe something extremely interesting. Some people believe that losing your virginity is impossible during rape because losing your virginity is a consensual act that you enjoy, and considering that sexual violence is not consensual and it is far from fun, it means you absolutely cannot lose your virginity during rape.

I cannot help but smile when I write about this reason.

If you adopt this definition then it means you can never lose your virginity to sexual violence, your attacker can NEVER take that from you and your virginity will always be yours until you decide this is the time and person you want to lose it too.

This definition is a great way to reclaim a small amount of power from your attacker. Your attacker will never take your virginity because they never had your consent and you did not enjoy it.

Your virginity is yours to keep, control and only *you* can "lose" it because it is yours and your attacker can never take it away from you.

What Do I Think Virginity Loss Is?

This is why I love writing about topics I am struggling with, because I am a virgin and I can't help myself but smile at that realisation. I am choosing (the fact I am actually making a decision is amazing to be fair) that my virginity can only be lost to someone I choose, someone I consent with and someone I can have fun with.

To me, you are only not a virgin if you have actual sex. Rape, sexual assault and any form of sexual violence is not sex.

Sex is when you form sexual acts with consent, enjoyment and attraction. To be able to have sex, there has to be a want, an interest and an attraction, so rape is never sex.

Rape seriously is not sex and that is a great thing to realise.

Therefore, all those years where the idea of having sex with a guy I was attracted to is still alive and that is still achievable. I can lose my virginity to someone I consent too and everything that kept me going during my extremely homophobic adolescence is still there and strong, and my rapist has not taken that from me.

He has taken so much away from me but I have something. I have something he will never take from me and after everything I have been through and after everything he has stolen from me, I can keep something.

And I love that. It is a great feeling to have.

Over To You

On the whole, at the end of this chapter, if your experience of sexual violence was your first sexual encounter like me, then you might want to think about your own personal definition of virginity, and how someone loses it. You've read a lot of different ideas and definitions in this chapter, so you might want to mix-and-match them, pick certain definitions and you can decide for yourself.

And even if you decide that after what happened to you makes you no longer a virgin, then please remember, that being a virgin is a social construct. It doesn't mean anything, so it's okay.

I hope this chapter gives you the information you need to make a decision about your virginity if you need to. Also, if you don't need to make this decision, then I hope it gave you some food for thought about our fellow survivors and what they might need to know to heal a little bit.

What's your definition of virginity?

DEALING WITH EXISTING FRIENDSHIPS AFTER SEXUAL VIOLENCE

As I continue this introductory section of topics that I want to say upfront so regardless of the point of your healing journey, you understand these critical basics. I want to talk about friendships in this chapter and then in a future chapter, I'm going to talk about making new friendships. Originally, I was going to put both friendship chapters together, but it took me until Week 12 or Week 14 to be ready to make new friendships and I would have panicked if someone mentioned new friendships at any point before then.

Therefore, in case you're like me and the very notion of making new friends makes you want to have a panic attack at this point in your healing journey, then that's okay. That chapter comes later and you can skip it and come back to it later if you want.

Existing Friendships After Sexual Violence

I know from my psychology degree that friendships and your social support network is a critical protective factor when it comes to your mental health. Typically, the more friends you have, the better your mental health will be and the following is a short extract from an academic article I wrote yesterday for a different project:

"This is critical considering people have a fundamental need to belong where they can experience ongoing relational bonds and these bonds have a plethora of mental health benefits (Baumeister & Leary, 1995). For example, social groups are protective factor against depression (Hellzen et al., 2011), stress (American Psychological Association, 2022), and Post-Traumatic Stress Disorder symptoms (Flanagan et al., 2016) amongst other benefits."

As a result, you can see how friendships and other social relationships help to protect us against negative mental health, and I've read articles over the past few months about how friendships are critical for rape survivors.

Personally, because of my child abuse and my autism, friendships are a very difficult topic for me naturally. At the time of writing, I only have two or three friends and there's only one friend (my best friend is referred a lot in this book) who I can talk about my rape with in any great depth.

You'll see through the book this led to a lot of guilt, bad mental health and it really doesn't help that I am very, very attracted to my best friend. This is a trigger for my rape stuff too so shortly after my rape, the friendship was very challenging for me but thankfully, it isn't any more and it is a brilliant friendship.

The only real "benefit" (the wrong-est word if there ever was one) of my assault was that it brought me and my best friend even closer together.

What Is The Point Of This Chapter?

Anyway, in the aftermath of sexual violence, when you're panicking, you're distressed and you have no idea what the fuck just happened to you. Your existing friendships can be utterly terrifying because you feel like you need to tell them because you want the support, someone to talk to and you want to process what happened. Yet you're scared of being judged, blamed and you might be scared your friends might cut-off contact with you.

As a result, the point of this chapter is to explain how I dealt with existing friendships after my sexual violence experience, and give you some more general tips about existing friendships.

By the end of this chapter, you'll understand some ways to tell your friends, why friends are important and how a disclosure of sexual violence might impact friendships.

This isn't as scary as it seems but it is so important to your healing process that you have friends you can rely on.

Always Start With Your Closest Friends

Even though I reference a lot of friendship content in the rest of the book, I want to spell it out clearly here that after you realise you've experienced sexual violence, I would recommend you tell your closest friends.

I say this because your closest friends are the people that know you best, the people that care about you the most and these are the friends that should be happy to support you, because you're a close friend to them.

You'll see in more detail in other chapters how my best friend was the first person I told about my assault. Granted it was stressful because they didn't see my messages for two days so I was very lonely in that time, I had to deal with a lot myself and it was rather hellish because I was processing what the hell happened to me.

However, my best friend is amazing, brilliant and they are one of the most caring people I know. Over the past few months, they have always been there for me no matter how distressed, self-critical and bad my mental health was. They were there for me.

They were always just a text away before we lived together, and now I'm living with them, they're always happy to listen to when I need to talk.

They are the ideal friend to have after experiencing sexual violence.

I truly hope everyone has a friend like mine.

In addition, when it came to how I told them, because they're my best friend I was extremely honest with them. Surprisingly enough, I know I share a lot of copies of WhatsApp messages I've sent in the other chapters (and I include some more below), I am not sharing these ones in this chapter.

Mainly because you can see how raw, panicked and distressed I was. You can see how I was in denial too for the first two days, and I hated rereading them.

However, when telling your best or closest friends about what happened to you, depending on the type of friendship you have, you can just be brutally honest. You can tell them the details, how it happened and just talk to them. Tell them whatever you need to be able to cope.

In my original text to my best friend, I was honest enough so they got the gist about how bad it was for me. Then whilst they were in Switzerland for the next three weeks, I texted them whenever I needed it and they learnt just how much I was struggling with everything and they might have been 600 miles away but they supported me.

Overall, when it comes to telling your closest friends about your sexual violence experience, just tell them and go into as much depth as you need to for you. You have all the power here and your closest friends will support, love and help you because your dear friends to each other.

Your closest friends are the people you're meant to feel safe with.

Finally, in terms of reaction, my best friend was extremely "sorry" about what had happened to me, and my best friend is not normally the type of person to send an extremely angry message directed at anyone. Yet to say my best friend was pissed off at my rapist was an understatement and it was actually lovely to read.

It was validating and that is what good friends do. They support you, validate you and listen to you.

How To Tell Other Friends?

Even though I don't have *that* many friends, there were still three other friends that I felt like I needed to tell. Yet unlike my best friend, I told these three friends when the situation popped up and I didn't really have a choice anymore.

Telling A First Friend

For example, I talk about this in another chapter but I have another friend who experienced sexual abuse as a kid and we are good friends. And as much as I didn't want to talk about it with him, my best friend wasn't getting back to me so I had to contact him and tell him.

I'll add a copy of the two messages I sent below that were sent about 30 minutes apart because I want you to see the differences between the messages I sent different people.

"Hi, hope you're okay.

Is there a chance I can talk to you about something that happened Saturday night please?

Yet this is to do with really bad sex stuff so you can say No. That is perfectly okay and I do have others to talk too. Your mental health and you are far more important. Say no if that's best for you. It's okay."

The second message.

"I've emailed the uni support services now so they'll help so it's okay. Sorry to bother you. I know this is a sensitive area. I shouldn't have mentioned it.

Hope you're doing well in general."

You see in this message I did want to talk to him but I was unsure about it, I was gently bringing up the topic to see how he would react and if this was an okay topic. I partly did this because I wanted him to know I respect him, his past and his mental health yet I wanted to gauge his reaction too.

You can see I got increasingly distressed in between these two texts being sent, and that's okay too. Telling someone about sexual violence is very scary and I was utterly terrified because of a possible negative reaction.

Thankfully, none of my friends gave me a negative reaction. They were all supportive, kind and lovely to me.

On the whole, what I learnt about doing a disclosure after talking to this friend was it's okay to go slow, approach the subject gently and it's okay to be distressed. Sexual violence is very distressing so it's okay to tell someone in a distressed way because you're processing a lot, depending on the friendship, you seriously don't need to downplay it.

In fact, you should never ever downplay sexual violence.

How I Told A Second Friend?

In a chapter later in the book, I talk about one of my friends Ruby (not their real name) and how they're living with me and my best friend next academic year. I really like Ruby, they are a great friend and I have a lot of great conversations with Ruby. Yet because of their age and their looks, I see them as a very innocent child (Ruby is 19 by the way) and because I didn't know anything about Ruby's mental health experiences up until two days ago. I was very nervous and resistant to have conversations with Ruby about what happened to me.

However, a few days before my assault I had contacted Ruby to see they wanted to meet up where they lived. That's about a two-hour drive for me but I wanted to see Ruby as I hadn't seen them in over a month.

Two days after my rape (yes Ruby is that bad at responding to texts), Ruby said to me they were excited to see me and that would be great. Yet the idea of one-on-one, going out and doing a lot of different things just seemed impossible to me.

So I had to tell Ruby what had happened to me in this text:

"That's okay about not responding sooner. Sorry, I'm no longer free next week because all I'll say is I was sexually assaulted a week ago, so I've got my therapy booked, I'm working Outreach at the uni and getting to get my life back to some sort of normal. Also, I'm a little sensitive to one-on-one situations at the moment.

In May when you're back, we'll meet up and do something.

Have a lovely rest of your easter."

Therefore, when it came to telling Ruby about my sexual assault, I was much more careful and limited in the details because besides from Ruby's reply about how sorry they are that happened to me and they hope I'm okay. This is all we spoke about it until very late May when me and my best friend met up with Ruby for dinner.

I choose to keep details light with Ruby because up until recently I didn't feel like I could have serious or traumatic conversations with them. I didn't feel like me and Ruby had that sort of friendship and I didn't want to keep having to tell different people.

Overall, whilst Ruby has been very supportive and lovely towards me, if you don't feel like you have the sort of relationship where you can talk in-depth about something as traumatic as rape and other forms of sexual violence. You can keep it very light so the other person has a general idea of what happened to you and then if you need certain things from that friend then you can ask and talk about it. For instance, in my text, I am essentially asking Ruby to be patient and understanding about why I cannot see them one-on-one for a while.

Thankfully, Ruby is very understanding.

How Did I Tell A Friend I Work With?

A final friend that I told in the initial aftermath of my assault was a friend who was my former supervisor for my psychology dissertation in my undergraduate degree. We became friends because we worked together really well, he knew I had great project management skills and he was the first person I told about my mental health, my extremely homophobic family and he was a great listener. He was there for me.

Granted he is still more of a work friend because of our age gap, we're different people socially and other factors, we wouldn't spend time together outside of a university environment together. But we still class each other as good friends.

Anyway, because he knows about my mental health, my past and he is honestly lovely and supportive. I would have liked to see him in the aftermath, so telling him was a little complicated. Since he is more of work friend than a personal friend, telling someone that you experienced sexual violence is a lot and I really, really didn't want him to see me differently because we have some great projects lined up together.

Therefore, I decided to tell him in a subtle, light way where I was asking more to keep myself busy and see a friend rather than wanting to have an in-depth conversation with him. Even though he did offer to have an in-depth conversation with me and I told him I would think about it.

"Hey, hope you're okay.

What days are you at the centre next week please?

Just asking because I was sexually assaulted Saturday night.

I've spoken to the specialist uni service, C and another friend of ours Y. I'm better than I was and this week I'm focusing on myself, chipping away at projects and seeing Y on Thursday (X's away). But I was wondering if next week I needed something else to do like helping at the centre, would that be possible?

I probably won't need it as I'm doing a lot of Outreach work but still. Thought I'll ask."

One major difference between this message and the message I sent Ruby was I went into slightly more depth because me and this work friend do have the type of relationship where bad things can be spoken about. Also, this friend knows a lot about other aspects of my life so I was okay going into a little more, and I know without a shadow of a doubt that this work friend is so lovely that he would support me no matter what.

Overall, when it comes to telling different friends about your sexual violence experiences, here are some tips for you:

- Tell your closest friends everything you want and you're comfortable telling them so you can process what happened.
- Only tell people you trust.
- It's okay not to tell people everything until later on.
- You can leave details out if that makes you more comfortable.
- Do what is right for you
- Think about the level of friendship you have with that person.

Ultimately, trust your friends to give you the support, love and listening ear that you need.

<u>How Did My Disclosure Impact My Different Friendships?</u>

This is the scariest aspect of telling your existing friends about sexual violence because I was concerned that my friends would:

- Not believe me.
- Blame me for what happened.
- Not want to be friends with me anymore.
- Tell other people without my permission.

I'm sure there were other concerns but these are the main ones, and from what I've read and heard from the past few months, these are the standard concerns of survivors.

Honestly, in my experience, my friends have been flat out amazing. I haven't had a single negative comment, a single piece of judgment and all my friends still want to be friends with me. All my friends have done nothing but love, support and listen to me whenever I needed it. They've been amazing.

In terms of specific friendships, me and my best friend have always been close but because of past friendships, I was very skittish because I was just waiting for my best friend to abandon me because everyone does that to me in the end. I was relatively insecure in that friendship until this happened. Also, my best friend wasn't entirely all-in in this friendship because I could be very intense at times and my best friend used to say a lot of "I need to get to know you more" in certain situations.

We were both close friends beforehand but both of us had things holding us back before truly committing to the friendship.

Thankfully, the disclosure about my rape made me and my best friend grow very close together. And we were talking about it the other night and my best friend agreed with me when I said my rape brought us closer together because neither one of us are letting things hold us back anymore. We're just enjoying being really close friends.

All because we've bonded through this trauma.

Besides from that effect of closeness, there haven't been any other noticeable effects on my friendships. My other three friends are very supportive and I know I can turn to them whenever I need it to some extent. I'm still not really close enough with my other three friends to have in-depth conversations about my rape, but they are there for me. As well as Ruby is a great listener even if they don't say too much because they have no idea how to respond.

I do have great friends and I'm glad I didn't isolate myself after what happened, I leant on my friends and thankfully it worked out brilliantly.

<u>Make Sure To Tell Your Friends What You Need</u>

In this penultimate section, I wanted to quickly mention that as part of dealing with existing friendships after sexual violence, it is perfectly okay (and needed) for you to tell your friends what you need from them.

If you need them not to touch you (like a hug), mention certain names or places or talk about certain topics (like sex or dating) then that is okay, your friends should/ will respect your wishes and you need to do what is right for you.

Some of my boundaries with my friends are:

- Not mentioning the name of my rapist (even if someone else shares the same name)
- We can talk about sex, dating and love but I have the power to shut down these conversations quickly if needed.
- Don't hug or touch me unless I give you clear permission

That's all the boundaries I can think of but my friends respect them and it helps to make spending time with them easier.

Furthermore, if you're going somewhere that is very triggering for you then feel free to tell them. Below is the text I sent Ruby when me and my best friend where coming down to visit them for a weekend. And I don't do well with crowded places, sleeping in new rooms and I just don't do well with going out much. I explain in a later chapter how hard this weekend was for me, but I explained to Ruby what might happen so everyone was on the same page.

"Hi Ruby, I like being honest and I know you're brilliant so you'll be okay with me telling you this, but

I just want to be honest. Mainly so I don't feel horrific guilt if stuff pops us.

I am excited and really looking forward to seeing you, but I am nervous. Because coming to Brighton and Seaford for a weekend is one of the biggest things I've done since I was raped. I went on holiday to Wales with my family but that was a disaster.

So I know if rape stuff pops up for me, it's okay, I can manage it and if I need to say no to doing stuff it's okay. And I do want you to stay for next week so you can see the house, do tourist things with me and more. But the first week after moving in was hell for me because it triggered so much rape stuff.

Point is, it will be a lovely weekend in Brighton because we're doing fun stuff and seeing you. And I'm looking forward to you living with us next week, but I'm reminding myself that if rape stuff pops up a lot, it's okay.

I have no clue if this text makes sense. And because you'll probably wonder, no thank you, there isn't anything extra I need from you. I can't predict my triggers so let's just have a fun weekend like normal and we'll deal with stuff if they pop up.

Looking forward to seeing you."

You can tell I was a little distressed by sending this text but it was okay to send and it was me doing what was best for me so I could have a nice time too.

You always need to give yourself permission to put yourself first so you can have a nice time too and live your life. Something else I talk about later on in the book.

Conclusion

Ultimately, I know following sexual violence, you're dealing with a hell of a lot of really, really scary shit from panic attacks to processing what the hell happened and your mental health changes too. This is why friendships are so critical but the idea of telling your friends is terrifying.

I hope after reading this chapter, you can see some different ways to tell different friends depending on your level of friendship with them.

In addition, I hope you can see how the vast, vast majority of friendships have positive reactions towards you after a disclosure. This means they'll want to support you, listen to you and help you with whatever you need.

That is what friends are for.

Sexual violence might seem like the end of everything and it can seem like it messes up your entire life and it seems like it can ruin friendships. Yet your friends love you, want to support you and your friends are the people you can hopefully feel safe with. So please, tell them, lean on them for support because you will need them so badly in the weeks and months to come.

But you can survive sexual violence with a little help from your friends.

Finally, just as a reminder, here are my tips again for when it comes to telling different friends about your sexual violence experiences:

- Tell your closest friends everything you want and you're comfortable telling them so you can process what happened.
- Only tell people you trust.
- It's okay not to tell people everything until later on.
- You can leave details out if that makes you more comfortable.
- Do what is right for you
- Think about the level of friendship you have with that person.

Ultimately, trust your friends to give you

the support, love and listening ear that you need.

MAKING NEW FRIENDS AFTER SEXUAL VIOLENCE

Something I really struggle with these days is the idea of meeting new people, forming new friendships and spending time with new friends. A lot of this comes back to me developing Post-Traumatic Stress Disorder and me associating new people with danger because my attacker was a new person, so as you can imagine I have a lot of social anxiety too.

This means the idea of making new friends is extremely hard for me to understand and it is a very scary idea.

As a result, it is only at Week 14 I am willing to talk about it because I have made a new friend and I am slowly approaching this friendship and developing it. Since even though Henry wasn't into me (he's straight), he was just very intense about wanting to get to know me and make a friend. And like me, he is very autistic so that explains a lot.

Therefore, as Henry is a new friend and he wants to be friends with me, this raised a lot of interesting points, including some scary ones about how to navigate certain things and I want to talk about it openly in this chapter.

Due to I know the idea of making new friends seems terrifying to a lot of survivors and a lot of us have social anxiety, so this makes it even worse for us.

Ultimately, in this chapter, I'll talk about my experiences of social anxiety, The R Conversation and managing friendships after experiencing sexual violence. This will obviously be based on my own experiences so it might be different for other people, and I will make more general useful points along the way too so this chapter can be useful for as many people as possible.

Social Anxiety

At this point in time, I don't do well when it comes to meeting new people, being in new situations and being out of my safe place. I've already spoken before about making sure you continue to live your life as much as you can and making sure you don't isolate yourself. This is why I put up with the anxiety even if it wrecks my mental health for days.

I want to limit how much my rapist steals from me, and each time I go out, live my life and experience happiness is an act of defiance against him.

In addition, when my best friend asked me why I found going to Brighton so stressful and triggering the other week from a social anxiety point of view, I explained that a few stressors run through my head at a million miles an hour:

- If I'm in a large crowd, that's a lot of people who could hurt me or rape me.
- I don't want to get trapped again.
- I don't want to get hurt.
- I don't want to get touched and groped and raped again.
- A crowd limits your options to escape.
- If I'm with new people then they could rape me again.

Of course, I acknowledge every single one of these is a biased, illogical thought that has no evidence supporting it. As well as a lot of these fears and thoughts aren't based in reality or what happened to me, they're actually based in the emotions I felt during the assault.

For example, I wasn't physically limited on me being able to escape, but I was so scared that my rapist would beat me, hurt me and pin me down if I made a wrong move. Since he was a lot bigger and heavier than me, it wouldn't have been hard. That the fear paralysed me and stopped me from being able to escape.

I never want to experience that feeling again.

Therefore, I have a lot of social anxiety about accidentally finding myself in another situation where I could get hurt and abused again, even I know in the grand scheme of things that is very unlikely.

Furthermore, I have a lot of anxiety about meeting new people because I know my pre-existing friends are not going to hurt or abuse me, but I am scared that new people will. As well as it doesn't help when my intrusive thoughts and dreams twist what happened to me to show me new friends (and sometimes old close friends) are beating and raping me.

All these different factors make meeting new people difficult for me.

However, I know I have to allow myself to meet new people, live my life and I never want to isolate myself. I recently found that the woman who attacked me because of her persecutory delusions was sexually abused as a kid by a woman and she started to isolate herself recently. I saw how she attacked anyone who did even the slightest thing wrong in her eyes and unless you supported her 100% she dropped you. She dropped my best friend (someone who moved heaven and earth for her constantly) just because my best friend defended me once against her.

I never want to end up like her so I will always be subtly open and try to make new friends, new connections and I want to live my life regardless of how many barriers my sexual assault puts up.

The R Conversation

As much as I hate to say this (and believe I wish I didn't have to), at some point in the friendship you have to have the conversation about what happened to you. And this does not have to be a detailed conversation, you never have to reveal anything you don't want to and actually, you don't have to tell them if you don't want to.

However, there might be a situation, a comment or a joke that makes you realise you need to have that conversation with your new friend so you can enjoy the friendship without getting triggered, have bad mental health and you can live your life without suffering.

There is no timeline for this conversation. You might want to or need to have the conversation within a few weeks of the new friendship, you might be able to wait months or you might never want or need to tell them.

Nonetheless, if you do want or need to have the conversation about what happened to you, my advice is the following:

- Be sure you want to tell them.
- Only tell them what you are comfortable sharing.
- Remember you are in full control of the situation, so you can tell them however you want to. For instance, in-person, on the phone or by text.

In addition, I would mention based on my own experience, this is actually more terrifying than telling your pre-existing friends. Since the friends you had before what happened to you occurred, you were already friends with them, your relationships were solid and your friends love you so a disclosure shouldn't have changed anything in that regard.

On the other hand, when it comes to new friendships, they don't know you before your sexual violence experience, they don't know what you're like and there is a fear they will react badly because your friendship is new.

Personally, before I told Henry about what happened to me (I'll show you how I did that in a moment), I was very scared that he wouldn't want to be friends anymore, he wouldn't just leave or he would react negatively to my disclosure.

I always knew I was going to have to tell Henry about what happened to me, because my best friend is going back home for a month, and we both want me to hang out with Henry so I get some social contact. As well as I have something to look forward to so I won't get hopeless and severely suicidality again.

Therefore, I wanted to push this conversation as late as I possibly could, so Henry could get to know me, the fun, cool person (I am so not cool) and not me The Rape Survivor. That is what I would have preferred.

Nevertheless, life doesn't always stick to my plans.

As a result of with Ruby being at the house this week and them bringing their Nintendo Switch, I knew Henry wanted to hang out this week and Henry is a massive gamer. And as me, Ruby and my best friend were playing Mario Kart 8 Sunday night, I was considering asking Henry to come round so I could get used to them without my best friend being there.

Something that would be very useful for when they go back. Since I am concerned about spending time with Henry one-on-one when my best friend isn't down here in Canterbury.

Therefore, I asked Henry if he wanted to come round and I wanted to get ahead of this so I effectively ripped off the bandage. This is what I sent on Instagram:

"Hey, are you free anytime this week? Maybe Wednesday?

My housemate Reuben's down for the week and they brought their Nintendo Switch and I know you're a massive gamer. I was wondering if you wanted to come round, catch up and play games for a few hours.

And you're a friend so I want to be honest with you. So I have PTSD because I was raped back in April and it can cause me panic attacks, intense social anxiety and so on. So one-on-one stuff is really difficult for me especially with a guy, so that's why I invite you to group things. Yet I really like you as a friend so even when X goes back to Solihull for a month in a few weeks, I will try to do things with you. And if there's anything you want to do, please ask and feel free to invite me.

I don't need you to treat or see me differently but I'm just telling you this because if I say no to things or ever have a meltdown in front of you (granted I rarely have meltdowns in public), it's nothing against you, you've done nothing wrong and I think you're a great guy. I do want to be friends with you."

The point of this message was to be honest and explain why I might struggle when my best friend goes back home for a month, so he doesn't feel like I don't want to be friends with him.

Originally, I was slightly annoyed at Henry's response because he disregarded my PTSD comments completely. Yet my best friend pointed out, he is very autistic (like both of us) so he might not know how to respond at all and he doesn't come across as the most emotionally mature person, so it's fine he didn't react.

At the time I completely disagreed with my best friend, because I wanted at least an acknowledgement. Yet now it doesn't bother me because we've still been texting, he shared a funny reel with me yesterday and he still wants to hang out with me.

He still wants to be friends.

Honestly, him still wanting to be friends is actually all I care about because Henry is still a friend I can do things with, have fun and I can live a little. Another act of defiance against my rapist.

Tips For Managing New Friendships

On the whole, when I was telling Ruby about me disclosing my sexual violence experience to Henry, they mentioned the following "if (a new friend) doesn't take your disclosure well then they aren't a person you should be friends with".

That is seriously true to be fair because we can want all the new friends we want, but unless they're respectful, kind and caring then I don't want them to be my friends. I am not so desperate for new friends that I am going to allow myself to experience disrespect and negativity from idiots who pretend to be my friends.

Friends are people who support me, care about me and are interested in knowing more about me.

If people react badly and unsupportively about my rape then I don't want them in my life.

In addition, when you find people who do respect you, are interested in you and want to support you as you deepen your friendship over time. Then here are my tips based on my own experience at Week 14:

- Go at a pace that is comfortable for you.
- You don't have to do anything you don't want to do.
- You can bring another friend along for in-person hangouts or whatever.
- Only have the R conversation when you're ready and if you want to have it.
- When you hang out, pick places and options that make you feel comfortable.
- Enjoy it.

Personally, the idea of picking places and options that make you feel comfortable is really important to me. For example, I flat out will not hang out at Henry's house for months because my sexual violence happened at a new person's house in their living room. So the idea of going into Henry's living room is terrifying.

Furthermore, it will take me ages to do something with Henry one-on-one but being in public is also distressing. Therefore, I will need to decide what's going to make me more comfortable because at some point, I will have to carefully spend time with him one-on-one.

Overall, making new friends is very possible after experiencing sexual violence and it is something you absolutely should do when you are ready and when you meet someone you want to be friends with.

Finally, please put yourself first. Protect your mental health, do what you need to do and make sure you enjoy the process of making friends. New friends are a great way to live your life a little after what happened and it can be a very rewarding process, if not a little scary to us survivors.

But just like surviving sexual violence, making friends is certainly possible, and making friends can certainly be fun, funny and very enjoyable indeed.

WHY DIDN'T I REPORT MY SEXUAL ASSAULT?

There are a good amount of chapters in this book that I seriously avoid writing for as long as humanly possible, because as you can imagine, a lot of these chapters are really hard and draining for me to write. Yet I want to get this content written down, I want to process what happened and I want to help people.

Therefore, I mention a lot of my triggers throughout the book but whenever I heard about someone reporting their sexual violence, I get very triggered because I feel inadequate. I feel like a failure for not standing up for my fellow survivors, I feel like I'm the reason why my attacker *might* hurt other people and so on.

Of course, none of these thoughts are realistic at all because if my attacker hurts anyone else, it is because of His decision to hurt them, not me. And I am not a failure for not wanting to report it because I know because *how* everything happened, reporting it would be relatively pointless because I fly in the face of so many rape myths and I am far from the "perfect" rape victim.

Hell, I am not even a victim, I am a survivor.

As a result, I'm finally comfortable enough to write this chapter exactly 15 weeks after what happened to me, because last night I read a woman's article from Candan on this exact topic. And it gave me peace of mind that I had made the right decision for me.

Important Note:

Despite everything I am going to say in this chapter, you absolutely have to do what is right for you, your situation and your mental health. If you want to report your sexual violence to the police then DO IT, if reporting it to the university, your workplace, wherever will help you then please DO IT and if you want to report it to see what happens then DO IT.

Everything in this book is just my experience, and you will have a different experience to me, so if you want to report your sexual assault then please do it.

This chapter is just to explain why *I* didn't report it in case a fellow reader finds this reassuring and comforting in case they didn't want to report it. As well as if you do want to report it, then this might encourage you to do so, so you can challenge some of these ideas.

And most importantly, hopefully put the bastard who did this to you behind bars.

The Article From Last Night

I want to share the article that I read last night because it's another perspective on everything I've spoken about in this book and it helps to show that whoever you are, the vast majority of us sexual violence survivors experience the same thing over time. Therefore, the article is "I was raped at university. Here's why I never reported it" by Meghan Simard, and I've added in the website link at the end of this section before I talk about my own reasons.

Essentially, Meghan consistently tried to report her rape to her university, the police and a range of other places but no one took notes, no one took her seriously and no one wanted to press charges against her attacker.

Mainly because what happened to her didn't fit with the idea that a lot of people had about rape, so even if it went to court, it probably wouldn't have ended up with a guilty verdict because she wasn't the typical "victim" in laypeople's eyes.

Even though in reality, she actually was the typical rape survivor in terms of she did what happens in 99% of rapes and sexual assaults, and her reaction during her rape was the same as mine. I really do recommend reading the article if you're up for it.

Personally, it just annoys me that laypeople (and honestly I was probably no exception before I was raped too) are so convinced they know what rape is and they have such fixed ideas that you are only a rape survivor if you kicked, screamed and fought off your attacker. And when someone who was actually raped comes forward, the laypeople call them a liar because their experience goes against all the myths.

On a little side note, this is so common in clinical psychology when we have to deal with laypeople too. Some clients believe they know what therapy is, what mental health is and they know what they need to do to improve their mental health, but when clinical psychologists try to help them, some clients think we don't know what we're talking about. Just because how therapy actually works is different from the myths.

I flat out hate myths.

Anyway, there is one paragraph in the article I love because it sums up my life and how much I love my best friend because they support me so well. As well as I am really grateful Meghan has a much larger social support network than me and I hope she's doing better now.

"The rest of my school year was more or less a garbage fire. Attending university classes with newly developed, untreated, and severe PTSD is hard enough, but I also had to see my rapist regularly on and around campus. I am indebted to my friends who held my hands through panic attacks and to my family who picked up the phone in the middle of the night when all I wanted to do was die."

Source-

https://www.cbc.ca/news/canada/first-person-campus-sex-assault-1.6189141

On the whole, you can experience massive challenges from the healthcare, university and Criminal Justice System when it comes to reporting your rape. This should never happen, it is outrageous and it is flat out disgusting that the very systems that are meant to protect us are failing us survivors so badly.

However, there are initiatives and policies and survivors fighting to change this, so hopefully over time this will change. For now, I will stick to doing occasional podcast episodes and books on sexual violence in an effort to change people's minds and reveal the truth about sexual violence, but it is a very uncomfortable topic for a lot of people. And I lose a lot of listeners each time I try to do these topics, but I need to do them sparingly unfortunately.

Why I Did Not Report My Sexual Assault?

When it comes to how sexual violence investigations work, like everyone else, my knowledge is limited but because I watch a lot of crime dramas, and a goodish amount of True Crime programmes and some of those episodes featured rape, I had an okay understanding of what to expect.

I knew I was the physical evidence and I understood that the "worst" thing I could do was shower, clean my teeth and the rest. Yet I was in denial about what had happened to me was classed as sexual assault and sexual violence until two days after it had happened.

Furthermore, I think I knew it was sexual violence because I refused to shower and clean my teeth when I got home. Maybe I was thinking I would realise what had happened in the morning and I would report it then. Yet these were not conscious thoughts of what I was intending to do because I was pretending I was perfectly okay and nothing had happened whatsoever.

However, when I got up the next morning as you read earlier I was so distressed that I would have been happy to cut off my own dick, so I did have a shower and I washed away the evidence on me.

That was one reason why I didn't report it because there was no physical evidence left. In all honesty, I still have my boxers from that night and there is a small chance His spit is still on them but I am not going down that road.

Another reason why I decided not to report it was because I was far from the stereotypical rape victim that jurors would expect. I'm male for starters and in society there is the stupid myth that males do not get raped.

Therefore, I would have to go through the embarrassment and stigma and social judgment from everyone that I (someone born male at birth) "allowed" themselves to get raped. Like fuck did I allow myself to get raped, but it is still what people believe.

In this situation, the myths and misconceptions that people have about male rape and male victims were massive factors that stopped me from being safe enough to report it to the police. This was only confirmed and reinforced by the negative reactions I've had from certain important people in my life who blame me completely for what happened and they think I'm making up how badly this is affecting me.

Also, I'm gay and transgender non-binary so there are times when my opinion is hardly positive about the police considering the heavy bias they have against gay and trans people.

Moreover, I know more than enough about the criminal justice system from my forensic psychology interest to know that in court, the defence would have to call me a liar. Now I have been called a liar before by important people in my life and I have no desire whatsoever to be called that disgusting term again.

Moreover, when I was being raped, I now realise all I wanted to do was survive as well as I was so scared to make a wrong move that I didn't fight back when he did stuff. Since I did not want to "offend" him and for him to turn violent. I was just focusing on surviving but that reason flies in the face of all the rape myths and misconceptions. Therefore, whilst that is what the vast, vast majority of rape survivors do during their attack, the defence would eat me alive through their stupid questions. Like:

- Why didn't you fight back?
- Why didn't you scream?
- Why didn't you leave after he grabbed you the first time?
- Why didn't you report it that night?
- He never actually hit you or threatened you so why are you making up that you felt in danger? Are you too sensitive?
- And on and on and on.

As much as I want to say in a court of law that the defence can fuck off because I just wanted to survive and the posh twat of a defence barrister could never even imagine what being raped is like, I know that would hardly make me look good and contemptible.

The criminal justice system itself was another reason why I didn't report it.

Finally, my main issue with reporting what happened to me was simply a lack of other evidence. The entire case would be "They said, he said," because I can't even prove I was actually there that night and we engaged in sex.

My rapist deleted the Grindr messages by the time I got home because I was going to take screenshots of them. Then without the messages there were no signs he wanted to have sex with me and I have no idea how you prove it wasn't consensual.

I've tried researching it online but consent is a very hard legal area to define and I don't know how you prove that the sexual activity I was forced to have against my will wasn't consent. I said it firmly wasn't but he would say it was (because he would have to unless he wanted to go to prison).

Therefore, without those Grindr messages, I have no idea how you prove I was there that night, let alone that he never asked for my consent, that he grabbed me against my Will a second time after I had said no and the rest.

There is no evidence that I could submit to a court of law so that's why I didn't report it because there would be no point.

How Has This "Decision" Affected Me Over The Months?

Firstly, I wouldn't call this a "decision" at all because a decision makes it sound like I had more than one option. I could have reported it but I have no evidence and there are other reasons above why I didn't report it, and I know there is a risk I could be charged with force reporting of a crime. And there would be a lot of dicks online that would twist my story and make it sound like I was "yet another" person making up rape stories.

In reality, so, so few people make up rape stories that it was outrageous that people think individuals would lie about this disgusting event.

Anyway, me not reporting what happened to me wasn't something I could control and because of the lack of evidence I couldn't take another option.

Over the past few months, me not being to report it didn't bother me until the end of Week 13 because it just started to annoy me and I felt a little grief towards that was yet something my rapist denied me and took away from me.

Also, before Week 13, it only played on my mind whenever I would hear news reports about how great, brave and courageous a sexual violence survivor was for reporting it to the police. I completely agree that survivor was amazing, especially because there was one time when it was a child) but I always felt like shit after hearing that. Then I would have a few panic attacks and so on.

At this current point in time at Week 15, I'm relatively okay about not being able to report it, because I'm still struggling. I am trying to move on, I know I couldn't handle the criminal justice system and I don't want to get called a liar by the defence.

And I'm at peace with the decision that my rapist might never see the inside of a courtroom and I will never get justice, but here's the thing. I'm alive.

I am alive.

Sure, as you'll see in future chapters, my rapist has taken so bloody much from me over the past few months and he will continue to interfere in my life so damn much. He has caused PTSD, severe social anxiety, suicidality and so on.

Yet I will recover, I will live a good life and I will date in the future. I have no idea how long that will be and who it will be with but I will not allow my rapist to ruin my life. He can make it as difficult as he wants because of that single outrageous event, and he will cause me many difficulties going forward.

Yet I am alive, I am sort of living and I am slowly accomplishing stuff over time. And I will continue to slowly get better at a snail's pace.

So yes, I am okay with not reporting my rape because I am alive and I am going to keep living in spite that what that bastard did. And each positive thing I do in my life is a middle-finger up to that bastard and everything he did to me.

Conclusion: Over To You

When it comes to deciding whether to report your experience or not, I know this is not an easy decision and you will have a million questions racing around inside your head.

You will be processing what the hell just happened to you, you will be wondering about how your friends and family will see you, and what the response will be from different areas of society including what your experience of the criminal justice system will be like.

Just stop and take a breath.

I strongly believe that the only aspect you need to be thinking about when you're thinking about whether to report it or not is you.

Just focus on yourself.

I would suggest you think about what do you need, what do you want and how are you going to feel if you report it versus not reporting it.

If you want to report it then you absolutely should and more power to you, because you are more courageous than I could ever be and I admire you for that.

However, if you decide not to report then that is absolutely okay too. It is what I've done, it is what 95% of survivors do and that's okay. It doesn't mean what happened to you matters or impacts you any less, and it still means you have a lot of healing to do.

Whatever decision you make, me and the rest of us survivors will support you because this is one of the hardest decisions you will ever have to make. And this is such a personal choice that is decided by a million different factors that only you can make this decision.

Let me repeat that, only you can decide whether to report what happened to you. No one else can or should ever decide it for you.

No one.

YOU HAVE THE RIGHT TO BE VULNERABLE AND CONFUSED

Originally I put this on my list of chapter ideas a few weeks ago so maybe around Week 12/ 13 because I felt so vulnerable all the time, as fragile as a child and I really didn't like this feeling.

However, once I accepted this feeling dealing with everything got a little nicer because sexual violence is so traumatic, so foul and so disgusting that it will rattle you to your very core. Hence, you will feel very vulnerable and fragile like a child because you might not know what your triggers are so you might be reacting to the so-called smallest of things and then you become anxious about becoming triggered and dealing with all the panic attacks and other trauma responses.

Nonetheless, I want to stress that this is okay. You need to remember that what you went through was traumatic, horrible and it will scar you but you can and will heal if you get professional help and you work through the trauma.

You will feel extremely vulnerable and fragile for a wide range of reasons. Including Post-Traumatic Stress Disorder so if you develop the condition, you'll be experiencing flashbacks, severe anxiety and nightmares so you'll be constantly on edge and hyperalert. This only makes you feel more vulnerable and fragile.

In addition, you might feel vulnerable and fragile because you might be scared that your attacker will hurt or harm you again or you might be scared other people won't believe you. Then it is this sense of fear that makes you feel vulnerable.

Personally, my main feelings of being vulnerable and fragile come from my anxiety and utter fear that someone else will hurt me again, and there is a minor concern that my rapist will find me again and do what he did to me again over and over.

The fear is where most of my psychological distress comes from.

Moreover, something I seriously struggle with is the sense of loss of control because rape is an awful act of violence that takes away our sense of control over our lives and our bodies. Thus, the lack of control that we feel leads us to feel helpless and very vulnerable.

Another reason why survivors feel vulnerable is because a lot of us struggle with guilt and shame even though what happened to us was never our fault. The fault only lays with the bastard that did this to us. And as I discovered a few weeks ago when me and my best friend moved in together, the feelings of guilt can be crippling and they are another major source of vulnerability in my experience.

By the way, I do expand upon these points in different ways in other chapters, but right now I want to give you the information.

Penultimately, the social stigma, myths and misconceptions surrounding rape is another reason why survivors feel a lot of vulnerability. Since the social stigma can lead to a lack of support and for us to feel isolated. This is definitely an issue I face because my best friend is literally all I have in terms of social support and as much as I love my best friend for always being there, I still want other people to support me.

Finally, physical injuries are another reason why survivors can feel fragile because if their assault included them getting injured physically then this only adds to the pain they experience. As a result, the physical healing process, something that sadly takes time, can be painful in itself but it can be a painful reminder of the trauma too.

On the whole, in this section of the chapter, we've looked at a wide range of reasons explaining why survivors feel vulnerable and fragile and I want you to know that feeling this way is okay.

It feels horrible, you might feel like a child,

you might feel weak and you might feel like you will never be strong or normal again. Yet I promise you that when you process things over time, when you accept yourself and your trauma responses then things get easier. This might take you weeks or months like it did for me, but you can get there and you can start to feel a little stronger over time.

And just remember, each time you get stronger, each time you experience joy and each time you can feel a little less fragile is a major act of defiance against what your attacker did to you.

Feeling vulnerable and fragile is a part of the healing process, and it never defines you.

HOW DOES SEXUAL VIOLENCE IMPACT EMPLOYABILITY AND PERSONAL FINANCES?

Last night one of my dear friends sat down with me and my best friend and told us some very personal things about their mental health, their past trauma and what had happened to them about a decade ago. I knew something had happened to them because of our conversations throughout this week and I had been laying the groundwork so my friend felt safe enough to talk about what was bothering them.

And last night, they thankfully trusted us enough to talk about it.

It was a very personal, deep and emotional conversation that brought all of us closer as friends, and the future should be a lot easier for this friend now whenever they stay with us.

However, I realised something very troubling during that conversation. I don't have the same level of empathy and emotions as I once did before I was raped. I still love this friend, I still said a lot of useful things and I've shown all week how I would happily move heaven and earth for them.

Nonetheless, when they were revealing what had happened to them, how it had impacted them and how they were refusing to talk about it and get professional help the one time I gently pressed them for it. I couldn't help but feel a little less empathetic for them because they couldn't see how much this event was hurting them, damaging their mental health and reducing them to a shell of the great friend I had spent the week with.

I understand this makes me sound like a bad person and a very bad friend. Yet there were tons of similarities between the symptoms me and my friend were experiencing. My friend wasn't raped but it was still trauma and they were having a lot of trauma responses.

And I understand this is just my psychology degree, psychology books and podcast that have helped me to understand how important talking, processing and getting professional help is for people. Yet it bugged me that I could see how much my friend was struggling and they didn't want to get help. They wanted to pretend it never happened and they were denying everything.

It brought up a lot of other feelings, including a lot of distress for me because hearing about their trauma experience was difficult for me. It triggered a lot of my own trauma about my rape and it caused a lot of things to pile up so I didn't sleep last night.

Considering I want to be a clinical psychologist in the future and improve lives, decrease psychological distress and give clients more adaptive coping mechanisms where I will have to hear a lot about other people's mental health, this is a major problem.

Leading us onto the topic of this chapter. How Does Sexual Violence Impact Employability And Personal Finances?

After I panicked about me not being able to be a clinical psychologist anymore as well as work in the mental health sector, I calmed down and I decided to look at the facts and any academic research on employment after sexual violence. There isn't a lot of research on the topic but I managed to find an excellent paper that I'll share below. It's very accessible, easy to understand, and I highly recommend reading it if you want to learn more.

Loya R. M. (2015). Rape as an Economic Crime: The Impact of Sexual Violence on Survivors' Employment and Economic Well-Being. *Journal of interpersonal violence*, *30*(16), 2793–2813. https://doi.org/10.1177/0886260514554291

Honestly, I almost cried reading this paper about four times because it revealed some hard truths about employment after experiencing sexual violence. Therefore, I'll take you through the results of the academic paper and then I'll explain my own situation.

The paper mentions how after experiencing sexual violence, employment can become very difficult for survivors for a range of reasons. For example, as mentioned previously, a lot of survivors go onto develop Post-Traumatic Stress Disorder including severe anxiety and flashbacks, and they experience other mental health difficulties or conditions. Such as depression, anxiety, substance abuse disorder amongst others.

As a result, the mental health impacts of sexual violence can cause survivors to feel the need to quit their jobs, especially if they were attacked on the way to or from work or if their attacker was someone they worked with. Also, a decrease in mental health can lead to decreased job performance so the survivor ends up getting fired in the end for no fault of their own.

In addition, the paper mentioned that survivors who told their bosses about being a survivor of sexual violence did better than the survivors who did not. Since the bosses and leadership team were able to attribute the signs of the survivor's mental health and decreasing performance to the sexual violence and not the survivor being bad at their job.

Moreover, the paper explains how dealing with the aftermath and mental health difficulties of sexual violence leads to a lot of costs over time. For example, needing days, weeks or years off work to recover, see doctors, liaising with the police and other members of the criminal justice system and so on. This cost or loss of money only increases if hospital and doctor's visits are needed, even more so in places that don't have free healthcare like the United Kingdom at the time of writing.

In addition, the aftermath of sexual violence can make some survivors need to quit work altogether because it is too much for their mental health, it is too triggering and they cannot hold down a job. For instance, the paper mentions how one woman who was raped 30 years ago has only been able to do minimum wage work ever since. As well as another woman had to do temporary work for 3 years after her rape because her mental health couldn't handle doing more than a week's work at a time.

This is why survivors who lived in states with progressive public benefits managed to do reasonably well, because they could get income support even if they were raped by an intimate partner.

On the other hand, the paper did explain how survivors who managed to access mental health support as well as counselling for their assault did manage to do better than those who couldn't access support after their sexual violence experience. For example, the woman who's sadly still doing minimum wage work after 30 years was never able to afford counselling for her rape, so she was never really able to recover. Whereas another woman who was able to afford counselling did *better* over time and she managed to return to full-time employment even though she's never managed to return to the same levels of earnings before her rape.

This is why counselling and mental health support is so critical, and more must be done to make it available to all survivors.

A final discovery in the paper that I want to talk about is the idea of Major and Modest Trajectory Shifts within a survivor's life. Due to it's very common for a survivor's life to change a lot after their sexual assault so their life effectively changes trajectory, so they don't end up doing what they wanted to do before they were raped.

One example in the paper is that one survivor needed to delay herself going to college by three years because she wasn't ready to do so before then. Another woman had to delay herself going to college by a year and the paper explained this took a year away from her future high earnings from her.

These two examples show you what a Modest Trajectory Shift looks like because these were temporary delays in what a survivor wants to do. As well as the definition the paper uses is as follows:

"modest trajectory shifts or delays, which are changes to survivors' employment or economic stability from which they eventually recovered and returned to their prior level of economic well-being."

This is a type of shift that makes me very happy and almost hopeful for the future because it shows that given the right amount of support (and a bunch of other factors), a survivor can go back to what they wanted to do before their rape in the end. Thankfully, modest shifts show that sexual violence doesn't have to change your employability forever, there is hope that you can reclaim your career choices given the right professional support and time.

In addition, there are lots of survivors who unfortunately experience major trajectory shifts, and this is something I am flat out terrified about. This is how the paper defines these types of shifts:

"major shifts, employment consequences that permanently changed survivors' occupational or earning pathways, 2806 Journal of Interpersonal Violence 30(16) including long-term unemployment, career change, and permanent disability. A lawyer explained major trajectory shifts this way: "It really spirals. Like I've talked to clients, literally, who 20 years later after the assault . . . the trajectory of their life is so totally different than it was the 10 seconds before the rape happened" (Provider 100)."

As you can imagine, this quote made me cry my eyes out because I'll talk about this more in a moment, but it goes to show that sexual violence can seriously interfere with every single aspect of our lives. Also, considering I have a future career in mind, I am terrified that I am never going to be able to do that, help people and improve lives.

I want to do my future career but I am scared that my sexual violence experience will stop that from ever happening.

How Has My Rape Impacted My Employability?

The major caveat to this section is that I am a Masters student but I still need to earn money, I am still a business owner and I am still a student ambassador with the university.

Therefore, it was only last night hearing my friend talk about their trauma experience and reading that academic paper that I realised just how badly my experience of sexual violence has impacted my employment over the past few months. In terms of being a student ambassador, it hasn't really impacted me too much because I am still doing the work, I am still signing up for work opportunities and Outreach still loves me because I always do an amazing job.

That is what external observers see.

In reality, I still love Outreach work, I love interacting with students and I really enjoy the wide range of work I get to be involved in to promote higher education. As well as give young people from disadvantaged, poor backgrounds hope that anyone can go to university regardless of their postcode.

However, I still have extreme social anxiety, panic attacks and I get triggered a lot at Outreach events. For example, I've had to hide in toilets to calm down at times, I've had to avoid certain students and teachers from outside the university like the plague and Thursday was very rough and you can see how bad I was in the following WhatsApp message:

"Mythbuster session was really good and I enjoyed it. There were only two people which is a shame but still.

Except the guy was fat, had long brown hair, jeans and a brown checked overshirt. He looked like a younger version of my rapist. Panicked a little in the session but managed to keep it under wraps. I've been sitting on the toilet for 20 minutes trying to calm down and I'm about to head back.

I'm going co-op now for some stuff now."

Therefore, as you can see this was a work situation because I was getting paid to deliver a Mythbuster session to a bunch of students (only two signed-up to the session but money is money and it was fun) but I was really distressed by the end of it.

And sometimes Outreach work does knock me out for a few days afterwards and sometimes it can trigger me for days. Thursday did kickstart a whole bunch of smaller events that led to me not sleeping last night, so I am very glad that Outreach work isn't 40 hours a week and I can pick and choose when I work, but that doesn't make it any easier.

Furthermore, when it comes to my writing business, this has been heavily damaged by my sexual violence. I have had to take a lot of time off to recover, to mentally and emotionally process what the hell happened to me and this all has a knock-on effect with my writing. I have written a lot less than I would have liked to at this point in the year, and this has a massive impact on my future income.

That's why I am so thankful and grateful

for my readers because you buying books helps to support me.

Then this lack of writing and lack of business work really negatively impacts my mental health, so I'm dealing with bad mental health on two fronts. The lack of writing and business because this is what I flat out love and it makes me so happy, and I'm dealing with the rape itself.

I have no idea how much money I've lost because of a lack of writing and business work as I try to process my sexual assault, but by the time I'm "okay" (whatever that means), it will be a lot unfortunately.

Finally, if we look towards the future and my possible career as a clinical psychologist where I get to help people improve their lives, give them control back and give them more adaptive coping mechanisms, then I am scared.

I used to be fine hearing about people's mental health, trauma and their maladaptive coping mechanisms. I used to be able to listen to these conversations in such a caring, compassionate and understanding way that I could offer really good tips, advice and other things to my friends and family. Yet I can only do this now with my best friend.

If I talk or listen to anyone else about their mental health and trauma then I find it distressing, triggering and all my rape stuff gets triggered over and over again. Hell, I tend to feel all the horrible physical sensations of me getting raped multiple times and my brain twists it horrifically so last night I had intrusive thoughts about my best friend beating and raping me.

I think listening to my friend talk about their trauma and bad mental health was the thing that broke my back and led to a terrible night of bad sleep.

I cannot do that every day and every night, but if I wanted to work as a clinical psychologist then I would have to. Especially when it came to building up my clinical experience when I would really need to work full-time to try and get as much experience as possible.

Last night, I went outside to process everything I had read in the academic paper and I really did cry.

I know not everyone reading this book will be psychology students or psychology professionals, but I flat out love clinical psychology. I love how it gives us the theories, the therapies and the interventions to transform people's lives. We can give them hope in their darkest hour, we can give them new ways to deal with stressful situations and we work with clients at every step of the way because our clients are proud, courageous and they deserve our full respect.

That is why clinical psychologists work so hard to improve the lives of our clients because they're great people that want to live their lives and we can support them doing that.

So the very idea that my rapist, that fat, ugly bastard could take that away from me is fucking outrageous. I flat out hate the idea that he could take away my ability to help so many amazing people who are suffering or are in need of psychological support.

I can deal with him impacting me, raping me and sabotaging my life. But how fucking dare he impact the lives of other innocent people who have nothing to do with him.

In the future, I should be helping them, supporting them and giving them hope, but if I cannot do that because of the hurt and trauma he has inflicted upon me then I hope he suffers somehow in the end.

I cannot stand leaving innocent people to suffer and live in pain, but unfortunately, if this is a major trajectory shift for me then I am concerned that I will not be the one to help clients in the future.

And that kills me inside.

You only have to read my books, listen to my podcast and talk to me in person to know how much I love clinical psychology and I want to be a clinical psychologist in the future.

However, unless I can find a way to work in mental health in a wide range of settings and be okay listening to trauma, psychological distress and maybe even the worst of humanity without it destroying my own mental health instantly then I am scared I cannot do the career I love.

And if that is the case then I know I will have to grieve that as well as everything else I am grieving as part of my rape.

Personally, if clinical psychology isn't available to me as a career path, I have considered going into academia and focusing on research. I do enjoy research these days and I do have ideas for a lot of different mental health studies for rape survivors and transgender individuals. I would enjoy researching my ideas, writing up papers and getting academically published.

This would require me to get a PhD so I would have the safety and security that being at the university gives me, as well as I could continue my Outreach work for another 3 or 4 years.

However, I know I don't actually want this, I have never thought about this before my rape and even for months after my rape I never considered or wanted this. I have always thought that a PhD was seriously not something I want and I do not want to work in academia because it is not my world.

This is just a rape reaction and it is not what I want for my life.

In a small way, it's funny because it was only the day before I met up with a friend I haven't seen since my rape and he asked me about future careers after my Masters. My words were basically "in an ideal world, it's still become an assistant psychologist, gain my years of experience and then apply for the doctorate of clinical psychology so I can become a fully qualified clinical psychologist. But in reality, it's what job I can hold down because I doubt I can do full-time work at the moment,"

It's weird that I already knew that deep down about how much I was struggling, hurting and not being able to function.

Thankfully, I should have my rape counselling starting next month but this is still hard. I want this to be a modest shift in my career trajectory but I'm concerned that it isn't, and maybe my rapist stole my chance of doing the career I flat out love and the one I've been working so hard for years to be able to do.

Yet I am not giving up on my future career without a fight.

Conclusion: Over To You

At the end of this chapter, I want you to know that if you're struggling with your employment after your experience of sexual violence that is normal, expected and if you get professional help, maybe talk to your employer and get other forms of support then things might be okay in the end.

This includes accommodations for you so

you can get the support you need and stay employed. For example, you might need extra time off if you need to talk to the lawyers or police or you might need to work from home for two days a week so you can work and get paid but you can look after yourself too.

Personally, reading this section within the academic paper was a massive relief because at the time of writing, tomorrow I have training for the Year 10 Residential summer school where over 50 14- and 15-year-olds will be staying at the university in halls for three days and two nights to experience university life. I'll be with other ambassadors but I am extremely nervous.

This will be a very intense four days for me because I have the training on the Monday and the summer school starts at 8 am on Tuesday and runs straight through until 5 pm on Thursday. Sure, I get a 1-hour or 2 hour break per day but that is it.

That is not a lot of time for me to look after myself if (when) something triggers me.

Additionally, I am very nervous about there being a student at the summer school with the same name as my rapist. Especially if this student is in my corridor that I have to look after, because I refuse, I just can't say his name over and over again this week when I'm looking after students.

I don't think I can handle that, but thankfully Outreach does love me, all the staff working at the summer school think I am amazing (their words actually) and I know they will support me. Therefore, this academic paper was a great reminder that it is okay to talk and ask for accommodations.

That is exactly what I will do this week if I need to. Please do the same for yourself if you need it.

Never suffer in silence.

Trajectory Shifts

You might experience a modest or major trajectory shift in your career and that is normal too. I understand you might be angry, rageful and you will grieve for whatever you feel like you have loss. I know I will in the end too.

However, the same guidance applies when dealing with employment issues than when it comes to mental health. Please be kind to yourself, be compassionate towards yourself and get professional help so you can work towards your recovery. Once your recovery is well underway your employment and job might get easier and your economic wellbeing might improve too.

To wrap up the chapter, here's some unofficial tips and advice you might want to do:

- Think about talking to your employer about what happened so accommodations can be made.
- Get professional mental health support
- Think about what would happen if you experience a modest and major trajectory shift.
- Process your feelings about your employment situation.
- Read the academic paper below.

Loya R. M. (2015). Rape as an Economic Crime: The Impact of Sexual Violence on Survivors' Employment and Economic Well-Being. *Journal of interpersonal violence*, *30*(16), 2793–2813. https://doi.org/10.1177/0886260514554291

IF YOU DON'T DEAL WITH TRAUMA, IT WILL DEAL WITH YOU

It's been at least three days since I've had a good night's sleep. I am currently emotionally and physically exhausted, I am a little depressed and I am terrified about going to sleep tonight because whenever I stop doing something and I lay down, I get intrusive thoughts and half-dreams about rape.

It is very rare that I write a chapter from the outset intending it to be for two different audiences that will find this content very useful. Therefore, this next chapter will be written with aspiring and qualified clinical psychologists as well as other people interested in psychology, and my fellow sexual violence survivors in mind. Since this next chapter will be packed full of useful insights for both groups of individuals.

This chapter focuses on the importance of processing and dealing with your trauma and realising you cannot deny your traumatic event ever happened. As well as for the psychologists reading this chapter, this chapter focuses on the lived experience of people who have gone through traumatic events, and the chapter helps to shine a light on some of the avoidance techniques that people with trauma go through.

In addition, another reason why I am using this chapter for both audiences is because I want to show survivors of sexual violence that psychologists only want to help you, support and there is no magic going on. In other words, a lot of the myths and misconceptions you have about therapy are just that. Anything weird and negative you've heard about psychologists and therapy almost certainly isn't true.

Overall, in the rest of the chapter, you're going to learn the heartbreaking experience I had with a friend recently that led me to write about this topic. Then I'll talk about why I allow myself to deal with my rape no matter how hard and distressing it is (and why I sometimes don't, which is not a good thing but I am still human) as well as through the chapter, I'll be adding in details and paragraphs for survivors and psychologists alike.

This is a very eye-opening and flat out critical chapter to read and enjoy.

What Recent Experience Made Me Want To Talk About This Topic?

I know I mentioned I haven't slept in three nights and this was a tiny factor in that massive problem. Since me and my best friend sat one of our friends down the other house because they were distressed, struggling and I had been laying the groundwork down all week helping our friend to realise that our house (they'll be our housemate in September) is a safe space and they can talk about whatever is troubling them.

Three nights ago, their last night at our house for a while, they told us about their trauma, what had happened to them and a whole bunch of other things that I was surprised about. I wasn't surprised something was causing their bad mental health because the conditions and experiences and even odd phrases they mentioned in passing made me know something had happened. Yet my friend wasn't telling us what had happened and I never pushed it.

Thankfully, they felt safe around me and my best friend to open up and explain everything.

However, the reason why this experience made me want to talk about this topic is because the trauma my friend experienced happened roughly 8 years ago. Now aspiring and qualified clinical psychologists know that to deal with trauma, time does NOT heal all wounds as well as it takes processing, professional help and talking openly and honestly about your trauma for you to heal.

Nonetheless, this friend, my dear sweet friend who I often refer to as a child and a baby because they are so young (okay, they're 4 years younger than me but they're very baby-faced and innocent) has believed for the past 8 years that if they simply didn't talk about it. Everything would magically be healed and they would be fine.

That is not how trauma works.

And what makes the whole situation even more troubling and concerning is that my friend was scared to death about talking about their traumatic experience. They kept saying how talking about it was "bad", "wrong" and they shouldn't talk about it because it's only going to get them hurt.

My friend had internalised so much shame, guilt and pain about the traumatic experience that they were refusing to talk about it for 8 years. And even when I gently and very subtly asked about going to therapy (which is free at the university), they didn't want to do that because it would make it real, it would involve talking about it which is "bad" in their eyes and it would involve telling others about their shame and guilt.

Yet from my perspective, as a friend, I hated seeing how shattered my friend was. This is the type of friend that is pure innocence, so kind and the person who you can laugh with about everything. My friend is always there for others, always kind and they never have a bad word to say about anyone.

My friend is the type of person who you want to protect at all costs because they are so innocent, so kind and so good. They are the sort of person the world needs more of.

However, three nights ago, my friend was so shattered, so broken and they were crying so much that I basically didn't recognise them. I could see their distress as they cried, I could hear their terror in their broken voice and I could feel them shaking on their end of the sofa.

They were really anxious, scared and they were having a major breakdown.

And yet my friend still believes not talking about their trauma, not processing it and not dealing with their trauma in any way is a good idea.

Me and my best friend gently and subtly suggested ways like therapy, talking about it whenever with us, learning about trauma responses and trying to understand why they've been depressed, anxious and occasionally suicidal for 8 years. Yet my friend doesn't want to do that and my friend is suffering so much.

On the whole, I understand why this is scary for my friend, and I am extremely privileged to know the power of psychotherapy and processing trauma because of my degree. As well as to some extent I am just as guilty of this when it came to my child abuse and trauma, I didn't get therapy until I had a breakdown in August 2023.

Nonetheless, my point is that my friend understands how badly they are struggling.

They have crippling depression, anxiety and that only makes their physical conditions worse. They understand this all links back to their trauma but they are refusing to process, talk and heal from their trauma in any way, shape or form.

They simply want to pretend their trauma never happened.

And I can see the result as clear as day now.

My friend is continuing to decide not to deal with their trauma, so their trauma is making them process the event in the worst possible way. And the saddest thing is that I know this isn't going to stop anytime soon unless my friend processes what happened to them in therapy and starts their healing journey.

Note: I highly recommend survivors read the section below as well.

<u>Why Is This Important For Clinical Psychologists To Understand?</u>

This is going to be a shorter section because I've already told in a range of places, including The Psychology World Podcast, my other books and my clinical psychology reflection books, about how clients can be resistant to processing their trauma and mental health.

Largely this connects to the topic of capacity to change where a client needs to be motivated and already to undergo the therapeutic process so they can talk, process and ultimately heal.

We can give clients all the tools and techniques that they need to improve their lives, decrease their psychological distress and develop new adaptive coping mechanisms. Yet unless they have the drive to bring about lasting therapeutic change and they put the effort in to use these tools and techniques, then the therapy will fail.

And that is heartbreaking.

Currently, therapy would be useless for my friend because they don't have the drive, motivation or capacity to change. They could go to therapy but they aren't at a point in their life where they would be engaged or motivated to let us work *with* them to improve their lives and start their healing journey.

My friend would be too resistant for therapy for any good to come from it.

Which is heartbreaking because all of us aspiring and qualified clinical psychologists are driven by our desire, need and I think it's a fundamental drive of our profession to help people. We know clinical psychology and different forms of psychotherapy can be immensely powerful and they can and do help millions of people each year.

Therapy has the power to transform lives for the better and our clinical work is some of the most rewarding work there is, in my opinion.

Because we make a difference using our expertise, working with clients and helping them to improve their own lives with the tools and techniques we give them.

Therefore, when someone is in distress like my friend and they are so clearly struggling and they would benefit immensely from therapy, and they don't want it, think it's valuable or a worthwhile use of their time. It is honestly soul-crushing.

I would love my friend to go to therapy because it means they could heal, they could feel better and they could feel safe around me and my best friend. Yet they don't want therapy and I cannot make them go to therapy as much as I would like to.

As a result, as their friend, this makes me sad because I want them to be okay but they aren't allowing themselves to process what's happening. So their trauma and brain is making them process it for them with devastating consequences.

Overall, whilst I lengthened this section so I could bust some myths about therapy and show to survivors therapy is a kind and collaborative process, my point is that when it comes to clinical work. We can give a client everything they need to improve their lives but unless they are willing to put in the work and have the motivation to change their lives then there is only so much we can do.

And it is heartbreaking but we are not miracle workers or gods or goddesses, we are just normal humans with human powers and a lot of psychology knowledge behind us.

We cannot make someone do anything they aren't ready for. Just be aware of that, that sometimes a person will not seek out therapy when they're struggling.

But when they are ready, we must always be ready to welcome them into our therapy room so we can help them improve their lives, decrease their psychological distress and help them develop more adaptive coping mechanisms so they can heal.

Maybe for the first time in their life.

<u>Why Do I Allow Myself To Process My Rape?</u>

If you're reading this in my book written for rape survivors (it doesn't even have a working title at the moment to be fair) then you'll be aware that in basically every chapter of the book, I explain how my rape negatively impacts my mental health, how it causes me extreme distress and I explore different aspects of my experience as a rape survivor.

I never really try to stop myself processing this stuff no matter how distressing it is. Although because I am human and I might be an aspiring clinical psychologist as well as a psychology author and podcaster, but I am still human. There are times when I do actively avoid processing stuff, like I sometimes only go to sleep when I'm so exhausted I can't process them in bed.

And you know what happened, if I delay processing an emotion, an experience or a trigger. It turns up at the next opportunity and it's ten times worse.

Therefore, I allow myself to process my rape and all the extremely distressing and wide ranging impacts it has on me because I want to heal. I can only heal if I allow myself to process what the hell happened to me, and I need to process this event by thinking about it, talking about it with my best friend and me writing about in this book. As well as hopefully starting next month at the time of writing, I will finally be having rape counselling so I can talk about it with a professional.

That will be brilliant.

As a result, as distressing as everything is, I know if I want to be okay, if I want to get to a point where I can live my life and have a boyfriend (the idea of that made me really smile) and live a relatively normal life then I have no choice but to process my rape.

For example, right now, I get horrific intrusive thoughts and times when I'm in bed and I'm in a light dream state and I imagine that people in my life that I'm even subtly attracted to are beating me, raping me and then killing me. I know this is me processing my fears and the emotions I was experiencing during my rape, and I fucking hate when this happens.

It's why I haven't slept much in three days,

However, I could be extremely unhealthy and go to bed at 2 am and get up at 7 am so I was purposefully so tired I cannot think about these thoughts. Yet I know this will have a worse impact on my physical and mental health over time.

I need to process this stuff as much as I can and I can process it more in therapy. And I am getting better and I am slowly healing over these 15 weeks (the time since my rape. In fact, it's 15 weeks and 2 days) so allowing yourself time to process stuff does help.

There are a lot of things I used to get extremely triggered by that I don't anymore. For example, whilst I have still have chronically bad social anxiety basically whenever I go outside and whenever I go somewhere I haven't been to before, I can get on the London metro system (the Tube) without having a full-on meltdown in public and crying my eyes out.

That is progress.

Overall, I will always hate every single little thing that bastard of a rapist has caused me to experience because it is so distressing and it wrecks my mental health so badly. Yet I am not going to avoid processing this trauma because I can see how badly it is affecting me and I don't want this to affect me for the rest of my life.

I know I cannot process my rape fully until I get my rape counselling next month (there was a 3-month waiting list) but I can take small steps to help me in the meantime. Like talking to my best friend, writing this book and researching and thinking about rape myself.

I can see how badly it's impacting and destroying my friend's mental and physical health. I don't want that for myself and as I keep supporting my friend and gently pushing them towards therapy over time. I hope that I can fully process my rape and I heal so I can live a full, relatively normal life that involves love, going outside and just living how people who haven't been raped do.

That is my dream, and I will only reach that dream by processing my rape myself and not allowing my rape to force me to process it in the only destructive way possible.

Conclusion: Why Is This Important For Survivors?

The purpose of this chapter flat out wasn't to say processing trauma was easy if you decide to do it yourself. That also isn't how trauma works because your brain will surprise you with intrusive thoughts, flashbacks and a whole range of other distressing mental health difficulties. Thus, the point of this chapter wasn't to say processing trauma was easy, that was the last thing this chapter would ever try to say.

Instead the point of this chapter was to highlight how rape is extremely distressing and it can damage your mental health in very scary ways. For example, earlier today, I was paralysed with fear for an hour because I had the intrusive thought that was my best friend's brother (who I have never actually met but I saw a topless photo of them yesterday and they have a great body) and a fellow university student who I'm working with this week were taking turns raping me.

For basically 65 minutes I had to live through the intrusive thoughts and physical sensations of two people who I find attractive raping me and occasionally beating me when my mind said no.

That is how distressing rape can be at times and processing this stuff is not easy.

No one will ever say processing is easy.

Nonetheless, in the long term, you have to process your sexual violence, and you need to take steps towards facilitating this processing. At first you might only want to talk to close friends then you might talk to a therapist and other people.

I would highly recommend that you talk to a therapist specialising in rape as soon as possible because that professional support is flat out critical in trauma recovery.

Just please make sure you take steps to deal with your trauma no matter how scary they seem. They never have to be big steps because they can range from you writing about your thoughts, feelings and your sexual violence to talking with close, trusted friends to seeing a therapist.

Just start your healing journey please somehow, and take steps towards processing what the hell happened to you.

Please don't be like my dear, sweet, innocent friend who breaks my heart by suffering, struggling and having extremely distressing thought spirals but not taking any steps towards healing.

You can heal if you seek out support.

Don't deny yourself healing. You deserve to heal because you are worthy, you are loved and there are people who care about you.

HOW TO CHANGE NEGATIVE SELF-TALK TO POSITIVE SELF-TALK AFTER SEXUAL VIOLENCE?

This is definitely a chapter that reveals that whilst I have a degree in psychology focusing on mental health, I am currently a Masters student in clinical psychology (mental health) and I live and breathe mental health through my podcast, I am still human at the end of the day. As well as just because I *know* all of this psychological knowledge about how our self-talk impacts our mental health, it doesn't mean I follow it.

Thankfully, I do now and my mental health is a lot better.

As a result, after rape and experiencing sexual violence, us survivors can have very negative self-talk. For example, we can call ourselves useless, pathetic, weak and a lot of other very negative words that are not healthy and it doesn't do anything good for our mental health.

What Is Self-Talk And Why Is It Important?

In fact, whilst I cannot go into too much depth about our self-talk impacts our mental health because this isn't a strict psychology book. Our self-talk impacts our feelings of self-esteem and self-worth so this leads to how we feel about ourselves. Therefore, if we talk negatively about ourselves then we feel down and we hate ourselves. Whereas if we talk positively we feel better about ourselves and it improves our mental health.

This is one of the reasons why you might notice a shift in language in the book towards the third month after my assault, because this is when my self-talk became more positive. I had to change the language I used to describe myself and who I am so I could improve my mental health and focus more on healing, instead of hating myself.

Moreover, this is why I prefer the term "survivor" instead of "victim". Since unfortunately, because of our society and the culture we live in, the term "victim" has a lot of negative connotations. For example, weakness, victim-blaming and it is a very disempowering term. Thus, "survivor" is a more helpful term as this has connotations of strength, courage and empowerment. Something that all rape survivors need to realise because we are strong, we are brave and we are empowered to deal with what happened to us.

So please use the term "survivor" instead to describe yourself, because you have survived. Believe me, I know at times your mental health will make it seem like you haven't survived your sexual assault at all. Yet you are alive and you have survived so you are a strong survivor.

Finally, a lot of rape survivors develop negative self-talk because we have low self-worth so we doubt ourselves, we question ourselves and whether *we* could have done anything differently to stop our assaults, and we experience a lot of shame and guilt and even feelings of responsibility over what happened to us.

None of these negative self-talks have any accurate basis in reality but I know, God I know when our mental health decreases it is impossible to see that.

On the whole, so far in this chapter, I've explained why self-talk impacts our mental health and why rape survivors experience negative self-talk. Now in the rest of the chapter, we're going to be deep diving into some examples of negative self-talk, why the negative things I said to myself wasn't right or helpful as well as how I changed my negative self-talk into positive self-talk using some examples from actual distressed messages I sent my best friend over time.

This is a critical chapter to read for your own mental health.

Most Important Tip In The Chapter

I wanted to put this here at the start of the chapter before I repeat it at the end too because this is the most important tip in the chapter and it will not make sense first of all but by the end of this chapter, it hopefully will. As well as when the penny does drop around this tip then your life and your mental health will improve, even if it only feels like a little bit.

You need to treat yourself how you would treat a dear friend.

This is what my best friend said about self-talk. If you wouldn't say it to a dear, close friend then certainly don't say it to yourself.

Of course, originally I didn't listen to my best friend but over the next week, I really tried and I kept trying to improve how I treated myself. Honestly, it was hard but now I am a lot kinder towards myself and my mental health is a lot better from a self-critical perspective.

That is a sign of progress and a win and I will happily take any wins I can get.

In other words, if you wouldn't say it to a dear, close friend, do not say it to yourself.

What Shouldn't You Say To Yourself?

I know I reuse this WhatsApp in a much later chapter but I wanted to put the message here because this is the worst, most self-critical message I have ever sent. This message wasn't healthy in the slightest and looking back with hindsight, I cannot imagine I would ever send a message like this nowadays at Week 15.

I'll copy the message below and then I'll explain what parts of the message wasn't healthy, why they're not accurate and what I would say instead:

"I don't think I can go to the Warhammer painting event Friday night. 5 hours is too long with new people in a small seminar room and there might be the person that looks like my attacker there judging from the Facebook photos of the club. Friday's causing me a lot of social anxiety, I don't want to have a meltdown, I don't want to suffer and I don't want to feel like I'm getting raped over and over again.

I know I'm just being a weak, pathetic victim but I just don't think I can. I've already done tons since my rape like endless outreach work, hanging out with friends, going to Group, playing DnD despite Tallis possibly being there and I've done well. The woman from the rape charity was pleased I'm still doing stuff. I'm just scared of going to this Warhammer thing.

I'll go in September to the Warhammer club for a normal session when it's easier to pop in and out instead of having to paint for a few hours. My counseling would be started by then too. I'll honestly probably find it a little boring too. I just wanted to do something new and different because I'm different now.

I'll rather just go to my great-aunt's for the evening, see her, get a goodnight sleep for Saturday so me not being tired slightly reduces the chance of Saturday going badly for me because of my child abuse, rape and Someone From My Past.

I'm sorry I'm a weak, pathetic victim at times. I'm trying I promise. (I know you don't doubt me but this is a lot to deal with and you're the only person I can talk to).

I hate waiting for counselling because I don't want to feel like a victim anymore.

P.S- Saturday's 8 weeks since The Event, and I had a nice day at Outreach today. Stuttered more than normal but it was a lot of fun being session lead. Tomorrow will be brilliant with my Psychology Society meeting.

Thanks for reading. I don't know how you can respond but thank you for always being there. I look forward to when counseling starts so this fear can go."

There was one very unhelpful and unhealthy idea I kept having during this text. *"I know I'm just being a weak, pathetic victim"* I used to say that so much up until my best friend basically moaned at me strongly for constantly hating myself. And I used to feel like this because of the Post-Traumatic Stress Disorder, the intense social anxiety and the sheer debilitating nature of rape. Even now I flat out hate how my rape stops me from doing perfectly normal things.

However, calling myself "a weak, pathetic victim" isn't healthy and it isn't positive. It shifts the blame, the pain and the focus of my rape to me. Yet it wasn't my fault, I am NOT the problem and there is nothing "weak or pathetic" about my actions. I am having perfectly normal trauma responses to an extremely abnormal situation.

I am not the problem so there is no reason to call myself a victim. I am a survivor, not a victim.

<u>Over To You</u>

I recap this discovery about positive self-talk later in the book but I want you to think about how you talk and describe yourself, both in your head and out loud. If you're not being positive towards yourself and if you're being self-blaming then you need to change because self-blame and negative self-talk only harms your mental health and make you feel worse.

Of course, I am flat out not saying you need to speak positively about your sexual assault (no one would ever do that), you don't need to talk positively about your trauma responses and you don't need to say you're okay when you're struggling.

That isn't what I'm saying at all.

Instead what I am saying is that you should never attribute your sexual assault, your trauma responses or your struggles to yourself.

You should **never** say or think:

- I caused my rape so I hate myself.
- I'm pathetic for always being anxious.
- I'm useless because I can't go to work without having a panic attack.

Instead a more positive self-talk version would be:

- I hate the bastard that raped me.
- I'm anxious because of what the bastard did to me, but I'll get professional help and improve over time.
- I struggle with work and panic attacks because of my sexual assault.

Even though these are fairly "basic" examples and believe me, I know us survivors have a much larger and more nuanced range of negative self-talk than that, but you see how I wasn't blaming myself in any of that. I was talking positively about myself by not self-blaming or self-criticising and I was laying the blame where it should be.

You should always blame your attacker.

Finally for this section, this is a skill that you will need to practice and improve over time. You're going to need to practice being kind to yourself, talking positively about yourself and this takes a lot of acceptance about whatever happened to you is NOT your fault. As a result, something you might want to do is practice saying kind things to yourself. For example:

- I am lovable.
- I am not to blame for what happened.
- I deserve happiness.

These might seem really simple and easy to say but these are equally extremely hard to say after experiencing sexual violence. I seriously wouldn't have been able to say these things until 2 or 3 months after my assault.

My point is, it's okay to have moments where your self-talk is negative but you need to learn that you aren't to blame, you deserve to be happy and you need to be kind towards yourself.

It's hard, I seriously know that, but you need to practice.

Improving A Little

I wanted to show how improving your self-talk is a process and it isn't a magical overnight thing. I never want to pretend dealing with anything around sexual violence is easy so me revealing a personal mistake on improving my own self-talk is another way of doing this honesty.

"Hope DnD was fun. I look forward to hearing about it Tuesday.

I think I just want to vent or something. Mum innocently saying "suck it" really fucked me up. I've had a good night. I recorded the podcast and me and Dad talked for hours in the garden. Still had flashbacks for 10 mins in the uni toilets, then even more throughout the whole evening. All leading to a really bad panic attack an hour ago.

I already sort of believe I'll die alone. So few would want to date me, the rape survivor. But what if I can never give or receive oral? Will guys and non-binary peeps hate me? I don't think they will but this is just disempowerment again. The cunt stole oral stuff from me. I don't know if I was ever into it. I can't remember or decide.

I looked at a job description earlier for the future. It would have been brilliant for me... Then I just got scared and triggered about the future. If a simple word can trigger me this bad, how am I meant to work in the profession I love in clinical psychology? Can I hold down a real job? What if he's stolen that from me too?

I'll probably recover well enough in the future but it's scary to think what if I don't. Will my life be worth living? And stop that silly thought train there.

Sometimes I just feel like a weak child and I don't want to.

That's the ultra-brief version of the few hours. Thanks for reading. I really liked dinner today. It was nice. Sleep well."

Whilst this message wasn't as bad or self-blaming as the last one, because I didn't call myself "pathetic" and I wasn't too hateful towards myself. I imagine if I sent this type of message a few weeks earlier I think I would be ripping myself apart about the employability and future stuff.

In addition, there is still a fair amount of negative self-talk, so there's an improvement but this isn't perfect. And honestly, no one is going to be "perfect" all the time but we need to be kind to ourselves.

In this message, I still called myself "weak" and "like a child" and I did a little self-criticism around other aspects of my life.

This message was progress but I still needed to work on getting better.

Example Of Good Self-Talk

Please note whilst these examples are a little dark because I was updating my best friend on what had happened the night before, these are still good examples of self-talk because I never blame myself for what I'm experiencing. None of these trauma responses are my fault and it is simply my brain trying to deal with an extremely abnormal situation.

Also, I know for some people these might seem to be very, very honest and intense messages. Yet this is perfectly fine within the context of mine and my best friend's relationship, so me being this honest isn't a problem at all.

"I guess I should tell you, last night was another rough night. It was better in the sense I wasn't getting beaten and killed. It was worse in the sense that because I think Your Brother has a great body (he doesn't do much for me in the face department), I kept having dreams and intrusive thoughts about Your Brother raping me, saying stuff like because I like his body that's consent and he kept doing stuff to me. Including saying how he enjoyed me struggling against him.

I know he is lovely in real life but I got fairly suicidal.

I hate it how whenever I find someone attractive even in passing. I get intense rape thoughts about them. Killing myself would be so much easier. I don't want to live if I'm constantly scared about finding someone attractive. Being attracted makes me feel good and normal until I go to sleep where I imagine them raping me.

How the fuck am I meant to meet your parents, hang out with A Certain Friend and go to Manchester if all I'm going to get is no sleep and rape stuff. That isn't a life.

But I know I can't kill myself because I do have things to live for and I can't hurt you. I despise anyone that hurts you so I never want to become one of those people. And if I don't do things then that makes me more hopeless and suicidal, and I enjoy living even if I have to deal with the consequences later.

I just want everything to stop. I want to be normal

allo-romantic and be able to admire attractive guys without imagining how they'll rape me, beat me and kill me.

I'm nervous about this week enough without my A Cute Guy I Work With concern. He is really attractive in a strange way. My mind tried to get him to rape me last night but Your Brother was scarier focus (because of his strength) so my mind went with that.

Enjoy your week. Text me if you need anything."

This is a good example of talking about distressing experiences without blaming yourself, because I never say these dreams or intrusive thoughts are my fault and I'm a failure for having them. Since I am not a failure for them at all.

Instead I say they're annoying, I don't like them and I find them deeply distressing, but I never imply they're my fault.

Additionally, whilst I "lash out" at my distress because me and my best friend are planning to go to meet their brother up in Manchester with another friend of ours. I know there's no reason to talk badly about myself because this is my brain trying to process what the hell happened to me.

Two Final Workplace-Based Examples

For context this week I'm working at my university at a summer school residential so 14 and 15-year-old students are staying overnight for two nights, but I stayed over the Monday night too. I was fairly concerned about the event and I had to do a lot of work around this event for my mental health, something I talk about in future chapters.

Yet even though I had a really distressing Monday night, I didn't blame myself as seen in the text below:

"Last night before bed was enjoyable. Got a lot of publishing work and writing done. Did about 3 hours total done then I wrote an email to My Three Supervisors about the accommodation I might need. I cc'd you in the email because I was so tired. Then because the other ambassadors made a group chat and An Ambassador put an implied rape image as the profile pic earlier in the evening that distressed me. I had to put a little message on the group chat. Everyone reacted well and 3 Ambassadors hoped I was okay.

I was extremely tired last night so that made my intrusive thoughts and dreams a little less intense. Yet it was still the normal A Cute Guy raping me (I'm definitely attracted to him in real life, and he's not completely my type but he's a little cool. He's autistic, plays DnD and yeah. I think I had internalised homophobia around him before) and your brother still rapes me in the dreams. I think because he has the strength and power that makes him a scary option in my mind. And there's still violence in my dreams. Like A Cute Guy killing me when I say no and dream Your Brother made threats against you if I said no. I still said no and... I dreamt about him doing his threat.

That was distressing as fuck.

Anyway I need to go for breakfast, catch up with the others and talk to A Cute Guy a little more if I can. Believe me, I know nothing can happen but he's nice. And I want to catch up with Another Ambassador and the others too.

Enjoy your day."

A final message example is:

"I've just finished 65 mins of lying on the floor paralysed by intrusive thoughts and half-dreams of Your Brother and A Cute Guy taking turns raping me.

I'm so emotionally and physically exhausted but I can't sleep or nap at the moment. I can't even ask Outreach for accommodations because there's nothing they can actually do, but if I think of something then I'll talk to them. I will break at one point because of the lack of sleep but I have energy now and the rape stuff has gone. So I need to do something to stop the rape stuff coming back for a while.

Thankfully I brought my laptop so I can write and do business things."

Brief Conclusion

On the whole, when it comes to self-talk, you need to remember:

- Never blame yourself
- If you wouldn't say it to a friend, NEVER say it to yourself
- Never criticise yourself for your reactions.

Moreover, having positive self-talk is never ever about undermining how distressing and traumatic your experience was and how you're dealing with it. That's why I picked these particular messages because they're filled with distressing content that different survivors might connect with, whilst showing you can still be kind to yourself.

This isn't easy and it has taken me months to learn it and even now I still slip up. Yet my mental health is better now because I am not hating myself because I am worthy, I deserve happiness and nothing that has happened to me was my fault.

You can have positive self-talk, it's hard but it is so doable with practice.

Most Important Tip In The Chapter

I wanted to repeat it here again because this is the most important tip in the chapter and it will not make sense first of all but by the end of this chapter, it hopefully will. As well as when the penny does drop around this tip then your life and your mental health will improve, even if it only feels like a little bit.

You need to treat yourself how you would treat a dear friend.

This is what my best friend said about self-talk. If you wouldn't say it to a dear, close friend then certainly don't say it to yourself.

Of course, originally I didn't listen to my best friend but over the next week, I really tried and I kept trying to improve how I treated myself. Honestly, it was hard but now I am a lot kinder towards myself and my mental health is a lot better from a self-critical perspective.

That is a sign of progress and a win and I will happily take any wins I can get.

In other words, if you wouldn't say it to a dear, close friend, do not say it to yourself.

WHAT IS DISEMPOWERMENT IN MENTAL HEALTH?

Disempowerment is a concept I've sort of heard a lot about in clinical psychology lectures, textbooks and in my own reading for The Psychology World Podcast, but no one has actually highlighted just how important it is to understand.

Since disempowerment refers to the lack of control and, well, power that a person feels like they have over their own life, decisions and what they do.

Furthermore, disempowerment targets a person's self-worth, self-perception and it can lead to feelings of shame and guilt. Granted I'm remembering what I read about disempowerment from sexual assault, but the same applies to other events and conditions too.

In turn, these feelings of guilt and shame that disempowerment can create and/ or reinforce can lead to a multitude of maladaptive coping mechanisms. Like alcohol and substance abuse, self-harm, suicidal ideation and more.

As a result, this idea of disempowerment is flat out critical to understand in mental health, because a wide range of mental health conditions are very disempowering. To some extent, this is probably why we don't really focus on disempowerment in mental health and clinical psychology, because we just know our clients are disempowered in their own lives so us, as aspiring or qualified mental health professionals, we don't really need to know or focus on it.

I agree to some extent.

However, I do believe we should think about mental health in terms of disempowerment from time to time, because once you start thinking about mental health conditions or difficulties as something that disempowers our clients. Then this opens up new ideas about how to conceptualise, understand and even empathise with our clients.

In addition, I should note that clinical psychology sometimes focuses on disempowerment in terms of minority groups and mental health services. I think I've actually spoken or reflected on this topic in a previous volume. Therefore, whilst it is flat out critical that therapists and services never disempower our clients, this isn't what we're focusing on in this reflection.

Instead, to give you some examples of mental health conditions as disempowerment, let's talk about social anxiety. This is the easiest example to understand but if a client has social anxiety then they likely feel like they can't go outside, they can't go out with friends and they can't do something that they want to because they're scared of feeling anxious, having a panic attack or being judged negatively.

Normally, we think about this in terms of normal social anxiety because these are symptoms, biased cognitive processes and some of the safety behaviours seen in social anxiety.

Nonetheless, if we think about this in terms of disempowerment, we can see that social anxiety as a condition and the biased cognitive processes has actually decreased the control and ability of the client to live their own life. The client wants to go out, be social and do things that bring them pleasure but it is the social anxiety that makes them feel like they don't have the power to do that.

Another example is depression, because a client feeling unable to get out of bed, they catastrophizing about everything and the client has a low mood. Through a disempowerment lens, you could argue that that isn't the client feeling that part, it is the depression taking away the client's power and ability to control what they do in their own life.

A final example which serves as a minor segway into our next section is Post-Traumatic Stress Disorder. Since the intense thoughts, flashbacks and panic attacks seen in PTSD robs a client of the control they have over their lives to the point where they get extremely distressed when triggered and they avoid potentially triggering stimuli all together.

Overall, my point is that a wide range of mental health conditions robs clients the control they have over their lives. Due to our clients want to improve their lives, they want to be able to do whatever they want and they want to regain their independence so their mental health difficulty or condition is no longer ruling their lives.

Of course, in an attempt to be balanced here, you could argue that there is no point thinking about mental health in this way because disempowerment is obvious. Of course, if you're anxious, depressed, whatever you're going to lack control over your life.

Therefore, you might argue that disempowerment is a waste of time and it's better to think of mental health in terms of the symptoms, interventions and what you're going to do to improve the client's life.

All of those points are valid.

Although, I would counter-argue by saying that thinking about disempowerment is important too for a very simple and important reason. Thinking about mental health as disempowerment is extremely humanising.

Instead of thinking about a client in terms of their symptoms, what can be done to help them so we can move onto our next client to reduce waiting lists (which is a very real, valid and understandable pressure we all face in mental health). If we think about a client in terms of what *they* have lost and how *they* are disempowered. Then we're taking a moment to think about the client and that's it.

And actually, I'm not going to explore it here but you might be able to get some useful information from disempowerment-thinking for your clinical formulation.

On the whole, I would argue disempowerment-thinking helps us to take a moment to think about the client, what they've lost and what they want to gain from the therapeutic work. This might help you understand the client so you can phase things in a certain way, help them and benefit the therapeutic alliance somehow.

Ultimately, disempowerment work is the main point of therapy.

Therapy is about subtly empowering our clients so using the tools and techniques we give them, the client can go back out into the world and conquer it. By empowering our clients we can obviously improve their lives, but we can decrease their psychological distress and give them control over their lives again.

And it is that sense of control that I'm focusing on in this reflection.

Since I'm actually going to come back in the next one and talk about why I'm discussing this and give you some examples about my own disempowerment in terms of my assault (which was a short extremely intense event) and my child abuse and trauma (a long-term, low intensity trauma that happened every single day for a decade).

Definitely turn over the page to see this disempowerment thinking in action.

WHAT DOES DISEMPOWERMENT LOOK LIKE AFTER SEXUAL TRAUMA?

The reason why I'm writing this chapter looking at disempowerment is because in the past two days, I've realised, truly realised how disempowering sexual assault can be. I've felt this way for a while but it took me some time and a good few internet searches to find the terminology.

Of course, once you know the terminology you feel like an idiot because you knew it all along.

Anyway, I'll get to the disempowerment I feel because of my assault later in the chapter, and please relax, I don't even talk about the assault itself so it isn't graphic at all.

Therefore, in this chapter, I'm going to be sharing my own experience of disempowerment in hope that this helps your own understanding, it might help you with your clinical work in the future and it might reinforce what we spoke about in the last chapter.

Disempowerment From Long-Term Trauma

I have to admit here that my long-term abuse and trauma that started in my childhood and went on for a decade thankfully stopped nine months ago, so my memory might be blocking some of the nuances of disempowerment but I remember the it for the most part.

And in fact a lot of my current difficulty actually stem from that disempowerment.

As a result of because my social world (a slightly vague term for who abused me) taught me, drummed it into my skull from 12 years old onwards and made threats and perform actions that made me believe those threats, I was terrified for my life for that decade if these people found out I was gay.

Therefore, because I couldn't afford to be gay because I didn't want to die, I didn't want to be beaten and I didn't want to be homeless. This was actually extremely disempowering and it's really interesting to look at my childhood in terms of disempowerment.

Since I basically had no control over large aspects of my life.

I couldn't really afford to have any gay friends because I wanted to protect gay people, and I didn't want these people to think I was gay. That would have been a direct threat to my life and safety.

Also, I couldn't date, have a first kiss or have anything that heterosexual teenagers enjoy as a matter of course. Again, experiencing any type of normal adolescent behaviour would have been a risk to myself, the person I was kissing or whatever and I didn't want to die.

It was as simple as that.

Also, these people in my social world were very critical of my friendships as it was so friendships were difficult enough as a young, gay autistic kid who struggled anyway.

Moreover, my entire family were deeply homophobic so combined a lack of familial support with a tiny and basically non-existent friendship network. My emotional dependency (you can hear more about that on the Psychology World Podcast) is seriously no surprise.

Since if we think about emotional dependency and how I was (to some extent) "addicted" to a close friend I made who accepted me for me. You might argue that my emotional dependency was me trying in an extremely unhealthy way to take control of my life again. In terms of me having a gay friend that liked me for me and wasn't berating or abusing me.

Overall, my current relationship and friendship difficulties certainly come from that disempowerment and lack of control I had over my own life. Since with disempowerment impacting someone's self-perception and self-worth judgment. I am awful for saying that I don't deserve love, no one will ever love me and I don't deserve happiness.

If not believing you deserve the same happiness everyone else has the right to feel isn't disempowerment, then I seriously don't know what is.

What Might Disempowerment Look Like

After A Sexual Assault?

Ever since my assault, even though I didn't realise it until yesterday, I've been feeling really disempowered because there are times my life feels like it's in freefall. I don't feel like I have control over my life and I am fearful what might happen in certain situations.

As I mentioned a few chapters ago, this mainly manifested itself after my assault as a crippling, intense fear of seeing my best friend again because I'm into them romantically. I was fearful of being alone with them, I was scared of sleeping in the same room as them and I was scared they would do something to me.

Of course that would never ever happen because they are the nicest person you would ever meet. Yet as much as it annoys me, sometimes when I think about my best friend it triggers thoughts of my assaulter. According to one of my other friends, that's a normal assault/ rape response because both are to do with physiological arousal.

As a result, when everything happened over my birthday weekend like my panic attack on the Tube, like my inability to sleep comfortably in the same room as my best friend and me having panic attacks at the social group I go to. That is such a disempowering feeling.

I don't know what I can do, where I can go and who I can be with so I don't have a panic attack or something else.

Below is a Whatsapp message I quickly sent my best friend and then I'll explain the context in terms of disempowerment:

"I acknowledge this isn't a logical concern but X isn't the type of person to touch and hug people she's only just met right?

I know she's lovely from our conversations. She's Y's girlfriend, right? I want to meet her.

I'm generally okay. Past few days have been nice.

Last night was tough. I'm just a little nervous about Friday. I'm coming no matter what but that's a lot of people in a (maybe locked) room. And I don't want to spoil it for people if I have a panic attack or something. If needed, I'll ask Z not to lock the door but I hate drawing attention to my discomfort. It just makes what happened even more real and reminds me I'm disempowered and it will take time to heal and get empowered again."

Firstly, I want to focus on getting back to a sense of empowerment does take time because it takes time to heal and for therapy to happen and for you to process stuff.

Also, the context for Friday is I'm going to a one-shot game of Dungeons and Dragons because a friend is doing it, he invited me and some others and I am refusing to let my social anxiety and assault control my life too much.

I don't want to accidentally lock myself away in my room because I'm too scared of being assaulted and hurt again.

Yet I am nervous about Friday for illogical reasons but to me they are very real. I mentioned some of the reasons in that text to my best friend, but there's another reason I will probably keep exclusively for these pages. I am scared about someone who's going to be playing this one-shot with us will be triggering to me.

There's a player and he's kind, very nice and we've spoke a few times. Yet he has long hair and he's slightly on the larger side of life and he has an oval-type of face. All those 3 things are similar to my attacker.

I think he might trigger me so there are very real but illogical reasons why I might have problems on Friday. Then I'm scared that a lot of negative thoughts will pop up about me not being able to enjoy my life anymore and stuff like that.

Personally, I know if something happens, no one will actually care in the sense that they won't judge me for it. Everyone but two of the seven people at the game knows to differing extents what happened to me. And that's something else I'm not thrilled about, I think I'm scared people are going to see me as a weak victim.

Of course, I know as an aspiring clinical psychologist that victims are flat out far from weak. But as a person, I feel a little weak, violated and I'm still reeling from what happened. I don't wish it on anyone and I don't want this to ever happen again.

That is why I feel disempowered because I feel like I don't have control over my reactions, my decisions to do things and I have this constant fear to be honest. Fear that something bad's going to happen, fear that people will judge me for having a panic attack and a fear that people will stop inviting me to stuff because they don't know how I'll react.

I know none of that is logical because my friends are amazing and even though I don't really care much about Dungeons and Dragons (sorry friends and readers), I want to be social and make sure I don't retreat into my room for the rest of my life.

Disempowerment isn't always pretty but if you give a client (or myself) time to process, heal and go to therapy then they can be empowered once more so they can retake control of their lives, decisions and more once again.

And that is an amazing feeling to have after being disempowered for so long.

ACCEPTING YOUR MENTAL HEALTH TRAUMA RESPONSES FOR WHAT THEY ARE

Now my best friend would probably be extremely proud of this next chapter because they would be seriously happy that I've finished accepting a lot about my mental health, my trauma and what I am able and not really able to do at the moment.

Of course, I'm referring to the outcome of my assault and my own frustration that my mental health simply cannot handle certain things, and I have certain trauma responses.

I've written about a lot of them in previous chapters, but when I wrote those chapters, I hadn't accepted that and I had been really annoyed that they were popping up.

In addition, what kicked off my acceptance of my trauma responses was a lot of small things that happened last week at the time of writing. Yet the following WhatsApp I sent my best friend was what really kicked it into high gear:

I don't think I can go to the Warhammer painting event Friday night. 5 hours is too long with new people in a small seminar room and there might be the person that looks like my attacker there judging from the Facebook photos of the club. Friday's causing me a lot of social anxiety, I don't want to have a meltdown, I don't want to suffer and I don't want to feel like I'm getting raped over and over again.

I know I'm just being a weak, pathetic victim but I just don't think I can. I've already done tons since my rape like endless outreach work, hanging out with friends, going to Group, playing DnD despite (Someone's Name) *possibly being there and I've done well. The woman from the rape charity was pleased I'm still doing stuff. I'm just scared of going to this*

Warhammer thing.

I'll go in September to the Warhammer club for a normal session when it's easier to pop in and out instead of having to paint for a few hours. My counselling would start by then too. I'll honestly probably find it a little boring too. I just wanted to do something new and different because I'm different now.

I'll rather just go to my great-aunt's for the evening, see her, get a good night's sleep for Saturday so me not being tired slightly reduces the chance of Saturday going badly for me because of my child abuse, rape and Someone's Name.

I'm sorry I'm a weak, pathetic victim at times. I'm trying I promise. (I know you don't doubt me but this is a lot to deal with and you're the only person I can talk to).

I hate waiting for counselling because I don't want to feel like a victim anymore.

P.S- Saturday's 8 weeks since The Event, and I had a nice day at Outreach today. Stuttered more than normal but it was a lot of fun being session lead. Tomorrow will be brilliant with my Psychology Society meeting.

Thanks for reading. I don't know how you can respond but thank you for always being there. I look forward to when counselling starts so this fear can go.

So as you could tell from that message I was distress to say the least, I was blaming myself for a lot and I was a little angry I was having these sort of reactions. I just wanted to be normal, able to do things and I wanted to start doing things.

That isn't possible at the moment.

Of course, my best friend was a little annoyed at me for blaming myself for so much. I cannot put their reply in these pages for copyright reasons but they wanted me to stop blaming myself and they mentioned I have PTSD.

Me being me was very dismissive (not to my best friend) about the idea of me having PTSD. Yet I looked into it and it turns out that about 81% of sexual violence survivors have PTSD in the first month and then that doesn't really drop too much even after the first month which is when you can actually get the PTSD diagnosis.

Again, I looked into PTSD itself a little more and let me include a list of PTSD symptoms from the NHS website:

- Flashbacks
- Nightmares
- Distressing and repetitive sensations and images
- Physical sensations
- Constant negative thoughts about the experience
- Including pondering the event
- Avoidance of being reminded about the traumatic event
- Hyperarousal
- Sleeping problems
- Difficulty focusing
- Mental health difficulties (like depression and anxiety)
- Self-harm or destructive behaviours
- Other physical symptoms

Well, even that list was rather fun (not) because over the past two months, I have certainly had the vast, vast majority of these symptoms. As you could tell from my WhatsApp message I'm no stranger to the physical sensations, especially when I feel like my sexual assault is happening over and over.

Therefore, me realising that I have PTSD

followed by me having a lovely time at my Great-Aunt's and some other things that happened over Pride weekend just made me realise I am sort of stuck for a bit.

And even as an aspiring clinical psychologist, I am willing to say this. I think this is okay for now because yes, I firmly do not believe I can do any *NEW* social situations at the moment. For example, I just cannot go to any new societies, meet-ups or group things, for the time being.

Even a social group I've been going to for months and months now I am finding harder and harder to be at, because there are a lot of people there, some of them are fat and it triggers a lot of assault stuff for me.

So yes, I have social anxiety when it comes to new things and that is okay. I have accepted that until my therapy, it is okay if I don't do any new things.

Yet I will not allow this to continue after my therapy because I need to start living fully again and I want to banish this social anxiety because of my assault. Even now to be honest, I am still doing a lot of things like being President of the Psychology Society at my university and I'm getting into a new situation in August. I'm working a year 10 residential at the university as part of my Outreach work.

That I am a little nervous about but I applied to work that before my assault and I'm committed to that now. I wouldn't really change it anyway.

In addition, I've accepted that I really don't bloody like enclosed spaces filled with people. I've already mentioned how I had a meltdown and cried on the Tube on my birthday because of the sexual violence notices on the Tube.

Well, I went on the Tube again yesterday and I thankfully didn't have a meltdown or cried and shook in public. Yet I was uncomfortable and I seriously hated the Tube coming back to the O2 arena (where my car was parked) because it was packed, I couldn't sit down and I couldn't have my personal space.

The problem I have with standing up is that my assault took place standing up, so sometimes it's like I can still feel him touching me and doing things if I stand up for a while.

Thankfully, my best friend was there so I sort of had to touch their coat and stare at them a little to ground myself in the present moment instead of the memories and physical sensations.

And once we got back to the O2, I basically sped-walked out of the underground station and didn't stop until I was past the pay barriers where I waited for my friend to catch up.

Therefore, I've accepted enclosed spaces with lots of people will be an issue for me. I am not avoiding going on the Tube, I am avoiding going to London by myself if I have to travel on the Tube, but if I'm going with my best friend then that's okay.

Granted, I am going to Kew gardens with my family at some point soon that will involve the Tube. But it's my family so I'll have to act like things are perfectly fine and just feel like I'm dying and getting raped inside.

The one silver lining about the Tube ride was I did not have a meltdown, cry or shake. That means the effect was less than it was before on me, so the more I travel on the Tube, the better I might be.

There is hope in that realisation.

Hope I am very happy about to be fair.

Another negative that made me realise I needed to accept I have PTSD is that my best friend, their friend and a mutual friend of ours were in the Pride Parade. The original plan was to have me and my best friend's friend stand together, watch the Parade and chat.

The mutual friend didn't know this but it was to make sure I was okay given my child abuse and my last reaction to Pride.

That didn't happen because the mutual friend wanted to join the Parade, there were spare wrist bands and I pushed him towards going in the Parade. I always like putting other people's joy ahead of mine.

So I was alone in Canterbury High Street watching the Parade.

It was a great Parade with great groups, great people and great music. Yet there were two sexual violence charities and I now know (and accepted) that I find anything referring to sexual violence to be extremely triggering.

So I had to self-harm to keep myself grounded and I had to bleed a little. It didn't stop all of the assault stuff coming back and the physical sensations taking over, but it sort of kept me grounded and there wasn't anything else I could have done.

I couldn't think of another way to distract myself.

Again, being alone in public without a way to distract myself, maybe this isn't something I can do at the moment either. Especially when my mind does just turn to those sort of things.

I need to keep myself busy, and I've accepted this difficulty.

<u>My Point For Aspiring And Qualified Clinical Psychologists</u>

My point is there comes a time in trauma, mental health and waiting for therapy that you just have to realise and accept what is happening to you. Now, I've truly accepted that I just cannot do certain things at this moment in time, I do feel more positive, happy and kinder to myself.

I no longer think of myself as a weak, pathetic victim. I am just a victim and I suppose a survivor, and I know in time when I start counselling with the charity that things will get better for me.

I will be able to do new things and I will be able to go out and do perfectly normal things without my best friend or anyone I lean on for support.

And in the meantime, what will I be doing?

Like always I will be writing, podcasting and running a business. I will also be having in-person meetings, emailing people and continuing to set up the Psychology Society for a September 2024 launch.

AND I will be seeing, meeting up and doing things with friends and I will be conducting and writing up my psychology research. As well as in September I'll be conducting research, supervising volunteers and helping Parkinson's clients at my university's Parkinson's centre.

Therefore, whilst I have extremely dark days and there are moments that I just hate because I feel like I am getting assaulted over and over again and I can't do anything to stop it. I am still living my life as best as I can and I am doing what makes me happy.

I will be even happier in the future when I can do whatever I want without a threat of a meltdown, self-harming or anything else.

That time will come. It will.

However, until that time comes, I need to accept that things will be challenging, difficult and there will be some things that will cause me too much distress to be worth it.

Yet there are a thousand other things that I can do, and it is the positives that I am focusing on and accepting.

Acceptance really is a powerful tool and it certainly has the power to make you feel more positive, happier and content with your situation until you start therapy. Just make sure you get the professional help you need because *that* is the thing that will truly change your life for the better.

APPRECIATING THE TRUE POWER OF SOCIAL NETWORKS

Whilst this isn't one of my clinical psychology reflection books where I normally reflect and tell aspiring and qualified clinical psychologists things that I've learnt through my own mental health experiences, this next chapter is partly based on a reflection. Therefore, I wanted to use this next chapter as a chance to partly reflect and write about something I have learnt after my sexual assault.

Due to you really learn who your friends are and how powerful social networks are after something as traumatic as a sexual assault.

I encourage you to keep reading because this isn't graphic and this helps you to deepen your understanding about how useful social networks actually are in mental health recovery and supporting victims. Since again, we can read as much as we want about mental health research and how important social groups are, but it isn't until something happens that we realise just how critical they are.

Especially when it comes to the darker side of sexual assault.

Also, I will add here that I wrote the previous reflection on lived experience 19 days ago and I haven't felt like finishing this reflection until now. A lot has happened in those 19 days and I am even more grateful for my friends and how I am building my social network over time.

Why Are Social Networks Important?

I won't spend too long on this section because we're all aspiring or qualified psychologists here, so we all know the benefits of having friends. For example, people with friends tend to be happier, have better mental health outcomes and have higher life satisfaction compared to people with few or no friends.

In addition, friends are great sources of support when something bad happens in your life. For instance, the death of a loved one, a major negative life event or you're struggling with something. Friends are people you can turn to for advice, they can listen to you and they are the people you can do fun stuff with to make you feel better.

We all know those basics and when it comes to mental health, sometimes I feel like a lot of our work is about human connection, and helping clients build better, more successful relationships in the future.

Such as, when it comes to social anxiety work, we are basically working with a client to give them the skills and coping mechanisms so they can go out into the world, make friends and get all the benefits of having a social network.

The same goes for depression, because we're working with a client so they have the techniques and coping mechanisms to stop isolating themselves, criticising them and stop their biased cognitive processes from limiting their social interaction. This allows them to go out into the world, rejoin their friends doing fun activities and they can deepen their friendships.

Finally, in Post-Traumatic Stress Disorder or any trauma-based work, we're giving client tools and techniques so they can move past their trauma, reclaim their life and they can start living again. This includes the part of life that involves going out with friends, doing silly things and just laughing until your stomach and jaw hurt.

That's my point of view on a lot of mental health work.

How Did My Social Network Help Me?

For the sake of context, I need to be upfront here and say I naturally have a very small social network. I have one close friend who I see often, we talk a lot and we're living together next academic year. I have another friend that we get on great when we're together and I am their closest friend, but they don't text me back. It isn't anything against me, they just don't respond and they always forget to reply to messages.

Then I have another friend which we aren't that close but we talk a fair bit, and I have more of a university friend who's a PhD student. We've helped each other a lot over the years and we are friends.

Anyway, I only really have two close friends. A lot of that is because of child abuse, trauma and undiagnosed autism to be honest.

And even though, I don't have endless amounts of friends, I am still so grateful to have each and every one of them in my life. They actually are some of the best people I know and they are all there for me in their own special way.

I love them for that.

Firstly, the morning after my assault when I realised how distressed I was I contacted my close friend despite them not being available. So the next day when they were available, we spoke and because they weren't back in the UK for another three weeks, we spoke a lot. They were very understanding, very calm and they were really supportive.

I seriously needed that because I was so scared of my best friend. Since I'm attracted to them and that was triggering a lot of assault stuff for me as I've mentioned before.

And ever since my best friend has been back in the country, they have constantly been there for me. We've had a lot of conversations, we've been out a lot and they've been interested in every step of my "recovery". Like tomorrow after I have my counselling assessment with a sexual violence charity, I'll be texting them about it because they want to know.

It's been lovely having a friend who is *that* there for me, and I know for a lot of people this is normal. Yet because of everything that's happened to me in the past, including a fair amount of friendship trauma and betrayal, this is surprising for me.

My other close friend, let's call them, Luke for the sake of ease. Even though Luke never replies to any messages because they forget, they were really nice about messaging me back quickly. We were planning to meet up a few times but I've had to cancel, because one-on-one situations with them was too hard for me. And Luke isn't the type of person I would want to have a meltdown in front of.

It's not because Luke wouldn't be nice about it, it's more because I would feel bad.

Yet I know Luke is a really good friend because they don't mind, they understand why I cancelled and why it took me so long to meet up with them. Then we went to a social thing and we were talking for hours and it was great.

That's what I appreciate about a social network and having different levels of closeness with people. Since my best friend is the person I tell everything to and who I panic and stress with in the moment and I have meltdowns in front of, but Luke is the type of person I talk to after the fact and we just have fun.

Thirdly, my PhD friend was lovely to because he works as a researcher in the Parkinson centre at my university, so I was going to spend some time helping him at work. It never happened because he was ill and then my mental health just died so I wasn't able to help, and I had exams anyway.

However, he was still there for me, he was still willing to listen and talk and I could talk to him about slightly different things compared to the others.

Finally, my last friend was able to offer me a very good perspective because he's a victim of sexual violence. He was raped constantly as a kid so it was actually something we bonded over. When I was feeling so distressed and whatnot and I wanted to give my best friend a little break, I could talk to him. We related a lot with each other, what we were going through and he told me different ways about how to cope with it.

That was nice and it was good hearing from someone with lived experience.

Of course, the "problem" with this friend is there are massive limits about what we can talk about because he's still reeling from his child sexual abuse and there are things he just couldn't process. Which I understand even if I was a little disappointed about because I wanted answers to certain questions and he couldn't give them to me.

Yet considering this was the first time me and this friend have hung out just the two of us and we talk a lot. It has been lovely having another friend who I can talk so openly with about some really dark stuff.

Conclusion

Overall, even though this has been a bit of a different reflection, I still hope you found it useful because you've been able to see the importance and the positive impact that my social network has had on me over the past six weeks. This is a useful reminder that our friends are great, we should always treasure our friendships and we should always be able to turn to our friends in our darkest hour.

Personally, I would hate to imagine what the past six weeks would have been like if I didn't have friends or the friends I have right now. The past six weeks would have been awful, lonely and I am willing to say, I doubt I would still be here.

I don't think that's inaccurate at all, because sexual violence is awful.

Moreover, this experience and this reflection on my own social connections will be useful in future clinical work. Since I'll be able to draw on examples when appropriate with clients about the power and the benefits of friends in difficult times. And this will make me focus and have a lot of enthusiasm for the social skills and the relationship part of our work.

Since I now truly appreciate the power, the hope and decrease in suffering that a good social network can provide, and I wish that everyone has the same opportunities that I do.

Friends really can be the light in the darkness of our lives.

ENJOY THE GOOD TIMES

You have to recognise, enjoy and celebrate the good times.

A lot of the content in this book deals with a lot of distressing topics like rape, negative mental health and occasionally suicidality. And whilst this reflects what the vast, vast majority of sexual assault survivors go through, I don't want this book to seem all doom and gloom because this isn't the message of the book.

This entire book is about showing you that your recovery and your healing will be tough and you will experience a lot of distressing mental health outcomes, but you can heal, you can thrive and you can have good times in between.

That's what I want to remind myself and you in this next chapter.

Today I've had an absolutely lovely day that marks a lot of progress to in my own recovery. Since Henry came around today to my student accommodation and I spent probably 3.5 hours with him, one-on-one and we had a lovely time. We spoke about video games and film lore. More specifically we spoke about Halo lore, his hangover, our student ambassador work a little more and so on.

He found it really nice as well, because he had to have a little nap because of his hangover. Yet before he went to sleep on my sofa, he mentioned he was really happy that he came round today because it was really nice talking to me. Something he repeated when I dropped him off home.

Personally, it was just such a lovely experience just being with a new friend in the comfort of my own home in a one-on-one situation without any rape stuff popping up. I didn't have a panic attack, I didn't have intrusive thoughts about him raping me and I didn't have any of my normal reactions to the idea of spending time with someone.

And as I write this shorter chapter, I couldn't stop smiling because this means a hell of a lot for me. It means I am healing, it might be slow and I might have seriously distressing hours, but I can actually do something that I flat out couldn't do even last week.

I *can* and I will spend time with new friends, just talking, being normal and just enjoying my life.

In addition, it proves that I don't *need* my best friend with me all the time in social situations. Our original plan was to have Henry around with me and my best friend talking to him, playing games and having fun.

However, my best friend has some resit assignments to do for their degree so they were going to be upstairs in their room working on that. They asked me if I wanted them to do downstairs sitting at the kitchen table so they were in the room to make me feel comfortable. I said no to that so I was comforted by the idea of them being in the house.

So my panicked mind could calm down about the fact that if Henry tried to hurt me (he never ever would) then my best friend would stop it and protect me.

The world had other plans.

Since my best friend took out of the university's rentable laptops and no one told them, the laptop does not work until you're on campus. Meaning my best friend had a serious conversation with me about whether I was comfortable being alone and if I wanted them to be here.

Honestly, if I really wanted them to be here, I could have said just work on my laptop.

I didn't really want them here just for me and my mental health, because I was feeling okay about Henry coming round. I told my best friend to go to campus so they could work on their assignments (which are a lot more important to be fair) and that's how a one-on-one situation happened.

And those three hours with Henry were some of the best, most positive moments I've had in weeks.

It isn't even because I had a nice time, because I've had a lovely week at the Year 10 summer school with my fellow ambassadors. And I've had lots of wonderful conversations with other people this week.

I think what made this time with Henry so lovely was it surprised me and gave me hope. It gave me hope that I seriously don't need my best friend to give me my social opportunities, I don't need them to accompany me whenever I want to do something social and when they go back home this week, I don't need to cut myself off from the world until they return.

I can be social and hang out with Henry in the meantime.

Of course, me and my best friend will still spend tons of time together and still do almost everything together because we are really close. Yet I am no longer restricted to only doing things with them.

I still know I will struggle socially in other respects. At the Year 10 summer school on Wednesday, we had a disco and that was extremely distressing for me, so I know I am not healed in certain ways.

However, I can trust people, I can enjoy spending time with them and I can enjoy my life after sexual violence. That is a win and I am grateful that I have these moments in my life.

Moreover, it probably helps that Henry is the complete opposite of my rapist because he's average and fit (not overweight), he's younger than me (unlike my rapist) and he's intensely kind (so not like my rapist). That was a massive help in making today successful, and I still know because of my best friend's Role-Playing Game group that I'll be joining in September for their Halo campaign that I still find very overweight men very triggering and distressing.

Therefore, this definitely isn't the end of my social anxiety and Post-Traumatic Stress Disorder. Yet it is still a win, a sign of progress and a sign of hope for my future.

Finally, as a quick note, a very small aspect of today that I'm excited about is I didn't realise that I could be genuinely attracted to Henry. Since he is lovely, he is fit and he is an attractive guy. Also, whilst he isn't gay so nothing can ever happen between us, the interesting thing for me was it didn't trigger anything for me. Me feeling attraction did not trigger any rape stuff for me.

That has never happened before.

Again, I know from the Year 10 summer school that this flat out isn't a fixed rule because attraction can make me severely distressed most of the time. Yet spending time with Henry goes to show that if I feel safe with someone, if I enjoy spending time with them and if my mental health is good then there is hope I can experience attraction without anything bad happening.

That is another massive sign of progress.

Two perfect discoveries to mark exactly 16 weeks since my rape.

On the whole, when it comes to your recovery, please focus, enjoy and celebrate the good times. You'll need to remember these moments in the dark times and sometimes these good moments will be uncommon, but that makes them even more special when they do happen.

You deserve to be happy, you deserve to be loved and you deserve to experience lovely times.

I know they can happen to you because if they can happen to me then they can happen to anyone, and most importantly, I believe in you.

MY EXPERIENCE OF REVEALING MY RAPE TO THE WORKPLACE

Week 15 was major for me in my recovery, my healing and me telling other people what had happened to me, because I told my bosses and the people I work with that I was raped.

Whilst I know I don't work in any "typical" job because I work as a student ambassador at a university on a very flexible contract where I work with students across Kent who come from schools with typically a low number of students who go on to higher education by supporting and/ or delivering a wide range of fun activities with them. There is a lot all of us can learn from this chapter, my experience and what response I got.

As a result of being a student ambassador is still a working environment where there are rather high expectations of me where I have to complete certain duties, responsibilities, behave in a certain way, report to a boss and so on.

Just because this isn't a typical office job, physical labour or anything that non-students would ever be doing, please do not dismiss this as me not having a job. Since this is a part-time job and revealing I was raped to my bosses was just as terrifying as it would be in any other job or profession.

If not more so because I was concerned if I revealed my rape and my bad mental health to my bosses then I would be put "on leave" because they might not have wanted me interacting with young students (under 18s) where I could possibly damage the reputation and image of the university.

That was a very honest concern I had.

Therefore, in the rest of the chapter, I'll give you the context for why I revealed my rape because I technically could have done it 15 weeks ago, but I didn't want to. Then I'll reveal how I did it and what the response was. As well as I'll explain why I told the other student ambassadors too and what their response was as well.

Why Did I Reveal My Rape?

This week I worked what's known as the Year 10 Residential summer school at my university. This was where 55 year 10 students (15-year-olds) came to the university from across Kent to stay for three days and two nights to complete a wide range of fun activities, so they could experience university life and they could take part in fun projects.

The overall theme of the summer school was Breaking Barriers, so showing students through some games, some group work and a group presentation that whatever barriers a person faces to their goals and future dreams. There is support for them at university or in other ways so they can overcome them and achieve whatever they want to.

In addition, there were other academic taster sessions, like law, forensic science, biology and film studies. They were all really good and the students loved them. As well as there were society tasters (for our international audience just think university social clubs formed around a particular interest) like singing, fantasy fiction, photography and mindfulness art (also known as painting).

Then we did quiz nights, meals and sports with them too. I would have loved to have been on the Nerf gun sport option but I was on the non-sport option. There was volleyball and ultimate Frisbee too.

As you can see we did a lot of things with the year 10 students over the three days. As well as there was a disco on the second night too.

Anyway, this was going to be an intense week and as I've mentioned before, I don't tend to do well meeting new people, doing completely new things and sleeping in new places. Hell, sleep is a fight that I lose most of the time.

I was very concerned about the summer school before I went and my concerns were only getting more founded.

Due to on the Monday (the day before the summer school), we had "training" so all 10 ambassadors who were working the event had spent 6 hours on the training. We went through the plan for the next three days, health and safety, safeguarding and a whole bunch of other things.

However, something I've read a lot about when it comes to rape survivors but I haven't really experienced it until the training was rape survivors struggle with concentration.

I kept zoning out of the training and that was a problem throughout the week. And I laugh about it now because whenever someone would give me or a group of people an instruction I would zone out and very quickly have to remember or figure out what the instruction was from the reaction of other people.

Thankfully no one noticed my zoning out but that was only because of some miracle.

That was a warning sign.

Then on the Monday night we could stay over at the university so we didn't need to travel back to the university the next day for the start of the summer school. Also, for context, there was an ambassador that I'll call Oaks (not his real name obviously) that I'm attracted to, and I've always been attracted to him before my rape. So my attraction to Oaks is genuine and not rape-related.

I checked into my room at 4:45 pm and I started having problems immediately. It's a student accommodation room so a sort of cheap hotel room. That means it's an enclosed space with only one way out and it had a double bed. I have massive problems with double beds because my mind twists them to say "oh, that bed's big enough for someone to climb in and rape you again".

Very helpful, not.

I tried to ignore my fears so I sat on the wooden chair and I started to take my shoes off like any normal person would. Yet I started getting intrusive thoughts about Oaks giving me a lap dance and sexually touching me.

This was distressing enough so I knew I couldn't sit on the wooden chair and flick through my phone after taking off my shoes. Also, I knew laying or sitting on the bed was a no-go so I laid on the floor and I quickly became paralysed for the next 65 minutes as the intrusive thoughts of Oaks and my best friend's brother took turns raping me.

I was so emotionally exhausted that it was just hell and you've seen the message I sent to my best friend about this distressing time in a previous chapter.

I knew my mental health was only going to get worse unless I did something. As well as I knew the disco was going to be extremely distressing for me and there was a genuine risk of being me finally having a very public and messy meltdown.

In reality, it was distressing but I managed. I did almost have a public meltdown and I was visually distressed at least twice and I did have to hide in the toilet twice. I did have full permission to go into the quiet room the university had setup but my normal reaction is hide in the toilets.

I knew I had to do something.

I knew I was finally going to have to tell Outreach about my rape so if anything happened then I had an explanation they were already aware of in place, so this would never be interpreted as something I was making up to explain away "bad" behaviour. Outreach would never be like that but I was distressed and so tired when I made this decision. As well as in case I needed anything from Outreach this week, I wanted them to know over an email what had happened because I am not brave enough to tell them to their faces.

So at 11 pm Monday night I sent the following email, and for context, please know I have a very good relationship with the three people in charge of the summer school. We're all very friendly (except for one woman in charge of the summer school who she just isn't approachable but I included her in the email anyway) and I am very well-liked within Outreach. Everyone is always happy to have me on an event because I'm very good at my job.

"Hi all, hope you're well.

I know we're all extremely busy getting ready for the summer school so I'll keep this as short as possible.

I would appreciate the possibility of a small "accommodation" please this week in the rare case I need it, and please appreciate this is a very hard email for me to write as this contains extremely sensitive information.

So I was raped 15 weeks, 2 days ago and all I'll say is as you can imagine it kills your mental health and affects you in basically every single part of your life. Some of the mental health consequences alone include panic attacks, severe social anxiety and Post-Traumatic Stress Disorder. So when these mental health difficulties get added to my mild autism, this is a very fun for me (not).

Therefore, whilst I would greatly appreciate you treating me like normal because Outreach work and the staff have been a lifesaver in the past 15 weeks for giving me normality in an extreme abnormal time and whilst I go through the waiting list for specialist rape counselling. I would appreciate the following:

- *If I ask to supervise or if an ambassador is needed for the quiet room when we're doing a major event (like the quiz or disco), then unless it is seriously inconvenience and it risks making the summer school not run smoothly. Then please let me do to the quiet room for a while and supervise whatever students are in there (or let me have a little bit of time in there please).*

- *If you need an ambassador for the quiet space, maybe ask me as a first pick or something please. I know this sounds nit-pricky but don't assign me the quiet space (if that's something you were going to do for ambassadors. I know it wasn't but I'm panicking as I write this email) because rape is extremely disempowering and I have enough trouble making basic decisions in my everyday life. So having someone innocently make a decision for me about my own mental health makes me feel even more disempowered.*

Besides from that, I don't think there is anything else I need or would like.

However, as an employee of the university, you've all worked with me over the past 15 weeks so you know I can do Outreach work really well and none of you have ever had been issue with me and my work on behalf of the university. Yet because this is a residential with a lot of intense parts, and it is effectively a new environment (especially looking after students in a corridor), this summer school might be challenging for me. As well as I haven't had a good night's sleep in three days because of trauma stuff and that might continue throughout the summer school.

In other words, chances are I will cope, the event will run fine and you won't be able to tell I'm a rape survivor with a lot of difficulties. But if there is a chance of me seriously struggling, I am telling you now so I feel able to ask for help.

I understand this is probably a tough email to read but thank you for reading. I was really hard for me to tell you all as my bosses. Yet all of you are lovely people and I enjoy working with each of you so I feel safe enough to tell you.

Thank you for reading.

I look forward to the summer school starting soon,

Connor."

With this email, I wanted to strike a balance between being seen as fully competent so there was no chance they would request I didn't work the next few days, and whilst emphasising I am not okay and I might need support.

In addition, I wanted to stress the need for them to treat me normally because if they followed the myths and misconceptions about rape survivors or so-called "victims" being weak, broken or any other negative myth about us. Then there was a very real chance of them making me feel worse and negatively impacting my mental health even more.

Of course, I am sure some of you reading this could never imagine being a mixture of formal and informal with your boss, and you will need to adapt your email or you revealing your assault to your bosses to suit your situation. Yet I've included this email in this chapter to give you a starting point or an idea.

<u>What Was The Response From My Three Bosses?</u>

At 7:30 am the next morning, I got an email from Nat, let's call her, and she is already a lovely lady that I have so much time for because she's been in constant contact with me for different Outreach events over the past few months and she cares about us ambassadors a lot.

Now I didn't see her email until an hour later after I had had breakfast with the other ambassadors and I had already seen her. I honestly hadn't realised she had read or seen my email because she treated me normally. She asked me *how was I* and *how did I sleep* but for her, that isn't an odd thing to ask at all.

Her response was basically something along the lines of *I can only imagine how difficult that email was to write so thank you for trusting us. That information will be handled sensitively and if there is anything you need just ask and we'll do it. You're really important to us and we're really lucky to have you on the summer school.*

I have a lot of time for Nat and later on in the day she did mention the quiet room to me and she said if we set it up, we'll ask you and only if you want you can do it. The conversation was half-serious because she wasn't sure it was even needed for the students and half-me-focused because she wanted me to be okay.

Then the other woman I sent my email too. She didn't treat me any different over the next three days and she didn't even talk to me about my email nor did she reply. Honestly, I wasn't expecting her to because the idea of her having an emotional or heartfelt conversation with anyone is funny. She has her nice moments but no one really likes her anyway because she is a very militant boss.

Anyway, the man I sent my email too was another great example of people treating me normally because I didn't think he read my email at all. Yet on the Wednesday night he spoke to me and it turned out he had read it Tuesday afternoon and simply hadn't had a chance to speak to me before the disco. Then he said he was really sorry for what happened to me and if there was anything I needed he wanted me to ask for it.

I asked where the quiet room was because I knew I was going to need it that night. It was even worse that after all the distress of the disco, I needed to start packing up my room because we were checking out straight after breakfast the next day. Yet I couldn't make any decisions so I had to text my best friend my thinking process so I could then make a decision. Thankfully, my best friend was asleep so I didn't have to have a reply.

Yet sending that text did help me a lot and I was able to pack.

On the whole, when it came to disclosing my rape to my bosses, it was hard but I am so glad I did it. This took a lot of the stress away and the summer school was a lot of fun. I do love Outreach work, interacting with students and doing a lot of fun activities.

It was nice to know that Outreach supports me no matter what and if you ask people not to treat you differently then they'll do it, and support you.

It was a brilliant thing to realise.

<u>How Did I Tell My Peers About My Rape?</u>

In an effort to be completely open and transparent with you, there has been a rough 5-week gap between me writing this section and the last section, because of my mental health. Yet that will be explored in a future chapter as well as the tips and tricks I used to manage my mental health as best I could.

Anyway, on the Monday night of the year 10 Residential, we created a WhatsApp group chat so we could all talk, relay information and sort out any problems during the Summer School if needed.

As I mentioned earlier by the time Monday night came along, I was already really struggling with everything and I knew there was a good chance I was going to get a lot worse, so I needed to protect my mental health.

This was made even worse when one of the less mature members of the Summer School, another student ambassador, made the group chat profile picture to be one of implied rape. Why the hell people working a school event would pick that is beyond me.

Well, this ambassador was a bit of an idiot too.

Therefore, when I saw that profile picture I got distressed, it triggered me and I was paralysed with rape sensations for another 30 minutes. I knew I had to get them to change the profile picture so I was going to have to tell them the reason why.

I posted the following on the group chat.

"Hey everyone, can we change the group chat image please?

Because all I'll say is (as hard as this is for me), I was raped in April so that sort of image is rather distressing to me and because this summer school is intense enough, there's a chance this event will be difficult for me. And I need to look after myself.

Apologies for this tough message, and please don't treat me any differently now you know I'm a rape survivor. I really like talking and working with all of you and I don't want that to change. Working with all of you over the past 15 weeks has helped me tons, so thank you all. Especially the summer core lot.

Sleep well everyone."

I went for this tone and sort of message in retrospect because I've worked with these people for a good few years, I really like them all and I was concerned they were going to treat me differently. Also, I had just spent the past month working with most of them every single working day on a wide range of Summer Core activities, and we had all become good friends.

As a result, the point of the message was to make sure they changed the image, that they knew what had happened to me and my biggest point was so they didn't treat me differently.

The worst thing for my mental health would have been for them to infantilise me, blame me or have a negative reaction.

How Did My Peers React To My Revelation?

I sent the message above at about 12:15 am because I was struggling too much to sleep beforehand and I had to get up at 6:30 am. I sent the message, put my phone on extreme power-saving mode so I couldn't receive notifications and I went straight to sleep.

Even when I got up the next morning, I showered, got changed and did French Duolingo before I even remotely thought about checking the messages.

Thankfully, there were lots of supportive messages considering the size of the group chat. There were 11 of us in the group chat so minus myself that's 10. When I checked the messages, there were 3 people who messaged saying how sorry they were that had happened, they're there for me if I needed any support and one of them changed the profile picture.

The idiot ambassador who made the silly profile picture in the first place never commented on this message. In all fairness, he probably felt too bad and I suspect he felt guilty because on the Thursday night (the end of the Summer School) we were all at a bar on campus and he made a comment and then he apologised to me. So he read it, remembered it and tried to change his behaviour.

That's good on him.

Then the next morning when me and another ambassador who I get along with brilliantly went into Canterbury city centre to pick up a student in a taxi, whilst we were waiting we were talking about random things then she suddenly said how brave I was, it was good I spoke up about it and she's sorry I had to go through that.

It was lovely.

That was all I got in terms of messages but

40% of people acknowledged it and made sure I was okay. That is still really good. As well as 0% of people treated me differently, negatively or judged me for my message.

That's all I care about.

In addition, one ambassador who I've known for years and we get on well he kept looking after me the next day. He would sit next to me and talk to me, he would subtly ask if I was okay and once we were in a talk and it was boiling hot so he kept giving me his tiny handheld fan.

It was really nice and I was surprised, but it was lovely.

<u>Over To You</u>

Ultimately, I know being a student ambassador who works part-time whilst being a university student isn't similar to your job. Yet there are still strong parallels because if you get on with your peers, if they actually care about you (a brilliant, resilient survivor) and if they're good people. Then they will listen, acknowledge and act on what you need to feel safe and get your work done.

I hope this chapter has shown you that it is possible to get support at work from your bosses, your peers and accommodations can be made.

It will still be difficult at times but if you need it, if your rape is impacting your ability to work then please consider telling your employer and asking for accommodations to be made.

If I didn't reveal my rape to my peers and bosses, I would have found the Summer School next to impossible and I think I would have had a very public and very bad meltdown that would have put my job at risk.

Please do what you need to do to keep yourself happy, able to work and safe.

You are more important than you'll ever realise.

THE GREAT COLLAPSE OF MY MENTAL HEALTH AND ALWAYS READ TRIGGER WARNINGS

Note: there are tricks and techniques layered throughout this chapter about how to cope with negative mental health, safety plans and how to heal from PTSD. Especially after the first two sections.

It pains me to admit this, but there's been a massive, very dark, very painful and extremely difficult 4-week gap in the writing of this book.

All because my mental health collapsed.

Of course, you've seen for the past 22 weeks how my mental health has ebbed and flowed, weakened and strengthened and how I've focused on the odd light in the darkness of this part of my life.

My mental health completely and utterly collapsed for the past four weeks, so much so my best friend has been really worried for me. They didn't sleep last night because they were so worried about me and so much has happened.

It's been impossibly dark most of the time between suicidal ideation, depression and even more depression. This is the worst my mental health has ever been and I have struggled so much just to function. It's one of the reasons why I haven't written this book for ages because I've been trying to focus on writing my academic paper, which I'm calling: *We Are Our Names: Transgender Individuals on Chosen Name Strategies and Mental Health Implications.*

I've managed to do everything for the

paper except finish the discussion section, conclusion, abstract and formatting it to be sent off to my supervisor. Since the past month has literally been a case of I have enough energy and mental capacity to do one major thing a day.

That is it and that is not how I normally am at all.

Anyway, in this chapter, I want to give you a brief overview of the past 4 weeks for me including my triggers, my experiences and how me and my best friend moved heaven and Earth to keep me alive.

What Happened?

My best friend went back up to the Midlands (for our international audience, this is the name of the region in the middle of England. Yes, the English are extremely creative with their names) to see family for 3 weeks starting on the 10th August. I met their parents for the first time on the 9th and it was lovely.

Yet me and my best friend, I finally need to give them a fake name so let's call them Purple (in all fairness that is trans and colour-blindness inside joke), were both concerned how I would cope being home alone for 3 weeks. I was going to see my parents, see my friend Henry and do some Outreach work but still.

We were concerned.

Anyway, that first week was really good. I flat out loved being home alone because I was being extremely productive, I was doing a ton of really fun writing and business projects and I was enjoying myself. I was doing 7-hour days, something I hadn't done since my rape.

However, my mental health kept dipping badly in the evening. It didn't help that I watched the first episode of *Young Royals*, two days after Purple left. It's a great gay royal romance TV series on Netflix set in Sweden. I'd been meaning to watch it for years but I hadn't and Purple had never really wanted to watch it.

They were gone and I needed a series to watch whilst I ate dinner.

Of course, in my 23 years of life, I have never ever had to read trigger warnings before so I watched it. At the 20-minute mark of the first episode there was straight sexual content, I screamed, jumped, had a panic attack and got depressed for 20 minutes until I texted Purple.

That is basically how my mental health started dipping and it kept dipping throughout the entire week. I really took a turn for the worse when Purple mentioned they were heading up to Liverpool to meet someone they met online for four days.

Now that actually did kill my mental health. 5% of it was probably jealousy that Purple wants to date someone who isn't me but 95% of it was just pure and utter grief that I cannot do that myself. I want to meet people, have a normal romantic life and enjoy that part of my life.

I will one day but when I'm depressed and struggling that just seems flat out impossible.

It was the Friday night of the first week that I learnt that Purple was going to Liverpool on Sunday to Wednesday. I knew my mental health was bad but I seriously didn't know how bad it was going to get.

When The Depression Started

On the Saturday morning, I woke up and really felt that something was wrong because I was so depressed, I couldn't get out of bed and I didn't see the point in anything. Luckily, I had

Henry coming round at 2 pm so I had to be ready before then so I forced myself to shower and do a little bit of hoovering.

And honestly, seeing Henry was lovely and it as exactly what I needed, but I didn't realise how the following message I sent Purple later on was just the tip of the iceberg in terms of me spiralling:

"It was lovely seeing Henry. He stayed for 4.5 hours just talking. We talked about Halo, Elden Ring, his parents and friends and social history. I spoke about my abusive upbringing and mentioned my parents' reaction to my rape. He was speechless about my parents both times.

A guy asked him out once. Edward kept talking to the guy but they drifted apart after that. I didn't have the heart to tell him, we thought he was bi.

He has a transwoman friend. Even though he only remembers her dead name which he knows how bad that is and he needs to talk to her more. She's great on a night out. Anyway, we had a trans conversation. He couldn't care less about my gender and his Mum thought I was a transman.

He has tons of friends, at least 20. He considers you a friend and there was my normal social awkwardness when he left. I think he wanted a handshake, I tried a hug then we settled on a hug. I think that was a bad idea because I think that's triggered me badly and I'm spiralling again.

I'm irritated you're the only one I can hug without having bad reactions.

It was nice seeing Henry. We're going to do something practical next time. He wants tennis. I firmly want something else but that involves me making a decision. Something... I will have to do it when I'm better.

I'm glad I have a friend I can see down here whilst you're away. It's a tiny light in the darkness."

Then as soon as Henry left I got slightly depressed because I was alone again and that set me up perfectly for the Great Collapse the next day. Below is a little extract from a podcast episode that summarises that particular Sunday for me:

"On the Sunday, it was even worse. And because it was so dark and so bad, I can't actually go into all of the details, but it was absolutely horrific.

All I'll say is it took me 3 hours and 20 minutes just to have a shower because the interesting thing about depression is that because it's a low mood, it really impacts your energy levels. So then what happened was that around 2:00 pm, I finally decided, right, I am gonna have a shower. I'm gonna move heaven and earth to have a shower.

Well, the issue with that is that you need to get up from the sofa, then you need to go upstairs, then you need to get your clothes, get your towel, go into the bathroom, have a shower, get changed, etc. So, when you think about it, there are actually quite a few steps to anything that we do. And normally, I can normally do that all in, like, 20 minutes.

On Sunday, it took me 3 hours, 20 minutes to have a shower. I mean, that was just like... It took me 15 minutes just to get up the stairs. But then I actually had to come back down, so I was depressed about that, and it was ridiculous. It wasn't until I actually got in the shower at 5:00 pm, and I was just like, there's no point in me actually having a shower because it's 5:00, and to me, that's pointless. But I was like, I've been trying to do this for three hours. I've got to try."

Afterwards, as the night went on my mental health got worse and worse. I self-harmed, I smashed my favourite mug in the entire world. It was a brilliant mug that I've had for 5 years now ever since I started my undergraduate degree and it was a 500 ml mug so it was great. I smashed it because I was so angry with my life, my rapist and my failing social support network. I still hate it that Purple is everything I have but it really got to me that night.

I was really bad and I wanted to kill myself and it just got to the point where I couldn't do anything.

Before Purple left, we had a discussion about how I could always text and call, and we had been texting every day that week. It was how they knew I was dipping throughout the week.

I called them on the Sunday night and we spent the next 75 minutes talking about me, we came up with safety plans and what we were going to do.

Moreover, it was so bad that I had to wrap up Purple's sharp knives in kitchen roll (I didn't want them to get dirty) and I had to throw them behind our tumble dryer because I kept trying to self-harm and kill myself with them.

We agreed to call every night basically regardless of what Purple was doing because they were going to make the time for me. And it worked out fine anyway because they could do whatever they wanted in the daytime, afternoon and evening and we would call between 10 pm and 11:30 pm depending on what they were doing.

In addition, we agreed that I would come up to the Midlands on the 30th August, because Purple would be back from a family holiday, seeing all their friends and Liverpool by that point. Then I would come up for the day and I would take them back to Canterbury the day after because one of our housemates (and really good friends) were moving in that day.

Furthermore, Purple made me go back to my parents for a few days so I wasn't alone, as well as I had a counselling appointment booked with my old therapist just so I could talk to someone in the meantime. And it was lovely talking to Purple because we spoke about how important we are to each other, how much better our lives are for having the other in it and we are just really good friends and Purple really, REALLY wants me around.

Therefore, I went back to my parents for three nights and three days and it was good. I wasn't alone when they were back from work, me and Purple called every night but I was still really depressed when I was alone. I couldn't do anything, I struggled to watch stuff and that was bad.

So that's basically how the next two weeks went, I was extremely depressed. I was still dealing with tons of PTSD, intrusive thoughts and "extreme" reactions to media and small triggers. I was a complete and utter mess most days and it was just impossible to function.

I had two really good therapy sessions but the "problem" was that my old counsellor isn't a rape specialist, so she couldn't help me too much. Yet it was lovely to talk to someone who wasn't Purple and to someone who had psychological training. Therefore, the first session was more me talking to her and educating her about the effects of sexual violence. Then in the second session, she gave me the following resources that are VERY useful and I **highly** recommend that you check them out for yourself:

- YouTube- Justin Haven All Trauma Is Treatable
- Dream Completion Technique- a technique to help PTSD nightmares
- Flash Technique- a great technique from EMDR.

As well as whilst I couldn't really do too much, I could manage one major thing a day which I dedicated to focusing on my academic paper and my psychology podcast.

Those two things were very important to me and I realised if I didn't try to focus on my academic paper then it would never be done and it's too "important" for that to happen.

A Potential Productivity Trick Whilst Depressed

One trick I did discover thankfully was I could manage doing one session/ sitting on my laptop before my depression and executive dysfunction kicked in. Then I would be depressed, disassociated or just spiralling for hours at a time.

However, I did learn after a while that if I wanted to force myself to do another session on my laptop or try to be productive. I could make myself a really nice Toffee Nut Latte with my Tassimo machine and promise myself that if I allow myself to have their luxury drink. Then in exchange, I need to do some stuff on my laptop.

It worked.

It was a good productivity hack on my "bad but not horrific" days and it allowed me to get some extra things done for my paper.

A Lovely Respite: Seeing Purple Again Wasn't The End of My Struggles, It Was The Midpoint

I thought Friday 30th August 2024 would be the end of my mental health struggles, and I would go back to what I was like before Purple went back to see their family and friends in the Midlands. In other words, still struggling, still having PTSD and everything I've spoken about in previous chapters. Yet not be depressed, unable to function and struggle as much as I had been.

I was wrong.

However, first of all, I went up to Midlands leaving at 7:20 am and arriving at Purple's house about 3 and a bit hours later but Purple was having an Osteopathic massage so I met their brother for the first time and spoke to him for ages. I'd been wanting to meet him for months because him and Purple got on well, he really supported Purple being non-binary and queer and that was such a violently alien concept for me that I wanted to meet him. And I thought I might be attracted to him (he's straight) but I'm still interested. I wasn't attracted to him in the end.

Anyway, Purple came back and we had a lovely lunch with their brother and Mum. We spoke for ages then me and Purple went Ice Skating, which was interesting.

Now I stressed to Purple in quite a few of our calls that I wanted to live, have fun and I wanted to be anywhere but indoors. Because I'd been stuck depressed and suicidal indoors for the past three weeks. Purple had suggested ice skating because there wasn't a great amount to do in the town they lived in that was filled with Rich Old White people.

Also, I am many things but I am not a sporty person. I've always wanted to go ice skating so I went and me and Purple had a brilliant 1.5 hours of skating. I laughed a lot, had a lot of fun and Purple really enjoyed it too.

However, the current joke (more like reality) is that I do not do sports because I am good at them. I do sports because I am so bad at them that I make everyone laugh.

I fell off so many times that I have 3 massive swallowed lumps on my right elbow, my right hip and under my right rib. Also, I had a minor swallowed lump at the base of my spine when I fell, hit my tailbone and let out an extremely loud scream that made everyone in the arena stop, look at me and go deadly silent until I got back up.

Anyway, it was great fun and I wouldn't change it for the world.

Afterwards, Purple showed me round their town and it was very nice. Then we went to Café Nero and had a coffee and something to eat, and I asked Purple about how worried they've been and how they're feeling.

They stressed that they're better now I was with them because they could keep an eye on me, but they were… they are worried about me. That change of tense was what they actually did in the conversation.

Only neither one of knew I was going to get worse still.

Following our coffee break we went to the park because Purple wanted to teach me some skateboarding, and because I wasn't in the ice ring anymore I took my hoody off.

The park itself was really nice with lots of young families laughing, smiling and running about as did young couples and dogwalkers. There was a nice warm breeze and the air was really refreshing, clean and calming.

So Purple talked to me about skateboarding, I tried, fell off immediately and scraped my already-swollen elbow on the path. So much so that there was a lot of dark red rich blood and we went straight back to their parents and their Mum fussed over me.

I bleed for a fair while.

We returned to Canterbury the next day.

<u>The Next Week: It Gets Worse</u>

At this point in the chapter, you need to realise that my mental health can be absolutely horrific, but one of my many superpowers is the ability to mask and act extremely well in front of other people. That is the survivor in me, it is what I have always had to be just to survive. It started in childhood and it is something I have just had to continue.

Then I crumble and collapse when I'm alone with someone I trust.

Therefore, me and Purple returned to Canterbury the next day and it was lovely seeing our other housemate and friend again. We caught up, we laughed, we talked and it was great.

Even though I realised I was still dipping very badly.

Over the course of the next week, I actually had some Outreach work. The first proper work I had in the past three weeks so it was nice seeing people again, but I was struggling. It was whenever I wasn't at Outreach work and I was home with my two friends. I was depressed and barely able to function.

I felt guilty that I was so bad, I was annoyed that I was openly being depressed in front of Purple and our other friend. It was awful.

However, Purple and our friend didn't mind, they understood and they were there for me. They're both really good friends even though Purple is the only one I can really talk to about stuff.

Honestly, most of that week is a blur because I was so depressed, it was two weeks ago and most of it was Outreach work and just crippling depression.

Nonetheless, we did go out and play Tennis with Henry and one of Purple's friends on the Thursday evening. It was "interesting" weather for it because the sky was grey, the air was moist and had a slight chill to it and the tarmac outdoor court had a slight slippiness to it.

Now, I am not good at Tennis but thankfully Purple's friend is horrific and even worse than me. It was a great, really fun and enjoyable time. It was a good escape from my depression and executive dysfunction for two hours.

Even though, my mental health was never going to leave me alone for two full hours especially when I was playing a game like tennis. A game that requires more mental capacity than I realised.

Around the 90-minute mark, I knew I was in trouble because I couldn't focus, I couldn't make decisions, I was terrified. Purple had already picked up something was wrong so we had a break and I went to the toilet.

Normally escaping to the toilet, getting depressed or calming myself down works when my executive dysfunction kicks in when I'm not at home. Yet that wasn't really an option at the tennis centre so I tried what I could in the toilet but I knew I was in trouble.

I went back we played light tennis for another 20 minutes including Henry and Purple (the two best tennis players) played against each other. Purple won.

Afterwards, we headed back to mine and Purple's place to hang out, but my executive dysfunction was so bad I couldn't talk. I needed to tell Purple that Henry wanted to do something about dinner but I didn't have the mental capacity to cook so I needed Purple to help me.

In the end, I wrote it on an email draft so they could read it.

Later on, I found out that Purple was really worried that I would go non-verbal for the evening. That's happened to them before.

Thankfully, I didn't go non-verbal and it was a lovely evening filled with talking, laughter and I just really, really like hanging out with Henry. He's cool and it's just brilliant to have another friend.

Highlighting A Tip

Just to make this tip very, very clear to all you wonderful readers, if we're experiencing executive dysfunction and you cannot talk to other people. You can **text** them or you can **write it down** so you can still communicate if you cannot form words.

Our Housemate Leaves, Purple Leaves, The Final-ish Week

It's honestly weird saying that it was the last week because the rest of this chapter covers the past 9 days but honestly it feels like a decade ago. I actually had to look at my calendar to remind myself what had happened because it was so bad and I've tried to block it out for the most part.

Saturday I can summarise shortly as our housemate left, me and Purple had a nice day together just talking, watching stuff and having some time just the two of us as close friends and we spoke about some stuff we couldn't talk about in front of our other friend. It was nothing bad or about my mental health, it was just other stuff.

Anyway, because my mental health was only getting worse, I said to Purple, the idea of me being alone for a week makes me want to kill myself. I was deadly serious about that.

Granted we had our final housemate moving in on the Wednesday (someone we kind of know but not really), and I was concerned I would feel even more lonely and depressed with our other housemate because they might be out a lot, they might be in their room a lot and so on.

Also, it really isn't the other housemate's job to provide me with social contact.

Purple suggested I come up on to the Midlands on Thursday because I had to be here on Wednesday to let our final housemate in, I had Outreach work Wednesday evening and all day on Thursday and Purple was seeing friends up until Thursday night anyway.

We both agreed that four days with Purple should be perfectly fine.

We were seriously wrong.

I went out with my "social environment" (I am trying to be anomalous here) on Sunday and that was a disaster. I realised just how negative, homophobic and disrespectful they were. It was a nice day with them in the sense that we caught up, we had a coffee, lunch and we did some sightseeing in Canterbury.

However, my "social environment" never asked me how I was because they don't want to know about my rape trauma because it hurts them too much, they were still homophobic and they don't respect my boundaries.

For example, I simply ask do NOT touch me without answering and do not touch me in certain ways.

They took me clothes shopping (I didn't want to go anyway) and I was already depressed and suicidal at this point anyway. And they kept touching me in certain ways that I will not tell you in case it triggers you, so I had a PTSD reaction and they shouted at me.

They believed they should be allowed to touch me because they are my "social environment" and I'm simply overreacting.

They dropped me off at my student house and I just disassociated for two hours, I was depressed, suicidal and Purple left 9 am that morning and they weren't available to call that night.

Sunday night was really bad.

When it came to Monday and Tuesday, they were only 8 and 9 days ago but I don't really remember them. I know me and Purple called Monday night and Purple was so angry with my "social environment" and we spoke for a good hour on the phone, and I was constantly dealing with PTSD reactions and intrusive thoughts about my "social environment" touching and doing things to me.

Then Tuesday, I spiralled so badly because I was so terrified of going to sleep. This sums up how horrific Tuesday night was for me and this is what I sent Purple at 2:30 am:

Please note: Purple later said to me, it's okay that you spiralled. You need to be kind to yourself when this happens. Please listen to Purple yourself.

"I'm sorry okay. I'm an idiot. I spiralled badly for the past 4 hours all because the images of Mum raping me because of those stupid touches and her shouting at me. I just wanted the thoughts and physical sensations to stop.

I kept disassociating but I was scared. I just wanted something else to focus on when the thoughts flooded me.

Nothing happened but I went on Grindr and talked to guys with the intention to have sex. I got close to setting stuff up. I didn't.

Maybe a fucked up part of me wants to get raped properly like Mum keeps saying. Maybe I want to prove I was raped whatever that means. Maybe I just want to get raped and killed.

I JUST WANT THE THOUGHTS TO STOP.

I'm sorry. I just can't do this anymore. I don't want to have images of every single person I meet raping me. No one cares about my rules, no one cares about talking to me. It feels I have to shout at the world to be heard even slightly.

That's why I need to die.

No I'm sorry. I'm so sorry.

I didn't mean it. I'm just spiralling. I need sleep but if I sleep the thoughts return.

I'm sorry. I'm probably hurting you and that's why I won't kill myself because I never want to hurt you.

I'm going to sleep and I'll wake up and have a better day. I won't but I want to wake up and be alive.

I'm sorry it's always you. I'm more sorry than you'll ever know. You never deserve this.

Good night. Hope you'll sleeping okay."

As you can see I was in a right state and I had terrified myself.

Wednesday was just more of the same sort of bad and depressed mental health, but Outreach work was fun. As well as I had a good two-hour conversation with our new housemate getting to know them and it was good.

In addition, I got my first rape counselling session scheduled because they phoned me. Yet the problem was I was too depressed to feel anything about the session that I've been wanting and hoping for for months. Purple was a lot more excited about the appointment than I was.

Then on Thursday, I had a fun day at the particular Outreach event I was working then it took me 4.5 hours to get to Purple's parents. Purple had another friend round when I arrived so I met this friend for about an hour (her and Purple don't see each other often) then I literally collapsed and let everything out when it was just me and Purple.

Purple held me for an hour whilst we watched stuff and I was really "out of it". I was shaking, disassociating and nothing felt real at times.

It was bad.

Fortunately, the next few days in the Midlands was fine in the daytime. Friday, me and Purple relaxed and watched stuff whilst their Dad was away on one of his projects. We watched the Dungeons and Dragons: Honour Amongst Thieves movie and it was good. Then I introduced Purple to a livestream of the game Space Marines 2.

It is brilliant.

Then Purple's Mum came home from being in France and it's always lovely seeing her.

My mental health always dies in the evening and at nighttime, which wasn't fun but I managed.

And the Saturday was surprisingly lovely because Purple was meeting up with a very old friend from secondary school who they hadn't seen for two years. This was arranged before my mental health died and me coming up to the Midlands this week wasn't planned until 4 days before I arrived.

So originally I was just going to do some academic work (and more than likely spend tons of hours depressed until Purple came home). Thankfully, Purple's Mum really likes me and I really like her so for the next seven hours (not including the two hours I spent doing laptop things) until Purple came home. We went for coffee and cake in town, we picked up medication where the pharmacist thought I was Purple, we went for a toastie, went in some shops, went for an hour long dog walk and then we spent a few hours in the garden with Purple's Dad. And because Purple's Mum is French we had an aperitif for an hour (just think a starter. Sorry, French people for the extremely cruel and slightly wrong definition)

Now the funny thing is that Sunday and Monday were literally two and three days ago. Sunday was just cooking a nice brunch for me and Purple before we drove back to Canterbury and Monday was working on my academic paper (for the first time in two weeks). I do not remember anything else about those days.

Then everything went to hell yesterday.

<u>The Climax Of Horrific Mental Health</u>

At the time of writing, it's Fresher's Week here in the UK so all the new university students are coming along to fun welcome events and trying to make new friends. Even though me and Purple are not first years, everyone still goes to these events to have fun and try to make new friends.

I was looking forward to yesterday because it was the LGBT+ coffee morning and then there were Board Games and other events going on. I wanted to make friends and I was going to try so hard.

However, I forgot how bad my mental health was so me and Purple went there, then me and Purple managed to attract a group of different people and they're very nice. Purple got on like a house on fire with them, I felt extremely lonely sitting at that table surrounded by my best friend and 8 others.

I didn't feel like I could connect with any of them because I don't share their interests. Purple later said they think I could but I need to try, keep contributing to conversations and effectively "use" going out with this social group to get introduced to other people I could connect with.

Anyway, during board games I went to the toilet, then I got depressed on the toilet for a surprising 45 minutes. I should have known I was in trouble but I kept going. I had a psychology neurodivergent event I was supporting too.

However, afterwards, I met back up with Purple and the group of friends we had made earlier in the day and we talked and did arty things for the next 2 hours. Then one of the friends mentioned they've been raped (they did ask for trigger warnings but I was silly and didn't mention it. I didn't want anyone to know I've experienced sexual violence. I had only just met them) so that distressed me.

Also, I got so depressed and suicidal sitting doing arty things and they had already made plans for the evening to continue late into the night. I couldn't do that and then sex conversations popped up.

I had to left then and I basically cried all the way back to my car, Purple had stayed thankfully and the rest of the night went to hell until Purple came back four hours later.

Now I cannot accurately describe how bad last night was myself so I'm going to show you what I sent Purple when I was extremely out of it. Thankfully, texting Purple helps me but sending these texts were next to impossible and then I want to caveat all this too afterwards:

"I do NOT want you home. I want you to enjoy your evening.

Make a decision for me please. I absolutely can't and I don't want to eat because if I don't eat I die sooner.

Should I cook or finish livestream?

Actually tell me to cook please. I'll do both. I'm likely to actually attempt the intensely difficult task if you ask me to do it.

Also, your small sharp knife is behind the microwave. I kept trying to slice my left upper arm but your knife isn't sharp enough to do that with small blade movements. So I splashed boiling hot water on my hand instead.

I'm sorry. I'm texting you. Everything's starting to feel real again, so I'm slightly better. I'll probably just be depressed. It's fine.

Please just do NOT come home until the evening's naturally ended. I WANT you to live your life with friends and do anything that makes me want to kill myself.

If you want a lift text me. I probably won't sleep tonight so yeah....

I better start cooking before the depression returns fully."

And I should note that I do send Purple very intense messages but we do have a healthy close friendship and I do leave them alone for the most part. For example, last night I was going through hell, depression and really wanting to kill myself, I didn't call them. I wanted to leave them alone and just allow them to have a nice evening with their new friends.

And even now, Purple's been out with another friend for 4 hours and I haven't texted them once. I haven't needed to. Granted they have just texted me saying they're on their way home.

My point is, these are extremely intense messages that make Purple seriously worry about me but we do have boundaries, we are healthy and Purple knows and will tell me if they need to step back.

Ultimately, when they came back, they were extremely fatigued because of socialising, health stuff and it was a long day. We spoke about their day, my mental health and we made enough safety plan because their sharp knives keep becoming an issue.

I'm banned from opening the draw and they're in and if I want anything in there for cooking I need to text permission.

It's a good safety plan. Annoying, but it will be effective.

And I know Purple was terrified for me because we always hug before we go to bed, it's what Purple does with their friends. Normally, their one to break the hug first and then I do. Last night, I went to break the hug and Purple just hugged me tighter and they spoke to me for a minute whilst tightly hugging me.

Then I learnt I was a big reason why they couldn't sleep last night. In addition to social anxiety and something they were doing this morning.

Overall, my dear readers, that is the past four weeks of my life. Just over 6,000 words on how my mental health has just died and the safety plans and other tips and tricks I have done just to still be alive when all I have wanted to do is kill myself at times.

However, life does get better and there are small positive moments that make everything worthwhile and worth living for. Because if I had killed myself, I never would have gone up to the Midlands and gone ice skating, I never would have had such a lovely time with Purple's Mum and I wouldn't have had the lovely conversations with Purple over the past month.

I am happy to be alive, and I want you to keep living too regardless of how bad your mental health is.

There is light, happiness and hope at the end of the tunnel no matter how pitch black the tunnel is in the meantime.

Never give up.

WHAT IS IT LIKE TO EXPERIENCE A MAJOR DEPRESSIVE EPISODE?

In the last chapter, I spoke about horrific my mental health has been for the past month and even though my rape counselling started today thankfully, I only gave you a brief overview. In our next chapter, I want to give you a more focused look at how mental health collapsed in the first week of this on-going depressive episode.

I wanted to include this aspect of my mental health in the book. Again, because I want you to know whatever you're experiencing it is normal, okay and you CAN survive it.

In addition, I normally say this to my psychology audience but whilst we learn a lot of content about different mental health conditions. It is only lived experience that can possibly help us to truly understand what a condition is like for a client or service user. Since we can all read as many academic papers or resources on depression but until you talk or listen to people who have or are currently experiencing depression then you will never be able to fully understand how depression impacts a person. Especially in their everyday life.

As a result, I am including this very personal chapter in this even-more personal book to help you understand what you might be experiencing. I hope it helps you, your loved one or the survivor in your life.

Why Am I Talking About Experiencing Depression?

Note: this is a cleaned-up audio transcription from the recording I made when I was experiencing a wave of depression. I did not realise I was as depressed as I was when I was making the record, so there will be grammatical errors. Since this is spoken word and not written word.

I've hinted at my depression and declining mental health in the past two episodes. Therefore, the reason why I'm talking about this is because since Saturday, so seven days now, I've been having quite a major depressive episode, and I've never actually had this before. Sure, I've had one or two days of being depressed, and I mean going through quite crippling depression, but I've never had it for seven days.

And yes, it's sort of gotten a little better, but I'm still quite depressed now, though. For example, the only reason why I can actually record this and sound relatively normal in terms of this is what I normally sound like, at least I hope so, is because I've just been texting my best friend because they wanted to know about what plant pot they had in their bedroom. And I was like, "Oh God, I'm gonna have to go and look."

So, I did that, and we were talking, and we were texting to and fro for a bit, and I was making fun of them for their mason jars here. Thankfully, this helped me to have quite a bit of energy. But I know that will seriously dip, though. I thought, right now I feel good, I've got to do this.

Overall, the reason why I'm talking about this is, one, because of the practical issue that I just spoke about. Two, as a future clinical psychologist, or maybe even qualified psychologists and people interested in lived mental health experiences, it is really important that we do understand not only what academia says about a mental health condition, but we also hear about it from those people with a life experience. Of course, I do not have a depression diagnosis. To be honest, I do have a scary feeling that I'm not actually gonna get any better by saying "over the next week." And because I have been feeling depressed for two weeks, this is just off the top of my head, so don't quote me on this, that's actually all you need for a depression diagnosis, of course, as long as you meet the other criteria too, though.

So, at the moment, I don't have a depression diagnosis, and I'm hoping that I won't ever have to get one. So, I'm talking about this just so we can all understand lived-like experiences here.

An Overview Of My Week

I already mentioned earlier that this all started on Saturday, but there's something larger that's going on here. So, as you guys know, I experienced sexual violence back in April, and that has really messed with my mental health. That has been quite debilitating, and I've been doing tons of different bits to try and get better in that sense. But I'm still on a waiting list for specialist rape counselling, which is taking a toll on my mental health because I need this support, but I can't get it because it turns out there's a lot of people that get raped. So, it takes a while for a place to open up for you, which is tragic. And I'm basically coping as best I can with my mental health getting worse as the months go by, especially my PTSD. And I mean, like, I think I've had two days of depression since my, so to like 19 weeks ago tomorrow at the time of recording.

I've not had it for seven days before.

In addition, what happened was that on Saturday, I started to feel quite depressed. I started to feel really down, and it was a struggle to get out of bed. Thankfully, I had a friend coming round at 2:00 just because we had already planned it, and I wanted to spend time with him because we get on really well. But the problem was, was that I couldn't get out of bed. It took me a long time to have a shower, not as much as the next day though. And it took me a while to do everything. So, thankfully, I was ready for when he came around at 2:00, but I wanted to do stuff before then. I wanted to do some writing, I wanted to do some podcast work and other stuff, but that really didn't happen.

Me and my friend had a really nice four and a half hours. It was really nice talking. We spoke about Halo Lore. We basically talked about a bunch of nerd stuff, then we talked about relationships and other bits and pieces, basically stuff you normally talk with your friends about. Then he left, and then I was just like, oh, right, I'm actually quite sad now. I'm actually feeling ridiculously lonely and everything. And then it was a full-on night of just PTSD. I mean, if there was a sound, I would have a massive reaction. There were tons of intrusive thoughts about sexual violence.

That was not fun.

On the Sunday, it was even worse. And because it was so dark and so bad, I can't actually go into all of the details, but it was absolutely horrific.

All I'll say is it took me 3 hours and 20

minutes just to have a shower because the interesting thing about depression is that because it's a low mood, it really impacts your energy levels. So then what happened was that around 2:00 pm, I finally decided, right, I am gonna have a shower. I'm gonna move heaven and earth to have a shower.

Well, the issue with that is that you need to get up from the sofa, then you need to go upstairs, then you need to get your clothes, get your towel, go into the bathroom, have a shower, get changed, etc. So, when you think about it, there are actually quite a few steps to anything that we do. And normally, I can normally do that all in, like, 20 minutes.

On Sunday, it took me 3 hours, 20 minutes to have a shower. I mean, that was just like... It took me 15 minutes just to get up the stairs. But then I actually had to come back down, so I was depressed about that, and it was ridiculous. It wasn't until I actually got in the shower at 5:00 pm, and I was just like, there's no point in me actually having a shower because it's 5:00, and to me, that's pointless. But I was like, I've been trying to do this for three hours. I've got to try.

And then, as the night went on, my mental health deteriorated. I broke my favorite mug. I smashed my favorite mug ever. Oh, God. I mean, I was actually quite devastated because it's this half-liter mug, which is just amazing. I've had it since 2019, since I first came to university, so I broke it, and then I just called my best friend, and we spoke for, like, an hour and a quarter, and then they were just like, "Right. You need to go home. You need to be around people," and, etc. So, I went...

I got back to my parents at half past midnight that night because me and my friend had a really heartfelt conversation. We'd had a really detailed one. Over the next two days, it was just constant depression. I was in and out of it because my parents work during the days, I was alone. Again, quite depressed. I couldn't really do anything. I had no energy. And then when they were back, it was fine because I was around people, so we could talk and stuff. Some stuff happened, but, I mean, that's just family.

And then I came back Wednesday because I saw my great aunt, who lives, like, nearby. Then I came back. Now, bear in mind, when my mug had shattered that night, I actually hadn't cleaned it up because I was just like... My mental health was so bad, I didn't have the capacity to actually clean it up. So, then I walked in at Wednesday, and I was just like, "Oh, my God, I'm back here. I've got to clean the mug. I've got to do tons of stuff." It took me an hour and 40 minutes just to clean that mug up. And that did not make me feel great. So that all happened.

Following on from this, yesterday, thankfully, I was able to do a few bits, but it was the energy levels that were really concerning me, because it was more of a thing about being in and out of depression and it basically not stopping and me not being able to reliably do stuff. I managed to do, I don't know, let's say four hours of stuff. It really wasn't that, it was more, like, two and a half because I tried to do some stuff. It was so unproductive. And considering I'm normally used to doing seven hours with ease of different bits and pieces, that was quite shocking, and that was actually quite bad. Quite bad.

Unfortunately, today it's just been more of

the same. There has been a lot of other very traumatic things going on in the background. But again, just to keep this podcast easy to listen to, or at least nice to listen to, I'm not gonna go into it.

I just had to pause the podcast because I thought I heard a noise outside. I thought I was going to have a bad reaction. And then I felt a massive hit of depression almost hit, though. So, I've got to keep going with this, otherwise, it's not gonna get done.

What Triggered This Depressive Episode?

As with all mental health conditions and difficulties, there are always goning be triggers and different aspects of this which make your mental health worse. Thankfully the only highlight of being depressed for seven days is that there are moments when you can actually think clearly. Oh, believe me, it happens extremely rarely, but they still happen.

As a result, the thing that really triggered my depression and the thing that keeps making me feel worse is one, of course, the sexual violence. Two, just being really lonely because I really don't have many friends. And my best friend, they went back to the midlands to see their family and spend time with their friends. As well as basically, everyone I know is out there doing really cool stuff. They're going away, they're having fun, they're seeing their other friends. And because of my PTSD, because of everything else, my issue is that I actually can't do the same.

Then there's also been some relationship stuff that were present. My best friends have been doing some relationship stuff. The LGBT+ society at my university, some of those conversations have been about past and current romantic relationships. And as someone who's been through sexual violence and also child abuse that was very homophobic, it's sort of like... I don't know if I can have that.

I know logically, I can, but I mean, like, there's gonna be so much work to actually do that for. So that really didn't help me. And also, PTSD is bad enough, but when it comes to going outside, that doesn't help. But also, something I've been finding a lot lately when I've been going outside, like, going shopping is a nightmare. For instance, I tend to forget a lot. I find it really hard to focus. So as you can expect, it's really tough going out. As well as in my mind, if you're going go out properly, like, you're going to go somewhere, you do tend to need a friend just to make it more, enjoyable. And you can do it as a shared experience.

But because my only real friend is actually not here at the moment, that's really tough.

What Are The Challenges Of Experiencing Depression?

Moreover, there are four main challenges which I'm really struggling with at the moment. The first one is an inability to watch stuff because it's bad enough when I'm in and out of being depressed, which is another major problem because I can just be going along, then a wave of depression can just hit me. It can also be linked to triggers. For example, I can be doing stuff, then an intrusive thought comes out that's really bad, quite traumatic. Then it knocks me for six, and then I get depressed, and I just lay on the stairs, on the sofa, or wherever I am for half an hour to an hour.

That's bad enough.

But when I'm depressed, I also have a massive problem. I can't watch stuff because I can't watch things on the TV or any streaming service because of sexual references and sex scenes, which never used to bother me whatsoever. But because that's how bad my mental health is at the moment, I can't watch any of that because it's too distressing, it's too triggering, which is annoying.

As a result, that was another reason why me and my best friend, we were on the phone for two and a quarter hours last night, as they were going through and compiling me a list of different series and films which I might be able to watch. But as I said to them, the main problem with that is, and just know I am extremely grateful that they did that. And I'm definitely gonna start watching some of it at some point. But some of it is that, yeah, you can have this list, you can have stuff to do, but you don't have the energy to actually do it, or you don't have the executive function to do it, which is an issue.

My third major challenging of experiencing depression is loss of pleasure. I've always known this is a depression symptom, but I've never had to experience it before. So, you can be doing stuff which you normally flat-out love. Like earlier today, I was flat-out loving doing some business stuff, but I wasn't enjoying it. It was just like, "Wow, this is actually quite boring." And sure, I sort of picked the more mundane aspects, but I still enjoy it. I still don't mind doing it. It's so important to me. I did not enjoy it.

Normally, I can do some reading, I can do a hobby, or I can do anything that I find really fun. No, not this week. I've just lost pleasure in most things, which is why I'm a bit concerned about this list that my friends put was they really love all of these programs. I don't wanna be the type of person who turns around and says, "Oh, thank you for doing this, but I really don't like this. I couldn't really care less about this." I'm pretty sure that's just the depression, but still, I don't want to do that even though I think that might be the case. But I will honestly try and enjoy this stuff.

But the main issue that I've been having is energy.

I know this is linked to a low mood, but the energy is that I really only have so much energy to be able to do stuff in the day. And I like to think of this in terms of spoons theory.

I've done an autism podcast episode maybe two years ago on spoons. So, the idea of this, and this is done by Christina someone, is that there's the idea that you only have so many spoons in terms of energy throughout the day, and every time you do something, you take away a spoon.

Let's say you have 10 spoons. Then what happens is that if you get up, then you could lose a spoon. If you go to work, if you have a shower, then you lose another spoon. Then if you get the kids ready, take them to school and get to work, that's another spoon. Then you have a really hard day at work, you have lots of meetings, you're working a very high-pressure job.

Let's say that actually takes five spoons away from you. That means you've only got two spoons left by the time you get home from work. But then let's say you've got to pick up the kids, and then you've got to do dinner. Both of those activities takes away your two spoons. Therefore, after you've cooked dinner, you might not have even served it up yet. You're completely exhausted, and you have no energy whatsoever. That's how you can think about energy levels in terms of spoons. That's something I found quite annoying yesterday, was that I was trying to do stuff, I wanted to do stuff, I had no energy after a while to do it whatsoever.

What am I trying to do to feel better?

I'm between a rock and a hard place.

The reason why I'm sort of in a rock and a hard place is quite simply because what I need is my rape counseling to start.

Nonetheless, that can't happen because I'm still on the waiting list. And my contact at this charity that I'm gonna be seen by, she's on annual leave until the 27th of August. That's five days away, at the very least. And in the meantime, I sort of keep suffering. Of course, it's not the charity's fault. This is just how life works. But she can't chase it, and she can't say, "Right, this person needs help ASAP. Can we please try and fit them in?"

So that's what I really, really need, and that's the sort of the solution. As soon as I start processing my rape and everything, then everything will get better. But until then, I am trying to do one or two things. I'm calling my best friend every night. We're having quite long conversations about each other's day, how I'm doing. And it's nice because it's social connection when I normally wouldn't get any social connection, which is quite a depressing fact, but that's just my life at the moment.

And then the only other thing which I'm really doing because this week's been quite difficult because, I mean, I can't go back to my parents again because they're away, and the whole point is that I'm lonely. So I can't just go somewhere else to be lonely. That defeats the whole point.

The only other thing I'm doing is I'm seeing my private therapist this week and next week. Both of us have agreed she's not a rape specialist. So, it's a case of me just talking to her. To be honest, like, I'm educating her about sexual violence because I've done so much research in the past 19 weeks. And I mean, it's nice just having someone to talk to, but I know it's sort of just sticking plaster on a very crumbling wall at the moment.

Oh, no. Actually, the only other last thing that I'm doing, though, is that next week, I'm going up to see my best friend in the midlands. So, we can see each other, we can go to this city that I've always wanted to go to, more for a laugh than anything else. But this got quite a reputation. And originally, I wanted to go by myself, but my best friend was like, "You can't. You just can't. Like, I don't think you'll be able to cope."

Of course, they said in much more polite terms than this, but I was just like, "You're right," and I'm really annoyed that I just can't go out without having a meltdown, without having an inability to make decisions and just getting overwhelmed, anxiety, PTSD, etc.

So, all fun, not.

As a result, I'm going up to see them, and their parents are going be there. And, I mean, I get on great with their parents. Their parents are lovely. And I might be able to meet their brother, which would be nice because I've been wanting to meet him for ages.

Ultimately, there's a lot's going on. I'm just trying to hang in there. And I don't know if this was a useful podcast episode, but I hope you got something out of it.

WHAT IS RAPE GRIEF?

Previously in the book, I've spoken a lot about how after my rape I researched sexual violence and Post-Traumatic Stress Disorder, because I wanted to understand what was happening to me, why I was having such extreme trauma responses and how I could heal. A lot of people who experience various types of trauma and mental health conditions do this and we all find various psychology facts, techniques and revelations that stick with us. For me, understanding rape grief was profoundly helpful, stabilizing and for the first time, it gave me words to describe a unique aspect of my rape and its consequences that no one had spoken about.

Therefore, in this chapter, you'll learn what is rape grief, why is this a powerful concept for rape survivors and more. If you enjoy learning about trauma recovery, healing from sexual violence and mental health, then this will be a great chapter for you.

What Is Rape Grief?

I think I found the concept of "rape grief" extremely powerful and important to me because it captured so much of what I was experiencing in the early days after my rape.

Therefore, grief is an intense emotional response to significant personal loss, and this painful emotional experience can include us wanting what we had lost back, concerns and fears about the future, as well as remorse for what we did and didn't do in a given moment.

Now everyone experiences grief at some point in their life and it isn't always around death despite popular opinion. For instance, yes, when someone dies we want our loved one back, we get fearful and concerned about how we will deal with them no longer being there in the future and we question whether they knew we loved them or not.

Equally, when it comes to jobs, we can yearn for that job promotion we never got, we can question if we said the right thing or not in an interview and we might question how we will work at the company now someone else is your boss or got the promotion.

We can experience grief around anything as long as there is that personal loss.

In addition, grief isn't a bad thing. Whilst it is a painful emotional experience, grief is a natural part of our lives and everyone will go through grief at some point in their life. It only becomes a clinical difficulty or "condition" if the grief causes clinically significant levels of psychological distress and impaired functioning in multiple domains of life. Like home life, work and school. As well as if it generates thoughts of self-harm, self-neglect and sometimes grief can be powerful enough to harm our own immune system.

As a result, when it comes to rape and other examples of sexual trauma, this "rape grief" follows the initial shock of the attack. This shock eventually leads to feelings of loss and fear amongst the sexual assault survivors because the survivors can lose a lot because of the attacker. For instance, survivors can feel a loss of their sense of safety and the following too:

- Loss of their lifestyle
- Loss of their physical and mental health.
- Loss of trust in other people
- Loss of their ability to work
- Loss of their hopes and dreams about the future

- Loss of virginity if their rape was their first sexual encounter
- Loss of important relationships. This is mainly if the attacker belongs to their family or group of friends.
- Loss of interest in physical intimacy
- Loss of ability to resume their normal roles like going to school.
- Loss of self-esteem

Personally, I don't believe there is a single one of those bullet points that I haven't experienced myself. Although, I will add in my book *I Am Survivor, Not A Victim* I do comment in there I firmly reject the idea that rape counts as losing your virginity. That was a very healing moment for me.

However, during the first 7 months of my rape, I felt a massive sense of loss because I had lost my sense of safety, my sense of hope about the future and the idea that I could ever work again or live a normal life. As well as I completely lost my ability to live my lifestyle and do my normal roles.

Moreover, when we consider how significant and how many of these sense of losses combine, it is no surprise that sexual assault survivors experience rape grief to extreme levels. The process of healing from rape grief isn't linear or easy or straightforward in the slightest. When I consider my own mental health journey, there have been major breakthrough moments where I thought my life was changed and healed forever, then new triggers, new fears and new experiences cause that all to change so this requires more healing. Trauma recovery ebbs and flows and it depends on the triggers that the client experiences as these act as reminders of what the client has lost.

In addition, one of the most annoying things but equally, it was this fact that I found healing. It is the fact that survivors experiencing rape grief will have conflicting emotions. For example, I remember this clearly because I had just found out about rape grief, I was sitting on the ugly red sofas in our shared house and me and my best friend had moved in together whilst the other two didn't until two months later. After a month, we were sitting on the sofa in the afternoon, I was depressed and I wanted to be alone. Yet I wanted to be with my best friend. I wanted to share everything with my best friend including the nightmares about them raping me (my best friend would never ever do that to me) but I didn't want to tell them because it would hurt them. And so many more conflicting emotions and thoughts.

I felt insane half the time.

And it is that simple realisation that it is okay for rape survivors to feel so many conflicting emotions.

It is normal. As difficult, insane and awful as you feel when you're experiencing all these different emotions, you are reacting normally to an extremely abnormal situation.

<u>Why You Should NOT Tell A Rape Survivor "Time Heals All Wounds"?</u>

There are a lot of different phrases and other rubbish that has been said to me as a rape survivor that have been the opposite of helpful. I cover a whole bunch of them in my book *I Am A Survivor, Not A Victim* but I flat out hate the phrase "Time Heals All Wounds" and "Give It Time".

Interestingly when it comes to this "well-intentioned" advice, this isn't helpful but it isn't done with malice. These pieces of advice simply reflect myths and misconceptions that people have about trauma and rape. Since this bad advice can create self-doubts within survivors as survivors can get concerned and fearful and their mental health can be further harmed if they believe they should be healing more because it's been months or more since their attack.

This was one of my major struggles after my rape.

In addition, "time heals all wounds" is a bad phrase because whilst it takes time to heal from grief and trauma, what actually impacts healing the most is the degree of support and acceptance that the survivor receives in the long term. I completely agree with this because it seriously wasn't the time since I was raped that healed me. It was living in a supportive and loving environment as well as my rape counselling. It was the support I got that made the difference, not the time.

Furthermore, if you tell a rape survivor to "just give it time" then this can seriously trivialise the gravity of the situation for the survivor and everything they are going through. As well as "just giving it time" doesn't help the emotional turmoil and hell that the survivor is going through and it makes the survivor feel powerless. Due to it explains to survivors that it doesn't matter what they do or how they try to cope, time (a factor that they do not control) will determine how long it takes for them to heal.

This suggests to the survivor that waiting is the only way to cope instead of any deliberate action.

Why You Should NOT Say "Don't Think About It" To A Rape Survivor?

When my mental health really got bad during August 2024 and I had to go back to my parents to stay with them for a few days, I remember one of them saying "Just don't think about it" and it annoyed me so much. I flat out hate this silly saying or piece of advice. Since the issue with "don't think about it" is that you are telling someone to ignore or bury these powerful feelings and it doesn't allow a survivor to create an emotional space where they can process what happened to them and heal. Instead "just don't think about it" encourages the survivor to not feel a certain way so this denies the survivor the right to truly feel how they feel and it can even imply that the survivor isn't good enough because they can't control their emotions.

This is similar to why "keep busy" isn't a good piece of advice either. Due to why I strongly encourage survivors to do self-care things that make them happy, give them structure and purpose. It is important not to "keep busy" because keeping a survivor busy doesn't make them "snap out" of the trauma, it simply allows them to escape processing and healing from what happened to them. I always like to mention that you can only go without processing trauma for so long. If you don't deal with your trauma, your trauma will deal with you. This can be depression, a mental breakdown, severe Post-Traumatic Stress Disorder (as if any form of PTSD isn't severe) amongst others.

Of course, like I mentioned in the last paragraph, there are mental health benefits to having structure and engaging in normal activities and routines. Like I found it extremely helpful during the worst of my PTSD to have my Outreach work at the university, my writing and my business. Then again, this is only useful if the survivor has a good support system around themselves, because keeping busy does not and will never eliminate the intrusive thoughts, feelings and other trauma responses.

"Keeping busy" is only ever a temporary distraction and trauma will be dealt with. It can be by the survivor with a social support network and therapy, but the trauma can make you deal with it.

What Are The Outcomes of This Misguided Advice?

When dealing with rape grief, this so-called advice that people give rape survivors just isn't helpful and it can be very harmful to their healing and recovery. For example, it can lead to the survivor becoming guarded in expressing how they feel to others out of concern for being judged or being hurt further. This is what happened to me because I only really open up to my best friend because I know they would never ever hurt me. It's only recently I've started to become less guarded around my family and a new friend that I'm making.

In addition, this unhelpful advice can make a survivor feel guilty about feeling or acting or not in a certain way. As well as this silly advice suggests that rape survivors should ignore or bury their powerfully distressing and negative emotions. This leads to the survivor becoming confused about what they're feeling or how they're expected to feel.

Ultimately, the reason why this is so harmful to survivors is because trauma healing is all about living in an environment that is supportive and allows the survivor to be honest with themselves and get in touch with their true emotions. If a survivor lives in an environment that isn't supportive and encourages denial, guilt as well as an inability to share their feelings with other people then they will not heal and their mental health will die.

Their sense of rape grief will only be prolonged and as a survivor myself, that is something we cannot allow.

That is why supportive friends, family and therapists are the most important thing in trauma healing. Especially after sexual violence which for me is the ultimate act of betrayal and violation. A violation so severe it creates an immense sense of loss and grief that must be overcome in order to heal.

It might feel impossible to heal from sexual violence but it is possible. It might be cheesy but this always makes me smile. I don't know who said it but I like the saying "Nothing is impossible because impossible actually reads I'm Possible,"

And that is even truer when it comes to sexual trauma recovery.

PART TWO: FACTS, FIGURES AND MORE ON SEXUAL VIOLENCE

WHAT ARE THE FACTS AND FIGURES FOR SEXUAL VIOLENCE ON UNIVERSITY AND COLLEGE CAMPUSES?

I've mentioned before one of the ways how I deal with trauma and understanding why different things happen in the world is through research. Therefore, in the months following my sexual assault, I've read a lot about rape, sexual assault and all the different facets of sexual violence. Sometimes this has only made me even more distressed and sometimes it has helped.

Therefore, one of the areas I came across during my rape research was related to the how common it is amongst the university or college population, and this seems to be a finding that applies to both the United Kingdom and the United States. Also, to be honest, I seriously doubt it is different anywhere else in the world.

As a result, in this chapter, I'm going to be explaining the facts and figures about how common sexual violence is amongst college students. You can see the full list of references at the back of the book in the reference section.

Introduction To Sexual Violence Amongst University Campuses

A moment ago, I mentioned that sexual violence is very common on university campuses because 13% of all university students (regardless if they're undergraduate or postgraduate) experience sexual assault or rape through physical force, physical violence or incapacitation during their time as a student. As well as, if we focus only on graduate and professional students then 2.5% of males and 9.7% of females will experience sexual assault or rape through physical violence, force or incapacitation.

Unfortunately, this increases when we focus on undergraduate students (probably because there are more of them) since 6.8% of males and 26.4% of females will also experience sexual assault or rape through physical violence, force or incapacitation during their time as a student.

Also, 5.8% of students regardless of sex or gender have experienced stalking since they started university.

This is even worse for transgender individuals because 23.1% of transgender, gender-nonconforming and genderqueer college students have been sexually assaulted.

Finally for this section, it's worth noting that regardless of whether a person is a student or not, being aged 18 to 24 means they are at a high risk of experiencing sexual violence. I was 22 years old when I was raped so I guess I'm proof of these statistics. Since there's a very interesting finding when it comes to risk factors because female college-aged students are actually 20% less likely than non-students of the same age to experience rape or sexual assault. Whereas male students are 78% more likely to experience rape or sexual assault compared to non-students of the same age.

Personally, I flat out hate all the statistics in this chapter because they are disgusting, wrong and so messed up. No one should ever be raped or experience sexual violence, and it is even more disgusting that university campuses seem to be a breeding ground for this sort of evil behaviour.

I know I can only speak for UK universities, but I know the research I'm basing this chapter on was done in the USA. And from everything I know about the USA's student population and their college hierarchy, I can unfortunately understand how these numbers are so common. There's a much larger focus in the USA on fraternities and sororities, drinking and having massive frat parties. Of course, the UK has a similar culture about drinking and having sex at university, but the USA version seems to be on an industrial scale by comparison.

My point is, I don't like these statistics. These are heartbreaking, troubling and outrageous. That's one of the reasons why I'm writing a psychology research-based book on sexual violence and a memoirish book on the aftermath of my own rape.

I want to educate people and help fellow survivors so maybe, just maybe these statistics can decrease in the future.

Sexual Violence Is More Common Than Other Crimes At University

Another tragic research finding is that sexual violence is more common than other crimes at university because in the general population, there are 5 robberies for every 4 sexual assaults meaning that robberies are more common to experience. Yet when it comes to college-aged women, there are 2 sexual assaults for every one robbery.

In other words, they are more likely to experience a sexual assault than being robbed at university.

That is flat out disgusting and that is rather soul-destroying for me. I've researched the consequences of criminal behaviours and the effects that crimes have on victims, and whilst being robbed can be very difficult for victims. Experiencing a robbery doesn't even remotely compare to being sexually assaulted.

Unfortunately, it's even worse that only 1 in 5 female survivors receive assistance from a victim services agency.

Now that really makes me uncomfortable because in the upcoming book, you'll see and hear how I've struggled immensely with my mental health since my rape, and I've been in contact with an agency. In fact, at the time of writing, I should be getting my rape counselling appointment in the next two weeks (at the very earliest). Therefore, I cannot begin to imagine how hard, how devastating and how bad their mental health has been if they didn't seek the support of some kind of agency.

I hope those female survivors are doing okay, but I unfortunately doubt it.

Moreover, there are certain times of the year when sexual violence is more common on university campuses. For instance, more than 50% of college sexual assaults happen in August, September, October or November. As well as students are at an increased risk of sexual violence in the first few months of their first and second terms at university.

Why Don't College-Aged Students Report Their Sexual Assault To Law Enforcement?

Now this is a fascinating topic because it is very uncommon for a sexual assault survivor to report it to the police. I didn't report my assault and I have an upcoming chapter explaining why this was the case. According to the research, I'm basing this chapter on, only 32% of nonstudent female survivors at college age report their assault to the police, whereas only 20% of female students report it to law enforcement.

This means 4 out of 5 students don't report their sexual assault to the police and 66% of nonstudents don't report their assault either.

Now if I had read this research before my own rape, I would have been confused, I wouldn't have understood why they didn't report it and I would have been judgmental because it was only after my rape I started to learn the truth about rape myths and misconceptions.

In addition, below are the different reasons why female students didn't report their sexual assault, and because participants were allowed to pick more than one reason, the percentages below don't add up to 100%.

- 4% reported it but not to the police
- 9% believed the police wouldn't or couldn't do anything to help them
- 10% didn't want to get their attacker in trouble
- 12% believed it wasn't important enough to report it
- 20% had a fear they would suffer some kind of reprisal for reporting it.
- 26% believed it was a personal matter and didn't concern the police
- 31% had other reasons not for reporting it.

Below is the list of reasons with percentages for nonstudents:

- 5% reported it but not to the police
- 10% believed the police couldn't or wouldn't do anything to help
- 14% didn't want to get their attacker in trouble
- 19% didn't believe it was important enough to report
- 20% had a fear of reprisal.
- 23% believed it was a personal matter
- 35% had other reasons for not reporting it to the police.

Interestingly, I actually agree with all those reasons based on my personal experience, and I've struggled with every single one of those factors, and I talk about why in a future chapter.

Yet I think it's always interesting to see why different survivors don't report it. If you did report it then more power to you and you have a hell of a lot of courage and I am proud of you for doing it. And even if you didn't report it like me, I am proud of you because you're alive, you survived and you are reading this book in an effort to recover.

It might not always seem like you survived or that you're healing, but you are. It might be extremely slow but you're being proactive by reading this book.

I'm proud of you for that.

WHAT HAPPENS DURING A COUNSELLING ASSESSMENT?

Regardless of your experience, the mental health difficulties or mental health condition you experience, it takes a lot of courage, bravery and motivation to reach out to mental health services for support.

If you've already done that then that is brilliant and I'm really proud of you.

If you haven't done that then please consider reaching out to mental health services because sexual violence is horrific and you cannot do this alone. You need professional help to support you as you heal and recover.

In addition, as part of this process, you'll undergo a counselling assessment and in an effort to demystify the process and make it less intimidating for non-psychology people, I wanted to tell you what happened in my rape one.

As a sexual assault survivor and a clinical psychology student, this was a lot of fun and I'm really glad that I did it. I've learnt a lot and it makes me look forward to having counselling with this service in the future.

Of course, every mental health service will have slight differences, but this is for information purposes only based on my own experience as a client (and a clinical psychology Masters student at the time of writing).

<u>What Happens During A Counselling Assessment?</u>

My counselling assessment for the sexual assault counselling was done over Zoom at 7:30 in the evening (again it was very suitable and a great time for me) and I always have a problem getting onto Zoom, but I managed it.

As I mentioned in few reflections ago, being a well-rounded person is critical within clinical psychology, because the lovely lady who was doing my assessment told me something. She told me about her dogs and that she was working at home and a takeaway person was going to ring the doorbell at some point during our call for other people in the house.

This wasn't her being unprofessional but it was her making it clear that her dogs would probably bark and she didn't want to alarm me. And honestly, I found this short conversation very reassuring because it showed to me that she was a kind, normal person and she was a person who I could get along with. As well as it showed me that even though I had literally only said "hello" that she already had my best interests at heart.

I appreciated that fact a lot considering how nervous I had been about this counselling assessment.

Next she explained how the counselling assessment was going to work and how long it would last, and she asked me some questions about myself. For example, what Doctors am I registered at, am I living in Canterbury and just some more information about me.

Afterwards, we spoke about the counselling itself. This included information on what I was hoping to gain out of this counselling, my physiological and psychological symptoms and what my availability was.

Now as a client, this shows the power of being a well-rounded and likeable clinical psychologist. Since in my last counselling assessment for the university, when the woman doing it asked me questions I would give her the answer but I wouldn't add context or additional information.

I didn't want to do this because I didn't like her. She was way too smiley, she interrupted and I didn't have a natural rapport with her.

However, the lovely lady at the charity, I was very open with so I told her about the physiological symptoms, me being suicidal the other week and I gave her more context than I normally would. She appreciated this and as an aspiring clinical psychologist, I think this goes to show how important it is to just be friendly, respectful and open with the client.

And try to build that therapeutic alliance or those interpersonal skills as soon as possible.

Especially, because the lady was able to add information to my assessment forms that would help the counsellor in the future. I think one of the "extra" notes was something in the next section about "have I ever thought that being dead would be easier". Now she asked on a Likert scale that I'll talk about in a moment and because it was "only" for one day, on the scale, it wouldn't be a lot but because I was honest and open with her she was able to add a note that would be useful for my future counsellor.

Furthermore, in this section, the lady asked me about past mental health, am I on any medication and those sort of general mental health questions. I am not on any medication but I do have past mental health and past trauma.

Leading to an interesting discussion about why if I ever requested my notes, I would see "Not For A Placement Counsellor" written on them. Since the charity has a handful of placement counsellors who want experience with sexual violence survivors, but the charity doesn't allow these placement counsellors to help survivors with additional trauma.

This might sound harsh but I seriously understand it.

Due to, I am only speaking for myself here, but my child abuse and trauma directly impacted my sexual assault. And to be honest, if I wasn't abused as kid then I never would have been sexually assaulted so they're connected in that way. Yet they are connected through the mental health impact after the sexual assault too.

For example, the same sort of abusive and negative thoughts that popped up in my childhood popped up after my sexual assault. My mind tried to use my sexual assault as proof that everything my abusers "taught" me in my childhood was true and so on.

There is a massive connection and overlap, and as a client, I would prefer a fully-qualified counsellor with a LOT of experience to help me.

Even as an aspiring clinical psychologist, I seriously wouldn't want someone like me as my first few cases.

Moving onto the final section of the counselling assessment, this is the section reserved for the mental health questionnaire. Now as psychology is a science, I am no stranger to questionnaires and I have made some questionnaires myself.

However, even I have to admit mental health questionnaires are almost funny at times because they are so cold and calculating that they miss so much nuance.

Although, my counselling assessment was a little messed up in this section because this week had been extremely weird in terms of my mental health. I wasn't dealing with rape or sexual assault stuff this week because I was spending so much time dealing with being publicly and privately attacked by someone I know who has Dissociative Identity Disorder with psychotic features.

Even though I will admit that as soon as all that was dealt with the sexual violence stuff returned with a vengeance. Unfortunately, this was after my assessment was done.

Anyway, there were 34 questions in total and some of them she didn't ask because I had already answered them in the other sections in response to other questions. As well as these were done as a Likert Scale ranging from "None Of The Time" to "Most of The Time" with "Often" and "Some of The Time" and "Occasionally" being in the middle.

In addition, the actual questionnaire has a timeframe of the past 7 days, but because of the weirdness of my week, the lady proposed the past 7 to 10 days which I wasn't going to reject.

I need the counselling way too much to not help myself.

For the rest of the counselling assessment, we went through the questions that asked how happiness, social functioning, suicidality, anxiety and a bunch of other domains of functioning too.

It was a good set of questions I admit and the lady did something I did appreciate.

She kept it fun.

She didn't make it seem like a deep, depressing task that would ultimately decide my future, and if I didn't answer something right it would be the end of the world.

No, instead she kept it light and fun and she worked with me as well. Due to let's face it, in my mind, there is very little difference between "Often" and "Some of The Time" so sometimes me and her did need to think about certain answers because the "real" answer was between those two points but I needed to put something as my official answer.

And that ability and patience to work with me was important. I am really grateful that she wanted to do that with me because she could have easily made me feel uncomfortable and awkward so I could say random answers to get it over and done with.

Yet she didn't.

She made me feel listened too, respected and she actually did some empowerment stuff without me or her even realising even now. She waited for me to give a response so I could make a real choice for the first time since my sexual assault.

And that feels amazing.

Now I'm realising that I actually made a choice for myself, that feels incredible and wonderful and I know for a precious few minutes, I don't feel like a weak, pathetic victim (yes I realise that self-perception is something I need to work on in counselling).

Then we wrapped up with whether I had any questions for her now, next steps and she spoke about how if I needed support or had a major meltdown I could reach out to the helpline or the woman at the charity who referred me to the counselling department because she is my dedicated sexual violence worker.

Personally, I still think I should have been given some kind of resource or a Brief Psychological Intervention, especially as the waiting list could be three months long. But the charity is brilliant and I am happy with my experience.

On the whole, when it comes to counselling assessment, as an aspiring clinical psychologist, I've learnt that you need to be kind, respectful and patient with the client. Since they will be nervous, they will be scared and they will probably be feeling so disempowered about the world around them.

Therefore, if you can give them a positive experience using your good interpersonal skills that make them feel respected, listened to and cared about. Then even though this is not a counselling session, you are going to have an insanely positive impact on them.

I've had a good and a bad counselling assessment and after comparing the two in my head, I know the main difference is the person performing the assessment. You are the main factor that will impact the client's experience.

Of course, the client has to want therapy, they want to have to change and improve their lives, and they have to want to work *with* the therapist. I know that.

However, if you don't treat the client with respect, patience and you don't empower them, like the first woman at my university. Then you might make them have a negative experience and that isn't what we want.

It will happen at some point in your career, that's normal and you can learn from the experience, but if you can nail it and make a client feel great and hopeful about the future. Then you already might have helped a client more than you could ever realise and it isn't even the first counselling session yet.

I know it can happen from my own experience, so I have no doubt it can happen again and again and again.

HOW TO BE A TRAUMA-INFORMED PARTNER?

I can never be 100% sure of the different reasons why people pick up my books, especially when it comes to psychology. You might be an aspiring or qualified psychologist, you might be someone you experienced a particular traumatic experience or mental health condition and you want to learn more or you might have a friend or loved one who experienced something and you want learn more in an effort to help them. Or you might be a combination of all three.

As a result, our chapter is more aimed at non-sexual assault survivors because this brilliant chapter focuses on how to date a survivor and the types of things you're going to need to know so you can support them and be informed. Interestingly enough, this chapter has its root in a podcast episode I did two months before I was raped, but it still stands up and I think this is going to be a critical resource for me and my future relationships.

I hope you enjoy it.

***

In recent years, there has been an increase in awareness within clinical psychology about the importance of a trauma-informed approach to mental health care. As well as considering trauma is relatively common, there is a chance we will meet and maybe form romantic relationships with people who have experienced trauma. Therefore, in this chapter, I wanted to combine clinical and relationship psychology to expand upon a list of tips and ways to be a trauma-informed partner. Since this will allow us all to become more trauma-informed and this might be an extremely useful guide if you learn your partner has trauma. This could be the difference between a relationship working or not. If you enjoy learning about relationships, mental health and trauma then you'll love this chapter.

Note: as always absolutely nothing in this book is any sort of official medical, relationship, career or any form of official advice.

Why Do We Need To Learn About Trauma-Informed Approaches?

Personally, I think there are three main reasons why it is critical to understand trauma-informed approaches. Firstly, this is a psychology podcast that aims at providing psychology students, professionals and other people with psychological knowledge and we mainly focus on clinical psychology. Since this is my main interest. Therefore, trauma-informed approaches are becoming more and more recognised and valued within clinical psychology so you need to learn about them. In fact, if you're in the UK, then you will probably be asked about trauma-informed approaches when you go for your interview to get onto the DClinPsych. You don't want to risk not knowing about an important area that might pop up.

Secondly, humans, like you and me, are social creatures, we all like social relationships, and these include romantic ones. Therefore, there is a good chance that at one point in our lives, we will date and maybe even fall in love with a person has experienced trauma. These relationships will have unique challenges at no fault of either party, but how these challenges are dealt with might become problems in their own right. Therefore, in this chapter, I want to give you the knowledge so you know how you might want to navigate these challenges and make your partner feel safe.

Finally, I just think this is a great topic and personally, I am fascinated by the concept of trauma-informed approaches because of my own abuse and trauma. I seriously want to understand this better and maybe I'll find some extra healing or relaxation in this knowledge. I don't know but that's why I'm here learning and having fun along the way.

Also, I should note the main points for this chapter came from the University of Kent's Student Support Service's Instagram page from a post they did on the 16th of February 2024.

Understand What Your Partner Needs

At first, this might seem like a very simple and almost silly point to make. Due to I can imagine a lot of people just dismissing this idea because surely we all know what our partner needs. They only need a bit of love, support and some fun and then they'll be happy. Surely, it's as simple as that?

Maybe in other relationships that don't involve trauma but even then I highly doubt it.

Since when it comes to trauma and life in general, we need to remember that everyone has had different experiences with intimacy, sex and sexual relationships. Some people would have had brilliant relationships and they have no relationship issues or baggage. Yet other people might have been abused, assaulted or hit in past relationships so this can bring complications into relationships.

As a result, it is critical that you try to understand your partner's experiences to find out what they were, how positive or negative they were and if they were negative then you need to approach this relationship with a trauma-informed manner or mindset.

Personally, drawing on my own experience here, whilst I have never been in a relationship, more than enough mental health and trauma stuff pops up in close friendships for me to understand (even roughly) how I would react in romantic relationships. And it's good that everything I do and all my reactions, I can trace back to a particular event so now it's just about overcoming them. Yet in a relationship I would need a partner who was willing to be patient, support and listen to my experiences.

Communication Is Key In Relationships

Of course, this is a brilliant rule for life because honest conversations are extremely powerful, but not everyone is ready to share in relationships.

One example I can think of, is how it took me two months to tell my closest friend about my past, how traumatised I was and everything that can happen to me at times because I was so scared of losing them because of it. That had happened before and then it took another two months for me to kill that fear outright, and now I am a lot more open with them. That's just an example of how people aren't always willing to open up about trauma, how it affects them and how all types of relationships can be difficult.

Therefore, when it comes to relationships, it's important that you try to create and encourage a safe emotional and physical space where your partner and yourself are both comfortable enough to share things openly.

Understand Trauma

Given how I sometimes feel that laypeople use trauma as a buzzword with absolutely no understanding of what trauma actually is, I can understand why some people in relationships might not understand the role of trauma and how it affects people. Yet if you truly care or even love your partner then you need to understand what trauma is.

Since trauma affects a person physically, emotionally and psychologically. No part of a person's life escapes trauma completely. When it comes to their physical body, your partner's nervous system will be affected by the trauma. For example, my heart rate can make me have extreme reactions in certain situations because of my trauma and what people have done to me before. Like two Sundays ago at the time of writing, my friend started texting me in a strange way because it turned out they wanted to ask me something massive. But considering I had made an innocent mistake a few days before (that turned out to be nothing) my heart rate was pounding because my trauma made me believe my really, really close friend was going to end the friendship with me.

It still took me another five minutes to get my heart rate back to normal, because it had "only" been caused by my friend texting me.

As a result, I wanted to highlight how trauma can make partners react in ways that aren't always in their control and most of it is just automatic. These responses aren't done on purpose and the partner isn't trying to hurt you, this is just how the trauma has affected them.

Then over time hopefully, as you both work on helping each other and your partner tries to improve their life and deal with the past, these responses will decrease or maybe stop entirely.

Be Observant In Relationships

There are a lot of different ways this point can be applied to relationships, but let's take the most innocent and probably most common one. You and your partner have just had a great night out, you had a lot of fun and you laughed a lot. Then you start acting flirty and you press them a little to come back to your place for a "nightcap". Even if you seriously mean it as a nightcap and no adult fun.

Watch your partner's body language.

It might change to show they're uncomfortable but they're too nervous or unsure how you'll react if they try to say anything.

If their body language changes then just

step back, relax and act if their feelings escalate. Since not everyone communicates verbally all the time.

For example, when a friend of mine stayed over a few months ago, I could tell they were uncomfortable and slightly bored whilst we were talking with my parents. And then later on they told me, they were anxious and nervous and they only did that for my benefit.

I know this was a friendship example but the same could apply in a relationship. If this was a relationship then I should have asked my friend what was wrong and if they were okay. They would have been better than noticing it and not recognising it for whatever it might have been. In this case it was anxiety. Which for this particular friend does go back to trauma.

Just Be Open

As we slowly take some steps towards dealing with adult activities in relationships, it's important to know you need to have open conversations. Since people who have experienced trauma can have very difficult relationships with sex and similar things.

That's why it's important to talk to your partner about both of your likes, dislikes and just talk about sex beforehand. You need to make them feel comfortable and what they need from you if they get overwhelmed.

Personally, I am flat out terrified of sex. I will happily admit that and I have no doubt it will cause massive issues in the future. Part of my fear comes from the touch difficulties in autism, but 90% of it is trauma-related because without saying too much, I am scared to let people close enough to me to touch me where they could hurt me. Logically, it is a silly fear but from a trauma perspective it is very practical.

Which is why there are only really four people that I've met in my 22 years of living that I wouldn't mind twice about having sex with. Simply because I know these four people would never hurt me, none of those things happened though.

Anyway, it just comes to show you how trauma can seriously affect sexual relationships and why it's important to be honest and open in conversations. Due to I know when I eventually find someone, I won't be comfortable with the idea of sex until a deep conversation about it. As that is another test to see if they care about me very much. If they don't want the talk then they clearly aren't that bothered by me.

Check In With Your Partner During Sex

I'll fully admit that I have never spoken about or said the word "sex" so many times in my life than this chapter, and you realise how uncomfortable you are with the idea when you struggle saying and writing it a lot. I suppose that's why I write sweet romance instead of steamy romances.

Anyway, building upon the last section, when you and your partner finally decide to have sex and it is perfectly okay if this doesn't happen for a while. Be it weeks, months or even years. It's important to check in with them during sex to see if they're still okay.

You can do this by occasionally asking your partner if what you're doing is okay and if they're still enjoying it. Also, you can remind that them you can stop at any time and they can withdraw their consent whatever they want. As well as you can agree on safe words or another way to communicate that means this needs to stop immediately.

This is just flat out critical I think to making anyone who's been through trauma feel safe, secure and cared for.

Learn Grounding Techniques

Finally, if your partner starts reacting or panicking or having some sort of negative reaction during sex then help them. One of the forms of help could be encouraging them to use grounding techniques so they become grounded in the present moment and not their traumatic past.

These grounding techniques can include reassuring them that they're safe, referencing the present location, date, time and other immediate sensations. Like anything you hear or whatever you see. This is all about helping to ground them in the present moment and making it harder for them to focus on the past and traumatic event they're re-experiencing.

Conclusion

At the end of the day, when it comes to being a trauma-informed partner, it's about realising none of us can remove all the harm that the trauma has caused our partner. It simply cannot be done. Yet what can be done is you can understand and support your partner by being patient and supportive and then you can do your best to minimise the harm caused by their trauma.

This isn't going to be easy and I have had friends that have found dealing with my trauma difficult to say the least. So I have no idea how a future boyfriend or partner would find it. Yet I know if they care about me or even love me, then they will be patient, understanding and supportive.

That's what you need to do to if you want to be a trauma-informed partner.

Therefore, just as a reminder here are the ways you can be an informed partner:

- Know what your partner needs
- Communicate with them
- Understand trauma
- Be observant
- Talk openly about adult activities
- Check in with your partner during sex
- Use grounding techniques

Just because a partner has trauma in their past, it doesn't mean they can never be loved. A relationship with a traumatised person can still be as magical, wonderful and loving as a relationship with anyone else. But only if you both put the work in and you become a trauma-informed partner that loves, supports and understands your partner.

WHAT IS POST-TRAUMATIC STRESS DISORDER?

The vast majority of people have heard of Post-Traumatic Stress Disorder (PTSD) before when it comes to veterans and soldiers. Also, we know this mental health condition involves flashbacks, intrusive memories and panic attacks, but beyond that a lot of laypeople don't know that much about Post-Traumatic Stress Disorder. I'm only starting to learn more about PTSD because I have it because of my sexual assault, so whilst I don't talk about it in this episode, my own experiences make this important to look at.

Therefore, in this clinical psychology podcast episode, we'll be looking at what is Post-Traumatic Stress Disorder, what causes Post-Traumatic Stress Disorder and what are the symptoms of PTSD. I won't cover treatments for Post-Traumatic Stress Disorder in this episode because that's a massive area and I've already spoken about that in different episodes on the podcast previously. So if you enjoy learning about mental health, trauma and clinical psychology then this is a great episode for you.

What Is Post-Traumatic Stress Disorder?

As you can imagine Post-Traumatic Stress Disorder is a mental health condition classed as a trauma and stress-related disorder that can develop in response to being exposed to an event or ordeal where severe physical harm or death was threatened or happened. People can develop PTSD after rape, violence, bombings, shootings, military service and rescue workers can develop PTSD too.

In terms of prevalence rate, I talk more about Post-Traumatic Stress Disorder in sexual violence populations briefly in a moment, but about 6.8% of Americans develop the condition in their lifetime. This information is from the National Institute of Mental Health.

Furthermore, Post-Traumatic Stress Disorder can develop at any age, including childhood, and women are more likely to develop it than men. Also, there is some evidence that PTSD runs in families, as well as Post-Traumatic Stress Disorder is often comorbid with conditions like depression, anxiety and substance use disorders. Then when these other conditions can be diagnosed and treated, the likelihood of the overall treatment being successful increases.

In addition, something we need to know about Post-Traumatic Stress Disorder is you can only get diagnosed with the condition if you have PTSD symptoms for over a month. If you have the symptoms for less than a month then you don't have PTSD (at least in diagnosis terms), instead you have Acute Distress Disorder.

Also, with the right care and support, a lot of PTSD symptoms can abate within trauma survivors within that first month so a lot of people never go on to develop Post-Traumatic Stress Disorder.

Interestingly, Post-Traumatic Stress Disorder can be delayed in its manifestations because this occurs if PTSD symptoms show themselves six months or more after the onset of the trauma.

Post-Traumatic Stress Disorder And The Military

I couldn't really do a Post-Traumatic Stress Disorder-focused podcast episode without talking about the military as this is where a lot of our common knowledge about PTSD comes from.

The prevalence rate of Post-Traumatic Stress Disorder in the military is moderately high because about 30% of the Vietnam War veterans developed PTSD, and 10% of soldiers who took part in Operation Desert Storm (the Gulf War) developed PTSD. As well as between 12% and 20% of soldiers serving in the Iraq war developed PTSD too.

As you can imagine, it is the combat element that increases the risk of developing Post-Traumatic Stress Disorder for veterans amongst other mental health conditions, because severe harm and death happens around them. There are other risk factors too, including the politics surrounding the war, the type of enemy the soldier faces and where the war is fought.

All these risk factors can interact to cause

Post-Traumatic Stress Disorder to develop and be maintained in a soldier.

Moreover, there is a type of trauma that is never spoken about in the military and this is Military Sexual Trauma and sexual assault or sexual harassment connects to this topic too. This certainly can cause Post-Traumatic Stress Disorder.

Since Military Sexual Trauma can happen to both men and women regardless of whether it's wartime, peacetime or during training with figures suggesting 23% of women have been sexually assaulted in the US military and 55% of women and 38% of men have been sexually harassed in the military too.

Personally, I suspect the real numbers are a lot, lot higher because no one likes to report this stuff and get it on public record. And I say this as a survivor myself, the people that made this research possible are amazing and a lot more courageous than me.

Overall, there are a lot of different traumatic experiences that can lead to a person developing Post-Traumatic Stress Disorder. Including terrorist attacks, natural disasters, sexual assaults and physical attacks.

Post-Traumatic Stress Disorder And Sexual Violence: Why Am I Talking About PTSD Now?

A few weeks ago leading up to Canterbury Pride in early June, I wanted to go by myself to a Warhammer event at my university with a Pride twist. I would be going alone and I wanted to go because it would be nice to meet new people, get back into Warhammer and it would be a good event. Yet I had a lot of social anxiety, I felt physically sick about going and I had seen photos of the Warhammer group at my university and some of the people there were rather triggering for me.

A lot popped up that week because of me wanting to go to this event.

I was really distressed so I texted my best friend and they mentioned I have PTSD, so I pooed-pooed. I wasn't listening to them, not that they knew it at the time. Yet I thought about it, researched it a little more and then found out it is very common amongst survivors of sexual violence.

This was hammered home last week too when I went to Wales because in the evening, my parents were asleep on the sofa and I was still watching the crime drama that had on and it turned out the killer was getting revenge on her rapists. And the programme showed the implicated rape scenes, so I got really distressed, I couldn't change the TV over so I shouted and it was a little messy.

There are other reasons why I'm certain I have PTSD and I'll probably sprinkle them in throughout the episode to help show examples of this in real life.

Anyway, the reason why I'm talking about Post-Traumatic Stress Disorder now is I want to understand it is more and it is scarily common. For example, Campbell (2009) who looked at studies dating back to the 1980s found that between 17% and 65% of women who experience sexual assault develop PTSD. As well as a peer-reviewed article from the University Of Washington School Of Medicine/Uw Medicine found 81% of survivors had PTSD one week after their attack and 75% of sexual assault survivors had PTSD a month after their attack. Lastly, an article from Verywell Mind in 2023 explained nearly 48% of survivors had PTSD after a year of being assaulted.

I want to note that the specific type of Post-Traumatic Stress Disorder that sexual violence survivors develop is known as Rape Trauma Syndrome.

So now we understand how common it is in another area besides military veterans, let's explore the symptoms of Post-Traumatic Stress Disorder in more depth.

What Are The Symptoms Of Post-Traumatic Stress Disorder?

A lot of people with Post-Traumatic Stress Disorder tend to relive and re-experience the traumatic event or different aspects of it. There is a wide range of triggers, something I am finding out more and more, but there are some common themes. For example, anniversaries of traumatic events and similar people, situations or places can trigger the distressing memories.

A similar person example for me was my attacker was very fat and very overweight so I can be extremely triggered when I see a fat man. This isn't me being fatphobic, it is just fat people trigger my rape memories.

In addition, Post-Traumatic Stress Disorder causes a person to experience flashbacks, intrusive thoughts, distributed sleep, anxiety, sadness, intense guilt, emotional numbness, outbursts of anger and dissociative experiences.

And whilst people with PTSD try to avoid situations that remind them of the traumatic event, they can still be surprised by what triggers them and when the symptoms last for longer than a month, a diagnosis of PTSD might be relevant.

Now I want us to look at the different types of PTSD symptoms.

What Are The Avoidance Symptoms Of PTSD?

Because no one with Post-Traumatic Stress Disorder wants to be reminded of the traumatic event, we all avoid certain triggers so avoidance symptoms include:

- Avoiding activities, places and people associated with the event
- Avoiding conversations, feelings or thoughts about the event

As I mentioned earlier, I avoid fat men like the plague because they remind me too much of my rapist, and I avoid any crime drama with a sexual violence theme. Thankfully, I never watched *Law and Order: Special Victims Unit.*

What Are The Reexperiencing Symptoms Of Post-Traumatic Stress Disorder?

When it comes to the reliving the traumatic experience over and over again, symptoms include:

- Experiencing intense emotions when you're reminded of the event
- Feeling or behaving as if the event was actually happening all over again (flashbacks)
- Having distressing memories and bad dreams of the event
- Having dissociative reactions and/ or loss of awareness of your present surroundings
- Having intense physical sensations when reminded of the event. Such as, feeling faint, feeling a loss of control, sweating, pounding heart and so on.

One of the ways I've experienced these symptoms include very distressing physical sensations all over my body about how he was touching and doing things to me, and that's all I'll say about that one. As well as I used to have this one a lot more but it has thankfully mellowed out a little nowadays, I would have a complete loss of awareness that worked with these physical sensations so I would need to use grounding techniques to get me to focus back on the present.

What Are The Reactivity and Arousal Symptoms Of PTSD?

When it comes to the reactivity and arousal symptoms of Post-Traumatic Stress Disorder, they can include:

- Feeling easily startled.
- Excess awareness (also known as hypervigilance)
- Sleeping difficulties including having trouble falling or staying asleep
- Difficulty concentrating
- Outbursts of anger or being irritable

An unfortunately good example of this area for me was during my Statistic Theory online exam in May. Since it was bad enough that I couldn't concentrate enough to do any revision whatsoever until a week before the exam, as well as because the exam was online and made up of 40 multiple choices, my mind wondered after question 20. Which led to a full-on meltdown and panic attack during my exam.

That wasn't nice but thankfully I passed, only by 3 points by still.

What About The Mood and Cognitive Symptoms Of Post-Traumatic Stress Disorder?

When someone has PTSD, they'll experience negative changes in their mood and thoughts, these symptoms can include:

- An inability to experience positive moods
- A lack of interest in social activities
- Feeling detached and numb from things
- Having difficulty remembering an important part of the traumatic event
- Pessimism about the future

In terms of clinical psychology, one thing I do want to mentiom is you can see why depression and anxiety are common conditions to find alongside PTSD. For example, a lack of interest in social activities and pessimism about the future, they're both common with depression too.

Going back to personal experience, I've already mentioned the social anxiety I have about going to something new and I have basically stopped that now, and even social events I've been going to since before my assault. It still takes me a while to actually go to them before I do. For example, I am not that ashamed to admit, I spent twenty minutes in the university toilets with my social anxiety before I went to a social last week.

Are There Other Symptoms Of Post-Traumatic Stress Disorder?

Some other symptoms of PTSD that don't really fit into the other categories include:

- Depersonalisation- feeling like you're outside of your body
- Derealisation- experiencing unreality of surroundings

These symptoms are rarer for people but some clients can experience them.

What Causes Post-Traumatic Stress Disorder?

Whilst we don't know the definitive cause of Post-Traumatic Stress Disorder, we know that there are biological, psychological and social factors that interact together to develop the condition. Since Post-Traumatic Stress Disorder causes changes in how the body responds to stress so it impacts our stress hormones as well as neurotransmitters that carry information between our nerves.

As a result, people who experience childhood abuse or other traumatic experiences are likely to develop PTSD months or even years after the trauma. Also, temperamental variables, like externalising behaviours or other anxiety difficulties, can increase the risk of developing the condition too.

Additionally, environmental factors can cause PTSD. For instance, childhood adversity, family dysfunction, family mental health history, cultural variables, and more importantly, the more traumatic the event, the greater the risk of developing Post-Traumatic Stress Disorder. This is why witnessing atrocities and severe personal injury are major, major risk factors.

Moreover, having maladaptive coping mechanisms, a lack of social support, financial stress and family instability can all worsen the mental health outcomes for people with Post-Traumatic Stress Disorder.

Personally, because my best friend is the only social support I actually have since my sexual assault because other people just don't know how to help me and the most important people in my life just want to pretend it never happened and I am perfectly fine. I am seriously not. That can decrease my mental health a lot because I feel guilt towards my best friend because they are all I've got until my specialise counselling starts and my best friend isn't always around, so I have had to do some maladaptive coping mechanisms just to survive.

Having more social support is critical when it comes to PTSD.

On the other hand, there are resilience factors that can decrease the risk of a client developing Post-Traumatic Stress Disorder. Some of these resilience factors are present before the trauma and other resilience factors can become more importantly learnt during and after the traumatic event. For example, seeking out support including mental health professionals, finding a support group, feeling good about your own actions in the face of danger, being able to act and respond effectively despite fear and having a coping strategy are all resilience factors that can help reduce the development of Post-Traumatic Stress Disorder.

Conclusion

We've covered a lot of ground when it comes to Post-Traumatic Stress Disorder because we've looked at what is PTSD, how common is PTSD in the military and sexual violence survivors, what are the symptoms and what are the causes. After this episode, we've all deepened our knowledge about this mental health condition a lot and I'm pleased that we've all learnt about PTSD more.

Since PTSD is a horrible, horrible condition to have but there is hope. There are treatments and you can still live a long, happy life with the condition.

Even though I've been having panic attacks, distressing memories, distressing physical experiences and so on, there are still happy, joyful moments. Like I love spending time with my best friend, I enjoy Outreach work at my university and I still love writing. There are moments of positivity so I focus on them.

And another reason why I liked today's episode is that I could start to see what I'm experiencing is normal and it's a natural response to an extremely unnatural situation.

I am not a problem and no one with PTSD is a problem.

Therefore, I want to conclude this episode by saying that if you ever meet, become friends with or get to know someone with PTSD. Offering them some social support (that accurately reflects the level of friendship of course), listening to them and signposting them to some mental health services could have a massive positive impact on that person.

And it really could change their life for the better.

PART THREE: ANXIETY

WHAT IS PANIC DISORDER AND ANXIETY DISORDERS?

I talk a lot about social anxiety and panic attacks in this book and a lot of us survivors know how it feels to be constantly anxious, especially if we develop PTSD. Therefore, I want to put in this anxiety content so we can learn what social anxiety is, why a survivor might develop it and what triggers social anxiety and how can social anxiety be treated through Cognitive Behaviour Therapy or Exposure Therapy.

As a result, in this next section of the book, I want to know on some psychology facts, theories and research findings on social anxiety so you can understand what and why your current or future clients might be feeling this way as well as I'll make you aware of some psychological therapies that your clients might benefit it, or some therapeutic models you might want to draw on in your own practice.

All the chapters in this section are taken from CBT For Anxiety, available anywhere you got this book from, so if you want to learn more definitely check it out.

Our first chapter focuses on understanding what are panic and social anxiety disorders.

Note: whilst the next few chapters is taken from a book aimed at psychology students, it should be still be accessible to you and help you understand what anxiety is, how and why it effects you and how psychological therapies are an effective treatment option for the condition and allow you to live a happier and less anxious life.

***

What Is Panic Disorder And Agoraphobia?

Personally, I always think that panic disorders are one of the worst anxiety disorders because this is a type of anxiety disorder that can be characterised by a person having repeated or debilitating panic attacks. With these attacks being a sudden episode of horrific bodily symptoms. Like: choking, chest pains and distress.

As well as whilst all anxiety disorders do involve panic attacks to various extents and normally a panic attack in any other disorder is limited to only the anxious stimuli like a social situation or spiders, but a panic disorder involves panic attacks that come out the blue.

For instance, whilst I once knew a girl that suffered from Social Anxiety Disorder so she had panic attacks in social situations, it was only those situations. Where a person with Panic Disorder would suffer from a panic attack in any situation. As well as panic disorders are found in 5% of women and 2% of men. (Barlow, 2002).

As a result, when it comes to understanding panic disorders, we need to look at the following three types:

- Panic disorder without agoraphobia
- Panic disorder with agoraphobia
- Agoraphobia without a history of panic disorder

Also, agoraphobia without panic disorders are the same as the above but this condition is focused on panic-like symptoms and not full-blown panic attacks.

What Is Agoraphobia?

Personally, I feel that agoraphobia isn't a very well-used word and it really isn't known about so agoraphobia is a form of anxiety coming from a person being in situations where escape is embarrassing or difficult or help isn't perceived to be available in the event of a panic or panic-like symptoms. For example, agoraphobia can be found in situations when a person is far from home because the person might not know who to turn to for help, and the same goes for travel and crowds.

Consequently, the person with agoraphobia will avoid these situations or if they go into these situations this will produce a lot of anxiety or they will need a companion to enter these situations. This helps with the issues surrounding the situation being difficult to escape and helping not being available. As well as if a person does want a diagnosis of agoraphobia then this condition needs to be able to explain the person's symptoms better than another disorder.

What Would A Panic Attack and Panic Disorder Diagnosis Require?

When it comes to getting a diagnosis, we all know that a set list of criteria has to be met in the Diagnostic and Statistical Manual Version 5 (DSM-5) for a diagnosis to be made, so all this information is from the DSM-5 (APA, 2013).

Therefore, for a person to meet Criterion A for Panic Disorders (and as this is the Criterion that gives you the best idea about the feelings a Panic Disorder gives a person, this is the only one we'll look at), a person must experience an abrupt surge from a calm or anxious state to one of intense discomfort or fear that peaks within minutes and during this time four or more of the following symptoms must happen:

- Sweat
- Tremble
- Shake
- Have a feeling of choking
- Experience palpitation, accelerated heart rate or pounding heart
- Experience chest pains or discomfort
- Feel dizzy, unsteady, faint or light-headed
- Have a fear of dying
- Experience a sense of smothering or shortness of breath
- Have a sense of numbness or tingling
- Nausea or abdominal distress

- Chills or heat sensations
- Fear losing control or "going crazy"
- Experience a feeling of unreality (Derealisation) or being detached from themselves (depersonalisation)

This is why I rather like looking at the diagnostic criteria for different mental health conditions, because they help to give a real sense about what it is like to experience these conditions, and then using this knowledge we can start to think about possible ways to treat these symptoms.

Social Anxiety Disorder (APA, 2013)

This definitely has to be the most famous anxiety condition so whilst I probably don't have to introduce it too much, I still really want to. As a result of social anxiety disorder is defined as high levels of fear or anxiety about one or more social situations where the person is exposed to scrutiny by others.

This fear and anxiety are caused by the person's fear that they will act in a way or show their anxiety symptoms that will lead to the other people negatively evaluating them. In other words, negatively judging them so the person will be humiliated, embarrassed and rejected by the other people.

Also when I was first learning this topic, I found it rather surprising that social anxiety disorder isn't one thing. Since a person could be fine at parties but have social anxiety disorder when talking in public, talking in a classroom or not at all. The entire point of social anxiety disorder is that a person's anxiety and fear could be provoked by a single type of social situation, most or all social situations. It really does depend on the person.

Furthermore, men and women are affected equally by this disorder as well as it typically manifests itself in childhood or adolescence (Robins and Regier, 1991).

A Social Anxiety Disorder Diagnosis

When it comes to a person wanting a diagnosis, there is a set list of symptoms and behaviours they have to meet. For instance, for a person to have social anxiety disorder they need to experience a high level of fear or anxiety about one or more social situations where the person is exposed to possible scrutiny by other people.

For example, the DSM-5 includes examples like social interactions, like meeting unfamiliar people and having a conversation, performing in front of others, like doing public speaking, and being observed, like eating or drinking.

In addition, the anxiety or fear they experience has to be out of proportion to the real threat posed by the social situation and the sociocultural context. This is an idea we'll return to in the Specific Phobia chapter.

Moreover, the social situation must almost always provoke a fear or anxiety reaction in a person, as well as the person must show that they avoid these situations or when they are exposed to these situations, the person has to endure them with intense anxiety or fear.

And then because the DSM-5 loves a good old time factor (a very common theme throughout the book), the person has to have a persistent fear, anxiety or avoidance of these situations for at least 6 months or more. As well as (by the end of this first section you'll be saying this with me) the fear, anxiety, or avoidance of social situations must cause clinically significant distress or impairment for the person in social, occupational, or other important areas of functioning.

INTRODUCTION TO COGNITIVE BEHAVIOURAL THERAPY

Now we understand what social anxiety and panic disorder involve, I want to point out some possible treatment options you might want to investigate more if you experience severe social anxiety. Therefore, in the next three chapters, you'll learn about Cognitive Behavioural Therapy, including this introductory chapter so you understand what Cognitive Behavioural Therapy (CBT) is, as well as Exposure Therapy. Both of these types of psychotherapy are highly effective for treating social anxiety.

And my favourite thing about CBT is that it is fascinating and a very fun read if you're interested in mental health, so please enjoy.

***

Now that we're getting onto the part of the book we've all been waiting for, let's start learning about the amazing topic of Cognitive Behavioural Therapy.

As a result, we first need to know both the cognitive and behavioural theories that Cognitive Behavioural Therapy is built on before we can ever hope to understand how CBT works for anxiety disorders.

Therefore, as you can probably imagine Cognitive Behavioural Therapy is based (at least in part) on the cognitive approach to behaviour. As well as Westbrook, Kennerley & Kirk (2007) noted that there is evidence that a lot of mental health conditions are associated with a wide range of cognitive factors. For example, many conditions cause people to have information processing biases, faulty belief schemas as well as dysfunctional ways of thinking.

Then if we apply this logic to anxiety disorders then we've already discussed in the book how anxiety causes a person to have faulty belief systems about how dangerous the stimuli is, the dysfunctional ways they develop to "cope" with the anxiety and their bias information processing because how they perceive the stimuli.

Also, the cognitive approaches to treatment were first pioneered by Albert Ellis (1962) and Aaron Beck (1967) with their aim being to incorporate cognitive processes into psychology, all whilst still maintaining an empirical approach to this because they wanted to avoid ungrounded speculation.

In other words, they wanted to make sure their findings withstood empirical scrutiny and it is a brilliant thing that they set out with this in mind.

In addition, when it comes to cognitive approaches, this view focuses on the idea that a mental health condition is caused by a person developing irrational beliefs, dysfunctional ways of thinking and biased information processing like we saw earlier. And this leads to the person's mental processes being impacted heavily.

For instance, the way a person behaves and emotionally reacts to a stimuli is strongly influenced by their cognition. Like their beliefs, thoughts and interpretation. As well as this impacts how a person reacts to an event too.

For example, because I personally don't find spiders anxiety-provoking, if I see a spider then I don't interpret this as dangerous, life-threatening and I'm not overwhelmed by the emotion of fear. Yet if an anxious person saw a spider then their cognitive processes would tell them this is a life-threatening situation and they will react completely differently to me because the anxious person has biased cognitive processes.

Furthermore, the cognitive approach believes mental health conditions develop and the mental health difficulties onset because of cognitive factors (obviously) but both functional and dysfunctional beliefs develop earlier on, and these beliefs may not cause difficulties for a long period of time.

And this is something that I personally find very interesting about mental health. A person could have depression, ADHD, autism or another condition and function absolutely perfectly. They can hold down a job, have tons of friends (if they want) and live a perfectly happy life, but it is only when they start to struggle and need help is when clinical psychology is really needed.

And something that I personally love to remind people is that a mental health condition isn't a death sentence like some people sadly believe it is. Sure a person with a mental health condition might need a little more support, guidance and treatment but given all of those things there is a good chance they could live a very happy and relatively clinically "normal" life.

Nonetheless, if the person does experience a critical incident event, also known as encounters the anxiety-provoking stimuli, then this would be a disturbing event to them, this could activate their negative beliefs and then lead to a distressing emotional response.

What's The Cognitive-Behavioural Approach?

Building on both the cognitive approaches, to form Cognitive Behavioural Therapy, this approach has to be combined with behavioural approaches. Therefore, whilst the cognitive approach focuses on a person's cognitions and beliefs and how these might lead to particular behaviours. It is these behaviours that are actually a core factor in maintaining or changing beliefs and emotions. Meaning this can become a very vicious cycle.

In other words, a person's negative cognition and beliefs cause negative behaviours. Then these behaviours reinforce the cognitions and beliefs and so on. Since it's the behaviour in a person's response to a negative experience or cognition that could have a significant effect on whether the emotion persists.

For example, if a person reacts badly to a spider then of course the person will want to avoid spiders to avoid this feeling again. Hence, they develop avoidance behaviours. Like, avoiding the situation and event completely, escaping it or engaging in safety behaviours.

Now personally, I love safety behaviours and I think they are truly fascinating because to be honest they have to be some of the biggest cons in psychology. Due to safety behaviours are fully intended to protect us from threat or prevent harm coming to us. As a result, these safety behaviours might reduce our anxiety in the short term, but they always have the unintended consequence of maintaining anxiety in the longer term.

That's why I think safety behaviours are very interesting cons that we pull on ourselves because we convince ourselves that we're helping ourselves to be less anxious, and if we don't do these behaviours we're going to basically die. But in reality, they're making us "worse", not "better.

Core Treatment Components

When it comes to what CBT actually involves, there are a few flat out critical elements that make up this amazingly effective and fascinating therapy.

Firstly, there is a lot of cognitive restructuring involved. This component involves challenging and modifying a person's negative thoughts as well as their dysfunctional beliefs. This is typically done by examining the evidence for a person's beliefs.

For example, we'll talk a lot more about cognitive intervention in two chapters' time but an anxious person will believe their safety behaviours save them and without their safety behaviours they will basically die. That is how powerful these behaviours are, so as you'll see in two chapters a therapist can challenge these beliefs by using experiments and testing whether or not there is evidence to support these beliefs.

Another core feature of CBT is it involves a therapist helping to modify a person's tendency to indulge in unhelpful thinking processes, this relates to the cognitive biases we spoke about earlier, so the therapist works with the client to modify and reduce these unhelpful mental processes. Like, how a person pays excessive attention to the threat, how they ruminate on the anxiety provoking stimuli and they engage in mental checking.

As well as when it comes to helping a person reduce their unhelpful behaviours, this includes things like reducing their avoidance, safety and checking behaviours. Also CBT involves behavioural experiments (definitely more on that later) and exposure and response prevention (again more on that in a later chapter).

Levels Of Cognition

Of course, we could never ever hope to learn about cognitive approaches and CBT without looking at levels of cognition, and this is absolutely critical when it comes to Cognitive Behavioural Therapy. Since a person's levels of cognition are as follows:

- Their automatic thoughts
- Their intermediate beliefs, attitudes and rules which are assumptions about the world and the self.
- Their core beliefs. Their basic beliefs about their self, others and the world.

And this idea about levels of cognition is flat out critical in CBT because a therapist has to be very careful when they do cognitive restructuring because you cannot hope to change someone's core beliefs automatically. That just isn't how things work but you can start off with challenging and modifying a person's automatic thoughts then their intermediate beliefs and then their core beliefs.

You need to work "slowly" and gradually for the therapy to work.

An anxiety example of how a therapist might go about finding out what a person's core belief is, is as follows:

- I'm terrified of spiders (automatic thought)
- I know if a spider gets near me it could attack me (potential intermediate belief)
- If a spider touches me then I know for a fact I'm going to get bitten and I'll be rushed to hospital (potential core belief)

Now I have to admit that it is far, far easier to come up with potential levels of cognitions with depression for teaching purposes but you get the general idea. A CBT therapist would have to effectively peel back the layers of a person's cognition to truly understand why they have these biased mental processes.

Thinking Errors/Biases

If you've studied depression then you might be familiar with this section of the chapter because there are a lot of commonalities between all types of CBT (at least "first-wave" therapies) and the types of cognitive biases and errors a CBT therapist would encounter. Therefore, here are the following cognitive errors a therapist is likely to encounter and I have broken them up so you can clearly see the error and an example of what it is like:

- All or nothing- if I can't love all dogs then I'm scared of all of them.
- Exaggerated standards/expectations- if I can't pet a dog then I'm a failure (a potential example at least)
- Catastrophising- my life is over because if I go outside I might see a dog and it might kill me.

- Selective attention to the negative/threat- a person is basically always drawn to anxiety provoking stimuli.
- Over-generalising- "I'm scared of my brother's pet dog so I'm scared of all dogs"
- Dismissing the positive- I might be able to stroke my sister's dog but I feel worthless and scary around all other dogs. I'm so lame.

- Magnifying/minimising- minimising the positive and magnifying the bad
- Jumping to conclusions
- Emotional reasoning- being irrational and basing your reason on emotion, not fact.
- Personalising
- Internalising/externalising

Again, some of those examples might sound similar to depression and that is to be expected considering there is a comorbidity between depression and anxiety in some people.

Role Of Avoidance And Safety Behaviours

Returning to my topic and building upon what we learnt earlier, a very good definition of a safety behaviour can be found in Salkovskis (1988, 1991):

"A behaviour which is performed in order to prevent or minimise a feared catastrophe"

As well as we know that safety behaviours have several effects on a person's beliefs. Like they prevent a person from getting disconfirming evidence about their beliefs (this is flat out critical for the information in two chapters' time), this can increase the sensation a person experiences like their anxiety and fear, and safety behaviours increase their rumination and preoccupation with the anxiety provoking stimuli.

Overall, all these effects on behaviour that safety behaviours cause are linked together to make the person focus on the stimuli they find threatening and this of course isn't helpful.

CBT FOR ANXIETY DISORDERS

Something that I really like about this book is that as the other chapters have shown us, there is an awful lot that goes into CBT, and CBT is nowhere near as straight forward as you might have previously believed since it is only now that we are getting onto CBT. As well as there is plenty more information after this chapter to deepen your knowledge even further.

Therefore, we know that anxiety disorders develop due to people believing that situations are a lot more dangerous than they really are. As well as this means psychologists need to help clients to consider alternative, less threatening explanations of their mental difficulty.

And yet, this isn't straight forward as each anxiety disorder has its own unique facets and this means a client has to learn and test these alternative ways of interpreting their experience.

Ultimately, this helps the person to make changes to their own unique, personal situation so CBT is critical in helping them to adopt and try out these new ways of understanding themselves, their experience and most importantly their future assumptions.

How Does CBT For Anxiety Work?

The entire point of all CBT models of anxiety disorders is to help the client consider their own threatening interpretation of the experience as well as how this is maintained by their emotion and behaviour as discussed in previous chapters.

In addition, all CBT models use behavioural activation and cognitive restructuring to help the client learn alternative ways of interpreting their experience and helps them to make changes to their situation by trying out their new ways of understanding themselves, others and the world.

But that is basically where the similarities end. Every CBT model is different for each anxiety disorder.

CBT For Panic Disorder

When it comes to panic disorder, the cognitive theory proposes that people have a relatively enduring tendency to interpret a range of bodily sensations catastrophically. In other words, people with panic disorder think their bodily sensations is the end of the world and they're going to die. That's an example of how exaggerated their biased cognitive processes are.

As a result, these bodily sensations are the ones that are mainly involved in normal anxiety responses, like heart palpitations, dizziness and breathlessness, but they aren't always triggered by anxiety. Hence, the person's catastrophic interpretation involves them perceiving these sensations as indications of an immediately impending physical or mental disaster.

And come on, anyone could find this absolutely terrifying and they would rightly have a major panic attack.

Afterwards, a person might start catastrophising these sensations but that doesn't mean they should automatically be maintained and a person should have these catastrophic interpretations forever, so what maintains panic disorders?

A lot of research finds that once a person has developed a tendency to interpret body sensations in a catastrophic way, then several other processes engage and it is these processes that contribute to the maintenance of panic disorder. For example, a person's safety behaviours, imagery, emotional reasoning and their selective attention to bodily cues.

Overall, when it comes to treating panic disorder with CBT, the therapy needs to focus on cognitively restructuring these catastrophic misinterpretations, reducing their unhelpful attentional processes and helping them to reduce their safety and avoidance behaviours. This is typically done through Behavioural Experiments (my absolute favourite topic in the entire book coming up in the next chapter).

CBT For Generalised Anxiety Disorder (GAD)

Additionally, if we look at Generalised Anxiety Disorder (this will be examined more in the free bonus essay at the back of the book), the cognitive model of GAD was proposed by Wells (1995; 1997; 2000; 2009) and he proposed that the excessive worry and anxiety common in GAD was maintained by a range of factors.

For instance, Wells found that GAD was maintained by a person's hypervigilance to threats, so they're always looking out for threats and I think we can all imagine how if a person is always looking for threats they will always find them in the end.

A GAD sufferer has information processing biases like attention and interpretation biases as well that have a maintaining role too. As does the person's dysfunctional beliefs about their worry and its function. Leading people to believe that it's perfectly necessary to run through this process of avoidance because they believe it is critical to avoid future catastrophes. Despite the worry this process causes them being uncontrollable and harmful. Then like always safety seeking behaviours and avoidance also play a role in maintaining GAD.

Therefore, when a CBT therapist comes to treating GAD, they focus on the self-monitoring aspect of the person with them constantly watching out for anxiety and worry.

This is done through cognitive restructuring by challenging the beliefs they have about the likelihood and cost of the negative events, they challenge the client's dysfunctional beliefs about their worrying as well as they carry out behavioural experiments to test out their beliefs about worry.

Moreover, the therapist would help the client to reduce and disengage from their worrying and reduce their safety behaviours, like reassurance seeking.

Overall, as you can see so far and we'll come back to this point at the end of the chapter, but CBT is like a core when it comes to anxiety disorders (and pretty much all mental health conditions) and it needs to be adapted and changed to meet the needs of the client with a specific mental health condition.

No two CBTs are the same because no two conditions are the same.

What CBT Works For Social Anxiety Disorder?

To wrap up this chapter, we'll look at one final anxiety disorder because Social Anxiety Disorder is always interesting to look at. Consequently, CBT for the condition aims to help clients reduce their negative mental processes and beliefs about social situations, their overly negative view of their performance in social situations, their excessive fear of negative evaluations by others as well as their excessive importance attached to social performance.

Additionally, to put this into a perspective for those of us without social anxiety disorder can understand, whenever we go to a social situation, we always want to do well, not look like an idiot and we want people to like us at these social situations but our entire identities aren't obsessed with that and our world will not end if we make a fool of ourselves.

But that is how social situations and negative evaluations feel to people with social anxiety disorder.

As a result, CBT for this condition seeks to reduce a person's self-focused attention, getting them to stop their safety and avoidance behaviours and get them to reduce their attentional bias to the social threat.

Ultimately, now that we've looked at CBT for three different anxiety disorders, hopefully you can see how CBT is adapted to each condition, and how there are similarities and there are some fairly stark differences as well.

And it is those differences that make this topic so fascinating to learn about.

EXPOSURE THERAPY

We seriously couldn't do a section on treatments for anxiety disorders without investigating exposure therapy, and this is a therapy that is so often used in books, TV and films that I just know a lot of people would have been disappointed if I didn't write about it. And personally, I would have been disappointed too because exposure therapy is flat out brilliant.

What Is Exposure Therapy?

Exposure therapy is a psychological treatment that was developed to help people confront their fears. Since whenever people are fearful or scared of something, they tend to avoid the feared object, situation or activity. For example, if a person is fearful of social situations or spiders then the person will avoid said social situation and spider.

Furthermore, as we know from earlier chapters, this avoidance behaviour might help the person to reduce their feelings of fear in the short term, in the long term it can make the fear even worse. Basically, this has the complete opposite effect than intended.

As a result, in exposure therapy, psychologists create a safe environment so the client can get "exposed" to the anxiety provoking, fearful objects, situations and activities that they avoid and find fearful. If the therapy is done correctly (more on that later) then this leads to a reduction in their fearful response and avoidance behaviour.

Moreover, exposure therapy isn't some guru rubbish that doesn't have supportive literature, it has been scientifically shown to be an effective treatment or treatment component for a wide range of mental health conditions. Such as:

- Social Anxiety Disorder
- Generalized Anxiety Disorder
- Phobias
- Obsessive-Compulsive Disorder
- Panic Disorder
- Posttraumatic Stress Disorder

How Is Exposure Therapy Done?

Now this is why I really enjoy learning about exposure therapy because the therapy really has come such a long way since its beginning. Especially since when I think about Exposure Therapy I only imagine a client looking at a spider in a glass box and it then crawling up on the client's arm.

Even though I don't have a spider phobia, I seriously couldn't imagine me willingly having a massive spider crawling up my arm. That's just goes to show how amazingly brave our clients are.

However, this is only one of the ways exposure therapy is done.

The first way exposure therapy is done is by what's known as "In vivo exposure" and this is basically what I mentioned above. Since this is when you directly face the feared situation, object or activity in real life.

For example, to use a different example, if a person is terrified of horses then they might be instructed to handle a horse, or a person with social anxiety might be asked to give a speech in front of an audience.

Another method is "Imaginal Exposure". This involves a person vividly imagining the feared situation, object or activity. And a great example here is from PTSD sufferers, because they might be asked to recall and describe their traumatic experience in great detail to reduce the feelings of fear.

Penultimately, Virtual Reality (VR) can be used as a form of exposure because in some cases, VR technology can be used in cases where In Vivo exposure just isn't practical. For example, we can all see that if a person has a fear of flying then the psychologist isn't going to rent a plane and take the client flying for the hour of their therapy appointment. It would be cool if they did but that really isn't practical in the slightest.

So VR comes in very handy in cases like this, especially as the VR equipment in the psychologist office's can be used to provide the sights, smells and sounds of an aeroplane.

Finally, "Interoceptive Exposure" can be used. This is a very interesting one because it involves bringing on physical sensations that are harmless to the client but fearful. Such as, if you're working with a client with panic disorder, they might be instructed to run on the spot to make their heart speed up so the person learns that the sensation isn't dangerous.

That's brilliant because the whole "problem" with a panic disorder is that the person is fearful of the physical sensation.

<u>What Is Graded Exposure?</u>

Originally in my weird little notes the three next sections were later in the chapter but as you'll see that just flat out wouldn't work.

Anyway, graded exposure is an absolutely critical feature of Exposure Therapy because it involves a fear hierarchy. This is a list of a person's triggers that makes them feel afraid or anxious, and these triggers are ranked from the trigger that is least anxiety provoking to the most provoking.

For example, if you have a client that is terrified of spiders then the least anxiety provoking situation might be seeing a photo of a spider, followed by watching a video of a spider, being in the same room as a spider and then allowing a spider to crawl up your arm.

This is a good example for a hierarchy for spider phobias, but of course a real one depends on the client.

Additionally, it's important in Exposure Therapy to try and have these items by distress number (another way of saying the amount of distress it causes goes up linear) so there are no big jumps. Then the idea is to make sure the client and the therapist work their way through the list from the lowest number to the highest number also known as the most anxiety-provoking.

Also, it's a good idea to make sure the theme of the list is relevant to the goals of the therapy. Therefore, a therapist could experiment with each item several times until the client no longer feels distress in that situation.

For instance, going back to our spider

example, a therapist wouldn't move from getting the client to look at images of a spider before moving onto watching a video. As well as the therapist might have the client look at images of small, medium and massive spiders to make sure the client no longer feels anxious after looking at images before moving onto the next one.

Equally, sometimes therapists might "only" keep experimenting until the distress in a given situation is about half of what it was. This makes sense because it isn't until a client reaches the top of their hierarchy that their anxiety responses are a lot better than before treatment.

That's the easiest way to explain it.

How Does Exposure Therapy Work?

This is what we all want to know because as psychology is a science, we want to know why and how something works. Therefore, there are four main mechanisms that help change to occur during a course of Exposure Therapy.

Firstly, the client goes through a process of habituation where over time, people find that their reactions to the feared objects, situations or activities decrease because of their exposure to them. This links with the challenging of their biased beliefs because if a client is being exposed to the feared object without the world ending then this helps them to learn that maybe their beliefs were wrong.

Secondly, the cognitive process of extinction occurs where exposure helps to weaken the previously learnt associations between feared objects, activities or situations and bad outcomes.

And yes, this has a lot to do with the psychology of learning, which you can read more about in *Cognitive Psychology: A Guide To Neuropsychology, Neuroscience and Cognitive Psychology*.

Thirdly, and this is something I think is so, so important in therapy work. A client learns about their own self-efficacy. Meaning the exposure helps to show the client that they're perfectly capable of confronting their own fears as well as they can manage the feelings of their anxiety.

This links to the brilliant concept of CBT Pie Charts, a very powerful and fascinating therapy tool, that I discuss more in *Clinical Psychology Reflections Volume 4*.

Finally, exposure therapy is great for emotional processing since during the exposure, the client can learn to attach new, more realistic beliefs about feared objects, activities or situations, and they can become more comfortable with the experience of fear.

What Are The Four Rules of Exposure Therapy?

I have to admit that psychologists love rules, methods and having to do things a certain way and this is definitely true for CBT, but when it comes to Exposure Therapy, these four rules are particularly important because if a therapist doesn't stick to the rules then chances are the therapy will fail and the client will only be worst off.

Therefore, the first rule of Exposure Therapy is the exposure absolutely has to be graded. If we look back at our spider example, you seriously cannot go from getting a client to look at photos of spiders to having a spider crawling up their arm. That will end so badly and the client will never improve and yeah, it will not be pretty.

Just don't do that.

In addition, and see this as a sub-rule of the first one, when it comes to creating the Hierarchy of Anxious Situations, it's best to start with the most anxiety-provoking and then work down. Remember, this is the creation phase because if a therapist asks a client about the object that causes them the least anxiety. Chances are they will not know.

They only know the *most* anxiety-provoking one so it's best to start there and then it breaks the ice, allowing you to ask more questions, investigate more and slowly work your way down towards the least anxiety-provoking ones.

Remember, therapy is a process and so is the creation of this hierarchy.

Secondly, these exposures have to be prolonged since the therapists need to wait until the anxiety comes down to about half of what it was before they started before they get the client to stop. Since if the therapist stops it too soon then they risk reinforcing the very behaviour they are trying to get the client to stop.

Thirdly, these exposures have to be repeated so the client should continue doing the exposure of the same activity until their pre-activity anxiety comes down to about half what it was when the therapist planned the activity.

Again, if a therapist shows a client a photo of a spider and the client starts rapidly breathing, they would wait until the rapid breathing decreases before moving on to the next task.

Finally, these exposures have to be done without distraction. The client has to be focused on these exposures and learn that their biased beliefs are not based in reality and the danger is nowhere near what they believe it is. And distractions only make this learning or unlearning even harder.

Exposure And Response Prevention

This next aspect is very similar to standard graded exposure and this is when a therapist and a client work together, much like how they do in CBT, to develop a hierarchy like we saw in the last few sections and the four principles still apply.

However, the difference is that the client needs to resist the urge to respond to a compulsive desire and it is important for the client to sit with the distress until it comes down to about half.

The clearest fictional example of this is with OCD. For example, a client might have the urge to start cleaning whenever they see dirt so their compulsion might be hand cleaning so at least they are clean. In this situation, the client would have to sit with that compulsion and *not* clean their hands.

Of course, this would cause a lot of distress and anxiety but it will also show the client that nothing bad will happen to them if they don't wash their hands the second the compulsion manifests itself.

What Are The Common Difficulties With Exposure?

Of course, nothing in psychology like life is straight forward and therapy is no different. Therefore, there will be problems a therapist encounters with their clients when it comes to exposure therapy. Some of these problems include:

- The client doesn't want to get started and the therapist can't encourage them.

You cannot do a therapy if the client isn't

willing to put in the work and at least try it, but exposure therapy is terrifying for people.

- Missing activities or missing steps in the hierarchy. That will almost always end badly.
- The client or therapist or both tries to do too much too soon.
- Jumping ahead in the hierarchy.
- The client doesn't drop their safety behaviours so they still believe it is their safety behaviours that are protecting them.
- Both the client and therapist have difficulties categorising activities in the hierarchy.

This is problematic because if a therapist can't categorise activities properly then it is so much harder to understand how to properly go up the hierarchy without the risk of jumping steps and trying to do too much at once.

- Stopping an activity before the anxiety drops.

How To Address Safety behaviours In Exposure Therapy?

Some of you might have realised that normally in CBT (which is completely separate from Exposure Therapy), you carry out cognitive interventions including behavioural experiments to challenge and address a person's beliefs and safety behaviours. And I'm sure there is a good argument that Exposure Therapy is a good form of cognitive intervention, but Exposure Therapy does not have a good way of addressing safety behaviours. At least from what we've seen so far.

The first step of getting rid of any safety behaviour is obviously identifying them, you can't get rid of something if you don't know what it is.

As well as we need to remember that safety behaviours try to distract us from the experience of our anxiety, and this is important because it reduces the opportunities for habituation. As well as this is why it's sometimes a very good idea to make a list of safety behaviours that might get in the way of habituation with the client.

As a result, a person might say to a therapist "I can look at spider photos if I do…"

We don't want them to say that. And whilst it is sometimes "okay" to allow a safety behaviour in order to make a jump in the hierarchy, this isn't ideal in the slightest, but when this is done, the next step should be completed without the safety behaviour before moving on to the next.

A practical example would be the one we've been using all chapter, if a client couldn't even look at a photo of a spider but we saw there was a decrease of about a quarter to a third in anxiety. Then maybe a therapist could allow them to do a safety behaviour before moving on to the next one.

Again, this really, really does come down to clinical judgement and the therapist's experience.

Overall, at the end of this great chapter, I have to admit that Exposure Therapy is definitely a serious but potentially fun therapy because we get to help our clients, and get very creative at the same time, and it is that creativity that I just love.

PART FOUR: THERAPIES FOR TRAUMA

WHAT IS EMDR?

Whilst I gave you a bit of an overview of Cognitive Behavioural Therapy in the anxiety section of the book, I wanted to give you some more information on different forms of psychological therapies. Since as sexual assault survivors, we will need psychological help if we ever want to recover, and this doesn't make you weak, damaged or any other of the myths and misconceptions about therapy.

Personally, I think if someone goes to therapy then they're brave, courageous and they're brilliant. Due to a lot of people need psychological help in order to heal, recover and improve their lives but a lot of people are too scared to get the help they need.

Therefore, in the next few chapters, I'll introduce you to different forms of psychological therapy that *might* be useful for sexual assault survivors. As well as whilst these chapters are based on psychology articles I wrote for my podcast, they're still easy-to-understand, engaging and they'll give you a good foundational understanding of the different options you might want to look at in more depth.

Enjoy.

***

EMDR stands for Eye Movement Desensitization Reprocessing and this is a type of psychotherapy that I've become more aware of in recent months. Since a close friend of mine mentioned they had EMDR and a good podcast I listened to mentioned that she went for EMDR too. And before this podcast episode, I knew it was an effective psychotherapy but I had no idea what it actually involved and I knew there was a sort of stigma around it within the psychology community. Therefore, in this clinical psychology podcast episode, you'll learn what is EMDR, how does EMDR work and much more. If you enjoy learning about mental health, clinical psychology and psychotherapy then you will love today's episode.

<u>What Is EMDR?</u>

EMDR isn't really a psychotherapy in and of itself, it is more of a psychotherapy technique that is designed to relieve the psychological distress associated with a client's disturbing memories. As well as it involves a client recalling a specific negative experience while following a side-to-side visual stimulus delivered by the therapist. A client needs to do this in EMDR because the lateral eye movements that following this stimulus causes that are thought to help reduce the emotional impact of this memory. This helps the negative experience to become easier to discuss with the therapist as the memory is effectively stripped of its power to trigger avoidance behaviours and anxiety within a client.

In addition, there have been a lot of empirical studies that show that EMDR works for some clients, but it is very, very controversial. There are a lot of reasons for this but one of the main reasons is that we just don't know how it works. There are a lot of theories that try to explain how EMDR works but there isn't a universally accepted theory.

Another reason why EMDR is controversial is because there isn't much clear evidence that EMDR is better than other forms of exposure therapy. Since EMDR and other exposure therapies are basically the same in terms of you have a client recalling a traumatic memory in the safe environment provided by a therapist. As well as the client repeatedly talks about the event in this safe context and this leads to a decrease in avoidance and fear responses.

Personally, when I first learnt those two reasons I wasn't very surprised, because I completely understand that EMDR is basically the same as other exposure therapies. They all follow the same principles and whilst it is good that we know EMDR works for some clients. Clinical psychology is a science after all, and we need to understand how and why EMDR works. Not just as a whole but why does it work for some clients and not others, and once we understand what are the important elements or components of EMDR then we might be able to distil EMDR and combine it with other treatment models. There is a lot of work to do in EMDR research as you'll see later on.

How Does EMDR Work?

Whilst as I mentioned a moment ago, there are no widely accepted theories that explain EMDR, but I'm going to tell you about some of the theories. None of these are conclusive and these are all just theories, but I think having at least a basic understanding of how EMDR *might* work is more important here.

Therefore, EMDR is meant to be based on the so-called Adaptive Information Model and this is meant to target the way a distressing memory is stored in the brain. The idea behind this is that the experience is distressing because of how it's stored in the brain so if you can change how the memory is stored then you can change how distressing it is to a client. As well as when these memories are triggered in the present they contain all the same emotions, physical feelings and thoughts as the experience did in the past. All because the experience wasn't processed properly in the first place.

I'm just going to say upright that I find this theory very suspect already, but let's continue.

Interestingly, there have been studies that have called into question whether the eye movement part of EMDR is even needed. Due to these studies suggest that EMDR actually works because the desensitisation involves recalling, confronting as well as reprocessing the aversive memories under the careful supervision of a therapist.

And you know what that's called. It's called exposure therapy.

On the other hand, there have been some new theories suggested in recent years to explain how EMDR works. For example, Andrew Huberman of Standford University supports the eye movements as an important part of EMDR because he proposes that the movements seen in EMDR copy optic flow and this decreases a person's fear system as well as temporarily decreases the sense of threat that the traumatic memory holds.

Additionally, the eyes are a part of the central nervous system and research Huberman conducted shows when the eyes are relaxed, a client adjusts their inner state to match. This is supported by additional research, including a study done by Dutch researchers and published in the *Journal Of*

Neuroscience.

Also, I want to add in this quote from Huberman that further supports his theory: "It makes sense from an evolutionary perspective. We've always been confronted with threats—animal threats, interpersonal threats. Forward movement is the way you suppress the fear response." Then when it comes to the visual system, he says, "is a steering wheel and brake of the nervous system. The brain will follow the visual system in many ways."

Overall, I think this theory makes a lot of sense because it helps to explain how EMDR works, the biological mechanisms behind it and how this has a knock-on effect for our mental processes. However, there are still other questions that have yet to be answered about EMDR's workings. For example, the interpatient factors that explain the variance in why it works for some and not others, and this almost sounds a little reductionist in a sense. Since this theory only focuses on the biological aspects of the eye movements. It fails to explain how the social factors, like being in a safe environment of the therapist's office, helps to explain how works.

<u>When Is EMDR Used?</u>

Whilst originally this therapy technique was developed to treat PTSD, it's now used for a wide range of conditions. For instance, anxiety disorders, depression, eating disorders, some personality disorders, obsessive-compulsive disorders and a few others.

However, it's important to note that for a client to be a good fit for EMDR, they need to be comfortable with some emotional discomfort. Also, they shouldn't be too easily overwhelmed by their feelings and not shut down emotionally when they face discomfort. As well as clients should be able to use their emotional and cognitive resources to help them reprocess their memories.

I will just add there that I don't think a single one of those points is actually unique to EMDR. I think they are basic assumptions of all clients going in psychotherapy because you can't do therapy successfully if you aren't willing to confront and process the past and you need to have a capacity for change too.

<u>What Should Someone Expect In EMDR?</u>

Whilst some clients might need fewer sessions, a typical course of EMDR lasts between 6 and 12 sessions that are delivered once or twice a week. With some studies showing that reprocessing a single distressing memory can be processed within three sessions.

Then after the client and therapist talk about the client's history and the therapist explains the procedure, the two work together to decide on which past experiences will be the subject of the treatment. Afterwards, the therapist activates the distressing memory by asking the patient to visualise and/ or experience their thoughts.

I find that term "activate" quite funny because it makes it sound like the therapist has a switch into a client's head.

Anyway, once the memory is activated, the therapist assesses the level of negative thoughts and feelings within the client about the event, and the positive beliefs the client wants to increase about themselves. Next, the therapist administers the bilateral visual stimulation.

In addition, the client can almost always expect to experience some physical and emotional discomfort here because they'll be recalling the distressing memories. Then as the procedure continues, new thoughts and feelings will emerge and these are discussed. Also, the therapist samples the nature and level of the client's emotional and cognitive distress as well as any physical distress.

Finally, the session ends when the client feels manageably calm and the therapist gives them instructions about how to handle any disturbing thoughts and feelings in-between their sessions. As well as in the following sessions, these begin with an assessment of the memories that might have emerged since the last treatment.

Conclusion

I have to admit that this has been a rather fun podcast episode for me because we've looked at how EMDR works, what EMDR is, what to expect in EMDR and more. And whilst I have made fun of EMDR in at least two sections of this episode, I think this therapy does have a place in clinical psychology. Of course, more research has to be done so we can actually understand how it works because psychology is a science and we have to use empirical tools in therapy. Also, there needs to be more research into how EMDR is different to other forms of exposure therapy because I am personally not convinced it's as different as it claims to be.

However, at the end of the day, there will be clients that need EMDR to improve their lives, decrease their psychological distress and function clinically normally. My friend's proof of that and so is the podcast host that I listen to from time to time. I think as long as we admit the limitations, we try to fix the limitations and we don't overstate how effective or great EMDR is compared to other therapies. Then this is a good compromise because EMDR is good for some people, but it isn't for others. And even for the people who it works for, we just don't know why.

And that little bit of controversy is why psychotherapy can be important, fascinating and seriously fun to think about.

WHAT IS COGNITIVE PROCESSING THERAPY?

Even though I flat out love trauma content because I find it really interesting, engaging and it's nice to understand my experiences through an academic lens, I wanted to return to some trauma-based therapies for this book on sexual violence.

So far in the book, I've outlined fairly "traditional" forms of psychotherapies that effectively help with a wide range of mental health conditions. Yet because of the traumatic nature of sexual violence, there are sometimes when these more "traditional" therapies like for depression and anxiety, just don't work for trauma. This is why psychology created some trauma-based therapies that we adapted off the more traditional therapies.

As a result, if you think a trauma-based therapy would be more effective for you then read about it, learn about the therapy and reach out to a qualified therapist practicing that therapeutic model to see if it's the right fit for you.

Also, I like learning about trauma because it's personal, I know how awful it is and I always like hope.

Hope that there is a post-trauma life.

And Cognitive Processing Therapy really helps with sense of hope because it is designed for trauma survivors and you can see how helpful and useful it is with my personal thoughts and examples in the article below.

Please enjoy.

***

I think when you get to a certain point in your clinical psychology journey, you start to realise what your interests are and what doesn't interest you at all. Sometimes this takes years or no time at all. I know undergraduate students that have known their areas of interest ever since their first year, some people don't understand their interests until Masters or beyond.

Personally, I didn't really know my areas of interest until at least my third year, and even then it was only looking back at the podcast episodes that I started to realise a pattern.

I love trauma-based content.

Granted in the grand scheme of things, we don't actually do that much on The Psychology World Podcast but I like learning about it because it's personal, I know how awful it is and I always like hope.

Hope that there is a post-trauma life.

And Cognitive Processing Therapy really helps with sense of hope because it is designed for trauma survivors and you can see how helpful and useful it is with my personal thoughts and examples in the article below.

Please enjoy.

***

It turns out that I have a minor interest in treatments for Post Traumatic Stress Disorder, so when I came across Cognitive Processing Therapy, I realised I had to do a podcast episode on it. Not only because the therapy is a treatment option for PTSD but also because this is a specialised form of Cognitive Behavioural Therapy, an approach that I really enjoy. Therefore, in this clinical psychology podcast episode, you'll find out what is Cognitive Processing Therapy, how does it work and more. If you enjoy learning about PTSD, trauma and different psychological therapies then you'll definitely enjoy today's episode.

What Is Cognitive Processing Therapy?

This form of psychotherapy is a specialised form of Cognitive Behavioural Therapy that is used to treat clients who have experienced traumatic life events. Such as violence, natural disasters, abuse amongst others, as well as it has been found to be an effective treatment for PTSD.

Cognitive Processing Therapy was first developed in the late 1980s and thankfully, it's been found to be a highly effective treatment for PTSD. All the references are at the end of the blog post but a large meta-analysis found that Cognitive Processing Therapy was more effective than a placebo immediately after treatment and at follow-up sessions regardless of the client's age. Also, the same conclusion was drawn whether it was group or individual Cognitive Processing Therapy with the American Psychological Association strongly recommending the therapy too.

In addition, Cognitive Processing Therapy is typically delivered in 12 sessions where the therapist helps a client who has had a traumatic experience evaluate their thoughts surrounding the trauma. Even more so for any self-blaming or maladaptive thoughts that might be maintaining or increasing the severity of the mental health difficulties. Afterwards the client will learn how to challenge these thoughts and take a new perspective when they need to with homework being used like in most other forms of CBT.

Now we'll look at this information in a little more depth in the rest of the episode.

How Does Cognitive Processing Therapy Work?

When we experience significant trauma, we can develop PTSD and this makes a person think about ourselves and our environment differently. At least when compared to before the trauma. For example, before my sexual assault, I was perfectly happy being in my bed or being in certain situations, but after the assault, I seriously wasn't okay in my own bed for a while. Even in different public situations, I was very, very nervous about because my assault changed how I saw certain environments.

Additionally, there tends to be five areas of life that people who have experienced significant trauma notice changes. Firstly, they see changes in safety in terms of the client might doubt their ability to protect themselves, others and their loved ones.

Secondly, the client might see changes in their intimacy, so they might feel incapable of connecting with and being understood by others, let alone accepted. To be honest, even though my abuse was spread over a decade period, this was my main concern and I was so closed off for so long and I refused to have any sort of emotional intimacy simply because I saw that as too dangerous.

Thirdly, the client might lack a sense of control so they don't feel capable or able of controlling their own life or influence the lives of the people they care about.

Fourthly, a client could see changes in trust. This means they might question the judgement and/ or intention of other people and they might doubt their own judgement.

Finally, esteem could be a massive issue because the client could see themselves and other people differently after the trauma and see themselves as "broken" and other people as "evil".

Personally, I'll talk about this briefly but it's that idea that you're "broken" or "messed up" or a "victim" that can be really hard for people who have experienced trauma. And it took me ages and a lot of therapy to start realising that I am a great person that isn't broken and my experiences don't define me.

Also, just today as I write this, I've learnt about the concept of Post-traumatic Growth which is an idea I love. I need to read and research it more but if you enjoy trauma work definitely learn that idea.

Anyway, these thoughts tend to lead our clients towards experiencing negative emotions, like guilt, fear, anger and anxiety and this can stop a person's recovery dead in its tracks. It seriously can. Therefore, Cognitive Processing Therapy can help people by teaching them skills that will help the person challenge their negative thoughts.

Overall, Cognitive Processing Therapy is based on the social cognitive theory of Post-Traumatic Stress Disorder. This theory argues that a client makes the traumatic event a part of their worldview and this is counterproductive and leads to maladaptive beliefs. As a result, Cognitive Processing Therapy focuses on repairing the damage the event has done to someone's beliefs about themselves, others and the world.

Typically, this is done by teaching the client and using specific cognitive restructuring techniques so a client can challenge these thoughts and instead gain a healthier perspective about their trauma in turn.

And before we move onto when is Cognitive Processing Therapy used, one almost heartbreaking example of how trauma impacts beliefs about the world is from my assault. Since about 3 weeks after the assault, my friend was returning from a little trip to celebrate my birthday with me and we were going to go to London, do a virtual reality thing and have dinner out. I remember begging my friend over Whatsapp to bring their brother who studied in London along because I was so scared of for starters being in a one-on-one situation because that was what happened in my assault. As well as I was so scared of the idea of needing a toilet that I really wanted my friend to come with me because I was terrified of something happening in the toilet.

Thankfully, therapy helped me get rid of that fear but it's an example about how trauma can warp a person's beliefs about the world.

<u>When Is Cognitive Processing Therapy Used?</u>

I've already mentioned a few different times in this episode that Cognitive Processing Therapy is an effective treatment for adult clients with PTSD, but it can be useful for people with other mental health conditions too. For example, older adolescents with PTSD is another ideal clinical population for this treatment.

Now, there is some research suggesting Cognitive Processing Therapy might be good for people who experience secondary traumatisation and people who anticipate encountering additional traumatic events. Such as, paramedics, police officers and other emergency workers. There isn't tons of research on this area, but this is thought to be good for these groups because the therapy aims to change the way clients process and interpret their trauma on an ongoing basis.

However, Cognitive Processing Therapy shouldn't be used for people without a diagnosis of PTSD nor if they have literacy difficulties, because this therapy involves written homework. Also, Cognitive Processing Therapy isn't a good idea for people with substance abuse, comorbid bipolar disorder or suicidal ideation. Instead people with these mental health difficulties should go for a research-supported trauma treatment called Prolonged Exposure Therapy.

<u>What Can A Client Expect In Cognitive Processing Therapy?</u>

When a client goes for this type of therapy, they can expect to either have group or individual therapy sessions or even a combination of both for 12 weekly sessions. Each session is about an hour to an hour and a half long depending on the needs of the clients.

The first few sessions are focused on the psychoeducation aspects of trauma so the client learns about PTSD as well as what they can expect to get out of treatment.

Afterwards, in the next few sessions, the therapist and client work together to identify and explore the different ways that the trauma has impacted and changed how the client thinks, feels and behaves. Then the therapist helps to pick out thoughts that act as barriers to the client's recovery.

Next the patient learns a set of strategies to challenge and modify the thoughts that aren't accurate and/ or unhelpful. Then the client practices these strategies with the therapist and with the homework in the form of exercises and worksheets.

And briefly jumping in here, trauma can make you develop some random thoughts that flat out aren't helpful. For example, since my assault, I've struggled with the idea of going out and even though I've managed to force my way through some rather intense episodes of social anxiety. I was talking about some of these thoughts and excuses with my therapist and it was almost funny saying them out loud because of how illogical and unhelpful they were. Of course, I laugh as a coping mechanism and because I've managed to get a little emotional distance from my Event, so I can look at it a little more psychologically. But working with a therapist and exploring these thoughts is absolutely critical for moving forward.

Moreover, the client might be asked to write about the traumatic event including some sensory detail or they might be asked to write more broadly about how their experience made them feel and how they tend to think it happened. Then if the client is having individual therapy then their writing might be read aloud during the session but the same isn't required for group therapy.

I can't even begin to imagine how scary that would be in a group setting.

On the whole, a client can expect Cognitive Processing Therapy to be very emotionally and cognitively intense, even more so when they're talking or writing about the experience itself. Due to clients tend to feel discomfort, and a lot of clients report that this discomfort was brief and the benefits gained from the therapy definitely outweigh the discomfort after completing the full course of therapy.

Again, I know I've never had Cognitive Processing Therapy but I like adding in some paragraphs here and there because I think it helps to bring the material alive. I had a therapy session yesterday related to my assault and I've been for therapy for other trauma before. But because my assault was more recent and acute, I was surprised at how draining it was emotionally. I normally have to do other stuff for about 30 minutes when I get home because I cannot be productive straight away after therapy.

This time it took a good two hours before I even thought about being productive, but I did feel a lot better afterwards.

<u>Conclusion</u>

I think I'll always have a soft spot for people with PTSD and other people that go through trauma. Maybe I feel a certain kinship, maybe I feel like I understand them a little better and maybe I just want them to be okay whatever happens. Personally, I think it's a mixture of all three.

Therefore, I really like Cognitive Processing Therapy because I've read a lot of psychology textbooks in my time and sometimes there is a sense of hopelessness and a lack of effective treatment options for people with PTSD. So I'm happy and grateful that there is an option for people with PTSD and other traumatic experiences so they can get support to improve their lives, decrease their psychological distress and have their lives effectively given back to them.

And that's what I love about our profession and I want to be a clinical psychologist in the future. We can help people to take back control of their lives, we help them feel better and to help them realise they can get past their trauma no matter how bad it seems.

Having the ability to do that is special and

that's why I'll always defend, advocate and encourage people to join or take an interest in clinical psychology. Because you never truly know what amazing things you can do until they happen.

WHAT IS TRUMA-FOCUSED COGNITIVE BEHAVIOURAL THERAPY?

For our final Cognitive Behavioural-based therapy in the book, I wanted to combine trauma and CBT together. Since to say I got excited about this therapy was a massive understatement for reasons you'll read in a moment, but this was a lot of fun to research, write up and I had a blast with it.

I hope you enjoy it as much as I did.

***

One of my many interests within clinical psychology is certainly trauma. Partly this is because of my own various experiences and I know first-hand how damaging it can be to our mental health. Therefore, I suppose my interest is me reminding myself that there is hope and there is a wide range of therapies to help people who have been through trauma. That's why in this podcast episode we get to learn about the combination of two of my major interests. Trauma-Focused Cognitive Behavioural Therapy combines my interest in trauma and Cognitive Behaviour Therapy. Hence, in this psychology podcast episode, you'll get to learn about what Is Trauma-Focused Cognitive Behavioural Therapy, how does it work, when is it used and more. If you're interested in mental health, trauma and psychological interventions then this is a great episode for you.

What Is Trauma-Focused Cognitive Behavioural Therapy?

This form of psychotherapy tends to be shortened to FT-CBT, and it is a therapy to support children, teenagers and families suffering from the effects of early trauma. Therefore, Trauma-Focused Cognitive Behavioural Therapy is very attuned for helping the specific and rather unique difficulties that children with PTSD and mood disorders experience. These mental health difficulties and conditions can be a result of sexual or physical abuse or violence, or grief.

Also, because the client in Trauma-Focused Cognitive Behavioural Therapy is normally a child, this therapy is rather unique in the sense that non-offending parents and other caregivers can brought into the therapy and it incorporates a lot of principles from family therapy.

This makes the therapy rather interesting I think because one, it is relatively uncommon to bring caregivers into a therapy setting, so it's interesting to know how this works. Two, I find it interesting personally because this is actually the second time I've tried to write this post. I couldn't even start writing the first time round because this therapy hit me in a few unexpected ways.

Yet the three main ways were, I had tried to write it originally less than a week after being sexually assaulted so that was a mistake. I might have been grieving because I would have loved to have had an option like this as a child myself. Thirdly, I hate the idea of another child going through trauma because I don't wish it on anyone.

So I just wanted to share that with you so you know my personal position on this therapy.

Moreover, Trauma-Focused Cognitive Behavioural Therapy was developed in the 1990s by a psychiatrist called Judith Cohen alongside psychologists Anthony Mannarino and Esther Deblinger. Originally, the therapy was designed to better help sexually abused children as well as adolescents. Then over the years, the therapy has expanded to include services for young people who have experienced over forms of severe abuse and trauma.

How Does Trauma-Focused Cognitive Behavioural Therapy Work?

I talk more about how the family therapy and the cognitive behavioural therapy aspects help Trauma-Focused Cognitive Behavioural Therapy to be the effective therapy it is towards the end of the podcast episode. Yet TF-CBT combines cognitive-behavioural techniques with trauma-sensitive approaches to help the client process their traumatic experiences, build resilience and develop more adaptive coping mechanisms.

In addition, Trauma-Focused Cognitive Behavioural Therapy is made up of the following five components that help to make it an effective therapy for trauma.

Firstly, there is a heavy focus in the therapy on skills-building. This is where relaxation techniques, emotion regulation strategies and coping skills are taught to the client to help them manage their emotion and any challenging situations.

Secondly, there is cognitive restructuring where the client's maladaptive thoughts, beliefs and behaviours are targeted and replaced to more with realistic and adaptive thinking patterns.

Thirdly, psychoeducation is important in Trauma-Focused Cognitive Behavioural Therapy because clients learn about trauma and its effects on us. This helps the client to understand their reactions and behaviours and this normalises their experiences.

Fourthly, trauma-narrative is another component. In this area of the therapy, clients are guided through the process of sharing and processing their traumatic experience in a safe and supportive environment.

Personally, this is a critically important area of therapeutic work, because when I was talking about my assault with my therapist it was lovely to have a safe space to talk about it. Of course, it was still distressing and really uncomfortable but I couldn't have processed it in another environment where I didn't feel safe and supported. This is why trauma-informed therapists are flat out critical, because they can help clients to feel safe enough to process and share what happened when other people can't.

Finally, gradual exposure is another important area of the therapy. Since this is where clients are gently exposed to trauma reminders in a controlled way to reduce their fear and avoidance.

Whilst I never had Trauma-Focused Cognitive Behavioural Therapy, after my assault, a small part of me did just want to crawl up in bed and never leave the house again. I didn't really want to see my friends, I didn't really want to see my parents and I just wanted to stay in my room because it was safe in there and I controlled it. Yet I knew that wasn't healthy but I did need to start slowly introducing myself back in the world and it's been lovely. And you definitely know what people think of you and how good they are as friends when you tell them you've been assaulted.

Things still pop up when I go out and when I introduce myself to situations, but doing it in a controlled way is very helpful and it minimises the risks.

When Is Trauma-Focused Cognitive Behavioural Therapy Used?

As mentioned earlier, Trauma-Focused Cognitive Behavioural Therapy isn't only for young people who have experienced sexual abuse. Nowadays, it's used for children and adolescents who have experienced a single or repeated incidents of mental, physical or sexual abuse or who young people who have developed post-traumatic symptoms, anxiety or depression.

Nonetheless, Trauma-Focused Cognitive Behavioural Therapy might not be the best option for children and adolescents who do show serious suicidal ideation, substance abuse or behavioural issues. In this case, other forms of psychotherapy might be better for the client, like dialectical behavioural therapy, as an initial intervention and then a trauma-sensitive approach could be used as a follow-up.

What Can Clients Expect From Trauma-Focused Cognitive Behavioural Therapy?

Trauma-Focused Cognitive Behavioural Therapy is a short-term psychological intervention that typically lasts anywhere from 8 to 25 sessions that can take place in a wide range of settings. For example, the therapy can be done in a group home, a community centre, school, hospital, in-home setting or an outpatient mental health clinic. Also, the therapy takes place with a non-offending caregiver or parent and often the therapy starts with separate therapy sessions for the child and caregiver. Then they advance into joint therapy sessions.

Furthermore, as this is a form of Cognitive Behavioural Therapy, a lot of CBT techniques are used to help modify the unhelpful and distorted thinking and the negative behaviours and reactions the child has because of the trauma. Then the child focuses on learning how to challenge their invasive thoughts of fear and guilt so they can reorganise their thinking in a more adaptive and positive way.

Subsequently, there is a major aspect of family therapy to Trauma-Focused Cognitive Behavioural Therapy too. Since the family therapy aspects focus on the issues the family members might be dealing with, because of the trauma suffered by the child. This is why a range of communication, parenting and stress management skills are taught here.

On the whole, research investigating the effectiveness of Trauma-Focused Cognitive Behavioural Therapy against other treatment models show that TF-CBT demonstrates significantly greater gains in the well-being for children and their parents.

Personally, this section reminds me about why I love clinical psychology and psychotherapies so much. Since family therapy and cognitive behavioural therapy alone would have only a positive on trauma work to a certain extent, because they focus on different things. But when you combine them and use cognitive-behavioural and family approaches together, now there is where the magic happens and that is where you can start to transform the lives of clients for the better.

I flat out love combining approaches to target a difficulty from different angles.

Conclusion

I have really enjoyed today's episode because I like looking at trauma and I like Cognitive Behavioural Therapy, so combining them into a single episode was great fun for me. And I know within clinical psychology, there is a shift towards becoming more trauma-informed so it is critical that we take every opportunity we can to learn and develop our understanding about trauma.

The last thing we ever want to do as aspiring or qualified clinical psychologists is to add to someone's trauma, because that is wrong, unfair and it isn't what the profession is meant for at all.

I think for me today's episode has reminded me that I like trauma work, therapy and it reminds me a lot about my own life. Sure, this is painful at times, but it is also reassuring. That there is hope for other people, trauma doesn't have to define a person and there is a good chance for recovery given the right tools and therapist.

For you, I hope that you're inspired to learn more about therapy, or at least you're inspired to think about combining and mixing different therapeutic approaches more. Due to the results, when done right and backed up by evidence, can be powerful, supportive and life-changing for our clients.

And as aspiring or qualified psychologists, that truly is all we want for them.

WHAT IS ACCEPTANCE AND COMMITMENT THERAPY?

Whilst our next therapy isn't one that is normally given as a treatment option for trauma survivors, I wanted to talk about Acceptance Commitment therapy (ACT) because there are a lot of useful ideas in the therapy that you can use in everyday life and this is an effective therapy for different conditions. Also, a large part of therapy work at times is accepting what has happened to you, accepting that you can't change it but you can heal through accepting that you can still live your life, recover and improve your life for the better.

On the whole, I really like this next chapter because it's interesting and it shows you a rather different sort of therapy compared to EMDR and Cognitive Behavioural Therapy. As well as this might give you some ideas about what you might want to work on in therapy.

Enjoy.

***

Within clinical psychology, there are a few types of psychological therapy that you hear about time and time again. These include cognitive behavioural therapy, interpersonal psychotherapy amongst others. As well as I often hear about Acceptance and Commitment Therapy but because this therapy isn't really available on the National Health Service in the UK, we don't really learn about it in any great depth. Therefore, in this psychology podcast episode, you'll learn what is Acceptance and Commitment Therapy, how it works, when it used and more. If you enjoy learning about psychotherapy, clinical psychology and mental health then you'll love today's episode.

Note: as always absolutely nothing on this podcast is ever any sort of professional, medical or official advice.

<u>What Is Acceptance and Commitment Therapy?</u>

Acceptance and Commitment Therapy is a therapy stemming from the more traditional behavioural and cognitive behavioural therapies. Since Acceptance and Commitment Therapy is an action-oriented approach to therapy because it gets the client to stop denying, struggling and avoiding their inner emotions. Instead, the therapy gets the client to accept their deeper feelings as appropriate responses in a given situation that they shouldn't prevent themselves from experiencing, because trying to stop these responses stops the client from moving forward in their lives.

As a result, Acceptance and Commitment Therapy gives the client an understanding that they need to begin accepting their mental health difficulties and commit to making the needed changes in their behaviour regardless of what's going on in their lives and how they feel about it.

Personally, I really like the sound of Acceptance and Commitment Therapy because I think all therapies need a touch of this to be successful. Since if we take Cognitive Behavioural Therapy for example, we need a client to accept that their depression, anxiety, whatever can't actually be cured. But if they commit to the therapy and have a capacity for change then they can develop adaptive coping mechanisms that will decrease their psychological distress and improve their lives.

So I could argue that the idea of acceptance and commitment is an undertone in all psychotherapies, but this therapy just focuses on it a lot more.

In addition, in the 1980s psychologist Steven C. Hayes from the University of Nevada developed Acceptance and Commitment Therapy based on his own experiences. Since the professor had a history of panic attacks and in the end, he promised himself he would no longer run from himself. Instead he would accept himself and his experiences.

How Does Acceptance and Commitment Therapy Work?

From a theoretical perspective, Acceptance and Commitment Therapy works because it is counterproductive for a client to try and control their painful emotions and their psychological experiences. As well as it is the suppression of these feelings that leads the client to experience even more distress.

As a result, Acceptance and Commitment Therapy proposes that a client needs to develop the belief system that there are valid alternatives trying to change the way they think. Including mindful behaviour, commitment to action and attention to personal values. This leads to taking steps to change their behaviour to decrease their psychological distress, but the client is still learning to accept their psychological experiences at the same level.

This eventually leads to a client changing their emotional states and attitudes.

What Should A Client Expect From Acceptance and Commitment Therapy?

Building upon this further, when a client works with a therapist for this type of psychotherapy, the client will learn to listen to their own self talk and this includes how they talk about problematic relationships, traumatic events, physical limitations and other challenges. Then it is up to the client to decide if a problem requires any immediate action or a change, or if the problem can be accepted for what it is whilst the client learns to make the behavioural changes to modify the situation.

To do this a client might have to look at their past to see what has or hasn't worked for them, and the therapist can help the client stop repeating the same thought patterns and behaviours as the past so they don't cause more problems in the future.

Additionally, after a client has faced and accepted their current challenges, the client can make a commitment to stop fighting the past and their emotions. Instead, the client can start practicing more optimistic as well as confident behaviour based on their personal values and goals.

Ultimately, Acceptance and Commitment Therapy aims to develop a person's psychological flexibility. A concept that encompasses emotional openness and the ability to adapt their behaviours and thoughts to better align with the client's own values and goals.

Personally, I really like the idea of psychological flexibility and a lot of what Acceptance and Commitment Therapy aims to do. Since being flexible in the way we think and feel in a given situation is critical to our mental health. We can't be strict and inflexible so we only feel a certain way in a given situation because this will make us feel awful and experience a lot of distress. Yet if start to explore other ways that make us feel slightly better then that will definitely improve our mental health over time if we accept and commit to changing our thoughts and behaviour.

A little personal example here is actually rather funny in a way, because I have a friend that I really want to date and everything, I asked them out and they said no. Fair enough, and we're both really open about the fact that I like them. Yet whenever they talked about them dating or seeing someone, I used to feel like utter rubbish and I had some very bad thoughts towards myself but that wasn't healthy. So over time I taught myself to think in other ways, accept how bad I felt and I have committed to take steps to change certain aspects of my life. Like, trying to meet other people. I know this isn't like professional Acceptance and Commitment Therapy at all, but what I'm trying to say is that the concepts are useful even outside of therapy.

Moreover, there are six core processes used in Acceptance and Commitment Therapy to promote psychological flexibility:

- Acceptance

This core process involves the client acknowledging as well as embracing the full range of their emotions and thoughts rather than trying to deny, change or avoid them.

- Being Present

This core process comes from mindfulness in the sense that a client should try to be mindful in the present moment, so the client can observe their feelings and thoughts without judging them or trying to change them. instead, the client should experience events clearly and this can directly help them to promote behavioural change.

- Cognitive Defusion

Thirdly, cognitive defusion involves a client distancing themselves from their distressing thoughts and feelings as well as changing the way they react to them. This decreases their harmful effects. Also, some ways how this defusion is done include singing the thought, labelling the automatic response the client has to them and observing a thought without judgment.

- Values

Fourthly, values are important for developing psychological flexibility because this encompasses a client choosing personal values in different domains of their life, and trying as hard as they can to live according to these principles.

Now this is interesting because this is in direct contrast to when a client's actions are being driven by their desire to avoid distress or to adhere to other people's expectations.

- Self As Context

Penultimately, self as context is the idea that expands the notion of self and identity because it proposes that people are more than their feelings, experiences and thoughts.

Something I completely agree with, because it is true. All of us are way more than our past, our thoughts and how we feel in a given moment.

- Committed Action

Finally, committed action involves a client taking concrete steps to incorporate changes into their lives that will align with their values and lead to positive changes. For example, the client could do some goal setting, skill development or expose themselves to difficult thoughts and experiences.

When Is Acceptance and Commitment Therapy Used?

Lastly, Acceptance and Commitment Therapy is a useful therapy for a wide range of mental as well as physical conditions. For instance, depression, anxiety disorders, psychosis, eating disorders, workplace stress, chronic pain, substance use disorders and obsessive-compulsive disorder.

Conclusion

I have to admit that I have rather liked this podcast episode because I have heard a lot about Acceptance and Commitment Therapy over the years through my lectures, but it is only now that I have learnt about the therapy in any great depth. And I know I say this in a lot of these therapy-based podcast episodes, but I think a lot of these concepts can be transplanted into other therapies too.

For instance, the idea of getting your client to accept that their experiences aren't something to be avoided, cured or ashamed of. That is nothing new and I know that is a large part of Cognitive Behavioural Therapy, which is where this therapy stems from in the first place.

Equally, getting a client to commit to taking actionable and concrete steps to improve their lives. Again, I don't exactly think that is anything new because surely that is the same as a client having a capacity to change.

Therefore, if you like the idea of acceptance and commitment but you don't practice Acceptance and Commitment Therapy, then maybe think about incorporating those concepts into your own practice in the future. It's just an idea but I know it's something interesting to think about.

What do you think?

WHAT IS PERSON-CENTRED THERAPY?

As a rape survivor and as I've mentioned in previous chapters, I'm on a waiting list for specialist rape counselling that will probably draw on a lot of humanistic and personal approaches towards mental health.

Therefore, you'll definitely get a greater sense of this approach to mental health in the chapter itself, but this type of therapy is very personal to me, I know from personal experience that it can be extremely helpful and life changing. Also, I think when we consider combining approaches to mental health, the personal or humanistic approach works wonderfully with a lot of other approaches.

This is going to be a fascinating chapter for sure.

***

Interestingly enough in August 2023, I started four weeks of psychotherapy to help me deal with trauma and abuse from my past and I have only recently learnt that the counsellor (or as I call her 'therapist') uses a person-centred approach to therapy. I have only just heard about this approach to mental health to be honest, so I want to explore it further. Since I found it rather useful. Therefore, in this clinical psychology podcast episode, we'll explore what is person-centred therapy, how does it work, what to expect and so much more. If you're interested in psychological therapy, mental health and clinical psychology, then you'll be in for a treat.

What Is Person-Centred Psychotherapy?

Person-centred therapy is a client-based psychotherapy that uses a non-authoritative approach to mental health difficulties that allows clients to take the lead in therapy sessions so they can discover their own solutions to their difficulties.

This particular approach to mental health was started by Carl Rodgers because he believed that every person is unique (which we are) and everyone's view of their world should be trusted. In other words, he believed we should never ever doubt our clients and how they describe the world, because to them that actually is how the world works.

Personally, I do understand this because everyone interprets different situations and events differently depending on their past experiences. This is basically what the cognitive approach is saying just with different words. Due to the cognitive approach believes it isn't the events themselves that cause mental health difficulties it is our beliefs and interpretations of them that lead to difficulties.

Furthermore, Carl Rodgers firmly believed in self-actualisation. This is the idea that all of us have the solutions, knowledge and power to make the changes we need in our lives. As well as this therapy is non-directive so the therapist doesn't take the lead and instead follows the client and doesn't engage in any direct discussions.

However, something I am seriously starting to notice is that all these different approaches to mental health are basically just rehashing what another has already said. For example, every single psychotherapy I can think of is about self-actualisation and making sure the client realises *they* can make the changes needed in their lives using the tools and guidance the therapist gives them. Yet only they can make the changes for themselves.

This actually isn't unique to any approach.

Moreover, I will admit that the non-directive part of person-centred therapy does require a bit of getting used to. Since I love cognitive-behavioural therapy, which is very structured, I had to let go of the idea that she was going to lead, and I had to lead instead. Thankfully I have so much mental health difficulties tied up in different parts of abuse and trauma that I have more than enough things to talk about, but it still did require a bit of relearning.

Anyway, during person-centred therapy, a therapist isn't the lead as we know. Instead the therapist is known as a "compassionate facilitator" because they listen to the client without judgement, they acknowledge the client's experiences without changing or moving the conversation and they are there to support the client without interrupting them. Or impacting on their own process of self-discovery.

In my experience that acknowledgement and "validation" in a fashion is extremely important and it does feel great to have someone else call your abuse and trauma, well, abuse and trauma. And I will happily admit that the process of self-discovery it is scary how much you can actually discover about yourself when we free yourself up. Like I literally cannot share everything I've discovered about myself on the podcast because that's like another twenty episodes in itself, but it's a lot of fun. And honestly, as much as really don't want to discover anything more about myself, I know I will and that's okay.

Overall, the reason why the therapist doesn't interrupt this process of self-discovery and lead is because it is down to the client to uncover what hurts them and what they need to do to repair it. That is a very powerful realisation when it hits you.

How Does Person-Centred Therapy Work?

The entire point of person-centred therapy is to step away from the more traditional psychotherapeutic models where the therapist is the leader and expert and instead the client is the expert in themselves. Again that is something I have mentioned a thousand times before on the podcast and in books.

Therefore, person-centred therapy has three central tenets that allow the therapy to be successful. Firstly, the therapist has an unconditional positive regard so they are empathetic and non-judgemental. Due to the therapist accepts what the client is saying as true and they want to convey to the client that they are understood, confident, trusted and they are valued. As well as the client is free to make their own better choices and decisions in their life.

This tenet I think is very powerful and helpful because I have tried to talk about my past before and there are only ever three outcomes really. None of which I blame on people. Firstly, they call me a liar because they don't want to hear it because what I have to say is too painful. Secondly, they are sorry for what's happening but they can ultimately never ever understand it at a deep level. Thirdly, they understand it but the problem with that is it is common trauma and abuse so they aren't comfortable listening to it and because of emotional dependency and other difficulties, I burn them out too much.

That's why having a therapist that can just listen to me talk is extremely helpful.

Secondly, there is congruence or genuineness so the therapists have no air of authority to them. Instead they present themselves as an accessible and their true self that clients can see is honest and transparent. And this is definitely true, I might be autistic so reading and understanding people is always going to be hard but I know my therapist is very honest and transparent.

Finally, there is empathetic understanding where the therapist wholeheartedly accepts and understands the client's views as well as feelings in a way that can be helpful in reshaping the client's sense of their experiences.

Normally, I think this final part is done by "accident" in a fashion because just by talking and listening and offering up good psychological insights. My therapist has helped me to realise a lot about myself and how I view my Self and my past and my relationships.

On the whole, in this therapy, whenever the therapy is working well the clients feel they are better understood in these sessions and this leads them to feel better understood in other areas of their lives as well. This does have research support, especially whenever a client identifies the unconditional positive regard in their therapist there is an increased chance in positive outcomes. Since the therapeutic relationship between the therapist and the client is a type of therapy in itself.

<u>When Is Person-Centred Therapy Used?</u>

A person-centred therapeutic approach might be used with groups and individuals, be it adults or adolescents in a short- or long-term fashion. The people that tend to take this approach and benefit from it are people that want more self-confidence, a stronger sense of identity and authenticity, increased trust in their own relationships and more success in establishing (and maintaining I will add) their interpersonal relationships.

In addition, like other approaches to mental health, the person-centred approach doesn't have to be used only because it can be combined with other therapies to treat depression, grief and anxiety. Although, it can also be treated to treat trauma, family stressors, abuse and so much more.

And because this is a client-led psychotherapy, it is the more motivated and determined clients that tend to do better and be more successful at the therapy.

Personally, even though I didn't choose person-centred therapy, I am more than glad I ended up with it. Since I've only had two sessions so far and I have found it so useful in understanding my own relationships, my identity, self-confidence and it has basically taught me to let go of what other people want from me and their expectations. I talk about this a little more next week in the Emotional Dependency and Locus of Evaluation podcast episode but person-centred therapy has been immensely useful to me.

<u>What To Expect In Person-Centred Therapy?</u>

Even though I've mentioned my own experience through the podcast episode, the only other thing I want to say is that the therapist might repeat your words. This isn't them trying to be annoying or anything, it is simply them trying to understand what happened, what you mean and how you feel. It is them trying to draw out a little more information from you too.

Of course, they might have misunderstood you and I think that's happened once or twice with myself. One time was when, because I laugh as a coping mechanism when I have seriously screwed up, she didn't understand why I was laughing about something extremely serious (well at least it was to me). This allowed me to rephrase my response in a way both of us could understand.

Moreover, there might be moments of silence in the therapy and this can be good because it allows us to process our thoughts and realisations. Since person-centred therapy is all about self-acceptance and self-discovery.

Or if you're like me and you have so many things to unpack, you basically don't stop talking for the entire session.

Then you end up at the end of the therapy feeling a little overwhelmed because of everything you've learnt, discussed and it can take a little while for you to realise what the takeaways are for you.

Conclusion

Overall, person-centred therapy is all about allowing a client to talk, explore their difficulties and find the solutions for themselves. This is extremely helpful in my experience but then again I've learnt recently I have very high emotional intelligence, which is funny because I used to be extremely bad at it.

A Person-centred Therapist should always have the ability to be calm in sessions and they need to let a client verbalise their frustrations and disappointments too. Since this can all help a client to gain insights into what's hurting them and most importantly how they can move forwards.

Personally, I am willing to say that person-centred therapy has already changed my life for the better and I still have two more sessions, so I am actually really excited to see what will happen, what will I learn and most importantly how else can *I* change my life for the better.

Therapy can be seriously fun, interesting and life changing if you want it to be.

CONCLUSION: YOU WILL HAVE YOUR HEALING MOMENT

Right now I am 100% sure I am meant to be doing my Seminar Report for my Neuropsychology Ageing module that is due in in less than 3 days, but I wanted to write this conclusion first. Due to it has been at least 6 weeks since I last wrote in this book, or I did any sort of sexual violence writing because my mental health has simply been too bad.

Yet I had my Healing Moment today.

What is a Healing Moment I hear you ask, well originally this conclusion was meant to be about how Therapy Is Hope, and therapy is an absolute must for any survivor, and this moment only came about because I'm in therapy and I got back to reading *Healing Sexual Trauma Workbook by Erika Shershun* today.

However, that original idea for the conclusion never felt concrete enough and at the time, I never really believed it myself and it didn't feel right me writing something I didn't believe in. Therefore, I wanted to try something else because I have had a Healing Moment.

A Healing Moment is when something just snapped inside you and your entire world changes for the better. It does not mean you are "cured" (whatever that means and that isn't how mental health works anyway), it does not mean everything will be plain sailing anymore and it does not mean you will never be in pain again.

I am actually tearing up as I write this section.

A Healing Moment simply means you realise that there is hope that everything can get better, you are definitely not a victim and if everyone is telling you that life gets better (hopefully they are or they shouldn't be in your life) that you realise it and internalise it as the truth that it is.

In addition, Healing Moments look different for everyone and what mine looks like will probably be completely different to yours.

Your Healing Moment might be tiny, yours might be massive, yours might make you cry or it might not.

It is *your* Healing Moment for a reason.

As a result, my Healing Moment happened today because I tried to kill myself twice last night in two different ways. I also found out I hurt my best friend by accident and I had done something wrong with a housemate that really hurt them. It was truly awful and I tried to kill myself.

Moreover, my mental health has been so bad for so long that I just couldn't see another way out. I've self-harmed, been suicidal for months and I have an eating disorder and on and on and on.

So I tried to kill myself.

Thankfully, my housemates subtly rallied around me and when I woke up this morning, I still felt suicidal but the idea of me hurting my best friend. Who I love romantically, who has always been there for me and the one person I have lived for for so long, I realised I had two choices.

Either I could keep trying to kill myself and ruin my best friend's life forever or I could find a new way of healing.

My best friend went to the gym with a new friend that I've made and getting close with, so I went into the library and started reading *Healing Sexual Trauma Workbook* again. I have not read this book in months because I used the possible "excuse" that my mental health was too bad that I didn't want to try it.

I had forgotten how great this book is for me personally. This book truly makes me feel understood and validated.

There was a simple exercise that changed everything.

The first chapter of the book focuses on feeling safe in your own skin and after the first few pages, the exercises focus on helping you to focus on the *feelings* of safety. For example, what does your body feel like when you feel unsafe then there's another question on what does your body feel like when you feel safe.

Those are not the actual wording of the questions and there are questions on thoughts during these times too, but you get the gist.

As a result, this is what I wrote for my answers:

When I feel unsafe, my body panics. My breathing increases but goes shallow, I shake and my thoughts go a million miles an hour.

When I feel safe, my body just feels 100% relaxed and untensed.

Now my counsellor has been wanting me to focus on my body for ages but maybe I was resistant to it, maybe I needed it to be worded differently, but that did not work for me.

However, me thinking and writing down how my body actually felt when I was safe was brilliant. It got me to label this feeling so I could savour it when I felt safe and I could focus on getting my body to that state.

In hindsight I did some weird stuff to savour that feeling. I went and sat in two different toilets at the university and I went into a very busy Co-Op (just think corner shop on campus) and each time I focused on feeling completely relaxed and untensed. I savoured that wonderful feeling of being relaxed and my body just not caring or being in survival mode.

I am relaxed because I am safe. I am always safe.

Then of course, I felt depressed and bad for the next few hours because I felt awful about hurting my best friend. Granted, they had already forgotten about it at that point, but I read a bit more of the workbook.

I did some more exercises but I did something interesting. I focused on feeling 100% relaxed in my own home in Canterbury with my three housemates in the house.

I realised ever since mid-August when I had my mental health collapse and everything happened. I had not felt safe in this house, this has never been my home and I know I haven't enjoyed living with two extra housemates as much as I love them. In a way, I suppose I have never felt safe in this house either.

I 100% relaxed today in my own home and I could do it so easily.

And this is my home now. I belong in this house with my three housemates, I belong in Canterbury and I am not a problem and all the million other things my mind tries to tell me.

I am not a problem.

It is a lovely feeling to know that I am home.

Something else I've been struggling with lately was my best friend has been focusing a lot more on another housemate who is going through hell-and-back at the moment. Also, my best friend deals with us in extremely different ways and I think I have been a lot more jealous than I want to admit.

My mind has tried to twist it repeatedly as my best friend not liking me, hating me and my best friend wanting not to be friends anymore.

But the following message highlights a large part of my Healing Moment:

I'm really sorry I'm chronically insecure a lot of the time because you're all I have in terms of real support.

And that it's taken me so long to realise that you focusing more on, spending more time with and doing more tasks for R isn't a reflection of you not liking, you hating me or our friendship breaking down so much so you're a carer, not a friend.

Mine and R's mental health manifests in very different ways and you are more comfortable with them anyway. R needs the constant help and support right now and for the next few months, and that's okay. Because you've offered the same to me since June without me realising it and now you can't be in two places at once.

I need to focus on my healing for me and I know you are always there for me when I need it most, but now I need to take back control because otherwise something might genuinely happen to this friendship without even one of us seeing it until it's too late.

So what I'm saying is... Thank you for being the most amazing and patient friend I can ever ask for. And I understand what I need to do to heal now a little better.

You're still there for me and I am ALWAYS there for you and it will still hurt like hell at times for me because of my trauma, but I now realise I don't need you to make me feel safe in my own home.

And here with R, L and especially you, you're all my home.

(Yes I teared up writing this. I hope this makes sense and I don't come off as a dick)

Thankfully, my best friend found that message really cute and sweet, and I need to send one to R and L later (don't you just love how creative I am with pseudonyms).

Ultimately, my Healing Moment boiled down to finally, finally realising that I am worthy of people liking me for me. I don't need to think I'm a burden, I don't need to think unless I am a certain way I'll be safe and I don't need to rely on other people to make me feel safe, because I am safe. And as long as I focus on that 100% relaxed and untensed feeling in my body then I know, I will truly know that I am safe.

Since when I'm distressed, it doesn't matter what I tell my body or tell myself, unless I *feel* safe in my own skin then I won't be safe and I will continue to be distressed.

That's why in the next book that focuses on therapy and rape counselling, I have a lot of new and exciting unofficial tips and tricks to share with you, because my life is worth living.

It will never be perfect, I will always carry this rape trauma with me and I will always be distressed at times. But I no longer have to feel unsafe in my own body and house and around other people, I am safe. I am loved. I am me.

And that's a great thing to me.

So I hope after reading this book as distressing as some parts would have been to both of us, you can see three things. Firstly, in whenever you are experiencing you are never alone, that as horrific as the past 6 months have been for me, there is light in the darkness and actually, there is healing.

It might take months or years and a lot more therapy than you ever imagined but it is possible to heal.

And never forget you are loved and worthy and you are so amazing.

You're not a victim, you are a survivor.

REFERENCES AND FURTHER READING

Linehan, M. M. (1993). Skills training manual for treating borderline personality disorder. Guilford press.

American Journal of Psychiatry

Annual Review of Psychology

Au, T. M., Dickstein, B. D., Comer, J. S., Salters-Pedneault, K., & Litz, B. T. (2013). Co-occurring posttraumatic stress and depression symptoms after sexual assault: A latent profile analysis. *Journal of affective disorders*, *149*(1-3), 209-216.

Biological Psychiatry

Brown, A. L., Testa, M., & Messman-Moore, T. L. (2009). Psychological consequences of sexual victimization resulting from force, incapacitation, or verbal coercion. *Violence against women*, *15*(8), 898-919.

Bullock, C. M., & Beckson, M. (2011). Male victims of sexual assault: Phenomenology, psychology, physiology. *Journal of the American Academy of Psychiatry and the Law Online*, *39*(2), 197-205.

Campbell, R. (2009). Trauma, Violence, & Abuse, Vol. 10, No. 3.

Campus Sexual Assault Study, 2007; Matthew Kimble, Andrada Neacsiu, et. Al, *Risk of Unwanted Sex for College Women: Evidence for a Red Zone*, Journal of American College Health (2008).

Canadian Journal of Psychiatry

Centers for Disease Control and Prevention. Intimate Partner Violence, Sexual Violence, and Stalking Among Men.

Cunningham, S., Hudson, C. C., & Harkness, K. (2021). Social media and depression symptoms: a meta-analysis. *Research on child and adolescent psychopathology*, *49*(2), 241-253.

David Cantor, Bonnie Fisher, Susan Chibnall, Reanna Townsend, et. al. Association of American Universities (AAU), *Report on the AAU Campus Climate Survey on Sexual Assault and Sexual Misconduct* (January 17, 2020). ("Victim services agency" is defined in this study as a "public or privately funded organization that provides victims with support and services to aid their recovery, offer protection, guide them through the criminal justice process, and assist with obtaining restitution." RAINN presents this data for educational purposes only, and strongly recommends using the citations to review any and all sources for more information and detail.)

Davies, M. (2002). Male sexual assault victims: A selective review of the literature and implications for support services. *Aggression and violent behavior*, *7*(3), 203-214.

Department of Justice, Office of Justice Programs, Bureau of Justice Statistics, Rape and Sexual Victimization Among College-Aged Females, 1995-2013 (2014).

Department of Justice, Office of Justice Programs, Bureau of Justice Statistics, Campus Law Enforcement, 2011-2012 (2015).

Diagnostic and Statistical Manual of Mental Disorders, Fifth Edition

DiMarco, D., Mizzoni, J., & Savitz, R. (2022). On the sexual assault of men. *Sexuality & Culture*, 1-9.

Dworkin, E. R., Menon, S. V., Bystrynski, J., & Allen, N. E. (2017). Sexual assault victimization and psychopathology: A review and meta-analysis. *Clinical psychology review*, *56*, 65-81.

Fuchs, S. F. (2004). Male sexual assault: Issues of arousal and consent. *Clev. St. L. Rev.*, *51*, 93.

Hippocampal Volume in Women Victimized by Childhood Sexual Abuse.

https://www.eurekalert.org/news-releases/630084

https://www.psychologytoday.com/us/conditions/post-traumatic-stress-disorder

https://www.verywellmind.com/symptoms-of-ptsd-after-a-rape-2797203#toc-symptoms-of-ptsd-after-sexual-assault

i. National Crime Victimization Survey, 1995-2013 (2015); ii. Department of Justice, Office of Justice Programs, Bureau of Justice Statistics, Rape and Sexual Victimization Among College-Aged Females, 1995-2013 (2014).

Jarero, I., & Artigas, L. (2016). Instruction for the Butterfly Hug Method.

Journal of Psychopharmacology

Journal of Traumatic Stress

Jubb, H. (2017). The effectiveness of self-soothing techniques for people with PTSD in secure units. Mental Health Practice, 20(5).

Khalfa, S., BELLA, S. D., Roy, M., Peretz, I., & Lupien, S. J. (2003). Effects of relaxing music on salivary cortisol level after psychological stress. Annals of the New York Academy of Sciences, 999(1), 374-376.

Malgaroli, M., Calderon, A., & Bonanno, G. A. (2021). Networks of major depressive disorder: A systematic review. *Clinical Psychology Review*, *85*, 102000.

Mohammed, G. F., & Hashish, R. K. (2015). Sexual violence against females and its impact on their sexual function. *Egyptian Journal of Forensic Sciences*, *5*(3), 96-102.

Mok, M. C., Schwannauer, M., & Chan, S. W. (2020). Soothe ourselves in times of need: A qualitative exploration of how the feeling of 'soothe'is understood and experienced in everyday life. Psychology and Psychotherapy: Theory, Research and Practice, 93(3), 587-620.

National Center for PTSD, U.S. Department of Veterans Affairs

National Comorbidity Survey Replication

National Institute of Mental Health

National Institutes of Health - National Library of Medicine

O'Callaghan, E., Shepp, V., Ullman, S. E., & Kirkner, A. (2019). Navigating sex and sexuality after sexual assault: A qualitative study of survivors and informal support providers. *The Journal of Sex Research*, *56*(8), 1045-1057.

Panisch, L. S., & Tam, L. M. (2020). The role of trauma and mental health in the treatment of chronic pelvic pain: a systematic review of the intervention literature. *Trauma, Violence, & Abuse*, *21*(5), 1029-1043.

Petreca, V. G., & Burgess, A. W. (2024). Long-Term Psychological and Physiological Effects of Male Sexual Trauma. *The Journal of the American Academy of Psychiatry and the Law*, *52*(1), 23-32.

Psychiatric Clinics of North America

Rice, S. M., Easton, S. D., Seidler, Z. E., & Oliffe, J. L. (2022). Sexual abuse and mental ill health in boys and men: what we do and don't know. *BJPsych open*, *8*(4), e110.

Shorey, S., Ng, E. D., & Wong, C. H. (2022). Global prevalence of depression and elevated depressive symptoms among adolescents: A systematic review and meta-analysis. *British Journal of Clinical Psychology*, *61*(2), 287-305.

Smith, M. M., Sherry, S. B., Ray, C., Hewitt, P. L., & Flett, G. L. (2021). Is perfectionism a vulnerability factor for depressive symptoms, a complication of depressive symptoms, or both? A meta-analytic test of 67 longitudinal studies. *Clinical Psychology Review*, *84*, 101982.

Steffen, P. R., Bartlett, D., Channell, R. M., Jackman, K., Cressman, M., & Bills, J. (2021). Integrating breathing techniques into psychotherapy to improve HRV: which approach is best?. Frontiers in Psychology, 12, 624254.

Thomas, J. C., & Kopel, J. (2023). Male victims of sexual assault: a review of the literature. *Behavioral Sciences*, *13*(4), 304.

University of Kent Student Service Instagram Post on 16th February 2024

US Department of Health and Human Services

Vidal, J., & Soldevilla, J. M. (2023). Effect of compassion-focused therapy on self-criticism and self-soothing: A meta-analysis. British Journal of Clinical Psychology, 62(1), 70-81.

Whiteley, C. (2022) Psychology of Relationships: The Social Psychology of Friendships, Romantic Relationships and More. CGD Publishing. England.

Whiteley, C. (2024) CBT For Anxiety: A Clinical Psychology Introduction To Cognitive Behavioural Therapy For Anxiety Disorders. CGD Publishing. England.

Whiteley, C. (2024) CBT For Depression: A Clinical Psychology Introduction To Cognitive Behavioural Therapy For Depression. CGD Publishing. England.

Whiteley, C. (2024) Social Media Psychology: A Guide To Clinical Psychology, Cyberpsychology and Mental Health. CGD Publishing. England.

Whiteley, C. (2024) Working With Children and Young People: A Guide To Clinical Psychology, Mental Health and Psychotherapy. CGD Publishing. England.

Widanaralalage, B. K., Hine, B. A., Murphy, A. D., & Murji, K. (2022). "I didn't feel i was a victim": a phenomenological analysis of the experiences of male-on-male survivors of rape and sexual abuse. *Victims & Offenders*, *17*(8), 1147-1172.

Wright, J. (2009). Self-Soothing—A recursive intrapsychic and relational process: The contribution of the Bowen theory to the process of self-soothing. Australian and New Zealand Journal of Family Therapy, 30(1), 29-41.

Sign Up Bonus

Keep up to date with exclusive deals on Connor Whiteley's Books, as well as the latest news about new releases and so much more!

Sign up to get a FREE psychology book boxset.

Sign Up Now!

https://www.subscribepage.com/psychologyboxset

Subscriptions:

Never miss an issue!

3 Month Subscription… $19.99

6 Month Subscription… $39.99

12 Month Subscription… $69.99

Subscribe Up Now!

https://payhip.com/b/eoQ85

www.ingramcontent.com/pod-product-compliance
Lightning Source LLC
LaVergne TN
LVHW080036210926
848481LV00011B/3210